MINING FOR JEWELS

Evgenii Zamiatin
and the Literary Stylization of Rus'

by

PHILIP CAVENDISH

MANEY PUBLISHING
for the
MODERN HUMANITIES RESEARCH ASSOCIATION
2000

Maney Publishing
for the
Modern Humanities Research Association

HONORARY TREASURER, MHRA
KING'S COLLEGE, STRAND
LONDON WC2R 2LS
ENGLAND

ISBN 1 902653 27 0

© The Modern Humanities Research Association 2000

Produced in England by
MANEY PUBLISHING
HUDSON ROAD   LEEDS LS9 7DL   UK

To Laura, Esme and Anouk

With love

CONTENTS

LIST OF ABBREVIATIONS

Dal´ Vladimir Dal´, *Tolkovyi slovar´ zhivogo velikorusskogo iazyka*, 4 vols, 2nd edn (Moscow–St Petersburg: Vol´f, 1880; repr. Moscow: Russkii iazyk, 1981). All references in the text and notes give the volume number in Roman numerals and the page number in Arabic.

D´iachenko *Polnyi tserkovno-slavianskii slovar´*, compiled by Father Grigorii D´iachenko ([n.p.]: [n. pub.], 1900; repr. Moscow: Moscow Patriarchate, 1993).

ES *Entsiklopedicheskii slovar´ izd. Brokgauza i Efrona*, ed. by I. Andreevskii, 42 vols and 4 supp. vols (St Petersburg: Efron, 1890–1907). All references in the text and notes give the volume number in Roman numerals and the page number in Arabic.

f.d. feast day. This refers to the day (or days) in the year on which the memory of a particular saint is celebrated by the Russian Orthodox Church. It is given in parentheses after the first mention of the saint concerned.

IMLI Institut mirovoi literatury imeni M. Gor´kogo Akademii nauk SSSR.

Kalinskii *Tserkovno-narodnyi mesiatseslov na rusi I. P. Kalinskogo* (1877), ed. by E. Malinina and N. Artemova, afterword by V. Anikin, Zabytaia kniga series (Moscow: Gosudarst-vennoe izdatel´stvo khudozhestvennoi literatury, 1990).

Maksimov *Sobranie sochinenii S. V. Maksimova*, introduction by P. V. Bykov, 20 vols, 3rd edn (St Petersburg: Prosveshchenie, [1908–13]). References in the text and notes give the volume number in Roman numerals and the page number in Arabic. The titles of works and volumes to which I refer frequently in this study are: *God na Severe* (Maksimov, VIII, 1–327; IX, 1–382; & X, 1–349); *Krylatye slova* (ibid., XV (1909), 1–455); *Krestnaia sila* (ibid., XVII, 1–235); and *Nechistaia sila, nevedomaia sila* (ibid., XVIII, 1–295).

'Perepiska' 'Perepiska s E. I. Zamiatinym i B. M. Kustodievym po povodu spektaklia "Blokha"', in Aleksei Dikii, *Stat´i:*

Perepiska: Vospominaniia, ed. by N. G. Litvinenko and A. G. Guliev (Moscow: Iskusstvo, 1967), pp. 279–356.

PPS   *Polnyi pravoslavnyi bogoslovskii entsiklopedicheskii slovar'*, 2 vols ([n.p.]: Soikin, [n.d.]; repr. Moscow: Vozrozhdenie, 1992). References in the text and notes give column rather than page numbers in Arabic.

PVL   *Povest' vremennykh let po Lavrent'evskoi letopisi: 1377g*, ed. by V. P. Adrianova-Peretts, translation, notes, and commentary by D. S. Likhachev, 2nd (revised) edn, Literaturnye pamiatniki series (St Petersburg: Nauka, 1996). All references give the year of the event according to the old method of calculation and the page reference in Arabic.

PZ   'Proizvedeniia E. I. Zamiatina', compiled by Aleksandr Strizhev, and published with an introduction by Vladimir Lazarev in *Sovetskaia bibliografiia*, 1989.3, 53–57.

RN   *Rukopisnoe nasledie Evgeniia Ivanovicha Zamiatina*, 2 vols, ed. by L. U. Buchina and M. Iu. Liubimova, Ruskopisnye pamiatniki series, 3 (St Petersburg: Rossiiskaia natsional'naia biblioteka, 1997). All references give volume number in Roman numerals and page numbers in Arabic.

SRIa   *Slovar' russkogo iazyka*, 4 vols, 2nd edn (Moscow: Russkii iazyk, 1981–84). All references in the text and notes give the volume number in Roman numerals and the page number in Arabic.

SRIa XI   *Slovar' russkogo iazyka XI–XVI vv.*, ed. by S. G. Barkhudarov and others (Moscow: Nauka, 1975–).

Srez.   I. I. Sreznevskii, *Materialy dlia slovaria drevnerusskogo iazyka*, 3 vols (St Petersburg: Imperatorskaia Akademiia nauk, 1893–1903; repr. Moscow: Gosudarstvennoe izdatel'stvo inostrannykh i natsional'nykh slovarei, [n.d.]). References in the text and notes give column rather than page numbers in Arabic.

Zabylin   *Russkii narod, ego obychai, obriady, predaniia, sueveriia i poeziia*, ed. by M. Zabylin (Moscow: Berezin, 1880; repr. Moscow: Kniga 'Printshop', 1989).

ZVS   *Zhitiia vsekh Sviatykh*, compiled by Father Ioann Bukharev (Moscow: Sytin, 1900; repr. St Petersburg: Voskresenie, 1996).

LIST OF ILLUSTRATIONS

PREFACE

The present study is devoted to the use of folk-religious culture in the work of Evgenii Zamiatin (1884–1937). It has been made possible by the deluge of new biographical and archival material which has become available since his semi-official rehabilitation of 1986 and the collapse of the Soviet Union in 1991. Naturally, the fact of this material emerging into the light of day is to be welcomed, and allows the scholar a special insight into Zamiatin's life and career which was denied to those writing in earlier, more repressive decades. It does not come without its problems, however. Much of this new information post-dates the editions of his work currently available in Russia and the West. For this reason even the most reliable of these editions contain errors either in relation to the dating of a particular text or, more seriously, in the content of that text. Even the archivists in charge of his manuscripts are not immune from this problem. Furthermore, this problem is exacerbated by the fact that there is currently no comprehensive edition of Zamiatin's works. A great deal of his writing (mostly critical) was published after his death; some of his fiction has been published since the appearance of the more comprehensive editions of his work; and new material is constantly appearing which could, potentially, cause one to revise opinions on matters relevant to the subject of this monograph.

Unless otherwise stated, all references to Zamiatin's *oeuvre* are taken from the émigré edition of his works published by Neimanis. This is the most extensive collection of his work to date and consists of the following volumes: *Sochineniia: Tom pervyi*, ed. by Evgenii Zhiglevich (Munich, 1970); *Sochineniia: Tom vtoroi*, ed. by Evgenii Zhiglevich and Boris Filippov (Munich, 1982); *Sochineniia: Tom tretii*, ed. by Evgenii Zhiglevich, Boris Filippov, and Aleksandr Tiurin (Munich, 1986); and *Sochineniia: Tom chetvertyi*, ed. by Evgenii Zhiglevich and Boris Filippov (Munich, 1988). All references to this edition in the text and footnotes give the volume number in Roman numerals followed by the page number in Arabic.

Since the publication of these volumes, and the wealth of material which has become available since the opening of the Zamiatin archives in Moscow and St Petersburg, a number of inaccuracies and lacunae have come to light concerning either the texts themselves, their date of composition, or their date of first publication. In those cases where the text is incomplete, or where fuller and more accurate versions have appeared elsewhere, I refer to those fuller versions where necessary and give the relevant references in the notes. On certain occasions, where there is a disparity between the date of composition and first publication, and this disparity is significant for the purposes of my study, I indicate in parentheses the time of writing and date of publication, e.g. 'Nadezhnoe mesto' (written 1918, first published 1924). Where it concerns those works published after Zamiatin's death, but written much earlier, I indicate the date of composition in parentheses, followed by the date of first publication and the reference to the Neimanis edition, e.g. 'Pis′mo Stalinu' (written 1931, first published 1955) (IV, 310–14). For those works published after his death, but not included in the Neimanis edition, I cite the relevant source where necessary and include the date of composition in parentheses.

Transliteration from Cyrillic follows the Library of Congress system without diacritics.

I would like to express my gratitude to all those who have helped and encouraged me during the writing and re-writing of this book. In particular, I would like to thank Julian Graffy at the School of Slavonic and East European Studies, who supervised this work at the doctoral dissertation stage and was painstaking in his rigorous corrections and suggestions; Dr Faith Wigzell, also at the School of Slavonic and East European Studies, whose advice in the sphere of ecclesiastical and folk culture has been invaluable; Professor Robert Russell, at the University of Sheffield, who invited me to publish with MHRA; and Aleksandr Galushkin, at the Gor′kii Institute of World Literature in Moscow, who arranged for me to inspect the Zamiatin archives, and has been an invaluable source of information and advice.

Philip Cavendish
London, 1999

INTRODUCTION

Драгоценные слова невозможно выдумать, они должны быть естественным, органическим свойством писателя, так же как отложения драгоценных металлов и образования драгоценных камней в горных породах. Замятин явился к нам с Урала, где драгоценные, благородные металлы и камни скапливаются, собираются тысячами, миллионами лет, лежат под давлением очень тяжелых и грубых пород и ждут. Жизнь идет. Драгоценные камни начинают светиться, становятся самоцветными и ждут веками настоящего ценителя и знатока, который подымет их из каменной толщи, высвободит и даст им простор сиять на весь свет. Вот это и есть Евгений Иванович Замятин — горный инженер нашего языка![1]

Alex M. Shane wrote his ground-breaking study of Zamiatin more than thirty years after his death;[2] since then, another thirty years have passed. During this period a great deal has changed in our understanding of this writer. His status as a key figure in the development of modern Russian literature, a status long accepted in the West, but vigorously resisted for almost six decades by the Soviet cultural establishment, is no longer a source of dispute. The situation could not be better for those interested in his achievement. His previously banned works of fiction have now been published, many for the first time since 1929, and his stories are part of the school syllabus. The archive holdings in the Gor'kii Institute of World Literature (IMLI) in Moscow are open for inspection.[3] The materials in the Russian National Library in St Petersburg, including the correspondence with his wife, Liudmila Nikolaevna Zamiatina (née Usova), have been published.[4] The criticism, journalism, translations, lectures, plays, screenplays, autobiographies, and private correspondence with his family, friends, and contemporaries has been printed or reprinted.[5] His notebooks, most of them held in the Bakhmetev archive at Columbia University, have been published.[6] International conferences and symposia dedicated to his life and works have been held both in Russia and abroad.[7] And the 110th anniversary of his birth was marked in 1994 by exhibitions, presentations, and readings in St Petersburg and Lebedian´, the town of his birth and youth (apparently, there are also plans to open a museum on the site of the Zamiatin family home).[8] Doubtless it is only a matter of time before a complete edition of his works, with a proper scholarly apparatus, becomes available in Russia, as has been the case with other proscribed writers of the twentieth century, such as Vladimir Nabokov, Mikhail Bulgakov, and Iosif Brodskii.

Despite the cornucopia of material which has accumulated over the decades since the appearance of Shane's study, it is striking nevertheless how relatively one-sided and narrow the focus of attention has been. In the West, for example, he is popularly known as 'Sir Zamiatin', the pipe-smoking engineer and Anglophile whose choice of sartorial fashion in the post-revolutionary era (tweed jacket and plus fours) was a deemed a deliberate provocation to the puritan and commissarial attire of the new Soviet authorities. He is the Bolshevik renegade, intellectual rebel, and heretic whose commitment to permanent revolution led to his increasing disdain for post-1917 ideological dogma and cultural philistinism. Furthermore, his best-known work remains the dystopian fantasy *My*, a work which, when published in the pages of the émigré journal *Volia naroda* in 1927, provoked a vicious and slanderous campaign against him and led four years later to his exile. It is symptomatic of this skewed interest in Zamiatin that the vast amount of Western scholarship published hitherto focusses exclusively on the fiction of the post-revolutionary period, in particular *My*, and the polemical articles of the 1920s in which he articulated his ideas on literature and revolution, energy and entropy, and synthentic art as a modernist phenomenon — this can be witnessed by the articles published over the last forty years, but also by two recent monographs by non-Russian authors.[9] For Anglo-American scholars, there is the added piquancy that Zamiatin worked as a shipbuilder in Newcastle during the First World War, and was well acquainted with both English and American fiction. It has been argued, for example, that his experience in Britain laid the foundations for his ideas on entropy and energy, and that the themes of *My* are to a great extent anticipated in his two English satires *Ostrovitiane* (1918) and 'Lovets chelovekov' [1918] (1921).[10] Zamiatin wrote about English science fiction (H. G. Wells), British theatre (Bernard Shaw, Richard Brinsley Sheridan), and the American short story tradition (O. Henry, Jack London), and had reviewed James Joyce's *Ulysses* as early as 1923. In many respects, he was a truly international and cosmopolitan figure, with a body of work which was cross-cultural in appeal and immediately accessible to Western readers. What could be more appealing than a figure who, in his celebrated letter of protest to Stalin in June 1931, contemplated becoming a writer in English, like the Polish-born Joseph Conrad, if forced into exile?[11]

In Russia, for reasons which are entirely understandable, and relate to his pariah status for most of the Soviet period until the beginning of his rehabilitation in 1986, a similarly skewed picture has emerged. Without risk of exaggeration, it is fair to say that the vast amount of scholarly material published since 1986 has been concerned with the 'blank spots' in his life and career as they pertain to the proscribed post-revolutionary period. Where biographical, this has tended to emphasize his position as a persecuted writer who fought to protect creative freedom against increasing ideological repression in the 1920s; and where critical, this has been aimed for the most part at introducing him to a new generation of readers and defining in general terms his position as part of the literary canon. There has been relatively little in the way of sustained analysis of individual texts. Furthermore, where that has occurred the overwhelming focus of attention is still *My*, the fiction and essays published after the Revolution, and the 'hidden' Zamiatin, i.e. works or projects which for reasons of official censorship were prevented from seeing the light of day during his lifetime. A survey of recent scholarship dedicated to his fiction is indicative of this phenomenon. Nearly one half of the papers delivered at the 1994 Tambov conference, for example, is devoted to *My*. The articles dedicated to Zamiatin in a recent issue of *Russian Studies* are centred almost exclusively on issues of censorship (the unstaged play *Atilla* [1928]); the post-revolutionary drama (*Ogni sv. Domnika* (1922)); the staging of his plays in exile (*Obshchestvo pochetnykh zvonarei* (1926) and *Blokha* (1926)); his work as a screenplay writer (his contribution to Jean Renoir's *Les Bas-fonds* (1936), the film version of Maksim Gor´kii's *Na dne*); his 'wanderings' while in exile; and his reluctant participation in the collectivization campaign of 1929.[12] And in *Novoe o Zamiatine*, a collection of essays published after the second Lausanne symposium, the contributors focus on his participation in the 1905 revolution; the circumstances of his arrests in 1919 and 1922; the 1929 campaign of victimization; his unfinished play about a British coal-mining strike (*Podzemel´e Guntona* [1931]); and his experience of emigration.[13] Suffice it to say, while these are valuable works of scholarship which undoubtedly extend our knowledge of his life and work, they do very little to correct what is still a chronic and disastrous distortion of our appreciation of Zamiatin as a writer.

Paradoxically, the vital element of his art which remains in the shadows, to all intents and purposes untouched and unexhumed, is his Russianness. By this, I mean not that he can be positioned within the neorealist and post-Symbolist phase of Russian modernism, but that

the early part of his career, and some of his later work, has its roots in
the folk-religious culture of the provinces and the oral tradition. In a
1937 obituary of Zamiatin, for example, his friend and erstwhile
collaborator Aleksei Remizov drew attention to this deeply Russian
side of his personality, and argued that his supposed 'Englishness' and
Anglomania was simply a mask which concealed his true self:

Замятин из Лебедяни, тамбовский, чего русее, и стихия его слов отборно русская.
Прозвище: 'англичанин'. Как будто он и сам поверил, а это тоже очень русское.
Внешне было 'прилично' и до Англии, где он прожил всего полтора года, и никакое
это не английское, а просто под инженерскую гребенку, а разойдется — смотрите:
лебедянский молодец с пробором![14]

Remizov is alluding to the fact not only that Zamiatin possessed a
strong emotional attachment to the area in which he was born and
brought up, but that his experience of the provinces and its vibrant
language was a fundamental and defining element in his art. As I will
attempt to demonstrate in this study, Zamiatin was deeply immersed
in the folk-religious culture of the *narod*. He possessed considerable
knowledge of peasant folklore, as well as the rituals, liturgy, and sacred
writing of the Orthodox Church. Furthermore, despite the eclectic
nature of his art, which revealed itself in his desire for constant
experimentation, and led him to modify and develop the stylistic
devices of his early provincial fiction, Zamiatin continued to exploit
this knowledge for much of his career. It supplies the imaginative basis
for such works as *Sever* (written 1918, first published 1922),
'Spodruchnitsa greshnykh' (written 1918, first published 1922), 'O tom,
kak istselen byl otrok Erazm' (written 1920, first published 1922), 'Rus''
(1923), 'Nadezhnoe mesto' (written 1918, first published 1924), *Blokha*,
'Slovo predostavliaetsia tovarishchu Churyginu' (1927), and 'Ela'
(1928). This is a rich vein in his work which continues the experiments
of the early period and illustrates the difficulty of attempting an all-
encompassing definition of his art. Ultimately it might be said that
Zamiatin was a Janus-faced writer, one whose *oeuvre*, very broadly
speaking, oscillated between two poles of influence, one represented by
Andrei Belyi, a self-consciously cosmopolitan and European writer,
and the other by Remizov, who was deeply immersed in the native
sources of Russian literature and culture.

While frequently acknowledged, this is a neglected and barely
investigated aspect of his art. In my view, a second rehabilitation of
Zamiatin is now required, one which gives due attention to the purely
Russian and folk-religious dynamic of his stories. In place of the

conventional reading of him as engineer and shipbuilder, scourge of the Bolsheviks, author of *My*, and victim of political persecution in the 1920s, I wish to present Zamiatin the neo-Populist ethnographer, collector of folklore, poeticizer of provincial life, and, to paraphrase Koni, geologist mining for precious jewels in the seams of the Russian language. This is an artist whose early career was launched in neo-Populist journals, who continued to maintain contact with his close friends and colleagues from the Socialist-Revolutionary Party well into the 1920s, who openly sought to revitalize the literary language through use of the vernacular, and who attempted the renewal of form through his borrowing of folk-religious genres and experiments in *skaz*. In an article ostensibly devoted to Nikolai Leskov, but prompted by Zamiatin's stylized adaptation for stage of Leskov's 'Skaz o tul'skom kosom Levshe i o stal'noi blokhe' (1881), the Formalist critic Boris Eikhenbaum defined this tendency as 'literary populism' (*literaturnoe narodnichestvo*).[15] He explained this tendency in terms of the 'fusion of "high" literature and *lubok*' (skreshchenie vysokoi literatury s lubkom), and spoke of the incorporation into élite prose of such folk materials as songs (*pesni*), folk tales (*skazki*), traditional epic songs (*byliny*), spiritual songs (*dukhovnye stikhi*), proverbs, folk theatre (*narodnye dramy*), saints' Lives (*zhitiia*), and ecclesiastical chronicles (*letopisi*), much of which had been collected and recorded by the Slavophile intelligentsia in the second half of the nineteenth century. In a later essay, also ostensibly devoted to Leskov, Zamiatin was located within a specific tradition of Russian prose which sought to move away from the 'written' forms of literature which had predominated in the nineteenth century towards oral modes of narration. Eikhenbaum included in this category Vladimir Dal', Nikolai Gogol, Leo Tolstoy (his folktales), Maksim Gor'kii, Mikhail Prishvin, Remizov, Pavel Mel'nikov-Pecherskii, Pavel Iakushkin, and Sergei Maksimov, all of them either novelists, short-story writers, or ethnographic belletrists.[16] Interestingly, a number of contemporary writers also located within this tradition — Mikhail Zoshchenko, Vsevolod Ivanov, Leonid Leonov, Konstantin Fedin, and Nikolai Nikitin — were all initially associated with the Serapion Brothers and had been taught creative writing by Zamiatin at the Petrograd House of Arts.[17] In his analysis, however, Eikhenbaum defined the contemporary phenomenon in terms of the 'stylization of *skaz*', rather than *skaz* proper; and it is important to note the distinction he drew between the modernist and essentially sceptical interest in these materials, and the Romantic tendencies of the Slavophiles — as he writes:

Наше современное литературное 'народничество' опирается, конечно, не на славянофильский романтизм, а на убеждение в том, что 'низовые' жанры (эпические, лирические и драматические) должны обновить и освежить 'высокое' искусство.[18]

The aim of this monograph is to investigate Zamiatin's fiction as an example of literary populism. The works considered are all *skaz* stylizations and incorporate a range of materials which pertain to the folk-religious imagination. Because these materials are obscure, and derive from a sphere of experience which has lain buried to all intents and purposes since 1917, the primary challenge consists of identifying them and providing a context in which they may be appreciated. If I describe these works as 'stylizations of Rus'', this is because they reveal a sophisticated, knowing, and modernist sensibility in their treatment of these materials.[19] While Zamiatin certainly sought to communicate the resonances and richness of the Russian folk-religious mind, he did so with an ambiguous, ironic, and playful attitude. Indeed, his works are a form of ventriloquy, at the heart of which lies the conceit of a provincial narrator whose language, social position, and imaginative outlook should not be confused with Zamiatin's own (according to Remizov, his public readings involved a similarly 'lumpen' mode of performance).[20] This mask, moreover, where rooted in the regions of provincial Russia, or where archaic and ecclesiastical, consists of a series of configurations which are harnessed to give an impression of authenticity. Zamiatin's art, in effect, consists of a multiplicity of disguises; and it is the objective of this study to subject these disguises to a detailed examination and to examine the ways in which they conform to the precepts of neorealism as outlined in his lectures on creative writing.

NOTES

1.   These are the words of Anatolii Koni, the lawyer, literary scholar, and contemporary of Zamiatin's. Cited in A. Shteinberg, *Druz'ia moikh rannikh let (1911–1928)* (Paris: Sintaksis, 1991), p. 158.
2.   *The Life and Works of Evgenij Zamjatin* (Berkeley and Los Angeles: University of California Press, 1968).
3.   See IMLI, fond 47, 625 edinits khraneniia (1903–32).
4.   *RN*, I, 13–436; & II, 439–545.
5.   For a list of Zamiatin publications during his own lifetime, see Shane, pp. 233–48. For a list of his publications both in Russia and abroad from 1937 to 1986, see A. Iu. Galushkin, 'Materialy k bibliografii E. I. Zamiatina', *Russian Studies*, 2.2 (1996), 368–413 (pp. 369–77). For a list of works published between 1986 and 1995, some of them for the first time, see Aleksandr Galushkin, '"Vozvrashchenie" E. Zamiatina. Materialy k bibliografii (1986–1995)', in *Novoe o Zamiatine*, ed. by Leonid Heller (Moscow: MIK, 1997), pp. 203–324 (pp. 205–36). For Zamiatin's correspondence with his family, see 'Iz perepiski s rodnymi', introduction and notes by Aleksandr

Strizhev, in M. Golubkov, 'Evgenii Zamiatin: "K razrusheniiu ravnovesiia"', *Nashe nasledie*, 1989.1, 104–19 (pp. 113–16). For publication details of Zamiatin's correspondence with various of his contemporaries, see Galushkin, '"Vozvrashchenie" E. Zamiatina', pp. 205–37. And for a collection of articles and literary journalism with a scholarly apparatus, see Evgenii Zamiatin, *Ia boius'*, ed. with commentaries by A. Iu. Galushkin and M. Iu. Liubimova, introduction by V. A. Keldysh (Moscow: Nasledie, 1999).

6. Those in the Bakhmetev archive have been published by Aleksandr Tiurin. See Evgenii Zamiatin, 'Iz bloknota 1931–1936 godov', *Novyi zhurnal*, 168–169 (1987), 141–74; Evgenii Zamiatin, 'Iz literaturnogo naslediia', ibid., 170 (1988), 77–86; Evgenii Zamiatin, 'Iz bloknotov 1914–1928 godov', ibid., 172–173 (1988), 89–127; Evgenii Zamiatin, 'Iz bloknotov 1914–1928 godov', ibid., 175 (1989), 103–34; Evgenii Zamiatin, 'Nezakonchennoe', ibid., 176 (1989), 109–33; and E. Zamiatin, 'O literature i iskusstve', ibid., 178 (1990), 151–93. See also Evgenii Zamiatin, 'Dvugolos'e. Iz bloknotov 1921–1928', ed. by Oleg Mikhailov, *Slovo v mire knig*, 1989.11, 76–85; and Evgenii Zamiatin, 'Duby (nabroski k romanu)', ed. by V. Tunimanov, *Novyi zhurnal* (St Petersburg), 2 (1993), 3–50.

7. The first major international conference dedicated to Zamiatin's work in Russia took place in Tambov between 21 and 23 September 1992. The contributions were subsequently published in *Tvorchestvo Evgeniia Zamiatina: Problemy izucheniia i prepodavaniia* (Tambov: Tambovskii Gosudarstvennyi Pedagogicheskii Institut, 1992). A second Jubilee conference, organized to coincide with the 110th anniversary of his birth, was also held in Tambov. See *Tvorcheskoe nasledie Evgeniia Zamiatina: Vzgliad iz segodnia*, ed. by L. V. Poliakova, 2 vols (Tambov: TGPI, 1994). In addition, there have been two symposia in Lausanne, Switzerland: the first took place in June 1987, with the proceedings published in *Autour de Zamiatine*, ed. by Leonid Heller (Lausanne: Age d'homme, 1989); while the second took place in December 1995, with the proceedings published in *Novoe o Zamiatine* (see note 5 of the present chapter).

8. The evening dedicated to Zamiatin in St Petersburg took place on 25 April 1994 in the Russian National Library and was accompanied by the publication of a literary supplement in his honour. See *Odnodevnoe blagotvoritel'noe literaturno-epistoliarnoe prilozhenie* (St Petersburg: Sankt-Peterburgskii fond kul'tury, 1994). The second event, held on 12 February 1994, involved a funeral service in a Lebedian' town church, the opening of an exhibition devoted to his memory in the Museum of Regional Studies, and an evening of presentations at the House of Arts. See Galushkin, '"Vozvrashchenie" E. Zamiatina', p. 309.

9. For an overview of the literature in English, see the bibliographical reference guide *East European Languages and Literatures*, ed. by Garth M. Terry (Oxford: Clio Press, 1978); and *East European Languages and Literatures*, ed. by Garth M. Terry, 6 vols (Colgrave, Nottingham: Astra Press, 1982–). For recent publications on the subject of *My*, see Rainer Goldt, *Thermodynamik als Textem: Der Entropiesatz als poetologische Chiffre bei E. I. Zamjatin* (Mainz: Liber Verlag, 1995); and T. Lahusen, E. Maksimova, E. Andrews, *O sintetizme, matematike i prochem: Roman 'My' E. I. Zamiatina* (St Petersburg: Sudarynia, 1994).

10. For a detailed discussion of his experience in Great Britain, see Alan Myers, 'Evgenii Zamiatin in Newcastle', *Slavonic and East European Review*, 68 (1990), 91–99; and idem, 'Zamiatin in Newcastle: The Green Wall and the Pink Ticket', ibid., 71 (1993), 417–27. For a discussion of the influence of *Ostrovitiane* and 'Lovets chelovekov' on the genesis of *My*, see T. R. N. Edwards, 'Zamiatin's *We*: The Necropolis of The One State', in idem, *Three Russian Writers and the Irrational: Zamyatin, Pil'nyak, Bulgakov* (Cambridge: Cambridge University Press, 1982), pp. 36–86. For a wide-ranging analysis of Zamiatin's interest in matters English generally, see O. A. Kaznina, *Russkie v Anglii* (Moscow: Nasledie, 1997), pp. 199–226.

11. 'Pis'mo Stalinu' (written 1931, first published 1955) (IV, 313–14).

12. See R. Gol´dt, 'Mnimaia i istinnaia kritika zapadnoi tsivilizatsii v tvorchestve E. I.
     Zamiatina', in *Russian Studies*, 2.2 (1996), 322–50; D. I. Zolotnitskii, 'Evgenii Zamiatin i
     "instsenirovka istorii kul´tury"', ibid., 350–60; T. D. Ismagulova, 'Evgenii Zamiatin na
     stsene teatra russkoi emigratsii', ibid., 361–75; M. Iu. Liubimova, 'O zakone
     khudozhestvennoi ekonomii, fabule i novykh kontsakh...', ibid., 375–87; V. A.
     Tunimanov, 'Poslednee zagranichnoe stranstvie i pokhorony Evgeniia Ivanovicha
     Zamiatina', ibid., 387–416; and A. Iu. Galushkin, 'Iz istorii literaturnoi "kollekti-
     vizatsii"', ibid., 437–78.
13. See Marina Liubimova, '"Ia byl vliublen v revoliutsiiu..."', in *Novoe o Zamiatine*, pp.
     56–71; Grigorii Faiman, '"Dnem i noch´iu chasovye..."'. Zamiatin v 1919-m i 1922-m
     gg', ibid., pp. 78–88; Aleksandr Galushkin, '"Delo Pil´niaka i Zamiatina"'. Pred-
     varitel´nye itogi rassledovaniia', ibid., pp. 89–148; Rainer Gol´dt, '"Podzemel´e
     Guntona": neizvestnyi stsenarii E. Zamiatina', ibid., pp. 149–75; and Leonid Heller, 'O
     neudobstve byt´ russkim (emigrantom)', ibid., pp. 176–202.
14. 'Stoiat´ — negasimuiu svechu pamiati Evgeniia Ivanovicha Zamiatina', in Golubkov,
     'Evgenii Zamiatin: "K razrusheniiu ravnovesiia"', pp. 117–19 (p. 118) (first publ. in
     Sovremennye zapiski, 64 (1937), 424–30).
15. 'Leskov i literaturnoe narodnichestvo', in *Blokha. Igra v 4 d. Evg. Zamiatina* (Leningrad:
     Academia, 1927), pp. 12–15 (p. 13).
16. 'Leskov i sovremennaia proza', in Boris Eikhenbaum, *Literatura: Teoriia: Kritika:
     Polemika* (Leningrad: Priboi, 1927; repr. Chicago: Russian Language Specialties, 1969),
     pp. 210–25 (p. 214).
17. Zamiatin gave a number of lectures on creative writing at the Petrograd House of
     Arts between 1920 and 1921. They were: 'Psikhologiia tvorchestva' (IV, 366–72); 'O
     iazyke' (IV, 373–89); 'O siuzhete i fabule' (IV, 390–99); 'O stile' (IV, 581–88);
     'Instrumentovka' (IV, 589–93); and 'O ritme v proze' (IV, 594–99). These are not,
     however, the fullest available versions of these lectures, and where necessary I refer
     to the texts published by Strizhev in 'Literaturnaia studiia Zamiatina', *Literaturnaia
     ucheba*, 1988.5, 118–43, and Evgenii Zamiatin, 'Tekhnika khudozhestvennoi prozy',
     ibid., 1988.6, 79–107.
18. 'Leskov i literaturnoe narodnichestvo', p. 15.
19. The term 'stylization of Rus´' is taken from J. van Baak's examination of Leskov and
     Zamiatin as writers occupying a similarly 'peripheral' fictional space within the
     general literary construct of Rus´. He writes: 'The concept "stylization" here stands in
     opposition to what may be termed the objectively-descriptive or, in other words, the
     positivist ethnographical position.' See J. van Baak, 'Leskov and Zamyatin: Stylizers
     of Russia', in *Literary Tradition and Practice in Russian Culture: Papers From an
     International Conference on the Occasion of the Seventieth Birthday of Yury Mikhailovich
     Lotman*, ed. by Valentina Polukhina, Joe Andrew, and Robert Reid, Studies in Slavic
     Literature and Poetics series, 20 (Amsterdam: Rodopi, 1993), pp. 312–24 (p. 312).
20. Remizov records that Zamiatin performed these stories 'with the voice of a
     "simpleton"' ('pod "prostaka"'). See 'Stoiat´ — negasimuiu svechu', p. 118.

CHAPTER 1

ZAMIATIN AND LITERARY POPULISM

Background

Zamiatin's experiments in the sphere of literary populism demand a very different emphasis as far as his life and early influences are concerned. In contrast to the post-revolutionary period, however, information about the early stages of his career is relatively sketchy. Much importance has been attached to his provincial upbringing as the inspiration for his most typically Russian stories. He was born on 20 January/2 February 1884 in the small town of Lebedian´, Tambov province (population of 6,678 in the 1894 census), and it was here that he spent the first years of his youth until sent to Voronezh at the age of twelve to attend a gymnasium.[1] There can be little doubt that the province of Tambov supplied him with the character models and *kolorit* for many of his early stories. In his 1930 essay 'Zakulisy', for example, Zamiatin recalled his (surprised) discovery that the real-life model for Chebotarikha, the merchant's widow in *Uezdnoe* (1913), was none other than the writer Mikhail Prishvin's aunt (IV, 303–04); in the same essay, moreover, he refers to a clerical worker in the local Lebedian´ post-office as the model for Kostia Edytkin, the central character of 'Alatyr´' (1914) (ibid., 301). Further testimony to the importance of his home town in shaping the language of his prose fiction, and the role of his grandmother as far as his folk education was concerned — she apparently instructed him in various forms of folk tale 'flourish' (*priskazka*) and love charm (*prisukha*) — is given in a letter to S. A. Vengerov in 1916 in which he responded to inquiries about his background and influences.[2] It is worth noting that Zamiatin continued to visit the Tambov region, describing it fondly as his *rodina*, well after his move to St Petersburg in 1903 and the death of his parents (his father died in 1916, and his mother in 1925).[3]

Equally important, and a fact not without consequence in view of the fashion for ethnographic fieldwork at the time, Zamiatin was extremely well travelled within the Russian Empire. While still only a student at the Polytechnic in St Petersburg, he visited a large number of areas

every summer on shipbuilding apprenticeship work. In an autobiographical article dating from 1929, for example, he mentions travelling
to such towns as Sebastopol, Nizhnii Novgorod, and Odessa in
'rollicking' (*pribautlivye*) third-class railway carriages (I, 28). After his
graduation in 1908, he spent three more years on shipbuilding work
proper — these expeditions included factories along the Volga river as
far as Tsaritsyn and Astrakhan, the Kama river, the Don Basin, Crimea,
the Caucasus, the Caspian Sea, Archangel, and Murmansk.[4] Two
further trips to the North were undertaken in subsequent years. The
towns of Kem´, Soroka (now Belomorsk), and the Solovetskii Islands
were visited in 1915 as part of his shipbuilding work during the First
World War ('Zakulisy' (IV, 301)); and twelve years later he travelled to
Aleksandrovsk (now Poliarnyi) for the shooting of *Severnaia liubov´*, the
film adaptation of his northern tale *Sever*.[5] Interestingly, all the stories
in which the specific location is indicated and genuine can be traced to
areas which Zamiatin knew well or from which strong impressions had
obviously been formed. His notebooks, for example, contain a
fascinating, ethnographic-style entry in which he records the customs,
matchmaking ceremonies, and popular etymologies of a rural
community somewhere in the Russian North — here he records such
dialect variants as *posidki* (the bridal party which takes place a few days
before the wedding nuptials) and *zaplachki* (the pre-marital farewell of
the bride to her parents), and makes brief notes on the funeral preparations for a young girl.[6] There is also strong circumstantial evidence
that conversations with local fishermen during the shooting of
Severnaia liubov´ inspired him to write 'Ela', the last story of his
northern trilogy.[7] Certainly, it is doubtful that he would have been able
to 'think with the imagination of a provincial' (*myslit´ po-uezdnomu*), an
expression coined during one of his lectures at the Petrograd House of
Arts ('O iazyke' (IV, 375)), without an intimate and detailed knowledge
of the Russian provinces. Furthermore, such evidence gives lie to the
claim, touted by those who were ignorant of his background, that the
language of his fiction was based not on his own experience, but
plundered second-hand from Dal´'s celebrated dictionary.[8]

Another aspect of his background worth stressing, and one which
has only recently come to light, is the religiosity of Zamiatin's parents.
It would not be exaggerating to say that from early childhood he was
steeped in the culture of Orthodox Christianity. His father Ivan
Dmitrievich, a lay priest serving in the local church dedicated to the
pallium (*pokrov*) of the Virgin Mary, was responsible for religious
instruction at the pre-gymnasium where Zamiatin was taught as a

boy;[9] while his mother Mariia Aleksandrovna (née Platonova), who was herself from a devout family (her father was a priest), used to embark upon regular pilgrimages to monasteries in the local vicinity and farther afield, frequently with the two children in tow.[10] One of Zamiatin's earliest memories of childhood was the traumatic experience of becoming separated from his parents on a crowded pilgrimage to Zadonsk ('Avtobiografiia' (1929) (I, 25)). This was a monastery situated to the north of Lebedian´ on the River Don, and famous as the grave-site of Tikhon of Zadonsk, the writer and former bishop of the diocese of Voronezh who had been canonized shortly after the inspection of his relics in 1861. In another autobiographical article, this time written in 1931, he recalled with evident nostalgia the religious processions which used to take place every summer outside his home: here he refers to the parading of the Icon of the Virgin Mary of Kazan, the sweaty pilgrims, the itinerant monks and nuns, and the Holy Fool 'Vasia "The-Anti-Christ"', whose cursing he described as a disturbing mixture of the sacred and the profane.[11]

This environment — by all accounts the family home was treated as a refuge by sundry pilgrims and itinerant monks (*stranniki*) — was crucial in determining the linguistic fabric of his *skaz* ornamentation. It is worthwhile speculating on the degree to which the numerous references to sacred literature in Zamiatin's stories testify to an intimate acquaintance with their contents. Serried ranks of menologies (*chet´i minei*),. prayer books or triodions (*triodi*), pentecostarions (*tsvetniki*), and patristic miscellanies (*izborniki otecheskie*) all line the walls of the priest's library described in the short story 'Neputevyi' (1914) (I, 101); and, as we will see in due course, Zamiatin recommended archaic ecclesiastical sources to his students at the House of Arts as linguistic material with which to revitalize the literary language. On the other hand, it is extremely doubtful that this interest was evidence of religious belief as such. Zamiatin's revolutionary activity in 1905, which resulted in a severe reprimand from his father and instant excommunication from the local church, suggests that at this stage of his life he was an agnostic, if not an atheist.[12] His attitude towards the heritage of the Orthodox Church must therefore be deemed ambiguous. Like Senia, the radical atheist and 'good-for-nothing' in 'Neputevyi', Zamiatin was fond of Russian monastic chants;[13] moreover, it is possible to speculate that his attitude towards Orthodox religion, like that of his fictional protagonist, was characterized by a fateful duality: one part of him, which had 'finished four institutes' did not believe; while the other part, which was attached to old Kremlin walls and churches, was not so resistant:

И ведь вот, не верит Сеня, конечно: какой там, к черту, ад у него. А сидит с стариком вот так и головою качает печально — не притворяется. Какие-то, будто, две половинки в нем: одной половинкой, которая четырех факультетов вкусила, не верит, а другой, которая к стенам кремлевским да к церквам старым привержена верит. (I, 102)

In this sense Zamiatin was typical of those members of the intelligentsia whose clerical background gave rise to an interest in the culture and mentality of Orthodox belief, but whose philosophical inclinations were anti-religious.[14] There can be little doubt, however, that this background was an advantage as far as the authenticity of his religious impersonations were concerned. He was certainly well versed in the scriptures (in a letter to his sister, he mentions graduating from school with top marks for religious education).[15] Furthermore, in those stories which take place in a monastic or clerical milieu, as well as those which parody ecclesiastical literature, an impression of authenticity is vital to the success of the narrative. With this in mind, it is interesting to note that Zamiatin adopted the name of his great-grandfather on his mother's side, Mikhail Platonov, as a *nom de plume* for the polemical articles written during the early months of the Soviet government, a time when he was criticizing the authorities for the destruction of culture and a deliberate policy of terror.[16]

Early Career and Critical Reception

Although the first story Zamiatin published was a fictional account of his time in prison after his arrest in 1905 — the short story 'Odin', published in the November 1908 issue of *Obrazovanie* — his career proper was launched with a series of tales and short stories which explored the concept of provinciality in Russian life. *Uezdnoe*, which appeared in issue number five of *Zavety* for 1913, made a massive impact and established his instant reputation. According to Sergei Postnikov, the chairman of the SRs who sat on the editorial board of the journal, there were three hundred reviews or references in a relatively short space of time.[17] This was followed afterwards by an account of military life in the Far East, *Na kulichkakh* (1914), which was branded semi-pornographic and seditious by the censors, and led to the confiscation of the issue of *Zavety* in which it had been published.[18] Over the next three years, Zamiatin wrote an eye-witness account of

the Potemkin uprising in Odessa, 'Tri dnia' (1914), and a number of
skaz stylizations also set in the provinces — 'Neputevyi', 'Alatyr'',
'Chrevo', (1915), 'Starshina' (1915), and 'Kriazhi' (1916) — all of which
appeared in his first short story collection *Uezdnoe: Povesti i rasskazy*
(1916). A trip to the Far North in August 1915 produced the short story
'Afrika' (1916), which he apparently read in the offices of
Ezhemesiachnyi zhurnal in November 1915.[19] This was followed by
'Pis'mennoe' (1916), two miniature tales for Gor'kii's journal *Letopis'* —
'Bog' (1916) and 'D'iachok' (1916) —, and a tale for children orphaned
by the war, 'Kartinka' (1916). In March 1916, Zamiatin left for Great
Britain on a shipbuilding contract with the Entente, and spent the next
couple of years abroad. It is known, however, that the first drafts of the
hagiographic parody 'O sviatom grekhe Zenitsy-devy. Slovo pokhval'noe' (1917) and the short story 'Znamenie' (1918) date from this
pre-revolutionary period.[20]

Although relatively little is known about this period in Zamiatin's
career — the pieces of the jigsaw puzzle are only gradually being put
into place — it is clear that his affiliations at this stage were primarily
with the neo-Populists. The editorial board of *Zavety*, for example, was
packed with figures whose aesthetic and political inclinations had
brought them into the orbit of the SRs: these included Postnikov
himself; V. M. Chernov (a political activist and SR luminary); V. S.
Miroliubov (along with Chernov, a radical Populist and former editor
at *Sovremennik*); A. I. Ivanchin-Pisarev (a close friend and collaborator
of the Populist writer Vladimir Korolenko); the SR journalist S. D.
Mstislavskii; and P. V. Ivanov-Razumnik, the critic who edited the
'Literature and Society' section of the journal.[21] The enthusiastic
reception of *Uezdnoe* put Zamiatin in a strong position vis-à-vis this
milieu; indeed, he was championed by them as a rising star, with
Chernov, in particular, keen to establish him in a stable of young
writers which would be associated exclusively with the journal.[22]
Zamiatin evidently enjoyed a good relationship with Miroliubov —
this is witnessed by the fact that after the latter had fallen out seriously
with Ivanov-Razumnik, and left *Zavety* to set up *Ezhemesiachnyi zhurnal*,
Zamiatin offered him a number of stories and reviews, as well as 'Tri
dnia'.[23] Nevertheless, he continued to retain close links with all these
publishers and editors well into the 1920s. Postnikov, Ivanov-
Razumnik, and Mstislavskii were involved in the publication of the
1918 Scythian volume in which *Ostrovitiane* first appeared. They were
also editors at the *Mysl'* publishing house, and were thus responsible
for the publication of Zamiatin's polemical essay 'Skify li?' (1918) and

'Znamenie'. Postnikov, along with Chernov, edited the relevant sections of the SR newspaper *Delo naroda* for which Zamiatin wrote several anti-Bolshevik articles under the pseudonym of Mikhail Platonov between 1917 and 1918. They also edited the SR supplement *Prostaia gazeta*, in which the satirical miniatures entitled 'Skazki-pobasenki Ivana Kochana' were published at the end of 1917. It is now clear that although political repression of both the Right and Left SRs forced Zamiatin to consider other outlets for his work after 1918, his affiliations with this group remained strong even after they had emigrated. It is known, for example, that he was communicating with Postnikov in Berlin via a secret SR Party postbox as late as May–June 1922; that he tried, again via Postnikov, to arrange for the publication of *My* in the Paris-based SR journal *Sovremennye zapiski* in the summer and autumn of 1922; and that Postnikov, in all likelihood with Zamiatin's explicit authorial sanction, was instrumental in securing the first Russian-language edition of *My* in the Prague-based émigré journal *Volia naroda* in 1927.[24]

Inevitably, bearing in mind the radical credentials of these publishers, Zamiatin's early stories tended to be viewed from a narrowly political perspective and compared with works which concerned themselves with the issue of Russia's identity after the twin disasters of military defeat and the brutal suppression of popular revolt in 1905. Parallels were sought with Ivan Bunin's *Derevnia* (1910), Gor'kii's *Gorodok Okurov* (1909–10), Ivan Vol'nyi's *Povest' o dniakh moei zhizni* (1912–14), Aleksei Chapygin's *Belyi skit* (1913), and Remizov's *Piataia iazva* (1912), all works exploring the dark side of Russian life as manifested in small provincial towns and villages.[25] Zamiatin's fiction was regarded as another contribution to the debate about the brutalization of the peasantry, and as a meditation on the vestiges of Tatar atavism in the national character. The critic Aleksandr Izmailov, for instance, interpreted *Uezdnoe* as an extrapolation of Dmitrii Merezhkovskii's warning in 1906 about the dangers of the 'yellow peril' — Baryba, the main protagonist, was the 'boor' (*kham*) whose vulgarity and sly, animal-like cunning was the embodiment of the lumpenproletariat on whom the Tsarist autocracy depended for its survival.[26] Zamiatin's 1916 collection reinforced this initial impression. While varying to an extent in terms of plot, the five other stories painted a brutal and depressing picture of life 'in the sticks', with hopelessness, oppression, corruption, brutality, and boredom being the dominant features. Stylistically, they were marked by a strong interest in material reality (*byt*), and this realism was saturated with a

grotesque exaggeration and vulgarity which only increased the sense of
a spiritual vacuum. In a second review, published on 8/21 March 1916
in *Birzhevye vedomosti*, but this time of *Uezdnoe*, the 1915 book
publication of the tale, Izmailov observed that Zamiatin's stance
towards this milieu was essentially merciless and condemnatory:

Ни любить, ни жалеть эту серую и темную массу, по примеру Гл. Успенского,
Замятин не хочет, проблесков в ней света глаз его не ловит — видит одно только
повальное свинство. Он не из благославляющих, а из проклинающих.[27]

This label would stick to Zamiatin in future years. Furthermore,
although the initial reception of his provincial fiction was favourable,
not everyone was enamoured of his prose. One critic characterized his
style in terms of 'artificial primitivism' (*iskusstvennaia primitivnost'*);
another deemed his language 'strange' and 'slightly artificial'; and a
third lamented that it was 'grey' and 'dismal', and a corruption both of
popular speech and the literary language.[28] In general, however, the
enjoyment of the narrative style seemed to depend very much on
individual taste. Aikhenval'd, for example, praised Zamiatin's
'colourful' and 'bright' style, which was 'Russian, too Russian', but no
less 'elegant' than 'artificial'; while in later years, Gor'kii continued to
regard *Uezdnoe* as the best thing ever produced by Zamiatin, describing
it as 'very Russian' and written 'with yearning'.[29] And Eikhenbaum
paid tribute to the power of the tale by remarking that: 'Про него не
скажешь: "он пугает, а мне не страшно"'.[30]

The Influence of Remizov and the Poetics of Neorealism

One of the most striking aspects of this first collection was the interest
in narrative masks and *skaz*-style techniques. In his early review of
Uezdnoe, for example, Eikhenbaum recognized immediately the kinship
and pigeon-holed Zamiatin within a self-designated Remizovian
'school'.[31] Other critics quickly followed suit, drawing comparisons
between Zamiatin's style of writing and that of the neorealists, a
literary tendency supposedly being championed by Ivanov-Razumnik
at *Zavety*, and one embracing such newcomers as Leonid Dobronravov,
Ivan Vol'nyi, A. Terek (the pseudonym of Ol'ga Forsh), and Prishvin.[32]
That such a 'school' existed is confirmed by the memoirs of Prishvin.
Here he pays tribute to the enormous influence of Remizov at this stage
in his career, recalling that the older writer used to host the writer's
equivalent of an artist's studio to which younger writers like himself
were invited on a regular basis. It is not clear, however, whether

Zamiatin also attended.[33] Remizov himself, while recognizing that new writers rarely emerged in a stylistic vacuum, mischievously recalled that Fedor Sologub had initially mistaken the author of *Uezdnoe* for him writing under a new pseudonym; he added that this was a general view at the time, and cited *Neuemnyi buben´*, his novel published in 1910, as the supposedly literary model.[34]

Although probably sensitive to such comparisons, Zamiatin responded to the inquiry by Vengerov in 1916 with the information that he had read Remizov's works 'only recently', and considered there to be an intrinsic disparity between their styles:

Ремизова лично узнал не очень давно и книги его стал читать сравнительно поздно. Кладовая языка у меня и у Ремизова разная: у него рукописи и редкостные книги, а я книгами почти не пользовался. Внутреннее мое несходство с Ремизовым чем дальше, тем, вероятнее, будет больше заметно. (IMLI, opis´ 3, ed. khr. 2)

The first independent evidence of his knowledge of Remizov's work appears in a 1914 review of two *Sirin* volumes: here he mentions *Neuemnyi buben´*, *Krestovye sestry* (1911), and *Tsep´ zlataia* (1913), the collection of tales which had appeared in the volumes concerned.[35] It is clear that *Uezdnoe*, however, if not directly influenced by Remizov, represented a radical break from the first stories of Zamiatin's literary career — 'Odin' and 'Devushka' (1910) — which were written in a conventional, non-stylized prose. By employing for the first time a rough-jewelled and *skaz*-orientated voice, one which sought to reflect the discourse of the distinctively urban lower-class and peasant milieu depicted in this tale, Zamiatin fundamentally reinvented himself as a writer. Furthermore, the degree of skill and sophistication with which he applied this technique can be gauged by the reaction of his commissioning editors at *Zavety* — they were surprised when the 'engineer from the Urals', as he was first imagined, appeared before them in person at a meeting of the editorial board and introduced himself.[36] Zamiatin was sufficiently amused by the critical reception of *Uezdnoe*, in particular the review by Izmailov (this mistook the coarseness of the narratorial voice to be a genuine reflection of the author's social status), that he mentioned it in a letter to his wife while recuperating in the military garrison of Nikolaev-Kherson in July 1913:

Разыскал (и украл) в библиотеке вечернюю Биржевку: действительно, там есть целый Измайловский фельетончик, посвященный Барыбе и … мне.

[…] Как же ловко, должно быть, умею я притворяться: такие чудные, на самом деле на меня не похожие, предположения обо мне. (*RN*, I, 140)

The same review is mentioned again in Zamiatin's autobiographical article of 1922, in which he mentions how Izmailov imagined him to be a shaggy-haired provincial with a walking stick, and his surprise when he learnt subsequently of his mistake (III, 14). In addition, his lectures on the art of creative writing reveal that he planned to mention this review in his discussion of narrative technique, along with anecdotes regarding his first meetings with Ivanov-Razumnik.[37]

By the time of these lectures, delivered almost six years after the first publication of *Uezdnoe*, the conceit of the provincial mask had been defined as a major stylistic device in a full-blown theory of neorealism. Although the lectures were envisaged as classes in the general techniques of creative writing, it is clear from their content that the lecturers often gave preference to their own tastes and aesthetic values. In the case of Zamiatin, moreover, they lay bare many of the formal devices which he pressed into service in his work, and can therefore be considered something of an artistic manifesto. In 'O iazyke', for instance, he drew attention to the way in which modern prose tended away from the lyrical towards the epic, giving rise to the kind of writing in which the author dissolved himself into the consciousness of his characters in the manner of an actor working in accordance with Stanislavskii's theory of acting. In his view, this technique ought to be extended to include all the objective remarks and descriptive passages of the author, so that he disappeared completely and assumed the guise of a representative *persona* whose language, consciousness, and imaginative viewpoint mirrored that of the milieu in question:

Если вы пишете об уездной жизни вы должны сами в этот момент жить уездной жизнью, среди уездных людей, мыслить по-уездному, вы должны забыть, что есть Петербург, Москва, Европа и что пишете может быть больше всего для Петербурга и Москвы, а не для Чухломы и Алатыря. Если вы пишете о Карфагене, о Гамилькаре, о Саламбо — вы должны забыть, что вы живете в 19-м веке после Р. Х., должны чувствовать и говорить, как Гамилькар. Если вы пишете о современном англичанине вы должны думать по-английски и писать так, *чтобы написанное вами по-русски имело вид художественно сделанного перевода с английского.* (IV, 375; emphasis in the original)

He stressed the importance of the author presenting the imaginary world of his creation as if he himself were a geniune and integral part of it, with all the devices at his disposal rigorously geared to the creation of an impression of authenticity. He also argued that all images and metaphors should reflect the consciousness of the given environment and the characters who inhabit it. At the same time, however, the language of the narrative voice should aim for a carefully synthesized *stylization* of the language of the relevant milieu, not necessarily a direct imitation of its lexicon, syntax, and intonational register:

У опытного мастера всегда есть уменье, не коверкая грубо язык, дать художественно-синтезированное впечатление подлинного языка изображаемой среды — будет ли это мужик, интеллигент, англичанин, эфиоп или лошадь. (IV, 377)

The writer's skill, he continued, lay in choosing only the colourful, rare, and original examples of colloquial speech, not the rough and substandard banalities.

Like other literary populists before him, Zamiatin considered the speech and expressions of ordinary people to be a rich linguistic seam which could be mined profitably for poetic effect and enfranchised within the bounds of literary taste. He taught his students to observe closely the speech of the common folk, to note the unexpected images, the subtle and humorous epithets, and the expressive phrases in order to incorporate them into their own writing (IV, 378). He believed that every milieu had its own syntactical pattern or arrangement of words (*rasstanovka slov*), and devoted a significant section of his lecture to outlining the features typical of what he termed 'popular language' (*narodnyi iazyk*). He drew the attention of his students to the frequent absence of subordinate clauses, conjunctions, and verbs. He also emphasized the use of diminutive and augmentative forms, idioms, colloquialisms, old forms of the adverbial participle, prepositions, particles, and collective forms, both singular and plural, all of which, in his view, imbued the language with an 'unusual expressivity and dynamism' (IV, 377–78). He argued that the Russian spoken in the central provinces and far-flung, peripheral areas of the North, such as Olonets and Archangel, was purer, more authentic, and intrinsically more interesting than the language of the metropolitan intelligentsia, which had been 'corrupted' by reading newspapers. Furthermore, he believed that it was the duty of every writer to travel to these areas and seek out such linguistic 'gems' for himself:

Все эти жемчужины надо откапывать не в больших городах, а в коренной, кондовой Руси — в провинции. [...] Только здесь можно учиться русскому языку, только отсюда можно черпать такое, что действительно может обогатить литературный язык. (IV, 378–79)

He equated this language with 'folklore' — 'Первоначальный источник и творец языка — народ. Фольклор' (IV, 378) — although by modern standards this must be considered a narrow definition.[38] He also referred helpfully to the three regions of Russia (Tambov, Kostroma, and the Far North) which had provided him with much of his linguistic material, and emphasized that this material had been 'overheard' by him — this was a hint that the language of his fiction was based more on living speech than on ethnographic collections (IV, 380).

At the same time, *pace* his remarks at this point in the lecture, and his earlier answers to Vengerov, Zamiatin advocated the consulting of certain literary sources as part of this enriching process. He mentions traditional epic songs (*byliny*), folk tales (*skazki*) and folk songs (*pesni*), and stresses that they should be read in their original versions, as recorded by the Imperial Geographical Society of the Academy of Sciences, rather than in modern, revised, and thus diluted editions (IV, 379). He encouraged his students to include ecclesiastical sources in their researches, in particular apocrypha, acathists (hymns in praise of the Virgin Mary, from the Greek *acathistos*), saints' Lives, both Old Believer and Orthodox, and ecclesiastical literature in general (*pamiatniki*) — in short, the kind of material which Eikhenbaum later characterized as *lubok* in his remarks on Leskov. These observations were succeeded by a list of Russian writers for whom such sources had served to enrich their literary language: Leskov, whose specialization lay in the field of ecclesiastical sources, folklore, and 'provincialisms', in the best sense of the word; Mel´nikov-Pecherskii, who used material published by the Old Believers and 'provincialisms'; Tolstoi, whose plays, such as *Vlast´ t´my* (1887), Zamiatin much admired for their richness of dialect and use of the vernacular; Gor´kii, in his so-called 'third phase' ('Eralash' (1916) is cited here as an example); the northern poet Nikolai Kliuev, whom Zamiatin characterized as 'an amazing specialist and master of language'; and Remizov, whose skill lay in his digging up of 'precious jewels' in old books, especially Old Believer texts (IV, 380).

'O iazyke' is primarily concerned with the linguistic resources of neorealism — as such, it provides a wealth of interesting information with regard to the sources for Zamiatin's pre-1918 fiction and his sense of himself as belonging to a specific literary tradition. Several observations are worth making in this respect. There is a palpably neo-Populist and neo-Slavophile tenor to the observations made in this lecture. The statement that the *narod* is the 'source' and 'creator' of all language; the view that the language spoken in the western areas of

Russia had become 'corrupted' due to Belorussian and Polish influence (IV, 379); the employment of words such as 'authentic' (*podlinnyi*) and 'pure' (*chistyi*) to characterize the areas of central Russia and the North (ibid.); and the choice of primary source material all place Zamiatin squarely within a neo-Slavophile cultural tradition. The vigour with which he stressed the importance of these sources and advocated that the aspiring writer should endeavour to experience this culture first-hand, rather than seek contact with it through the intermediary of secondary sources, echoes the Populist practice of 'going out among the people' (*khozhdenie v narod*) — as he makes quite clear:

Перечисленные авторы могут служить второисточниками для изучения языка. Но этими второисточниками нужно пользоваться только для того, чтобы войти в дух языка, полюбить язык, научиться пользоваться им. Черпать материалы из таких второисточников не годится. Впечатление оригинальности, своего языка, вы можете создать, конечно, только в том случае, если будете обращаться непосредственно к первоисточникам. (IV, 380–81)

It goes without saying that these precepts on the need to revitalize and enrich literary prose through popular language belonged to a wider artistic phenomenon which was gathering pace during the first decades of the twentieth century. They come close to duplicating, for example, the theories of the *Opoiaz* group, later known as the Formalists, on the need for poetic language periodically to renew itself in order for lived experience to be re-experienced as if for the first time. Indeed, although there is little evidence that Zamiatin was acquainted with the figures who later came to form this circle at the time of writing his early stories, his words reflect strongly the thesis first expounded by Eikhenbaum in his review of *Uezdnoe*;[39] moreover, they were echoed later by such critics as Aleksandr Voronskii, who spoke of the 'newly-minted' quality of Zamiatin's early prose and compared it to the 'dull coins' of conventional language which had remained 'too long in circulation'.[40] Zamiatin himself spoke of the need to 'democratize' the written word, and the importance of bringing the literary language and the vernacular closer together ('O iazyke' (IV, 383)). He saw himself fighting a battle against conservative adversaries who, like the 'archaist' Admiral Shishkov in the era of Pushkin, were supposedly seeking to protect 'high' literature from 'vulgar' contamination (ibid., 382–83). At the same time, he pointed towards parallel developments in the work of certain Western writers — for example, the French novelist Henri Barbusse, O. Henry, and the Italian disciples of Gabriele D'Annunzio (Zuccoli and Papini) —, all of whom, he argued, were striving for an effect of immediacy, dynamism, and spontaneity.[41] Although not nearly as iconoclastic or ambitious in scope, his interest in linguistic enrichment can be compared profitably to the trans-sense innovations of the Russian Futurists. Baryba, for example, the richly euphonic sobriquet given to the brutish and square-jawed hero of *Uezdnoe*, and the inspiration for which had derived apparently from the name of a railway station on the line from Moscow to Lebedian´ ('Zakulisy' (IV, 301)), had already featured in *Iar´*, the 1907 volume of poetry by Sergei Gorodetskii, and would later be employed as an example of *zaum* in Kruchenykh's 1921 manifesto 'Deklaratsiia zaumnogo iazyka'.[42] Like the Futurists, Zamiatin favoured the invention of neologisms, declaring in 'O iazyke' that this was a natural process which mirrored folk practice (IV, 381–82). A similar stylistic revolution, triggered by Gauguin's theory of synthetism and the Pont-Aven school of painting in 1880s France, was rapidly acquiring momentum in the other fields of the arts. The role of Diagilev's journal *Mir iskusstva* in promoting folk-inspired modes of book illustration, drawing, and painting; the adaptation of *lubok* techniques in the neoprimitivist work of Mikhail Larionov and Natal´ia Goncharova; and the use of folk songs and dissonant sounds of the street in the works of such modernist composers as Igor´ Stravinskii (in particular, see the music for the two ballets *Zhar-ptitsa* (1910) and *Petrushka* (1911)) were part of a wider cultural movement which sought to invigorate outmoded and outdated forms of expression.

Skaz *and the Invisible Author*

Despite the undeniable interest of 'O iazyke', it is limited as a framework within which to explore Zamiatin's individual brand of literary populism. It is important to know that he recommended folk-religious sources for the weaving of a modern prose fabric. However, the linguistic composition of this fabric is only one stylistic element in his stories and, as we will see, frequently operates in complex ways. A related issue is the problem of how the poetics of neorealism as outlined in this lecture is achieved in practice. It is noteworthy, for example, that nowhere does *skaz* feature as a technical term to describe his narrative style. This occurs for the first time only in his 1922 article on the Serapions ('Serapionovy brat´ia' (IV, 533)), and its absence in the lecture is all the more surprising in view of the fact that Eikhenbaum's initial investigations into the field of *skaz*, the essay 'Illiuziia skaza', had already been published in 1918, and that he was lecturing at the House of Arts at the very same time.[43]

In a later essay, Eikhenbaum gave the following definition of *skaz*:

Под сказом я разумею такую форму повествовательной прозы, которая в своей лексике, синтаксисе и подборе интонаций обнаруживает установку на устную речь рассказчика.[44]

However, with the exception of 'Pravda istinnaia' (1917), a narrative ostensibly written in the form of a letter from a peasant girl to her mother, there is no explicit 'tale-teller' as such in Zamiatin's early fiction. Rather, as suggested by Kastorskii in relation to *Uezdnoe*, we are dealing with an implied tale-teller who should not necessarily be identified with the author:

The narrator does not appear in person in the tale, but in the tone of the entire narrative it is felt that behind the author there is hidden some provincial man to whom the story has been entrusted.[45]

This formulation leads to the problem of whether the author is truly absent from the literary text as the poetics of neorealism seems to demand. V. V. Vinogradov, the Formalist linguist, drew attention to this problem in an article on *skaz* in 1925:

Стилистические устремления Андрея Белого, Ремизова, Пильняка, Евг. Замятина, К. Федина и др. рисуют теперь нам разные стадии и разные формы этого процесса обновления литературно-художественного построения примесю сказа. У них часто не сказ, а сказовая окраска повествовательной прозы, крутые неожиданные скачки многообразных, чисто письменных сооружений в плоскость повествующего устного монолога. Это горнило, в котором куется синтез отживающих форм литературного повествования с разными видами устной монологической речи, горнило, в котором предчувствуется образование новых форм литературно-письменной, художественной речи.[46]

In a recent analysis of *Uezdnoe*, moreover, it has been argued that while Zamiatin's implied narrator consistently preserves the illusion of orality throughout, the presence of an author is detected through the sophisticated musical orchestration and ornamentation of the text.[47] Bearing in mind the nature of the conceit, there exists in his fiction an inevitable tension between actual author and implied narrator, one which becomes even more acute when we come to examine the presence of such poetic devices as metaphor, metonymy, synecdoche, symbolism, and so on, all of which are employed in the early fiction and imply the presence of a highly developed literary consciousness.

Eikhenbaum's initial view that the author of *Uezdnoe* was self-effacing, and that the language of the narrative belonged not even to a fictional provincial *persona* as such, but to the 'voice of the provinces', is stimulating and provocative.[48] However, it is untenable as it stands. In practice, the devices of neorealism are conceits designed to give the illusion of spontaneity to a narrative which is in fact extraordinarily carefully crafted. For this reason, in my view, it would be preferable to discuss Zamiatin's stories in terms of their 'author-narrators', rather than 'author' and 'narrators', since in fact they are not so easily distinguishable.

The notion that the narrative conceit of these stories creates a tension or space between the author-narrator and the milieu described has further implications as far as the author's attitude to folk-religious materials is concerned. Eikhenbaum argued that the narrator of *Uezdnoe* was a folk tale teller (*skazitel'*) who was essentially objective and did not comment directly on the subject of his tale:

Рассказчик не только беспристрастен, каким должен быть художник, но и бесстрастен. [...] Здесь не рассказчик, а 'сказитель'. Он закрывает глаза, когда ведет свой рассказ, и никому нет дела до его собственной души. Это истинный эпос, и вот к нему-то обращается теперь наша художественная проза.

Повесть Замятина рассказана так, что от автора нет в ней ни слова. Не знаешь, что сам Замятин думает и каким языком он сам говорит.[49]

This is only superficially true. As observed in relation to the English satires, Zamiatin's artistic manipulation of the text, especially his extensive use of metaphor, gives rise to the suspicion that there is an outsider present in the narrative whose values and imaginative viewpoint are communicated, at least indirectly, to the reader — this can be witnessed not only by means of the objective remarks which adopt an ironic tone of voice with regard to the tales' middle-class inhabitants, but also by means of the grotesque leitmotifs which are employed in relation to both positive and negative characters.[50] Furthermore, while it is true that these two English satires represent the acme of this procedure, one known as the 'synthetic method', and typical of Zamiatin's so-called 'middle-period', the same devices can be detected in embryonic form in the provincial works as well. The result is an additional tension or interplay between the imaginative consciousness of the milieu portrayed and that of the author-narrator, but one deliberately exploited for poetic effect rather than denied or concealed. It is an abiding paradox of Zamiatin's art that while his stories evidently attempt to convey the charm, humour, and beliefs of the folk-religious imagination, there is a rational spirit at work which places these qualities in an ironic and sometimes tragic light. Indeed, the more minutely Zamiatin's impersonations of provincial voices are investigated, the more the extent to which his own personality is an integral and irresistible element in the disguise can be appreciated. His art is the product of two sensibilities — the folk-religious and the élite, the provincial and the metropolitan — which merge and blend to form a fresh new synthesis.

As Voronskii rightly observes, Zamiatin was a 'word-worshipper' (*slovopoklonnik*).[51] Like a poet, he manipulated exotic and obscure words not only for their iconic and textural value, but also for their punning and allusive potential; indeed, it is often through his use of these words that the space between author-narrator and milieu is located. An illustrative case in point, one which testifies to his acquaintance with the symbolism of obscure Orthodox feast days, is the word *prepolovenie* as used in the short story 'Afrika' (I, 283). At first glance, this word appears quite innocuous. This is the name given to a mobile religious festival falling exactly half-way between Easter Sunday and Pentecost (the etymology of the word derives from the Russian word for 'half', i.e. *polovina*).[52] As an ancient festival, one celebrated by the Orthodox Church from the very earliest days of its existence, this word clearly operates within the tale as a conventional indication of time. Further research into the subject, however, reveals that the rituals performed on this day have a symbolic resonance directly related to the situation of the main protagonist. According to Sergei Maksimov, the Festival of Prepolovenie was associated in the folk-religious imagination with the element of water — basing their actions on Christ's speech to the Pharisees at the Jewish Feast of the Tabernacle, a speech in which water was employed as a metaphor for the restorative powers of the Holy Spirit, priests in Russia celebrated this feast day by conducting special blessings of rivers, streams, and springs in the vicinity.[53] Furthermore, Maksimov recounts a curious apocryphal legend associated with the festival which tells how the Virgin Mary was miraculously delivered from drowning as she tried to escape bandits by swimming across a river with the baby Jesus in her arms — hence the colloquial expression for the festival, *preplavlenie*, which literally means 'a swimming across'.[54] Zamiatin seems to have been peculiarly alive to this resonance. In 'Afrika', the festival is mentioned in the context of the hero's decision to embark on a journey overseas (a symbolic crossing of water), and follows a three-paragraph fragment on his predilection for 'swimming' in snow-drifts when drunk (I, 282). The verb *plavat´* is employed on four separate occasions during the course of this tiny fragment, the final instance (*proplaval*) being a direct echo of the name of the festival itself (ibid.). What we are witnessing here, therefore, is the orchestration of the text around an apocryphal legend, and the juxtaposition of parallel narratives for ironic, parodic effect; in other words, what functions initially as a device for establishing the time-frame of a particular event, one which testifies to Zamiatin's familiarity with an obscure religious festival in the Far North, becomes a vehicle for poetic manipulation at the hands of a playful author.[55]

It is important to appreciate that comic and parodic elements often underpin Zamiatin's treatment of the folk-religious imagination. Not only do they provide a corrective to the often expressed view of his fiction as grey and depressing, but also, as an exemplary illustration of Eikhenbaum's thesis, they force a distinction to be drawn between the ironic exploitation of such materials in his own work and the attitudes of his predecessors, such as Remizov and the Symbolists, in whose work folklore is attributed with an intrinsic, mythopoeic value. These artists were greatly influenced by the nineteenth-century mythological school of social anthropology. They had imbibed specialist ethnographic collections, in particular Afanas´ev's three-volume compendium of Slavic myth *Poeticheskie vozzreniia slavian na prirodu* (1865–69), and tended to view all manifestations of folk culture as relics or vestiges of a primitive, pagan, and mythological past. Remizov, for example, seeking to rebut the charges of plagiarism levelled against *Posolon´* (1908), explained that his aim had been 'to recreate popular myth', fragments of which he recognized in rituals, games, Christmas carols, folk beliefs, omens, proverbs, riddles, charms, and apocrypha.[56] The world of the folk presented these writers with a rich source of poetic inspiration. Some were drawn to the rituals of liminality, such as weddings and funerals. Others were fascinated by magical practices, the lives of picturesque outsiders — for example, Holy Fools (*iurodivye*) and the wandering beggars who performed spiritual songs (*kaliki perekhozhie*) — and Old Believer sects (see Belyi's use of the Flagellants or *khlysty* in *Serebrianyi golub´* (1909)). Although individual exploitation of this material varied (Belyi's novel, in particular, is a fascinating display of variegated *skaz* performance), there is rarely ironic distance in the works of these writers. On the contrary, folklore is celebrated as the embodiment of the irrational, primitive, and transcendental; indeed, it belongs to an alien sphere which, while often disturbing and violent, is nevertheless considered superior to the deadening rationality of modern urban existence.[57]

By comparison, Zamiatin's ambitions are modest and grounded in realism. A revealing contrast between his fictional imperatives and those, for example, of Belyi can be found in their respective treatment of the witch figure. In *Uezdnoe* (I, 64–65), the old crone Ivanikha is a comic figure. She intones an evil charm (*zagovor*) in order to 'spoil' the health of Baryba, but this illness is easily countered with modern medicine (additional irony is gained from the fact that it is monks from the local monastery, for whom folk beliefs regarding *maleficium* are presumably relics from a pagan past, who have asked for her assistance). By contrast, the pockmarked Matrena in *Serebrianyi golub'* occupies a mysterious world of dark, mystical, erotic, and apocalyptic fantasy. The scene from Zamiatin's tale is accurate from the strictly ethnographic point of view — the text of the charm, cited verbatim, matches exactly a charm in the published collections of Sakharov and Zabylin.[58] Furthermore, it belongs to a mass of detail which contributes to the rich texture of his exotic, provincial *kolorit*, and the presence of which in the story is motivated by the conceit of narrative authenticity. We can see, however, that the presentation of folk-religious elements goes well beyond a mere depiction of *byt*. Reality is comically and grotesquely manipulated in Zamiatin; and the shifting perspective of the author-narrator, one in which he seems to share the imaginative viewpoint of his protagonists, and yet at the same time adopts an ironic stance with regard to this viewpoint, gives rise to some complicated and unexpected ambiguities. As his career progresses, this stance itself undergoes gradual transformation. The satirical and somewhat brutal thrust of his earlier fiction is tempered by an earnest lyrical expressionism; and the sceptical stance towards the imaginative world of the folk is replaced by a romantic pathos, as a result of which the world of popular fantasy, while not embraced fully in the myth-making manner of his Symbolist predecessors, is poeticized and accorded more sympathy.

The Scope of this Study

The texts chosen to illustrate Zamiatin's brand of literary populism belong to a stage in his career which extends from 1914 to 1926. In terms of the dominant reading of his fiction, which privileges the accessible over the obscure, and considers *Uezdnoe* the only *skaz* stylization of the provincial period worthy of discussion, they are not in general well known. It is these works, nevertheless, which reveal Zamiatin's exploitation of folk-religious masks most fully and rewardingly. Furthermore, with the exception of the two hagiographic parodies, which were designed with specific, polemical purposes in mind, they are marked by an absence of satirical intent and grotesque exaggeration.

The texts can be divided into three distinct categories. The first consists of 'Poludennitsa (Kuny)' (1914–16), 'Kriazhi', and 'Afrika': these are short stories set in the three locations mentioned in 'O iazyke', and are typical of the provincial period. The narrative is colloquial in register and employs regional dialect and slang; the plot, characterization, and imagery, like the peasant woodcut, are simple and expressionist in design; and the folk-religious world inhabited by the male and female protagonists is treated with a simultaneous blend of irony and pathos. These three stories are also linked thematically. The main protagonists are poor peasants who harbour illicit sexual passions, or suffer from obsessive desires, the fulfilment of which remains beyond their reach; in two cases — 'Kriazhi' and 'Afrika'— these obsessions lead to their deaths. Shane reads these stories as testaments to Zamiatin's maximalist approach to life and his belief that human beings 'should die striving for their goals rather than live to discover them to be false illusions'.[59] In these stories, however, this philosophical position is underpinned by a political imperative. There is a social dimension to the predicaments of Zamiatin's fictional protagonists in that the illicitness of their obsessions involves a transgression of social hierarchy and a challenge to conservative sexual and moral norms. The main female protagonist in 'Poludennitsa (Kuny)', for example, a simple peasant girl, desires a priest who has been widowed. The main male protagonist in 'Kriazhi' is too poor for the object of his love to consider him a worthy marital prospect. And the hero of 'Afrika' develops an obsession with a female guest from overseas who is his social and intellectual superior. This case is symptomatic of the general utopian impulse which lies concealed behind these parables of unrequited love. 'To live anew' (zhit´ po-novomu), the mantra which inspires Zamiatin's poor hero to embark on his journey abroad, is a euphemism for a better and more rewarding life in the widest sense of the word. These texts are thus quintessential Zamiatin narratives which contain, in embryonic form, many of the themes of his mature fiction.

'Znamenie' forms the second, separate category, since it is a tale which unfolds against the background of a symbolic, rather than region-specific setting, and involves a modification of Zamiatin's earlier *skaz* style. Folk beliefs, biblical eschatology, the cult of the Virgin Mary, the legendary powers of icons, and the events of apocryphal legend are blended together to communicate the fantasies of the folk-religious mind against a background of revolutionary threat to pre-Petrine, Holy Rus´. 'Znamenie' also provides a convenient bridge between the early provincial fiction and the hagiographic parodies. The *skaz* stylization of the early period, which depends for its effectiveness on the illusion of a provincial *skazitel´*, is here replaced by the illusion of an ecclesiastical chronicler steeped in the sacred literature and imaginative world of the Orthodox tradition. It might be objected that these 'voices' are fundamentally at odds with each other, and that the hagiographic tradition which Zamiatin sought to imitate belongs to the sphere of élite, rather than folk culture. Such an objection, however, would be misguided. In the pious regions of provincial Russia, the legends of the saints were an integral part of peasant double-faith (*dvoeverie*). Furthermore, it was generally in the language of the folk that archaic and ecclesiastical expressions were best preserved. It is common, for example, to stress the importance of the folk in creating the legend of the saint, and thus in giving shape and expression to his or her life — the historical figure of the martyr and confessor saint is transformed and embellished through the inclusion of legendary achievements and miracles into an exemplary but largely fictitious character whose actual life bears little relation to the subsequent *vita*. The Bollandist scholar Father Hippolyte Delehaye has argued that the early hagiographical legends constitute the 'folklore of the saints', and that behind the ultimate author who puts them down in writing there is the 'hidden author', i.e. the anonymous and manifold masses, whose memory stretches back through the generations;[60] it is a commonplace of hagiographic scholarship that the improbable and miraculous episodes of these accounts are often the products of popular fantasy and can be traced directly to folkloric *topoi*.

The last category consists of the play *Blokha*, which Zamiatin himself described as an experiment in dramatized *skaz*.[61] As a work of stylization first produced at the Second Moscow Art Theatre in February 1925, *Blokha* enjoyed enormous popularity among audiences throughout the 1920s. More importantly, the transferral of the play to Leningrad prompted one of Zamiatin's clearest statements with regard to the artistic manipulation of folk-religious materials — the essay 'Narodnyi teatr' (1927) — in which he explored the possibility of a popular theatre in the post-revolutionary era. In this essay, Zamiatin was careful to draw a distinction between the kind of theatre foisted on the *narod* 'from above', supposedly for its own enjoyment and edification, and the 'ancient', 'sturdy', and 'distinctive' forms of drama which had been developed by the folk themselves over the centuries for their own entertainment (IV, 424). Furthermore, he appreciated that not all these dramatic forms were equally impressive or lent themselves productively to professional adaptation in the modern era; thus the artistic potential of each form was assessed with rigour. His watchword here was 'revitalization' (*omolozhenie*), a word coined ostensibly in the context of Efimova and Simonovich's modern versions of the Petrushka puppet theatre (IV, 426), but one which could equally well have been applied to his own approach. Zamiatin argued that only by harnessing the dramatic, spontaneous, and vigorous formal elements of folk drama could a new artistic synthesis be achieved. Indeed, he placed himself in the company of a range of artists who had exploited similar materials, but from other spheres of folk culture. These included peasant sculptors specializing in wood and stone (Sergei Konenkov); artists specializing in naive modes of painting and illustration (Boris Kustodiev, Nikolai Rerikh, Kuzma Petrov-Vodkin); composers who had both recorded and adapted folk music (Modest Musorgskii, Nikolai Rimskii-Korsakov, Igor´ Stravinskii); and Sergei Diagilev, the choreographer and impresario who had presented revolutionary dance techniques in the form of his Ballets Russes (IV, 425). It is within this wider context, as part of a neoprimitivist and expressionist movement in Russian culture at the turn of the century, that the texts analysed in the ensuing chapters deserve to be judged.

NOTES

1. Zamiatin, 'Avtobiografiia' (1929) (I, 27).
2. Zamiatin's letter to S. A. Vengerov dated 2/15 December 1916, as cited in N. N. Primochkina, 'M. Gor´kii i E. Zamiatin (k istorii literaturnykh vzaimootnoshenii), *Russkaia literatura*, 1987.4, 148–60 (p. 149).
3. Zamiatin describes Lebedian´ as his *rodina* in his obituary of the painter Boris Kustodiev. See 'Vstrechi s B. M. Kustodievym' (written 1927, first published 1957) (IV, 176). For the date of his father's death, see 'Iz perepiski s rodnymi', p. 115n. For the date of his mother's death, see Zamiatin's letter to his wife dated 20–21 December 1925, in RN, I, 295–96 (p. 295).
4. See 'Avtobiografiia' (1929) (I, 30); and 'Avtobiografiia' (written in 1931), ed. by A. Galushkin, *Strannik*, 1 (1991), 12–14 (p. 12).
5. Shane, p. 44.
6. 'Iz bloknotov 1914–1928 godov' (1988), pp. 91–92.
7. As the shooting of *Severnaia liubov´* came to an end in the summer of 1927, Zamiatin wrote to his wife that he would be staying a few days longer to 'hang about' (*povalandat´sia*) with the local fishermen, among whom he boasted a number of

'friends' (*priiateli*). This was followed six days later by a letter in which he announced his intention to write a 'simple story'. See Zamiatin's letters to his wife dated 11 and 17 July 1927, in *RN*, I, 320–21. The first draft of 'Ela' (initially entitled 'Elka') is dated 14 August 1927 (IMLI, opis´ 1, ed. khr. 94).

8.   See, for example, the opinion ventured by Boris Pil´niak, who later became a close friend: 'Вы ведь знаете, что он свое "Уездное" написал, сидя в Петербурге, по Далю, России не видя, восприняв ее Ремизовым — нам, провинциалам, все это видевшим на месте, ясно, что Замятин *очень талантливо* — врет, причем пишет таким языком, которым *нигде* в России не говорят.' Emphases in the original. See Pil´niak's letter to V. S. Miroliubov dated 26 July 1921, cited in Igor´ Shaitanov, 'O dvukh imenakh i ob odnom desiatiletii', *Literaturnoe obozrenie*, 1991.6, 19–25 (p. 21).

9.   'Iz perepiski s rodnymi', pp. 114–15n.

10. Strizhev mentions monasteries in Lebedian´ and nearby Troekurovo, as well as those in Zadonsk and Voronezh, presumably to venerate the relics of Tikhon of Zadonsk (1724–83) and Mitrofanii of Voronezh (1683–1703). The family also visited the monastery in Sarovskaia pustyn´, where Serafim of Sarov (1759–1833), an important mystic canonized by the Orthodox Church in 1903, lay buried. See ibid., p. 116n.

11. 'Avtobiografiia' (written 1931), p. 12.

12. 'Iz perepiski s rodnymi', p. 115n.

13. Remizov, 'Stoiat´ — negasimuiu svechu', p. 118.

14. For a more detailed discussion and background, see Margaret Ziolkowski, *Hagiography and Modern Russian Literature* (Princeton: Princeton University Press, 1988), pp. 17–18.

15. 'Iz perepiski s rodnymi', p. 114.

16. L. V. Poliakova, 'Evgenii Zamiatin: tvorcheskii put´. Analiz i otsenki', in *Tvorcheskoe nasledie Evgeniia Zamiatina*, pp. 7–83 (p. 31).

17. S. Postnikov, 'Stranitsy iz literaturnoi biografii E. I. Zamiatina', published as a supplement in R. Iangirov, 'Prazhskii krug Evgeniia Zamiatina', *Russian Studies*, 2.2 (1996), 478–520 (pp. 516–18 (p. 518)).

18. For a more detailed discussion of this affair, see Shane, pp. 14–15.

19. This information is given in the notes which accompany the publication of Zamiatin's letter to his wife dated 17/30 May 1916. See *RN*, I, 202–03.

20. For relevant publication details of Zamiatin's early work, see *PZ*, 54. For draft versions of 'Znamenie' and 'O sviatom grekhe Zenitsy-devy. Slovo pokhval´noe', see IMLI, opis´ 1, ed. khr. 39–42, & 58–61, respectively. Further discussion of the dating of these stories can be found in Chapters 5 and 6.

21. For further information on these figures, and the launch of *Zavety* in April 1912, see Julian Graffy and Andrey Ustinov, '"Moi deti – moi knigi"': From Evgenii Zamiatin's Letters', in *Themes and Variations: In Honour of Lazar Fleishman, Stanford Slavic Studies*, 8 (1995), 366–75 (pp. 346–49).

22. This ambition was expressed in a letter to Ivanchin-Pisarev dated January 1914, cited in ibid., p. 348.

23. 'Perepiska E. I. Zamiatina s V. S. Miroliubovym', ed. by N. Iu. Griakalova and E. Iu. Litvin, *Russian Studies*, 2.2 (1996), 416–37 (p. 416).

24. For information regarding the publishing activities of these figures during the immediate post-revolutionary period, and Zamiatin's later contacts with Postnikov, see Iangirov, 'Prazhskii krug Evgeniia Zamiatina', pp. 481–87. For publication details of Zamiatin's work during this period, see *PZ*, 54. And for the publication details of the 'Skazki-pobasenki Ivana Kochana', see the Neimanis edition (IV, 75–76).

25. Michel Niqueux, '*Uezdnoe* (*Choses de province*) de Zamiatine et le débat sur le peuple russe après la révolution de 1905', in *Autour de Zamiatine*, pp. 39–55.

26. A. A. Izmailov, 'V literaturnom mire: Prishedshii kham', *Birzhevye vedomosti*, 28 June/11 July 1913. For the original reference, see 'Griadushchii Kham' (1906), in D. S. Merezhkovskii, *Polnoe sobranie sochineniia*, 17 vols (Moscow: Vol´f, 1911–13), XI (1911), 1–36.

27. Cited in Poliakova, p. 22.
28. Cited in ibid., pp. 22–23.
29. Cited in ibid.
30. This remark is made in his review of *Uezdnoe*, which was entitled 'Strashnyi lad'. See B. M. Eikhenbaum, *O literature: Raboty raznykh let*, ed. with commentary by M. O. Chudakova, E. A. Toddes, and A. P. Chudakov (Moscow: Sovetskii pisatel´, 1987), pp. 290–91 (p. 291) (first publ. in *Russkaia molva*, 17/30 July 1913).
31. Ibid., p. 290.
32. E. Lundberg, 'Literaturnyi dnevnik', *Sovremennik*, 1915.1, p. 214.
33. Cited in Poliakova, p. 21.
34. 'Stoiat´ — negasimuiu svechu', p. 118.
35. 'Sirin. Sbornik pervyi i vtoroi' (IV, 499). For information regarding Remizov's contribution to the volumes in question, see *Bibliographie des oeuvres de Alexis Remizov*, ed. by Hélène Sinany (Paris: Institut d'Études Slaves, 1978), p. 106.
36. Shteinberg, p. 148.
37. 'O iazyke', as published in 'Tekhnika khudozhestvennoi prozy', p. 80.
38. A book which introduces folklore to the general reader gives the following definition: 'Folklore consists of all lore (knowledge, wisdom, action) transmitted by tradition. [...] A brief review of recent folklore publications reveals such varied interests as cookery, costume, impudent gestures, hoaxes, children's games, songs, events, and even hangover cures.' See K. W. and M. W. Clarke, *Introducing Folklore* (New York: Holt, Rinehard & Winston, 1963), p. 8.
39. '"Сказывать" нужно забавно, нужно словами и прибаутками сыпать, чтобы у всех уши поразвесились и рты прораскрылись. Как же сделать язык забавным для городских, "литературных" читателей? Надо допустить диалекту, надо освежить застоявшуюся и изломанную метафорами речь областными говорами.' See Eikhenbaum, 'Strashnyi lad', p. 290.
40. 'Evgenii Zamiatin', in A. K. Voronskii, *Stat´i* (Ann Arbor: Ardis, 1980), pp. 57–91 (p. 58) (first publ. in *Krasnaia nov´*, 1922.6, 304–22).
41. 'O iazyke', as published in 'Tekhnika khudozhestvennoi prozy', p. 85. It is not clear why Zamiatin mentions these Italian writers. He is clearly referring to the poet, dramatist, and prose writer Gabriele D'Annunzio (1863–1938), and the prose writers Giovanni Papini (1881–1956) and Luciano Zuccoli (1868–1929). Only Papini, however, whose *Esperienza futurista* appeared between 1913 and 1914, could properly be described as an experimenter in the avant-garde mould.
42. A. Kruchenykh, 'Deklaratsiia zaumnogo iazyka', in *Manifesty i programmy russkikh futuristov*, ed. by Vladimir Markov, Slavische Propyläen series, 27 (Munich: Fink, 1967), pp. 179–81 (p. 179). See also the commentary to 'Strashnyi lad', in Eikhenbaum, *O literature*, p. 480.
43. For the text of 'Illiuziia skaza', see B. M. Eikhenbaum, *Skvoz´ literaturu* (Leningrad: [n. pub.], 1924; repr. 'S-Gravenhage: Mouton, 1962), pp. 152–56 (first publ. in *Knizhnyi ugol*, 2 (1918)).
44. 'Leskov i sovremennaia proza', p. 214.
45. See S. Kastorskii, '*Gorodok Okurov* i povest´ E. Zamiatina *Uezdnoe*', in idem, *Povesti M. Gor´kogo* (1960), cited (and translated) by Shane, p. 164.
46. 'Problema skaza v stilistike', in V. V. Vinogradov, *O iazyke khudozhestvennoi prozy: Izbrannye trudy*, afterword by A. P. Chudakov, commentary by E. V. Dushechkina (Moscow: Nauka, 1980), pp. 42–54 (p. 54).
47. Niqueux, p. 53.
48. 'Strashnyi lad', p. 291.
49. Ibid., p. 290.
50. See Eric de Haard, 'On Zamjatin's Narrative Art — "Lovec čelovekov"', in *Voz´mi na radost´: To Honour Jeanne Van der Eng-Liedmeier* (Amsterdam: [n. pub.], 1980), pp. 169–81 (p. 171).
51. Voronskii, p. 57.

52. *PPS*, II, 1901. It is perhaps worth noting that Leskov had earlier used the word
     prepolovenie to mean 'half' in 'Zapechatlennyi angel' (1873). See N. S. Leskov, *Sobranie*
     sochinenii, ed. by V. G. Bazanova and others, 11 vols (Moscow: Gosudarstvennoe
     izdatel´stvo khudozhestvennoi literatury, 1956–58), IV (1957), 320–84 (p. 353).
53. Maksimov, XVII, 142–43 (p. 142). See also the entry in *ES*, XXV, 69.
54. Maksimov, XVII, 143.
55. Maksimov makes great play of the fact that most people in Russia, when asked to
     state the significance of the Feast of Prepolovenie, have no idea at all why it is
     celebrated: 'Праздник Преположение принадлежит к числу тех, истинное значение
     которых совершенно непонятно для народа. Даже люди образованного круга, на вопрос:
     что такое Преположение — отзываются сплошь и рядом полным неведением.' See ibid.,
     p. 142.
56. Cited and discussed in Charlotte Rosenthal, 'Remizov's *Sunwise* and *Leimonarium*:
     Folklore in Modernist Prose', *Russian Literary Triquarterly*, 19 (1986), 95–111 (pp. 95–
     96).
57. For further discussion, see Catriona Kelly, 'Life at the Margins: Woman, Culture and
     Narodnost´,' in *Gender Restructuring in Russian Studies: Conference Papers – Helsinki,*
     August 1992, ed. by Marianne Liljestrom, Eila Mantysaari, and Arja Rosenholm,
     Slavica Tamperensia series, 2 (Tampere: [University of Tampere], 1993), pp. 139–59
     (p. 153).
58. Zabylin, p. 382. Zabylin indicates here that the source for the text of this charm is
     Sakharov's *Skazki russkogo naroda* (1841).
59. Shane, p. 112.
60. *The Golden Legend of Jacobus de Voragine*, translated and adapted from the Latin by
     Granger Ryan and Helmut Ripperger (New York: Longman, Green, 1948), x.
61. Iurii Annenkov, *Dnevnik moikh vstrech*, 2 vols (New York: Inter-Language Literary
     Associates, 1966), I, 266.

CHAPTER 2

(TAMBOV)

POLUDENNITSA (KUNY)

'Poludennitsa (Kuny)' is an incomplete text which Zamiatin offered for the approval of the military censors at some point between 1914 and 1916.[1] The manuscript, made available to the editors of Neimanis by Natal'ia Borisovna Sollogub, and published for the first time in 1988, consists of some twenty pages, along with two alternative introductions, and is a typed version of the draft variants preserved in the Zamiatin archive in IMLI (opis´ 1, ed. khr. 79 & 80). The fact that one of these introductions features a village constable called Baryba (43) suggests that the writing of the narrative might even pre-date *Uezdnoe*, the chief protagonist of which boasts the same name and profession (Zamiatin was working on this tale between 1911 and 1912). The fourth chapter, 'Kuny', which is the only chapter in the story to bear a title, was later reworked and published with minor modifications in 1923 in Lezhnev's journal *Rossiia* (PZ, 55). Thus it is the only text from the post-revolutionary period which owes its inspiration to an idea first mooted, if not entirely executed, before 1917. This circumstance justifies the examination of 'Poludennitsa' and 'Kuny' together as early provincial stories, and for the purposes of this chapter they will be treated as an artistically uniform unit, but analysed separately.

Shane's remark that the 1923 version of 'Kuny' signals 'a nostalgic return to the provincial Russia satirized in the early works' cannot be sustained in the light of the facts now known.[2] Unwittingly, however, his reading of the story touches upon an important facet of 'Poludennitsa (Kuny)', namely the tonal gulf which separates them from the other tales usually lumped together in the early provincial bracket. While these are all *skaz* stylizations in the sense that they are written in a style which attempts to communicate the syntax, lexicon, and register of popular speech, Zamiatin's pre-revolutionary period shows striking development in terms of his attitude to the imaginative world of his fictional protagonists. This is detectable even in tales situated within the same milieux. The harsh, satirical vision gradually softens, moving away from the brutal perspective of *Uezdnoe* towards the colourful, vibrant, and lyrical expressiveness of 'Afrika' (1916); the grotesque and ugly imagery is transmuted; the grating and harsh dissonances of the language develop into something less shocking and disharmonious; the violence of the syntactical reversals is radically tempered; and what appears at first glance to be nihilism generally is replaced by a gentler comic and ironic spirit which is more exuberant, celebratory, and positive.

The choice of 'Poludennitsa (Kuny)' for analysis is motivated less by their artistic quality (the unfinished state of the former makes such a statement superfluous) than by their interest as indicators of the important shift which takes place between 1914 and 1916. These stories reveal a newly discovered, or better to say more consistently explored fascination with the folk-religious mind as far as it pertains to rituals, songs, games, double-faith, and the celebration of feast days. In the earlier stories, for example, the use of this material functioned primarily as *kolorit*. The humorous portrait of the witch in *Uezdnoe* has been mentioned already in the first chapter of this study.[3] In addition, one could mention the references to dream-books (*sonniki*), portents (*primety*), and love charms (*prisukhi*) in relation to the merchant's widow Chebotarikha (I, 41); the stylized treatment of St Elijah's Day (I, 49–54); and the penny-dreadfuls (*lubochnye knizhonki*) which Baryba reads in his spare time.[4] These are random, isolated, ethnographic, realistic details, and testify to the implied narrator's close acquaintance with *byt* in all its local and class-specific manifestations. Furthermore, while these stories occasionally exploit religious symbolism and sacred genres, usually with the purpose of subversion — *Uezdnoe*, for example, has been approached from the point of view of anti-hagiography, and as a reversal of Christ's Parable of the Prodigal Son[5] — nowhere is folklore integrated into the text as a theme in its own right, or as a self-contained imaginative world with its own codes and signifiers. By contrast, the rituals, customs, and beliefs of the pious folk in 'Poludennitsa (Kuny)' carry a poetic burden and symbolic significance crucial to the overall design. We are dealing here not with a naturalistic diet of the quaint and exotic — the staple fodder on which the progressive intelligentsia nurtured its hopes and dreams of the *narod* during the second half of the nineteenth century — but with a poeticized and stylized expression of an imaginative consciousness, one as if composed by a genuine insider, against which the themes of the story are juxtaposed and elaborated.

The action of 'Poludennitsa (Kuny)' is set in the province of Tambov, not in the Far North, as initially surmised by Shane.[6] The village mentioned in the narrative, Kuiman´, is a real village situated in the Izbishchensk district some fifty kilometres south of Lebedian´, the small town in which Zamiatin was born and spent most of his youth. The villages of Kalikino and Dobroe, which are mentioned in the main body of the text (26), and the county of Dankov´, which is referred to in one of the introductory variants (42), can also be found in this locality. The actual status of Kuiman´, however, is difficult to gauge on the basis of a pre-revolutionary map. It lies on the road between Lebedian´ and Lipetsk, and looks like a large village or market town (*selo*), rather than a small village or hamlet (*derevnia*).[7] In 'Slovo predostavliaetsia tovarishchu Churyginu' (1926), a satirical *skaz* narrative composed in the form of an after-dinner speech to commemorate the tenth anniversary of the Revolution, Kuiman´ is offered as an emblem of marginality and pre-revolutionary backwardness. The speaker of the title, a country bumpkin whose grasp of Bolshevik ideology functions only on the level of revolutionary argot, claims Kuiman´ as his *rodina*. Furthermore, he refers to it in terms of a *derevnia*, and gives a brief account of its characteristics:

Вся природа у нас там расположена в сплошном лесу, так что вдали никакого более или менее уездного города, и жизнь происходит очень темная. (II, 84)

Churygin's boast about his humble origins need not be taken at face value: it is hyperbole, intended to impress upon the audience his genuine proletarian credentials. Nevertheless, like Lebedian´, Kuiman´ plainly belongs to a semi-urban, semi-rural cultural space with a provincial set of norms and patterns of behaviour, many of which may have been inspired by Zamiatin's own memories of his youth (as we will see, the presence of the priest in the story, and the galaxy of eccentric characters employed by the church under his care, are strongly reminiscent of his own family background).[8] Suffice it to say, whether based on the real Kuiman´, or merely an ethnographic conceit, the Kuiman´ in the two Zamiatin narratives conforms to the category of location increasingly favoured in his provincial fiction, namely the peripheral backwater in which ancient customs, double-faith, and colourful, authentic speech have remained untouched by the impact of modern civilization.

PART I: 'Poludennitsa'

The plot of 'Poludennitsa' spans a period from the beginning of the
Lenten Fast to the Assumption of the Virgin Mary (15 August). The
opening paragraph introduces the reader to four characters living
together in a small house behind the local church: in the 'clean half',
the priest Father Viktor and his young wife; and in the blackened *kurnia*,
grandmother Pelageia and the young Marinka.[9] The exact nature of the
relationship between these people is never properly explained in the
course of the narrative. Pelageia is clearly Marinka's grandmother, and
presumably employed as a cook and home-help; nothing, however, is
said about the young girl's parents. Written in the third person, the
narrative concerns the growing relationship between the priest and this
young girl after the successive deaths of the grandmother and the
priest's wife, Liudmila. Marinka initially develops what appears to be a
maternal and protective attitude towards the young man as he
desperately mourns his wife's death and wrestles with the implications
for his religious faith. Soon, however, this attitude develops into an
obsessive, fatal passion. As Marinka is well aware, such a love is
destined never to be consummated (in such circumstances an Orthodox
priest would not have been permitted to remarry).[10] Nevertheless, as
the priest's faith begins to wane, its source of strength dampened
irreparably by the tragic loss of his wife, so his moral defences begin to
crumble. The climax of the narrative occurs when Marinka, having
failed to elicit a response from him on St Elijah's Day (20 July),
confesses her passion during the festival to celebrate the Assumption of
the Virgin Mary. The narrative concludes abruptly and ambiguously,
with indications that the young girl will succeed in her aim of seducing
him.

Charting the process by which 'Poludennitsa (Kuny)' becomes
transformed into the 1923 version of 'Kuny' is an illuminating exercise,
since it illustrates the degree to which Zamiatin opted for a shift in
dramatic and poetic focus, away from the figure of the priest, and
towards his young heroine; in effect, by stripping away the rest of the
tale, and leaving only an abridged version of its fourth chapter without
the final two segments, he consigned his youthful priest to oblivion.
The draft introductions show that during the initial stages Father
Viktor was envisaged as the main protagonist — evidence, perhaps, of
Zamiatin's intention to narrate the story directly from the priest's point
of view, and therefore concentrate on his crisis of faith. Variant A, for
example, opens with a letter from his brother Gleb, in which he is
urged to give up his cassock, return to his home town of Kazan, and

'live for life, not for death' (40). Discreet mention is also made of his
sexual initiation as a young boy at the hands of his forty-year-old
nanny, an experience which causes him feelings of guilt and anxiety
(41). His conversations with the sexton Afrikanych produce a
potentially interesting observation:

— Ведь всякое наше движение, всякий цвет, слово, улыбка — отпечатывается где-то
там, колебаниями какими-то, больше ведь это ничем не выражается. Весь мир как бы
один огромный кинематограф, видимый умершим, изредка — нам. (42)

This is an indication, perhaps, that Zamiatin aimed to approach the
painful subject of death through a semi-mystical prism (it is especially
intriguing to see mention here of the new medium of cinema — apart
from the role it plays in 'Alatyr´', the cinema features rarely, if at all, in
his early fiction). Yet, as we know when all the variants and texts are
compared, this is not pursued any further. Beginning with the two
alternative introductions, through the main body of 'Poludennitsa', to
the version of 'Kuny' as published in the journal *Rossiia*, we witness the
gradual erasure of the priest and his relegation to the status of marginal
figure. He moves from the individualized to the general and symbolic;
indeed, identified already in 'Poludennitsa' with the iconic image of
Christ, by the time of 'Kuny' his individuality has been altogether
purged and he exists purely as an embodiment of the Orthodox faith.
His interior world, and his struggle to keep the faith and survive the
death of his wife, become non-existent issues, drowned out by the
imaginative world and interior voice of Marinka.

The reason for this radical change in direction can only be speculated
upon. It is, however, the first such narrative in Zamiatin's fiction (for a
non–*skaz* treatment from a female perspective, see 'Aprel´' (1915)), and
one of the very few narratives in Russian literature which is written by
a male author but seeks to project in direct fashion the imaginative
world and voice of a young woman.[11] Part of the explanation may lie in
his desire for experimentation (the challenge of a female, as opposed to
a male, form of ventriloquism); but it may also lie in his growing
fascination with the vitality of the world which Marinka herself
represents. This process can be seen at work in 'Poludennitsa' by the
extent to which the narrative voice and point of view regularly merge
with her own; indeed, it is signalled at the beginning of the story with
an extraordinarily arresting portrait of her grandmother, a woman who
dominates her early years. The relevant passage is a stylistic *tour de
force* and deserves citation in full:

Эх, бабушка! Да николи ее Маринке не забыть. Сказочница, прибаутница, стряпуха
— у самого Куйманского барина такой, поди, нету. Шаньги какие пекла, заспенники,
обыдники, пироженники — эх! А сказки... Бывало, зимой на дворе морозяка лютый,
бревна трещат, а тут, в кухне, теплынь. Печка огромная, как ведмедь в сказке, так и
пышет. На печи — ячмень сплошь насыпан, сушится, там-то вот и есть ребячье да
бабкино царство. Ребятишки налезут и дьячковы, и Аверьяна лабазника, и солдатки
Прасковьи, и еще нивесть чьи — соседские, на ячмене-то тепло да мягко — ну, тут
бабка Пелагея им и рассказывай. Очки нацепит, ниткой круг уха обведет,
коклюшками пробрякивает — и уже такого наскажет. И про лису, и про зайку-
всезнайку, и про курицу — отчего она петухом поет и к чему это, и как быть, если
икона со стены упадет. А то еще про белую лошадь: ночью в поле едешь — вдруг,
нивесть откуда — рядом с санями белая лошадь, бежит да бежит, и не отстанет, пока
всех покойников не помянешь. [...]
    Весело было с бабушкой Пелагеей. (23–24)

This is a celebratory piece of writing, the like of which cannot be found
in any of Zamiatin's fiction prior to this moment. Furthermore,
although it may well reflect the rich influence of his own grandmother
on his education, it is more than merely a nostalgic (and banal) portrait
of the old woman as transmitter of folklore.[12] Its strategic position
within the text as a whole, its incorporation of several references to
actual folk tales, and the careful manner in which the world of tale-
telling is evoked ensure that the passage will be read as a trope for
Zamiatin's own *skaz* conceit. The wonderfully inventive image of the
old woman pulling her woollen thread 'around the ear' (*krug ukha*) is a
clever, visual approximation of the action of knitting, yet at the same
time it can also be interpreted in the context as a trope for oral
narration, the impact of which depends primarily on acoustic reception. Such a trope focuses attention on the intimate relationship
between speaker and audience necessary for the telling of tales, and the
importance of sound generally. Furthermore, the depiction of the entire
scene, with its freezing frost outside and cosy warmth inside, is an
archetypal evocation of the folk tale-telling world. The degree to which
the narratorial voice identifies with this world, at times giving the
impression that it is blending with Marinka's own interior monologue,
is striking. The colloquial tone and register of the language (the
repeated use of the exclamatory *ekh!*); the persistent use of diminutives;
the regional dialect (*vedmed´* instead of *medved´*); the illusion of shared
participation ('a tut, v kukhne, teplyn´'); and the disavowal of authorial
omniscience (he affects not to know the identities of the other children
in the kitchen when grandmother Pelageia tells her tales) indicate a
provisional merging of viewpoint between author-narrator and
fictional protagonist.

In several key respects the description of Grandma Pelageia in this opening paragraph has an important bearing on the ensuing narrative. She is a great teller of tales (*skazochnitsa*) and a walking dictionary of proverbs, sayings, and pithy observations (*pribautnitsa*). She is also an expert on portents and omens, able to tell the meaning of an icon falling off the wall and the significance of a chicken crowing like a cock.[13] The contents of the old trunk in which she keeps her special personal belongings, and which Marinka inspects after she has died, suggest some sort of folk-healer or herbal doctor (*znakharka*).[14] There are objects here with healing properties, some of them medicinal, and there are others which are clearly antidotes to various forms of maleficium (*porcha*). We learn, for example, that the ten dried mosquitoes (*koramora*) can be applied as a cure for malarial fever (*likhomanka*).[15] The other herbs, however, such as the *alateinyi* and *kupyrnyi* roots, and those which are not named because Marinka does not know them, may well have magical properties.[16] The revelation that Grandma Pelageia knows all the 'evil charms' and 'love charms' — 'Все пригубы да присухи ведала' (25) — is significant: the former refers to a knowledge of incantations and charms (*zagovory*) which cause harm, even death;[17] while the latter alludes to a range of charms supposedly known only by witches and sorcerers.[18] The suspicion arises on the basis of this information that there is a much darker dimension to her character than at first sight appears to be the case.[19] There is a strong hint in these opening lines that the old woman's dabbling in magic may ultimately have led to her downfall, or led to her becoming the victim of someone else's maleficium. She disappears mysteriously the day before Forgiveness Day (*Proshchen den*'), having left to go outside for a bucket of water from the well, and is later found dead in a ravine some distance away with the bucket by her side (24). The author-narrator, indirectly expressing Marinka's thoughts, observes that this object may have played some role in her death: 'Надо быть — не без него тут дело обошлось' (ibid.). This is an indirect admission that she might have been performing some sort of *zagovor*, since this was often done with the aid of water, and the ravine in folklore was widely associated with witches. A little while later, after the priest's wife has died from an inexplicable fever, the author-narrator records the rumour that the priest's house has been 'cursed' — 'Напущено это было на попов двор' (24): this is an explicit allusion to the practice of spoiling (Dal', II, 457).[20] Pelageia's disappearance, which takes place at the end of the carnival season, and ironically just before a festival in which people forgive each other's sins, thus comes to appear in a new and sinister light.[21]

Marinka's powerful attachment to her grandmother — understan-
dably, she is much more upset about her death than the death of the
priest's wife — is significant within the context of this opening section:
it establishes her symbolic kinship with the old woman and serves as a
displaced indicator of her own imaginative world. This sphere belongs
to the realm of double-faith, a characteristic of the peasant's
imaginative world in the nineteenth century which involved simultaneous belief in the Orthodox faith and supernatural spirits.[22] Marinka
and her grandmother belong to a number of characters in the narrative
who inhabit a similar belief system (the most amusing example is the
inebriated Afrikanych during the final hours of St Elijah's Day), and it
is important to realise that the hold of Orthodox religion on all is
tenuous. The symbolic division of the house, with its 'clean half'
reserved for the priest and his wife, and the 'dirty half' inhabited by
Marinka and her grandmother, encourages a reading of the text in
terms of the deliberate juxtaposition of two imaginative worlds: the
former is 'pure' and rooted in Orthodox Christianity; while the latter is
'impure' and rooted in folk belief. Herein lies the central conceit of
Zamiatin's narrative. Concealed among these seemingly random
revelations about Marinka's grandmother lies a pattern of meaning
which revolves around spoiling and incitement to love, offering a
parallel 'folk' explanation for the amorous folly which ensues. It is an
axiom of this perspective, one anticipated by the early mention of icons
falling off walls as a sign of bad luck, that the illicit and forbidden love
of Marinka for the priest is viewed as the result of malevolent intervention which causes them to act immorally in the eyes of the Church.

It is symptomatic of the folk-religious symbolism of the text that
Marinka's obsession with Father Viktor takes place against a background of concern about marriage and the prospects of finding a
husband (*suzhenyi*). As was customary in rural communities, these
thoughts are linked symbolically with the arrival of spring and the start
of the festive season. As Marinka emerges from church on the ninth
day after a remembrance service held for her grandmother — an
indication, therefore, that this is the second day of Catkin Week
(*Verbnaia nedelia*) — she espies the first rook of spring.[23] Her thoughts
move naturally to the launch of the festive season: the painting of eggs,
the swinging on swings (activities associated with Easter Week and the
weeks which followed), and then the round dance season, which we
learn begins in Kuiman´ during *Rusal´naia nedelia* — in other words, the
week leading up to Whit Sunday.[24] Her youthful mind looks forward
in ambiguous anticipation to the meeting with her intended:

Девичью ль сердцу горевать, когда суженый впереди: худо, когда суженый есть — прощай девичья воля, — худо, когда милый не любит — прощай суженый. (24–25)

A crucial episode in the acquisition of her intended occurs when Marinka is visited by the neighbouring matchmaker Petrovna, who has waddled over to the house on hearing that the young girl has discovered three 'chicken gods' (*kurich'i bogi*) belonging to her grandmother (significantly, these stones were associated symbolically in rural areas with fertility).[25] The characterization of Petrovna, obviously a key figure in the betrothal process, is typical for the rural matchmaker. She is regarded as something of a witch — the description *staraia Iaga* refers to *Baba Iaga*, the wicked old witch of Russian magic tales, while the word *koldun'ia* is standard for rural areas — and for good measure we are referred to a growth (*kila*) the size of a nut on her forehead which she conceals beneath her headscarf in order to avert suspicion.[26] Marinka rightly suspects that Petrovna wants these stones in order to perform some 'evil magic' (*nagovory*) of her own. At the same time, while trying to bargain with Marinka by offering her a drug in exchange which will make her intended fall in love with her, she makes a surprising revelation:

— Коли дашь, девушка, одного божка — и я тебе снадобья дам такого, что с ним живо суженого своего обратаешь. А суженый-то молод, пригож, на попа похож. (29)

The mention of such a drug echoes back to the earlier mention of *prisukhi* in relation to Marinka's grandmother. Yet the revelation that her intended is handsome and looks like the priest proves shocking and intriguing; being clairvoyant, a gift which all witches and sorcerers in Russia were reputed to possess, Petrovna seems to have guessed Marinka's secret. Marinka refuses to give Petrovna any of the stones, however, and despatches her firmly from the house (she decides not to strike her because this might bring bad luck).[27] Nevertheless, the seed of hope has been firmly planted in her mind. And this sense of foreboding is heightened when, after Petrovna walks off with an ambiguous warning and Marinka has returned into the house, a jug crashes off the wall. This is clearly a bad omen, and signals the beginning of 'malevolent' interference in her fate.

Marinka's initial reaction to Petrovna's prediction is to pray before a holy icon of Christ, asking that she be saved from the 'midday demon'. The words spoken at this moment ('Господи, спаси от беса полуденного и сряща' (30)) are a direct citation from the Old Testament, Psalms 90. 6, and refer to the calamities which strike in the middle of the day (the archaic *sriashch* here, from the Greek *sumptoma*, refers to accidents and unforeseen events).[28] It would appear that she believes that an irresistible and malevolent force is taking hold of her, and the theme of love as the fulfilment of evil prophecy is spurred into action as a possible explanation for the ensuing events. At the heart of this nexus lies the word of the title. This can refer to a fever contracted in the middle of the day (Dal´, III, 251), and thus recalls both the fever which kills Father Viktor's wife at the beginning of the story, and the various cures for malaria found in Pelageia's trunk. There is more than a hint, however, that Zamiatin's *poludennitsa* refers, not merely to a fever, but to the female spirit with whom that fever was identified in the folk-religious imagination of the southern province in which the story is set. Fevers were so common in Russia that peasants divided them into different types, each one associated with a particular female spirit. Furthermore, Zelenin gives *poludennitsa* as a synonym for *rusalka* (i.e. water-spirit), noting that in southern areas rural communities employed three different terms — *utrenniaia*, *poludennitsa*, and *vecher-nitsa* — depending on the time of day when she was believed to be most dangerous (this echoes back to the original prayer in front of the icon, and something of this kind is also intimated in *Uezdnoe* with the mention of the belief that one should not sleep or swim in the middle of the day for fear of the *bes poludennyi* (I, 41)).[29] It is possible that Zamiatin's *poludennitsa* is a corruption of *poludnitsa*, an apparition invoked by adults to prevent their young from stealing from other people's gardens during the midday siesta period (Dal´, III, 251). According to some sources, this spirit took the form of a beautiful tall girl in white who was believed to walk the fields at noon when the grain was ripe.[30]

'Poludennitsa' suggests that all these interpretations apply to the South of Russia. An analogy is drawn, for example, between the intensifying heat of the summer months and the growing intensity of Marinka's feelings towards the priest; this is reinforced by images juxtaposing the 'chasteness' of night against the 'wantonness' of midday, a reversal of the usual poetic opposition:

Жуткая, жаркая, полуденная тишина не страшнее ли тихой полночи? Полночь — монахиня, спрятавшая под черной скуфейкой жаркий блик молодых глаз своих; полдень — монахиня, сбросившая с себя черные покрывала, раскрывшая широко глаза и губы. Разве не страшна красногубая, жадная женщина? (30)

The possibility that Marinka, like the *rusalka*, is a potential undoer of the male sex has been indicated at the beginning of the narrative by her grandmother, who was fond of reminding her that it is a bad sign to have eyebrows meeting in the middle: 'Ox, не люби никого, Маринка — одного полюбишь, и того погубишь' (25). As Marinka becomes more feverishly obsessed, so she adopts the tactics of the archetypal *femme fatale*, seeking to arouse the priest by rushing into his room with the buttons of her shirt deliberately undone. This is followed by several passages in which she herself is associated with the idea of the midday heat and the *poludennitsa*: 'Валится все из рук, слушает, стиснувши зубы, шепчет что-то становится сама полуденной' (30). Later, at the moment she decides to confess her sins personally to Father Viktor, Marinka recalls the words of her song during the round dance, and has a vision of the 'shameless' spirits whirling around in the mid-day heat:

Желтые, горячие поля исходят сухим зноем. Вьются над полями бесстыдные полуденницы, шевеля ноздрями, как собаки, втягивая знойный, вещающий грозу воздух. (39)

During the confession, the metamorphosis is complete: 'Нельзя смотреть — это первое — и поднимает на нее отец Виктор глаза: прямо перед ними — ярая полуденница, пышет, губы раскрыты' (40). It is symptomatic that the priest's last attempt to resist her involves pressing his cross against her lips.[31]

'Poludennitsa' is the first Gogolian obsession text in Zamiatin's fiction, one which seeks to explore the lives of people possessed by an idea or another person, living on the edge in a state of delirium and ready to hurl themselves into the abyss.[32] In so far as it constitutes a fictional exploration of a young girl's imaginative world, and charts her sexual awakening, it may be compared both to 'Devushka' (1910) and 'Aprel'' (1915). The folk symbolism, however, and the peasant milieu in which the action takes place, give rise to an entirely different reading experience. Marinka, as well as being a young girl, is emblematic of the *narod* and the folk-religious mind. The drama of her love for the priest is thus essentially a symbolic one. She is torn between two modes of consciousness and spirituality which are ostensibly at odds with each other, but which in Russia had become confused into the phenomenon of double-faith. Her transmutation into a hissing spirit, the sound of which echoes the hissing of the stove and the *vedmed´* of the folk tale in the second paragraph, signals the abandonment of all pretence of Orthodoxy in favour of the pagan and 'devilish'. Her closeness to the earth, moreover, suggested by the regular references to her domestic duties (calving, milking the cows, collecting eggs from the henhouse, baking of bread etc.), and her symbolic identification via the image of the *poludennitsa* with fields of rye ready to be harvested, indicate a view of the world in which birth and fertility are vital preoccupations. In 'Kuny', both as a chapter within 'Poludennitsa', and as a self-contained text, these forces are given a more intense and concentrated symbolic focus. There is a greater degree of emphasis on the carnivalesque spirit with which the world of the folk is imbued; and the duality of the text, with its spatial division between church and village common, and its juxtaposition of ecclesiastical and folk rituals, becomes more apparent.

PART II: 'Kuny'

Unlike 'Poludennitsa', 'Kuny' (written 1914–16, first published 1923) charts a single day in the life of the village of Kuiman´. It is St Elijah's Day (*Il´in den´*), an altar-day (*prestol´nyi prazdnik*) in this particular rural community, and one with a symbolic resonance for the Russian peasantry as a whole.[33] The inhabitants are shown celebrating in traditional fashion. There is a service held at the local church in the morning conducted by the parish priest; this is followed in the afternoon by games and round dances on the village common, an age-old pastime performed primarily by the young girls of the community throughout the spring and summer months. In the morning, Marinka is shown praying before an icon of Christ, her concentration fixed intently on the priest performing the eucharist, evidently in the hope of some indication, however small, that her feelings of passionate love may be reciprocated. After the service, however, disappointed that she has been ignored, Marinka reluctantly joins her friends for the dance celebrations. Quickly she succumbs to the spontaneity, vitality, and energy of the occasion. Whirled around and intoxicated by the heat of the sun, she performs a teasing, erotic dance before the blacksmith Iasha Grebenshchikov (partly, we suspect, to avenge the fact that she has been snubbed by the real object of her passion). Later, out of caprice, she is tempted to succumb to her handsome partner and arrange a rendezvous with him for the evening. Having met him, however, she thinks better of this idea and reprimands him when he tries to take advantage of her. The day ends as sadly as it began: Marinka's love remains unrequited, she is unable to accept a substitute for the true object of her passion, and her life remains balanced precariously between conflicting wishes and desires.

As a *lubok* stylization, 'Kuny' is a striking example of the devices enshrined later in Zamiatin's lectures on the art of creative writing. Prominent among them is the conceit of narrative authenticity, according to which the author-narrator insinuates his thorough familiarity with the language, customs, mores, and imaginative world of the milieu. The information that St Elijah's Day is Kuiman''s *prestol´nyi prazdnik*, a term used to denote the feast day of the saint to whom the local church has been consecrated, suggests more than merely a nodding acquaintance with the district. So too does the recording in meticulous detail of the traditional costumes worn by the peasant women who have travelled from Korovinsk (presumably a satellite village) to attend the service: Zamiatin mentions the headdresses studded with silver coins, the silk veils, and the woollen skirts and sarafans, homespun in blue wool, with red gussets, fringes, and detailed patterns — these are costumes, we are told, which have been handed down from generation to generation and preserved for such special occasions as this one. Further ethnographic detail is supplied during the description of the market. The edible items, such as the gingerbread biscuits (*zhamki*), the biscuits baked in honey (*makovniki*), and those baked in the shape of goats (*prianiki-kozuli*); the toys for children, such as the slate-grey, laminated boards, clay whistles, and birchwood boxes; and the traders themselves, such as the raffish gypsy horse-dealers dressed in blue jerkins (this detail was added for the 1923 version (III, 79)), the manes of their horses combed and lubricated with *kvass* — all are topographical details pertaining to this particular southern region. The conceit of authenticity is further reinforced by the use of regional dialect. *Kuliberda* (33) is presumably a variant of *beliberda*, and thus means 'nonsense' (nota bene: this word is spelt *kuleberda* in the 1923 version (III, 79)). *Paneva* (33) refers to the woollen skirt of traditional peasant costume (Dal´, III, 14). And *razvytnyi* (34) means 'capable', 'hospitable', and 'high-spirited' (Dal´, IV, 20).

A key word in this context, one with a resonance far beyond the merely exotic, is the title of the story itself. This is a word with an ancient pedigree in Russian folk culture. In the singular, with the stress on the second syllable, *kuná* is a synonym for *kunítsa* or 'marten', the small, weasel-like animal valued in Russia and America for its fur (Dal´, II, 218). In ancient times, this word also referred to the small metal coins which came to replace fur as a means of payment for trade (ibid.), and it is found with this meaning in Russia's first annalistic chronicle, the *Povest´ vremennykh let* (*PVL*(6523), 62). Parents often demanded marten fur as the price for giving their daughter's hand in marriage — thus *kuná* became a metaphor for the bride during matchmaking ceremonies (this was especially true in the South of

Russia, where the bride and groom were referred to respectively in betrothal speeches and wedding songs as the 'black marten' (*cherna kunitsa*) and 'black sable' (*cherna sobol'*)).[34] Such phrases as 'virgin marten' (*devich'e kunichnoe*) and 'wedding marten' (*svadebnaia kunitsa*) were common expressions in Europe and Russia to denote the (compensatory) tax levied by feudal lords on newly wedded women if they were marrying into another demesne.[35] Furthermore, this custom was still prevalent in certain parts of Russia at the end of the nineteenth century.

Certainly, on the basis of Zamiatin's story, it would appear that *kuná* had retained its traditional connection with the custom of betrothal, at least as far as the province of Tambov was concerned, as late as the twentieth century. Both as a chapter within 'Poludennitsa', and as a self-contained fragment, 'Kuny' is a narrative in which anxiety about marriage and the prospects of securing a future partner are omnipresent in the mind of the heroine. In the opening paragraph, for example, the word of the title is given a semantic context in the form of a local variant for the term *khorovod* or round dance, a ritual which played an important role in rural communities as far as courtship was concerned.[36] The St Elijah round dances (called the *Il'inskie kuny* in the 1923 version of the story (III, 77)) are Marinka's last opportunity to secure a partner, or she will remain single until the beginning of the round dance season next year:

Уж теперь поздно, отошло их время, прошла Русалочья неделя, не успели залучить себе парня, девушки останутся еще на целый год. Одна надежда на куны: закружатся парни в кунных кругах, завихрят их девки, запутает в серебряную паутину паук-месяц: может, попадет какой по ошибке в русалочий хоровод. (32)

Later in the narrative, this ritual is described in detail. Initially, all the 'old maids' in the village (*devushki-vekovushki* (34)), dressed solemnly in dark headscarves, walk out on to the village common, form their own circle, and sing remembrance songs (*pominki*). All the young girls under marriageable age, the women who have not been able to find a husband, and those whose husbands have been conscripted into the army (*nemuzhnye zheny-soldatki*), all in red headscarves, then step onto the common and form a circular palisade to defend themselves against their 'undoers' (*pogubiteli milykh*) — in other words, their 'grooms'.[37] Marinka, the proud 'princess' (*tsarevna*), stands in the middle of this ring, the so-called 'marten city' (*kunnyi gorod*), and starts moving in the opposite direction to those standing around her. She launches the dancing with a humorous song about the 'enemies' (*vorogi*) who live outside the city with 'purses of gold' (ostensibly a reference to the young men and boys who are standing and watching by a willow tree nearby). She chooses to dedicate a song to the local blacksmith, Iasha Grebenshchikov, who is then crowned her 'prince' (*tsarev syn*). She switches to another song — 'U nas v gorode tsarevna, tsarevna' (35) — and then in another song, only two lines of which are cited, refers to the choosing of girls and the waving of kerchiefs. The *kunnyi krug* whirls faster and faster until Marinka orders the participants to stop ('Ekh, zhist´, otopris´'): the ring is broken so that the 'prince' can enter. There follows a teasing, erotic dance which builds up towards a climax before the sequence abruptly halts, shifting to a quieter moment later in the evening when the couple are alone together.

Although there were different kinds of round dance game in rural Russia, varying in terms of composition, type of song, and performance, Zamiatin's description of the *kunnyi krug* suggests that it is a popular game (*igra*) which symbolically re-enacts the rituals of courtship and betrothal. It is well known, for example, that the individual stages of the marriage process were dramatic spectacles with well-established, ritualized patterns of behaviour, and were popular among the folk as subjects for entertainment; this also applied to round dances and the various games associated with them. In this sense the *kunnyi krug* may be considered an example of folk theatre.[38] One such game, described by Kallash and Efros in their history of the Russian theatre, bears a striking resemblance to the spectacle in 'Kuny':

В игре, изображающей выбор невесты, в песне поется о том, как жених подступает под каменный город, разбивает стены и выводит красну девицу; изображающий жениха в это время ходит между двумя рядами девушек, выбивает у них из рук платки и, наконец, берет одну из них за руку и уводит с собою. Выбрав таким образом невесту, молодец обращается к соседям с распросами о ней. Оказывается, что 'соседушки-собратушки' не хвалят ее; тогда он выбирает себе другую, которую соседи 'схвалили'.[39]

A similar type of *igra* is mentioned by Propp in his introduction to a modern edition of Russian popular songs and ballads, many of them reprinted from nineteenth-century collections. He notes that the peasant *khorovod* was often depicted in terms of a 'town' or 'city' (*gorod*), with the performance involving a male person outside the circle who is challenged by the female participants to break through the 'wall' or 'gate' in order to acquire a prize within in the form of a young unmarried girl.[40] Interestingly, one song to which he refers in connection with this spectacle was recorded by the composer Milyi Balakirev some fifty years before Zamiatin in a region not very far from

Kuiman´ — it was subsequently included in his collection of folk songs for voice and piano.[41] Furthermore, Sobolevskii's nineteenth-century collection of folk songs contains a series of variants modelled on this type of courtship game.[42]

Although none of them match precisely the word sequence of the second song in 'Kuny', there can be little doubt that this song belongs to this round dance category. The references to the *vekovushki*, for example, their fate of remaining single for ever ('Им свой почет, поминки, вечным девушкам' (34)), and their euphemistic description as 'blind' (*slepye*), 'unwanted' (*nenuzhnye*), and 'dying' (*umershie*), establish the theme of their isolation and the importance attached to the securing of a husband. The opening lines of Marinka's first song, moreover, with their allusions to 'enemies' and 'purses of gold', refer metaphorically to the prospect of attracting (i.e. fighting) a rich husband.[43] The opening lines of her second song, with its references to cities, princesses, and princes, borrow from the imagery of the standard song type; the actions of the dance mirror generally the movements described by Propp; the two lines from the third song ('Он из тысячи любую выбирает/Он и белым платочком махает') echo the movements of the bride game outlined by Kallash and Efros; and the verb *otdat´* ('Вот она, царевна наша, бери — отдают, лукаво — покорная'), which means 'to give away', is employed in the folk sense of 'to give someone's hand in marriage'. Bearing in mind the fact that Zamiatin planned to use a similar game for the stage production of *Blokha* in 1925, it seems likely that he himself had witnessed the *kunnyi krug* in action.[44]

'Kuny' is an excellent illustration of how a single word can trigger a series of specific resonances within a given text, resulting both in irony and pathos. Part of the pathos of the story derives from the importance attached to the *khorovod* as a courtship ritual within the typical rural community — in other words, as a means for teenagers of both sexes to meet, become acquainted, and begin the marital process in accordance with the highly conservative and rigorous codes of conduct observed at the time.[45] It is also testimony to the tremendous gravity with which marriage itself was regarded by young women in these communities — as one scholar has commented recently: 'Other than birth and death, marriage constituted the most important event in the lives of Russian peasants.'[46] Thus, to employ a round dance in the form of a betrothal game, and one which would have been the very last of the festive season (unless there was an altar-day later in the year, the round dance festivities usually ended on St Peter and Paul's Day, i.e. 29 June),[47] lends Marinka's dilemma a dramatic urgency. She becomes powerfully established as a young girl on the threshold of womanhood, concerned with securing a partner and anxious about the prospect of remaining single.[48] It also provides an ironic commentary on her reluctance to accept a partner other than the one on whom her heart is set. Blacksmiths, for example, largely as a result of their profession, figure prominently in romantic songs and wedding songs: to 'forge a wedding' (kovat' svad'bu) was a standard expression in rural Russia. The marriage which Marinka has turned down symbolically is poignantly echoed during the scene in which she bursts into tears at the end of an emotional day: her 'groom' showers her with unwanted kisses, the expression used — svadebnyi khmel' (37) — being a conventional expression for the high and drunken spirits at a wedding. Furthermore, in order to understand the gravity of her refusal, it is worth being reminded of the disgrace and ignominy with which women were viewed in the peasant community if they did not manage to find themselves a suitable partner at the right age.[49]

The khorovod was a standard feature of peasant life, and one depicted in both lubok engravings (see Plate II) and the work of professional painters interested in folk pastimes. Zamiatin's treatment of the round dance theme in 'Kuny' is a sensuous, earthy affair, and the dance itself is far more exuberantly portrayed than the rosy-cheeked, but essentially wooden and surprisingly sombre versions produced by peasant engravers and their academic imitators.[50] Paradoxically, since the khorovod reflected a pattern of social relationships in which women were more or less passive spectators in the negotiations which decided their fate, Zamiatin accurately conveys the mood of the rural event and celebrates the mixed khorovodnaia igra as a sexual ritual. On the one hand, it is deliberately juxtaposed with the passionless rituals of the Church on St Elijah's Day;[51] and on the other hand, the sexual symbolism implicit in the dramatic gestures of the dance is exploited to striking effect. The palisade which surrounds the young (virginal) woman may be viewed as a symbolic hymen which is then punctured by a male figure who enters her terrain: this is made explicit by the references to the 'desired enemies' ('Крепким частоколом оборонились от желанных врагов' (34)), desired because they bring the prospect of marriage, and yet at the same time instrumental in the compromising of virtue and chastity, and thus 'undoers' (pogubitelei milykh) of the fair sex. The pagan undercurrents of the ritual, and its association with the worshipping of fertility, are never far below the surface. The exuberance of the dance, possibly reflecting the influence of Stravinskii's Vesna sviashchennaia (1913), is characterized in terms of a

primitive, semi-Dionysian frenzy, and in several ways anticipates the
erotic imagery of the later 'Lovets chelovekov': here the houses of
central London are seen dancing a slow *khorovod* around the gigantic
stone phallus of Nelson's Column (I, 347). In common with this
narrative, the golden orb of the sun in 'Kuny' is a symbol of
Bacchanalian energy and fertility. It is equated with the round dance
itself, an allusion to the belief prevalent at the turn of the century that
the round dance developed historically from pagan cults of fertility
worship: 'А жизнь неспешная, древняя, мерным круговоротом
колдующая, как солнце — здесь на выгоне' (34).[52] Furthermore, there is
a semantic echo which connects the lyrical images of the very first line
of 'Kuny' to the song with which Marinka launches her performance —
this suggests that while Marinka symbolically represents the fields of
wheat awaiting harvest, the 'enemy' with the 'purse of gold' is none
other than the sun itself:

Все выше взмывает солнце, все беспощадней. Вороха лучей насыпаны в ржаном поле
— и рожь стоит золотая, жаркая, и тихонько, матерински-довольно колышет колосья.
(32)

This may be compared with the words of the song which follows later:

Как за городом живут вороги,
Золотой казны у них ворохи,
Нет у ворогов военной головы. (34)

The acceleration of the dance, the intensifying heat, and the giddiness
caused by the relentless spinning are all emphasized. Marinka is
whipped into a sexual frenzy by the dancing, ready to yield herself to
anyone; so too is Iasha, who enters the ring and is instantly intoxicated
by the sight of her nipples pushing firmly through the material of her
red jacket. The dance ends with the promise of final consummation as
Marinka teases Iasha with her lips and shoulders: like the pine trees,
the couple are described as ready to uproot and throw themselves
down on the grass.[53]

Marinka's fundamental dilemma is that her natural inclinations do
not accord with the precepts of the Church. It is another ironic paradox
that the restraint which she displays in church — noted by her friends
(33) — is symbolically paralleled by the absence of rain during the
course of the day. Central to this paradox, and to the idea that Marinka
and the community are somehow 'punished' for her illicit passion, is
the folk-religious symbolism associated with St Elijah's Day. As several

commentators have observed, this was an important religious festival for the rural population of Russia in the last century.[54] As one of the hottest days of the year, the symbolism of this festival depended on the expectation of intense heat which would ultimately result in powerful rainstorms, thunder, and lightning; its theme, reflecting the character of the Old Testament prophet himself, was thus that of divine wrath. Folk commentators speak of Elijah's golden chariot careering across the skies, releasing bolts of lightning, and causing death and destruction wherever he goes; as a result of this, it was forbidden to work in the fields on St Elijah's Day or do anything sinful which would provoke his anger. At the same time, the prophet was also venerated as the giver of rain for the harvest. The absence of rain is twice remarked upon in the story, and on both occasions as something undesirable. The first observation belongs to the implied narrator: 'Да нет ни капли. Вот тебе и Ильин день. Хоть бы одна дождинка на смех' (36); while the second belongs to the sexton Afrikanych as he lies by a mound and stares at the sky: 'Эх, все пошло не по-человечьи, где же видано, чтобы Ильин день без дождя?' (ibid.). Elijah's withholding of rain is thus the symbolic equivalent of the priest's witholding of love (in the 1923 version Zamiatin makes this explicit by describing Marinka's ardent passion in terms of the parched earth).[55] Simultaneously, it can also be viewed as divine punishment for her pagan sinning. This is the view of Afrikanych, whom Marinka encounters on her way to her night-time rendezvous, who blames the absence of rain on her dancing and high spirits: '— Сама ты эх! Развытная больно! Непутевая. Плясавица. Из-за вас Илья дождя не дает' (36). The irony lies in the fact that Marinka's misdemeanour is not the conventional one of high-spiritedness, but the less obvious, because concealed, sin of harbouring passionate thoughts about the local priest.

Marinka is the prototype for several young women in Zamiatin's later fiction who feel the need for passionate fulfilment and do not shrink from expressing it, even if they are ultimately unsuccessful in evoking a reciprocal response. This urge is treated positively as a powerful natural instinct, as it is in many expressionist and neo-primitivist works of this period; indeed, it is one which features frequently in Zamiatin's fiction, and seemed to preoccupy him greatly, possibly because he and his wife were unable to have children.[56] In accordance with the stylistic conceit of the narrative, Marinka is a *lubok* type, rather than a subtle and intricately elaborated personality. Nevertheless, like other female protagonists in his early provincial fiction, she possesses distinctive features which emphasize her passionate nature

and semi-pagan, taboo-breaking, and carnivalesque spirit. Her description as 'lead' or 'first singer' (*zapevala, pervaia pevun'ia nasha* (36)), while
obviously an indication of her musical talent, refers also to her
prominent position within the hierarchy of girls in the village and the
important function she assumes in both round dance and matchmaking
ceremonies.[57] The use of such epithets as *zateinitsa* and *zadornitsa* (33),
both possessing a folk resonance, refer to a mischievous sense of fun,
an argumentative, quarrelsome nature, and an ardent spirit.[58] Her
skipping to the movement of a folk dance already on the church parvis
('— Постой, постой, на паперти, что ли?' (ibid.)) symbolizes the strength
of her underlying pagan allegiance. Moreover, her verbal brio is
indicated when Zamiatin reports her use of the vulgar expression
nalizat'sia (36) — literally, 'to get pissed' — in relation to the drunken
sexton Afrikanych. It should be pointed out that Zamiatin's colourful
and positive depiction of his protagonist constitutes something of a
novelty when compared to the female peasant types of nineteenth-
century fiction. She is neither the noble, virtuous, pathetic type of the
sentimental tradition, often a helpless victim of external machination
(see, for comparison, Karamzin's *Bednaia Liza*); neither is she the harpy,
virago, or shrew, denoted by the derogatory term *baba*, who was considered in some quarters responsible for the erosion of the patriarchal
hierarchy in the village (see, for comparison, Tolstoi's *Vlast' t'my*).[59]
Marinka is a new type in Russian fiction, a young woman on the
threshold of sexual awareness whose participation in the round dance
is essentially a ritual of liminality; as such, she exhibits sexual predatoriness and romantic longing in equal measure. While coquettish, and
therefore displaying all the tendencies of a turn-of-the-century *femme
fatale*, her situation is not without tragic pathos. The story ends on a
dispirited, downcast, and defeated note, with the long year until the
next St Elijah's Day stretching out before her, and only her dreams to
give her solace. We see a young woman who is trapped and struggling
to break free of the cultural and sexual conventions which bind her.

In his exploration of this woman's imaginative world, Zamiatin
poeticizes her sense of entrapment by means of a second folk-symbolic
analogy, one which, while certainly a convention of Romantic fiction, is
here treated with a considerable degree of originality. The first
paragraph, a lyrical introduction ostensibly belonging to the voice of
the implied narrator, but one which (again) seems to merge
imperceptibly with the interior voice of Marinka herself, refers to the
tragic situation of the *rusalka*:

За Куйманским лесом пруд весь зарос темной зеленью, из пруда по ночам выходят русалки и напролет до утра, заломивши руки, тоскуют на берегу, неутоленные, неутомленные. (32)

In retrospect, it becomes clear that this is a poeticization of Marinka's own dilemma. As the narrative progresses, the parallel between herself and the water-spirit is developed with increasing emphasis. Having left the church in the morning, for example, Marinka and her friends encounter a drunk on his way back to the village and are said to whirl him around and pinch him, giggling, like *rusalki* (34). During the description of the dance, moreover, there are several more such explicit references. In a direct echo of the opening paragraph, the challenge which Marinka issues to her 'prince' in the round dance is described in terms of casting a devious net: 'Поет царевна насмешливую песню, закидывает хитрые сети' (34). And later, her teasing of her opponent is described as capricious and tormenting: 'Эх, потешиться хоть над этим, замучить, защекотать по-русалочьи' (35). In the evening, the drunken Afrikanych accuses Marinka of secretly disappearing to participate in a *rusalochii khorovod* (36); and as she and her male consort walk across the common together, her voice is described as malicious and *rusalka*-like (37). As the narrative closes with a restatement of the original refrain — the *rusalki* sit crying among the branches, wringing their hands in despair at having failed in their search for a partner (ibid.) — there can be little doubt that this refers to Marinka and her sense of disappointment with the day's events.

This overarching symbolism in 'Kuny' is interesting both as ethnographic fact and as a good example of Zamiatin's neorealist tendencies. On the face of it, the opening paragraph seems to be recounting local folklore; as such, it might be said to reflect faithfully the fabulates in southern Russia about *rusalki* and the seasons of the year with which they were associated.[60] In the imagination of the folk, for example, the *rusalka* was a spirit of the 'unclean dead': she was believed either to be the ghost of a girl who had accidentally drowned or committed suicide, or the ghost of an infant who had died before being baptized.[61] The theme of the *rusalka* myth was thus the combination of danger, beauty, and treachery. As a spirit associated with water (she was believed to reside in ponds, pools, and rivers), she belonged to a category of supernatural being which acted in league with the 'unclean force' (*nechistaia sila*). In southern Russia, moreover, she was usually envisaged in the form of a beautiful, ethereal being, and thus the Russian equivalent of the Greek *naïad*, German *undine*, and French *ondine*. As indicated in the opening paragraph of 'Kuny', *rusalki* emerged during celebrations to welcome the onset of spring and then moved into the fields and woods during the summer. *Rusal´naia nedelia* (the week before Whit Sunday) was the period when they were considered at their most dangerous. Fabulates relate how they would emerge from their pools by the light of the moon and sit on the banks, combing their hair, singing enchanting songs, and dancing round dances in the hope of luring unwary travellers into their midst and drowning them; they were also portrayed as swinging on the branches of trees, whispering to each other, giggling, crying, and lamenting their unhappy fate. If the pathos of their situation derived from the fact that they were trapped in a miserable fate, it was also believed in certain communities that if a *rusalka* could deceive a village lad into marrying her, then she would miraculously regain human form.

Zamiatin's exploitation of the folk-myth in connection with Marinka is striking for the absence of any Romantic/Gothic conceit. His description is stripped of the enchantment and mystery which accompany the treatment of the theme in Romantic fiction — most strikingly, for example, in Gogol´'s Ukrainian-based 'Maiskaia noch´, ili utoplennitsa' (1831).[62] On the contrary, the tone of the narrative voice in the opening lines of 'Kuny' is factual, almost as if the lore of the region were being imparted for the sake of ethnographic record. Indeed, Zamiatin's treatment of the theme reflects the way in which the images and activities of the *rusalka* mirrored closely the social activities and romantic concerns of young girls in rural communities during the spring and summer period. As Zelenin observed in this context:

Молодежь весною занята веселенями: песнями, хороводами, играми, плясками, качаньем на качелях, заботится о своих нарядах и украшениях, а также прельщает и увлекает во свои сети молодых мужчин.[63]

The ethnographic fidelity of the description, nevertheless, offers opportunities for ironic counterpoint. The pathos of the water-spirit lay in her sense of imprisonment — hence the controlling emotional tone of yearning or *toska* with which Zamiatin's text is imbued. Furthermore, if in Romantic literature the tragedy of the water-spirit lay in her inability to cross from one realm to another in order to achieve or regain her heart's ambition, Marinka's sense of hopelessness derives from her recognition that the true object of her desires, metaphorically speaking, belongs also to a different realm (i.e. that of the Orthodox Church). Through Marinka, Zamiatin encapsulates and poeticizes the paradoxical qualities of femininity: innocence, sexual predatoriness, and malevolence, balanced by romantic longings and sad premonitions of an unhappy fate. Unlike the evil and dangerous *rusalka*, however, Marinka's threat consists only of a challenge to sexual and religious convention.

Despite its roots in the folk-religious mind and expressionist leanings, 'Kuny' is a relatively modest affair. Because of its commitment to realism, it does not seek to articulate the more menacing and violent impulses with which pre-Christian sexuality was represented in the avant-garde work of this time. Stravinskii and Diagilev's *Vesna sviashchennaia*, for example, set ostensibly in the dark and distant past of the ancient Slavs, combined the primitive ritual of the round dance with a marriage by abduction and a human sacrifice to the God of Spring and Light (Iarilo), and was much more radically neoprimitivist in spirit and design.[64] In essence, this reflected the difference between the poetics of neorealism and the mythological treatment of folklore by the Russian Symbolists. Furthermore, if the use of dialect and colloquial language sought to expand the parameters of the linguistically acceptable, and represented a challenge to conservative literary norms, the instrumentation of Zamiatin's 'Kuny' nowhere approximates the shocking and barbaric dissonances of Stravinskii's score. One does not have to agree entirely with Shane's definition of the story as a eulogy to Old Russia in order to appreciate, despite its ending in a minor key, the Kustodievan sense of carnival which underlies the description of the fair.[65] It suffices only to compare 'Kuny' with the treatment of St Elijah's Day in *Uezdnoe* (the same motifs of heat, rain, thunder, and impending punishment are all deployed, but without the sense of colourful exuberance), to comprehend the degree to which Zamiatin's vision of provincial life had become positive and life-affirming even at this relatively early stage in his writing career. Such an impression is reinforced when we come to examine 'Kriazhi', a tale about spurned and unrequited love which also exploits the lyrical beauty and harmony of nature as an ironic commentary on the refusal to recognize instinctive urges.

NOTES

1. See the editors' note in the Neimanis edition (IV, 23). Henceforth, unless otherwise stated, all references are to the Neimanis version, but without the volume number.
2. Shane, p. 180.
3. See Chapter 1 of the present study, p. 26.
4. The titles of these three stories are given as *Tiapka – lebedianskii razboinik, Prestupnyi monakh i ego sokrovishcha*, and *Kucher Korolevy Ispanskoi* (I, 60). The first two can be said to anticipate the plot in the sense that they give Baryba the idea of stealing the savings

of his friends in the monastery; thus they introduce a metafictional element into the narrative.

5. Tat´iana Davydova, 'Antizhanry v tvorchestve E. Zamiatina', in *Novoe o Zamiatine*, pp. 20–35.
6. Shane, p. 171. He also maintains that the story takes place on Midsummer Night's Eve; this is an error which will be further discussed in due course.
7. This would seem to be confirmed by the mention of a church in the two narratives, a feature which distinguished the market-town from the village. For indications of the relative size and amenities of both types of community, see Mary Matossian, 'The Peasant Way of Life', in *Russian Peasant Women*, ed. by Beatrice Farnsworth and Lynne Viola (New York: Oxford University Press, 1992), pp. 11–40 (p. 13).
8. 'Iz perepiski s rodnymi', p. 116n.
9. *Kurnaia izba* (*kurnia* is presumably a local variant) refers to the primitive hut of the poor peasant in the nineteenth century, which was so called because it did not have a chimney, thus causing the smoke and fumes from the stove to blacken the interior. See *ES*, XVII, 91; and also Matossian, p. 14.
10. Eve Levin, *Sex and Society in the World of the Orthodox Slavs, 900–1700* (Ithaca, NY: Cornell University Press, 1989), pp. 264–69.
11. Remizov's treatment of female folk types may well have been influential here. See 'Russkie zhenshchiny', in Aleksei Remizov, *Dokuka i balagur´e* (St Petersburg: Sirin, 1914), pp. 13–91.
12. In his 1916 letter to Vengerov, Zamiatin paid tribute to the educational influence of his grandmother: 'Учился языку я в Тамбовской гувернии, в городе Лебедяни... А учительницей была всего больше бабушка... Присказок... и присух всяких знала множество.' Cited in Primochkina, p. 149. This is confirmed in an autobiographical article which Zamiatin wrote in 1923: 'Чудесные русские слова знала моя бабка, может быть кое-чему научился от нее.' See '"Avtobiografiia" E. I. Zamiatina', ed. by V. V. Buznik, *Russkaia literatura*, 1992.1, 174–76 (p. 175).
13. '*Курица петухом поет* — не к добру; тогда суеверные хозяева свертывают ей голову и бросают чрез порог, приговаривая: 'на свою голову, не пой курица петухом.' Отсюда даже возникла пословица: '*не пой курица петухом, не бранись баба с мужиком.*'' All emphases in the original. See Zabylin, p. 268.
14. The definition of the word *znakhar´*, and the identification of such a person in a given rural community, is fraught with difficulties. In general, this was a 'wise person' (*znatok*) whose knowledge, powers of healing, and suspected links with the 'unclean force' put him on a par with fortune-tellers, sorcerors/wizards, sages, and whisperers (*sheptun´ia*), all of whom were believed to possess the ability to 'spoil' and heal their victims. For further discussion of this complex phenomenon, see Maksimov, XVIII, 184–96; Linda J. Ivanits, *Russian Folk Belief* (Armonk: Sharpe, 1989), pp. 103–24; and Samuel C. Ramer, 'Traditional Healers and Peasant Culture in Russia: 1861–1917', in *Peasant Economy, Culture, and Politics of European Russia: 1800–1921*, ed. by Esther Kingston-Mann and Timothy Mixter (Princeton: Princeton University Press, 1991), pp. 207–32.
15. *Korámora* refers to a particular species of mosquito popularly known in Russia as a *dolgonozhka*. Although this sounds like the English daddy-long-legs, it is in fact harmful and malarial.
16. Russian herbal doctors prided themselves on their knowledge of botany, some claiming to know as many as ninety-nine different grasses, herbs, and roots. Twelve of these were compulsorily kept at home by every self-respecting practitioner: *tsikuta, semena beleny, koren´ lapchatka, bogoroditskaia trava, volch´i iagody, koren´ morkovnika, koren´ paporotnika, kurich´a slepota, pautinnik, zemlianye orekhi, kunavka, buzinnyi tsvet*. See Maksimov, XVIII, 192, note 1. Zamiatin's selection is eclectic, however. Of the two mentioned in the story, the *kupyrnyi koren´* is identical to the *koren´ morkovnika* (Dal´, II, 221), and thus belongs to Maksimov's list. The *alateinyi koren´* would seem to derive

from the altei plant (*Althea officinalis*), and thus belongs to the same family as the English dog rose (*sobach´ia roza*) (ibid., I, 12).

17. The word *priguba* is probably dialect for the more common *paguba*. For the importance of spoiling in the life of rural communities, see Ivanits, p. 103. And for an anecdote which humorously draws attention to the continuing prevalence of spoiling even after the Revolution, see Zamiatin, 'Iz bloknotov 1914–1928 godov' (1989), p. 119.

18. Rendering assistance in gaining the affection of a loved one, or causing someone to fall out of love, was one of the major functions of the various practitioners of magic in the Russian village: 'Мимо ворожеи не пройдут ни удалые молодцы, ни красные девицы, ни обманутые мужья, ни ревнивые жены, потому что и нынче, как в старину, живет в людях вера в 'присуху'. Не надо ни лысых гор, ни придорожных расстаний, достаточно и деревенских завалинок, чтобы, узнавая сокровенные тайны, усердно заниматься приворотами и отворотами любящих и охладевших сердец.' See Maksimov, XVIII, 155.

19. 'Они [знахарки — РС] охотно берутся 'снимать тоску' с того человека, который лишился любви, но заставить полюбить не могут, так как 'присуха' — дело греховное и дается колдунам. В этом собственно и заключается существенная разница между колдунами и знахарями: то, что наколдуют чародеи — знахари и знахарки снимут и поправят.' See ibid., p. 194.

20. Zamiatin was aware of the danger malaria posed in southern Russia, since his own father had been struck down for several days in 1909 by a fever (*likhoradka*), although Zamiatin's mother was not certain whether it was malarial. See her letter to Zamiatin dated 25 April/8 May 1909, in 'Iz perepiski s rodnymi', p. 116.

21. It is instructive to compare this passage with the spoiling in *Uezdnoe*. Ivanikha initially asks the two monks whether they have come for a 'love charm' (*prisukha*). She then uses a bowl of water in order to enact her 'spell' (*zagovor*), and having drunk some tea with this water in it, Baryba, the intended victim, is soon afflicted with a 'fever' (*likhomanka*). See *Uezdnoe* (I, 64–65).

22. This was still the case at the end of the nineteenth century. Ivanits, for example, cites a correspondent from Tambov Province, V. Bondarenko, who wrote in 1890 that 'under the cover of Christianity, still understood only in its external form, many remnants of paganism have been retained'. Cited (and translated) in Ivanits, p. 4.

23. The chronology of this section can be established from the information given in the text. We are told, for example, that Marinka's grandmother dies on the Sunday before the first week of the Lenten Fast (*proshchal´noe voskresen´e*); while Father Viktor's wife dies during the fourth week of Lent (*krestopoklonnaia nedelia*). See PPS, II, 1493, & 1932 respectively. *Panikhidy*, which were special funeral services in memory of the dead, were held on the second, third, and fourth Saturdays of Lent (ibid., 1958). The fragment which begins with Marinka thinking aloud to herself about the death of her grandmother can therefore occur only nine days after the fourth Saturday of Lent, known in Russia as *verbnaia nedelia*, during which time it was customary to observe the arrival of birds back from their emigration and the first stirrings of spring. See A. Ermolov, *Narodnaia sel´skokhoziaistvennaia mudrost´ v poslovitsakh, pogovorkakh i primetakh* (St Petersburg: Suvorin, 1901), pp. 108–11 (p. 110).

24. The round dance season began in some areas as early as Easter. For others, it began on *Krasnaia gorka* (the first Sunday after Easter), or the week leading up to Pentecost. See M. M. Gromyko, *Traditsionnye normy povedeniia i formy obshcheniia russkikh krest´ian XIX v.* (Moscow: Nauka, 1986), p. 168.

25. A *kurichii bog*, more commonly known as a *kurinyi bog*, is a smooth, round fieldstone with a small hole in the middle which was employed by peasants to ward off evil spirits from the henhouse. See Ivanits, p. 57. Zamiatin's description is interesting from the ethnographic point of view because it considerably extends the known parameters of this stone's powers. Marinka believes that it drives mice away from larders; that it can be washed and added to water in a cow-trough to increase the

richness and quantity of the milk yield; and that it increases the egg yield when hung above the chicken-coop.

26. Witches were supposedly distinguishable from ordinary folk primarily by means of their tails — see Ivanits, p. 98. However, any form of (concealed) deformity was usually regarded with suspicion. Zamiatin's use of the word *kila*, which refers normally to a disease-hardened swelling afflicting animals and vegetables, may derive from the colloquial expression *nasazhivat´ kilu*, which refers to the process by means of which sorcerers cause healthy people suddenly to be struck down by illness or madness. See Maksimov, XVIII, 142. Dal´ (II, 108) notes that this swelling could also be inflicted by the actions of a *znakhar´*.

27. It was commonly believed that a sorcerer could spoil simply by striking or pinching his intended victim. See Maksimov, XVIII, 189.

28. D´iachenko, 656.

29. D. K. Zelenin, *Ocherki russkoi mifologii* (Petrograd: Tipografiia A. V. Orlova, 1916), p. 167.

30. Ivanits, pp. 74–75.

31. According to Russian folklore, *rusalki* were rumoured to be afraid of the sign of the cross. See Zelenin, p. 191.

32. For 'Poludennitsa' as a typical example of the Gogolian obsession text, see Julian Graffy, 'Zamyatin's "Friendship" with Gogol', *Scottish Slavonic Review*, 14 (1990), 139–80 (pp. 148–49).

33. The folk-religious symbolism of St Elijah's Day will be analysed in due course. For the meaning of *prestol´nyi prazdnik*, see Dal´, III, 381.

34. Zabylin, p. 118.

35. Ibid.; and Dal´, II, 218.

36. Theoretically, the term *khorovod* refers to any pastime outside work hours which involves a collective, circular action, or any other dance configuration during which songs are sung; these may take place on village streets, in fields and meadows, or under the open sky. In the strict sense, however, the word refers to a number of specific dance routines of varied composition — mixed, female-only etc., — which involve dramatic scenes. For a detailed discussion of this phenomenon as an important part of the social calendar in rural areas during the nineteenth century, see Gromyko, pp. 161–68.

37. The word *gubitel´*, which means 'undoer' (Dal´, I, 405), is frequently used in songs and laments to refer to the wedding groom.

38. V. V. Kallash and N. E. Efros, *Istoriia russkogo teatra* (Moscow: Ob''edinenie, 1914), p. 8.

39. Ibid., p. 9.

40. *Narodnye liricheskie pesni*, ed. with an introduction by V. Ia. Propp (Leningrad: Sovetskii pisatel´, 1961), p. 17.

41. The song was originally recorded in Spasskii County, Tambov Province, and first published in M. Balakirev, *Russkie narodnye pesni: Dlia odnogo golosa s soprovozhdeniem fortep´iano* (1866). For the reprinted text of this song, see *Narodnye liricheskie pesni*, pp. 190–91.

42. A. I. Sobolevskii, *Velikorusskie narodnye pesni*, 7 vols (St Petersburg: Gosudarstvennaia tipografiia, 1895–1902), VII (1902), song numbers 533–60, pp. 490–508.

43. The *zolotaia kazna* (34) echoes the sense of *kuna* as an item of currency. Furthermore, the verb *voevat´* and the noun *vorog* (i.e. *vrag*) were standard metaphors in songs referring to the pre-nuptial viewing of young brides. See, for example, Soboloveskii, VII, song number 578, pp. 524–25.

44. His draft proposal, sent to the director of *Blokha* on 3 February 1924, contains the following exposition for the opening scene of Act II: 'Тула. Хороводная игра о цареве сыне и царевне. Царев сын — Левша, царевна — тульская девка Машка. Величают их, Левша целует Машку. Тульский купец, конечно, это видит: он отдает Машку за Левшу

только, если тот предоставит червонцев на сто рублей, да серебра на тридцать, да ассигнациями — пуд и три четверти' ('Perepiska', 282).

45. For the classical *khorovod* as a viewing opportunity for the participants, as well as their watchful parents, see Elizabeth A. Warner and Evgenii S. Kustovskii, *Russian Traditional Folk Song* (Hull: Hull University Press, 1990), p. 50.

46. Christine D. Worobec, *Peasant Russia: Family, Community in the Post-Emancipation Period* (Princeton: Princeton University Press, 1991), p. 119.

47. Gromyko, p.168.

48. This sense of urgency is reinforced by the mention of the 'old maids' in the context of the dance, but has also been anticipated earlier in the opening paragraph with the images of ripe apples in the priest's garden: 'Яблоки в садах стали томно-желтыми и качаются, каждый миг готовые отдать кому-то свою сладость' (32).

49. For the disdain with which Russian peasants treated unmarried women, and the variety of pejorative names applied to them (*vekovushka* being one such example), see Worobec, p. 124.

50. See, for example, the engraving entitled *Russkaia pesnia* (1871), in *The Lubok: Russian Folk Pictures: 17th to 19th Century*, introduction and selection by Alla Sytova (Leningrad: Aurora, 1984), illustration no. 166. For a comparison with the professional painters of Zamiatin's time, see Boris Kustodiev's *Khorovod* (1912), in V. Lebedeva, *Boris Kustodiev: The Artist and His Work* (Moscow: Progress, 1981), illustration no. 65. In order to distinguish this work from her earlier book in Russian on this painter — see *Boris Mikhailovich Kustodiev* (Moscow: Nauka, 1966) — I shall henceforth refer to these two works respectively as Lebedeva (*EV*) and Lebedeva (*RV*), with the relevant illustration numbers or page numbers.

51. It has been suggested that the songs in mixed *khorovody* sometimes overstepped the normal social barriers prohibiting open discussion of sexual matters. See Worobec, p. 130.

52. B. Rybakov, *Iazychestvo drevnei Rusi* (Moscow: Nauka, 1987), p. 120. It has also been noted by Propp that the standard *khorovod* moves 'sunwise'. See *Narodnye liricheskie pesni*, p. 16.

53. Unfortunately, this was not a genuine possibility bearing in mind the strict conventions of the time. For a discussion of the sexual taboos which still applied at the turn of the century, see Worobec, pp. 137–39.

54. For more detailed descriptions of the folk-religious symbolism of this festival, see Maksimov, XVII, 188–95; and Ermolov, pp. 379–84.

55. 'И такие у ней губы — жадные, сухие, раскрытые, как трещина в бездорожной земле' (III, 78).

56. It is not clear why Zamiatin and his wife did not have children; it has been suggested, however, that the absence of children weighed heavily on their relationship. In her memoirs, Irina Kunina makes the following remark about the couple: 'Замятин умел быть веселым, чаще всего вне своего дома, где была, как мне в молодости казалось, какая-то чуть унылая преданность его подруги, словно чувствующей себя виноватой из-за не данного ему ребенка, или будто несуществующая детская могилка разделяла их.' See Irina Kunina, 'Vstrecha s Blokom', *Literaturnoe obozrenie*, 1991.9, 92–97 (p. 96).

57. *Zapevala* refers to the soloist who launches the singing, and whose tune is picked up by the folk choir, often in the context of wedding songs. See Warner and Kustovskii, p. 14.

58. *Zateinitsa* literally means 'inventor' (*SRIa*, I, 581). Its rural connotation, however, derives from the expression *zateiat' igry*, which refers to the organizing of games and pranks either at Christmas time or in the summer. *Zadornitsa* refers to someone who is always picking arguments and fights (Dal', I, 573).

59. See Cathy A. Frierson, *Peasant Icons: Representations of Rural People in Late Nineteenth Century Russia* (New York: Oxford University Press, 1993), pp. 161–80.

60. See Ivanits, pp. 75–82; and E. Pomerantseva, *Mifologicheskie personazhi v russkom fol'klore* (Moscow: Nauka, 1975), pp. 68–91.

61. Zelenin, p. 127.
62. N. V. Gogol', *Sobranie sochinenii*, ed. by S. I. Mashinskii and M. B. Khrapchenko, 7 vols (Moscow: Gosudarstvennoe izdatel´stvo khudozhestvennoi literatury, 1976–79), I (1976), 54–80 (especially pp. 74–76).
63. Zelenin, p. 196.
64. *Vesna sviashchennaia* was composed by Stravinskii between 1911 and 1913, and first performed as a ballet on 16/29 May 1913 in Paris. See Eric Walter White, *Stravinsky: The Composer and His Works*, 2nd edn (London: Faber and Faber, 1979), p. 207. It is not known whether Zamiatin attended the first Russian concert performance under the baton of Sergei Kusevitskii in Moscow in February 1914. It is unlikely, however, that as a music lover and player of the piano he failed to hear about the scandal which erupted after the opening performance in Paris.
65. Kuiman´ Fair is the first *iarmarka* to be portrayed in Zamiatin's fiction. It is not inconceivable that he was influenced by the paintings of Kustodiev, in particular the two works on this theme which he painted in 1906 and 1908. See Lebedeva (*EV*), illustration no. 42; and Lebedeva (*RV*), p. 117.

CHAPTER 3

(KOSTROMA)

KRIAZHI

When the speaker in 'Slovo predostavliaetsia tovarishchu Churyginu' describes his native Kuiman´ as a place buried amid deep forest, miles from any provincial town, and one in which life is dark and ignorant (II, 84), he might equally well be talking about the village depicted in the short story 'Kriazhi'.[1] The opening lines, which picture a forest so dense that a person can walk for an entire day without meeting another soul, establish the themes of isolation and marginality with an explicitness rare in Zamiatin's prose fiction. For the first time, moreover, this entity is given a sobriquet, Rus´, with all its connotations of primordial solidity, strength, and durability. Symbolically, the murmuring pine trees that stand as yet untouched by the ravages of modern industrial civilization belong to the same solid and primeval forest which serves as the central metaphor for Old Russia in Zamiatin's ambiguous lament for the pre-revolutionary era, the aptly titled 'Rus´' (II, 44). They are 'wise' (*mudrye*) and 'grand' (*vazhnye*), and stand as guardians of ancient wisdoms and protectors of religious propriety until later metamorphosed by the winter snow into 'old nuns in white cowls praying silently for the living'.[2] From the very beginning, therefore, 'Kriazhi' is advertised as part of a certain cultural space, one which is located in the provincial heartlands of the Russian imagination, and in which the ancient conventions and traditions of conservative rural society have been preserved intact against the encroachment of modernity. It is against this background of age-old purity and permanence that the ensuing narrative demands to be interpreted.

Unlike Kuiman´, the village of Pozhoga in 'Kriazhi' would appear to be a fictional location. It does not exist on any pre-revolutionary maps, and it probably owes its name to the Russian verb for 'to destroy by fire' (*pozhech´*), which often provided the place-name designation for villages in isolated northern areas, near rivers or lakes, where dense forest had been burned away and cleared for settlement.[3] Nevertheless, the general vicinity in which this village is situated is quite specifically indicated. In 'O iazyke', as we have seen, Zamiatin mentioned three areas in connection with his collection of folklore — Tambov, Kostroma, and the North — and it is significant that on three occasions in 'Kriazhi' a river is named — the Unzha — which features as an agent of death in the narrative (267, 268, & 270). This river is genuine: its source is located in the very northernmost tip of the Kostroma region, and from there the river winds southward for approximately two hundred kilometres before joining the Volga near the town of Iur´evets. Interestingly, the lower section of this river south of Makar´ev is notable for the narrow ridges or *kriazhi* which run parallel to the left bank all the way to its confluence with the Volga; in addition, a famous expanse of primitive forest lay both to the east and west of these ridges, occupying a thick swathe of territory between the Unzha and the Vetluga rivers all the way south to the bend of the Volga at Nizhnii Novgorod (*ES*, XVI, 408–10). By all accounts, this was a sparsely populated, isolated region; indeed, it was so secluded that the ridges were referred to as mountains because the local population had never seen proper mountains before (ibid., 408). Pavel Mel´nikov-Pecherskii, whose celebrated ethnographic novel *V lesakh* (1875) describes an area of the forest which lay to the east of the Volga between Rybinsk and Kerzhenets, emphasized the purity and antiquity of its way of life and customs.[4] Furthermore, an ethnographic expedition to the northern section of this forest, undertaken eight years after 'Kriazhi' was published, and thus six years after the October Revolution, recorded that it was still a backward region untouched by urban civilization, and one in which belief in devilry, sorcery, and 'fire-breathing dragons' remained powerfully entrenched in the imagination.[5]

At the turn of the century the stretches of the Unzha below the town of Makar´ev were accessible by ferry and paddle-steamer (*ES*, XVI, 410); thus it is conceivable that Zamiatin visited the region during his days as a student on technical assignments, or later in a professional capacity. Certainly, the ethnographic conceit of his story, and the weaving of local dialect into the linguistic fabric of the narrative, depend for their effectiveness on an impression of authenticity. This is reinforced by his use of a tree-dominated *couleur locale*. The cutting down of trees and the logging of timber during the summer months was a major source of income for the villages situated along the lower section of the Unzha (ibid.); and it is entirely in keeping with this reality that the two main protagonists in 'Kriazhi' are shown earning a meagre living by means of this material: Ivan is clearing a copse owned by the local priest; while Mar´ia is depicted in the opening chapter selling blocks of wood at the local market. Furthermore, the forest from which the young couple make their living functions simultaneously as an integrating metonym, its trees embodying the very qualities of the local inhabitants themselves. The multiple layers of meaning contained within the title serve to highlight this with maximum poetic effect. The noun *kriazh* can refer to a narrow ridge of low mountains, but also to a solid offcut or block of wood, as well as a thick log or tree-stump; in addition, the adjective *kriazhistyi* which derives from this noun — meaning 'strong' (*krepkii*), 'hard' (*tverdyi*), and 'thick' (*tolstyi*) — can often be employed in a human context to denote qualities of sturdiness, toughness, and strength (Dal´, II, 208). Elsewhere in his early provincial fiction (see, for example, the characterization of Baryba in *Uezdnoe* and the store owner Kortoma in *Sever*), Zamiatin employs the adjective *kriazhistyi* to indicate both physical sturdiness and an obstinate, implacable tendency.[6] Indeed, both senses are duly echoed in 'Kriazhi'. In the opening chapter, for example, commenting on the refusal of Ivan and Mar´ia to act upon a powerful and mutual attraction, the author-narrator emphasizes their rigidity and attachment to convention: 'Oba — kriazhi, norovisty' (265).[7] Later, as witnessed by Mar´ia's desperate words at the end of the tale as Ivan lies dying, the meaning of toughness and durability is implied: '— Отживе-еет еще, у нас народ крепкой, кряжистой' (271). Thus, like the ancient and sturdy trees with which they are symbolically associated, these young protagonists belong to a world which is stubbornly conservative and deeply rooted in convention.

'Kriazhi' lends itself to a variety of readings, depending on the particular critical focus. Since it opens with an incident involving a stone idol, and plays deliberately with the notion of idolization in the sense of 'to love someone passionately, to bow down to someone, like a god' (Dal´, II, 8), it is only natural that the story be interpreted as a statement on the primacy of passionate love over convention. Shane, for example, writes that:

The story 'Krjaži' expresses Zamjatin's opinion that neither pride nor convention should stand in the way of the realization of love. Through stubborn pride, the strong physical attraction between Ivan and Mar´ja remains unrealized.[8]

Although there is no reason to take issue with this particular interpretation, it is insufficient as an appreciation of the text's aesthetic appeal. The most striking aspect of 'Kriazhi' — its *skaz* stylization — is a vital textural ingredient which endows the tale with an expressionist and neoprimitivist flavour; and it is perhaps worth noting that the description of the characters in terms of wood has analogies in the neoprimitivist sculptures of certain artists at this time.[9] When Shane talks about convention, it is important to identify the nature and role of convention within this particular community and its influence on the protagonists' behaviour. Likewise, the subtle poetic nuance of several episodes in the narrative, largely ironic and subversive in intent, can be missed without some understanding of folk-religious culture. The imaginative viewpoint of the implied narrator, and the degree to which it effectively disguises the cultured author, is intrinsic to this aspect of the story. This problem has been raised in Chapter 1 of the present study, and is the subject elsewhere of an interesting, albeit cursory, analysis within the wider context of oral narration in modern Russian literature.[10] The authors argue that while the poetic passages of 'Kriazhi' compromise the colloquial tendency of the narrative voice, the use of folklore identifies the implied narrator closely with the imaginative world of his characters. As we will see, the implied narrator displays an easy familiarity with the symbolic resonances of certain Orthodox feast days; in addition, he exhibits an acute sensitivity to the passing of the seasons, and the significance of even the most minor deviations in the pattern of the weather. This, according to the Populist writer Gleb Uspenskii, was an important litmus test for the authenticity of the peasant imagination.[11] At the same time, there is a distancing effect in operation which can be witnessed not only in the relatively sophisticated artistic organization of the narrative, but also in the author-narrator's ironic treatment of folk belief and double-faith. Zamiatin manages both to project and subvert the imaginative viewpoint of the folk, and it is the ambiguous tension between these opposing tendencies which I propose to examine in detail in this chapter.

The ostensible theme of 'Kriazhi' lies in the fierce clash of temperaments between two characters which prevents them from recognizing a powerful, mutual attraction. Mar´ia, the female protagonist, is sketched with *lubok*-style simplicity. The words used to characterize her, many of them imbued with a strongly colloquial appeal, emphasize her physical prowess and athleticism, her sense of initiative and playfulness, and her indomitable spirit. She is variously described as a prankster (*konovod* (267)), a ringleader (*zavodilo* (267)), a daredevil (*otorviazhnitsa* (268)), an athlete (*bogatyrikha* (268)), and a firebrand (*boi-devka* (268)).[12] Her initial encounter with Ivan reveals a hot-blooded temper. Moreover, she is later witnessed tampering mischievously with the nets of the local fishermen on St Peter and

Paul's Day (29 June), and catching a sheat-fish in the river with her bare hands — an indication of her fearlessness, presumably, since this was the largest fish in European fresh waters and generally feared on account of its aggressive tendencies.[13] Mar´ia represents a challenge to the idea of male dominance in a patriarchal society: she appears uninterested in men, lives alone with her mother, and works the farmstead on her own. But ultimately it is convention which causes her to spurn Ivan — the reason she gives to the village gossips is that he is poor and has no property of his own. However, there is also an element of injured pride, if not deliberate defiance, which is triggered by the initial encounter with Ivan. Certainly, Mar´ia is the prototype for a number of powerfully erotic, strident, and independently minded female figures in Zamiatin's fiction — see, for example, Pelka in *Sever* and I-330 in *My* — all of whom, as noted sardonically by Remizov, are characterized physically in terms of their breasts.[14] Unlike these later heroines, however, it is Mar´ia's failure to act upon her feelings, rather than that of her male counterpart, which leads to a self-inflicted disaster in the form of Ivan's death.

For his part, Ivan is unable to cope with this wild, untameable opponent. A poor, simple, and apparently parentless *muzhik*, one who scrapes a living by chopping down trees on a piece of land owned by the village priest, he is initially attracted to Mar´ia physically: 'Эх, хороша девка. […] Может, кабы не такая была, а свернул бы Иван' (265). Moments later, when a button bursts off her white tunic as she raises her fist in anger, he becomes aware of her erotic attractiveness. After the clash of tempers which gives rise to his initial interest, he becomes increasingly obsessed and tries to engineer situations in which he can impress her through his physical prowess and bravery. The plot, however, contrives a series of humiliating failures: his plan to kill a snake plaguing the local community after St Cosmas and Damian's Day (1 November) is ruined when someone else in the village gets there before him; his reckless journey by horse and cart in the middle of a winter's night — an open invitation to forest wolves to attack both him and the geese he is transporting back home for Christmas — passes off unchallenged; finally, his attempt to impress Mar´ia by being the first to cross the river Unzha after its winter 'bridge' has formed leads to his death. Undeniably, Ivan's concept of the courtship ritual is primitive and based on traditional notions of male supremacy; indeed, it is a teasing challenge from the women on the other bank of the Unzha, questioning his virility, which provokes his foolhardy decision to cross the ice in the first place.[15] His passion, moreover, has its disturbing and violent moments. It is a measure of his frustration that he can hack down a tree with an axe and imagine that it is Mar´ia submitting to his indomitable will, gradually falling to her knees in obeisance like a tree trunk slowly crashing to the ground:

Хекал-свистел топор, брызгали щепки, сек со всего плеча — будто не сосна это была, а Марья да та же все. И сейчас подкосится, сломится, падет на коленочки и жалостно скажет:
— Ой, покорюсь, ой, Иванюша, помилуй ... (269)

This is a grotesque moment in the narrative, and reveals the degree of obsession to which Ivan has succumbed.

A reader accustomed to the sophisticated plots of most modernist fiction might find this plot banal. He or she would be right in this view, although it would miss the point of Zamiatin's *lubok*-style conceit, and would involve overlooking many deft and subtle artistic touches. Shane, for example, has drawn attention to the lyrical expressiveness of certain passages in the narrative, and analysed well Zamiatin's exploitation of the rhythmic and musical potential of language, a feature of his work which has been noted in relation to *Uezdnoe* and tends in any case to compromise the purity of his *skaz*.[16] Moreover, closer examination of the narrative reveals the careful use of parallelism and ironic reversal with regard to the tragic fate of the male protagonist. The three main episodes, for example, echo each other in terms of images of nominally lifeless bodies wriggling vigorously back to life. The sheat-fish, which the peasant fishermen claim is sleepy, suddenly springs back to life after it has been dragged out of the water by Mar´ia and her companions: '— Со-онный, говоришь? — как соскочит Марья с сома, рыбина как сиганет, мужики как попятятся ...' (268); while the snake, which has been plaguing the local community, is still writhing after it has been captured and decapitated: '— Копается-шша? Ну, и живуч, омрак страшный!' (269). Ironically, both verbally and visually, these episodes anticipate Mar´ia's desperate plea for Ivan to come back to life after he has been pulled out of the frozen water: '— Качай, ребята! Отживе-еет еще, у нас народ крепкой, кряжистой ...' (271). Another symbolic anticipation of this death can be found in an earlier passage which plays on the nuances of the Russian word *dur´*. This can mean 'obstinacy' and 'idiocy' (Dal´, I, 502), and thus refers to Ivan's unreciprocated obsession with Mar´ia; but it is also a slang term for vodka (ibid.), and thus insinuates that Ivan has been celebrating St Michael's Day (8 November) in an orgy of alcoholic self-abuse (apparently such behaviour was typical for rural communities on this particular feast day).[17] The passage in question, therefore, as well as indicating Ivan's desire to free himself from his crazy obsession, refers also to the commonly-adopted method of recovering from a hangover:

Морозу бы теперь лютого, так чтоб деревья трескались! Да выбежать бы в одной рубахе, окунуться в мороз, как в воду студеную, чтоб продернуло всего, чтоб ногами притопнуть — живо бы всю дурь из головы вон… (270)

Ivan has indeed been 'submerged' in 'freezing water' by the end of the tale — this time, however, the regaining of his sanity has been achieved only through death. The two episodes are further linked by the creaking of the trees in the severe cold and the cracking of the ice across the surface of the Unzha ('Krugami shel tresk' (271)); and it might be argued that both sounds hark back audibly to the initial 'croaking' (*kriakan´e* (265)) of the wooden axle as it strikes the pagan idol.

Alongside the sophisticated artistic organization of the text, there is a pattern of folk-religious imagery which raises important questions about the narratorial point of view and lends the story a universal resonance and tragic pathos. From the point of view of *lubok* stylization, for example, the characters of Ivan and Mar´ia are stock figures of the folk imagination. Their Christian names are common in Russia and, as the authors of *Poetika skaza* have observed, the couple are typical and healthily attractive representatives of their respective genders:

'Как надо' выглядят и главные герои новеллы 'Кряжи': их нормативность подчеркнута и традиционной парностью мужского и женского имени (Иван да Марья), и соединением в образах обоих персонажей физической красоты и нравственного здоровья.[18]

Zamiatin emphasizes in a variety of ways that it is only natural for this couple to be paired as a love match. The draft versions of the story, for example, employ their names as a subtitle, which suggests that the names themselves, and their immediate juxtaposition, are significant (IMLI, opis´ 1, ed. khr. 26). This is reinforced in the actual text itself by the constant repetition of their names in close proximity to each other — this occurs on three separate occasions in the opening section: 'Через эту самую нечисть пошла вражда между Иваном да Марьей' (265); 'Скоро проведали, какая пошла раздеряга между Иваном да Марьей' (266); and 'И разгасятся они оба, Иван да Марья' (ibid.). It is possible that this emphasis on the natural bond between these two young protagonists derives from Russian folklore. When juxtaposed in this fashion, both visually and audibly, the names of the young pair echo the name of a wild flower, the cow-wheat flower (*ivan-da-mar´ia*), which is distinguished by its yellow and blue petals, and functions in certain works of Russian literature as an emblem of natural harmony and Russianness.[19] It was also reputed among the folk to possess health-giving qualities. In *V lesakh*, for example, Mel´nikov-Pecherskii records that young girls used the *ivan-da-mar´ia* in steambaths on the Eve of St Agrippina (22 June) as part of their preparations for the courting rituals which traditionally took place the next day, i.e. Midsummer Night's Eve; it was believed that the flower would make girls young and beautiful so that the young men of the village would fall in love with them.[20] In view of the plot development of 'Kriazhi', therefore, the choice of names for the young pair is ironic; indeed, the absence of the hyphens when these names appear together, which would form the name of the flower proper, graphically underlines the disruption of an unbreakable natural bond between them.[21]

As well as exploiting the symbolism of names, Zamiatin weaves into his narrative a number of allusions to the folk lyric song. The names of Ivan and Mar´ia, for example, feature widely as the 'ideal pair' in songs of this type, and it is significant that both are given the physical characteristics of the typical lyric song hero and heroine. Mar´ia has eyebrows of sable-fur — 'Эх, хороша девка, брови-то как нахмурила соболиные!' (265) — and is later described in terms of her rosy cheeks and healthy complexion ('А в кругу Марья ходила, веселая, червонная, пышная' (268)). While Ivan is described initially by the locals in terms of his athletic build and blond hair ('Da kudriavyi, da statnyi' (266)), and mention is made later of his 'curly locks' (*kudlami rusymi* (269)). These epithets are the customary stock-in-trade of the folk lyric song.[22] Furthermore, several of the lyric song's standard themes, such as the offering of gifts and the round dance as a symbolic enactment of marriage proposal also figure in the narrative.[23] As in 'Poludennitsa (Kuny)', the expectation of marriage is the background against which the relationship fails to develop. Ivan, albeit half in jest, is singled out by the village gossipmongers as a potential match for Mar´ia because of his strength and good looks: '— Эх, Марья, работник-то попов, Иван-то. [...] Да курдявый, да статный: вот бы тебе такого в мужья! Не пойдешь говоришь?' (266).[24] Even at the turn of the century, however, convention dictated that love was a secondary consideration when compared to the economic prospects which a bride would gain through acquiring a rich husband.[25] Thus Ivan, without a penny to his name —

indicated by use of the colloquial expression *bez kola-bez dvora* (266) — is simply not a serious proposition for Mar′ia.[26]

Having established this state of natural expectation on the part of the reader, the rest of the narrative is geared towards extracting the maximum possible pathos from the young couple's situation. The central episodes, orchestrated around both a shift in the cycle of the seasons and a number of Orthodox festivals, reinforce the unnaturalness of their unfulfilled match. This operates on two levels. As celebrations in which the community as a whole was expected to participate, every mention of a feast day serves only to emphasize the chasm which separates the two protagonists against a general background of collective merriment. Furthermore, the themes of isolation and marginality with which the story opens begin to assume a more ominous dimension as Ivan finds himself more and more cut off from the rest of the village. The first section concludes by evoking the loneliness of sleeping at night on one's own (266); the second section ends with Ivan watching from a distance as the young boys and girls of the village participate in a round dance (268); and the third section contrasts a mushroom-picking expedition by the villagers with Ivan's solitary work in the forest, followed later by his decision not to show his face in public for the rest of the winter (269). The festivals in question possessed important resonances in the folk imagination as far as courtship, matchmaking, and marriage were concerned. This serves only to increase Ivan's sense of desperation, and explains indirectly why he is prepared to risk his life in a futile show of virility at the very end of the story.

The first festival mentioned is St Peter and Paul's Day (29 June). As an ancient Orthodox feast day to commemorate the apostles Peter and Paul, it was a celebration with special relevance for fishermen — communities in which fishing played a vital economic role would thus lay out their nets and pray to the saints for a good catch. It was also the point in the year when the sun reached its zenith, hence the custom among the folk of treating the day as a sun festival. More significantly, unless there was an altar-day in the remaining weeks before the harvest, St Peter and Paul's Day usually marked the end of the festive season, and thus was the last opportunity to indulge in round dance celebrations. Furthermore, because it was nearly always one of the last major festivals of the summer season, it was also traditional for the young to permit themselves a joke at the expense of the older village inhabitants.[27]

As an ethnographic record, Zamiatin's description of this festival is very much a series of impressionistic snapshots. The opening words of the second section — 'Петров день скоро, великий праздник летний' (266) — imply that St Peter and Paul's Day, rather than *Ivan Kupala* (24 June, known in English as Midsummer's Day), was the more significant summer festival, no doubt because it was a fishing village. As the festival day approaches, the villagers are already engaging in outdoor celebrations ('Uzh i poguliaiut v Pozhoge' (266)); the peasants are getting drunk on vodka ('Pokhlebaiut vina do dna muzhiki' (ibid.));[28] and the young are taking part in traditional round dances ('Nakorogodiatsia devki da parni' (ibid.)).[29] On the day of the festival, the red-hot sun burns like a bonfire. The peasants lay their fishing nets across the river early in the morning, and can be seen later dozing in the shade of the trees on Horse Island, presumably having returned to recover from their drinking bouts. The local girls go bathing in the mid-afternoon and decide to play a traditional trick on the fishermen by pulling in their nets. Mar'ia, having fearlessly landed the sheat-fish, trades it for money, and buys animal-shaped cakes (*kozuli* (268)) and honey for the traditional meals or *gostintsy*.[30] In the evening, the round dances take place in the shade of the pine trees. The participants sing traditional songs — Zamiatin quotes two lines from a song which resembles one recorded by Rimskii-Korsakov[31] — and Mar'ia is chosen several times by the young men in the dance. Finally, as the sun sinks below the horizon, and the moon slips out into the night sky, the older peasants disperse tipsily home.

While it is interesting to compare these images with the picture of St Peter and Paul's Day celebrations as presented by Mel'nikov-Pecherskii, it is the subversion of the festival's main theme which is most striking.[32] Zamiatin plays deliberately with the notion of trapping as it reflects the fishermen's preoccupation on this feast day, and transforms it into a general metaphor for the process of acquiring a bride. The marital context for this episode is supplied in the second paragraph of the section. The statement that there are many attractive young women in the village from whom to choose — 'Есть откуда выбрать в Пожоге: пригожих много' (267) — and the image of Ivan furiously polishing a copper comb which he has inherited from his grandfather and obviously plans to present to Mar'ia — 'Ox, выбрал, должно быть, Иван, кому гребень отдать!' (ibid.) — establishes the expectation that this festival will be the occasion of his proposal of marriage.[33] What follows, however, is a reversal of this expectation, and an ironic commentary on the theme of subjugation in so far as it relates to the traditional role of men and women in the betrothal process. Crucial in this regard is Zamiatin's pun on the verb *obrotat´*, which means 'to harness', and is usually employed in relation to horses and other domestic animals, but which in peasant slang possessed a sexual and marital connotation as well.[34] The news that Mar´ia has 'harnessed' the sheat-fish — 'Как Марья сома обротала' (268) — endows this episode with a symbolic dimension, and suggests that the animals themselves are substitutes or displacements for their human counterparts. Ivan is thus associated with the sheat-fish (aside from its aggressive tendencies, its shape and length give it a phallic dimension); while Mar´ia is associated with the untamed horse (it is symptomatic that the action of this episode takes place on an island on which horses are 'tamed' every year).[35] The struggle, therefore, is not between Mar´ia and the fish as such, but between herself and Ivan for supremacy and domination in their relationship. If Ivan is intent on offering her a gift, and thus on 'trapping' the object of his devotion, it is Mar´ia, ironically, who makes the catch and offers a gift of her earnings to the boys and girls among her friends. The difficulty she experiences, first in removing the nets from their stake, and then in hauling in the sheat-fish (' — Tiani-tiani-tiani!' (267)), parallels but reverses Ivan's struggle to capture her. Moreover, this episode is another ironic anticipation of his eventual fate, since a very similar appeal is made by Mar´ia to bystanders when Ivan is fished out of the water half alive at the end of the story ('— Kachai, rebiata!' (271)). Disgruntled that his prey has managed to escape, Ivan absents himself from the dancing, the last courtship opportunity of the season. His isolation is reinforced symbolically by his standing outside the round dance circle and watching the ritual from a distance; while his failure in general is stressed by mention of Mar´ia being chosen by the other boys in the *korogod* — a reference within the semiotics of the dance not only to the other boys' desire to choose her as a partner, but also, symbolically, to their desire to marry her.

St Cosmas and Damian's Day (1 November), known in rural areas as *kuz´minki*, is the second festival mentioned in the narrative. The symbolic connotations of this holiday for the Orthodox Church and the common folk were at slight variance. For the Church, this was a festival to commemorate the martyrdom of the Eastern saints Cosmas and Damian, the twin brothers and blacksmiths who acquired a legendary reputation in their native Cyrrhus for working miraculous cures and practising medicine without charging fees.[36] As physicians and patron saints of the poor, they were regularly invoked by rural folk in Russia

whenever they or their farmstock fell ill or suffered from disease.
However, they were also regarded as protectors of the family hearth
and the happiness of married couples. According to Maksimov, young
girls were placed in charge of the household on St Cosmas and
Damian's Day, and songs were sung in the evening and at night which
testified to its importance as a matchmaking festival; this was one of
several such events which accompanied the onset of winter in rural
communities.[37] The matchmaker invoked in these songs, a fictitious
personage named Madame Kuz´ma-Demian, was the product of a pun
on the verb meaning 'to forge', as in 'to forge a marriage' (kovat´
svad´bu), and 'to forge metal' (kovat´ zhelezu), the customary activity of
the blacksmith.[38] In this context, it is worth stressing the close
identification between marriage and fertility: Cosmas and Damian
were also known as protectors of hens, largely because they were paid
with gifts, rather than money, and these gifts sometimes took the form
of eggs.[39]

In 'Kriazhi', the author-narrator demonstrates straightaway his
awareness of the festival in terms of its significance for wives, young
women, and hens: 'С кузьминок — бабьего, девичьего да куричьего
праздника — дождь пошел' (269). Although there is no ethnographic
detail in this episode, the theme of sickness and health is brought into
play and manipulated for ironic effect. Just prior to the mention of this
festival, for example, at the beginning of the third section, Zamiatin
mentions the local priest's legendary ability to cure ailments by means
of herbal medicines; one of these ailments is given as 'carnal desire'
(bludnaia strast´).[40] This is a comic touch, since the Church authorities
would no doubt have taken a dim view of such healing. Nevertheless,
the reference is followed a few lines later by the insinuation that Ivan
himself is suffering from precisely such an ailment: the image of him
felling a pine tree, imagining that it is Mar´ia submitting to his wishes,
is an image of violent subjugation symptomatic of a serious and
disturbing sexual passion. This introduction to the theme of the festival
is succeeded in turn by the episode in which a boy is poisoned by a
snake after an expedition to gather· mushrooms to the local forest: he
dies, an anticipation of Ivan's fate, and an ironic commentary on a
community which believes in miracle health cures. At this point,
however, the marital subtext of the festival is introduced. The snake
which poisons the boy is transformed (presumably by rumour) into a
terrifying 'serpent' (zmei strashnyi (269)), and it is important in this
context to recognize the associations of serpents in the folk-religious
imagination with the abduction of brides.[41] If Ivan sees this as another

potential opportunity to impress Mar´ia — 'Никому другому — Ивану надо змея убить' (269) — he is doubtless influenced by traditional epic songs and fabulates about St George in which the latter features both as a dragon-slayer and a protector from snakes and poisonous insects.[42] As with Mar´ia's trapping of the sheat-fish, the slaying of this particular 'dragon' by someone else in the village is a symbolic form of castration or emasculation (shaped like the fish in terms of its width and length, the snake might also be said to function as a phallic object).

These two episodes demonstrate Zamiatin's willingness to subvert the traditional symbolic associations of certain religious festivals. He continues this strategy, moreover, during a third sequence which should, technically, be considered as a separate section in its own right. The words 'Zabeleli utrenniki, zaziabla zemlia' (269) introduce a new episode into the story which is also orchestrated around a series of festivals and predicated on the notion of expectation reversal; in this case, however, it takes the form of an exceptional fluctuation in the weather which leads to the abnormal delay of the winter freeze.[43] As various commentators observe, it is characteristic of the peasant farmer to try and predict the harshness of the forthcoming winter: it is thus an indication of the author-narrator's closeness to the earth and his familiarity with the relevant portents (*primety*) that he should allude in this section to a series of popular sayings from which weather lore was derived.[44] Rainfall on St Cosmas and Damian's Day, for example, was generally regarded as something unusual, since this was the day on which the populace, especially in the North, expected the first signs of winter — in the words of one *primeta*: 'Кузьма-Демьян кует на всю зиму.'[45] The mention of St Michael's Day — 'И на Михайлов день — снег повалил' (269–70) — refers to another occasion on which the peasant farmer sought an indication of future weather patterns; and indeed, while it was usually expected to be mild, tradition suggested that it should reverse the expectation already established on St Cosmas and Damian's Day.[46] In 'Kriazhi', however, this does not occur — the snow arrives, and the earth frosts only slightly: 'А морозы не шли, все больше ростепель' (270). At this point the narrator expresses surprise at the continuing absence of a severe winter freeze and the rise in temperature, as a result of which by the time of *sviatki* (6 December onwards) there is still no winter path across the Unzha.[47] This is described explicitly as an 'unusual event' (*nebyvaloe delo* (270)), and reflects the general preoccupation with the arrival of the winter frost during the festivals of St George (26 November), St Sabbas (5 December), and St Nicholas (6 December). Surprisingly, the winter path across the Unzha is still only two days old by the time Ivan tries to cross it at some unspecified point after St Nicholas's Day (but obviously near Christmas), and is still not firm enough to cross safely. The reader is left in little doubt that there is something profoundly odd about this situation, almost as if it were the result of some inexplicable force interfering in the normal functioning of nature.

While the delay in the onset of winter is not ultimately responsible for Ivan's untimely fate (his eagerness to impress and foolhardiness are clearly more to blame), there is a hint in 'Kriazhi' that this unexpected reversal in fortune, caused by the fragility of the ice across the river, is due to bad luck. For the peasant farmer, moreover, prone to belief in supernatural spirits, bad luck rarely occurred without good cause. From the very opening of the story, with its description of a pagan idol found in the priest's threshing barn, Zamiatin seems willing to play with sinister explanations for events which have a mundane solution in reality. Indeed, it is a curious aspect of this story that on several occasions the characters are shown in what appears to be a state of fear and panic with regard to certain objects, both animate and inanimate, which were viewed by the folk as malevolent and associated in their minds with the 'unclean force' (*nechistaia sila*). This could be accepted as a realistic (and comic) expression of the backwardness of the region, and something which would accord with its known ethnographic profile. On the other hand, it could reflect the influence of a malevolent force inadvertently angered by human action. One conceit of this tale, surely, is that the two protagonists unwittingly come into contact with an 'unclean force' which eventually causes them harm. If the failure of Ivan and Mar´ia to unite in passionate love is interpreted as an inexplicable event, or as a breakdown in the normal pattern of behaviour, then the allusions to peasant fears and anxieties with regard to malevolent forces cast an equally curious and inexplicable pall over the development of events. It is as if Ivan owes his death not to some wild recklessness on his part, but to the workings of a sinister mechanism beyond the control of ordinary human beings.

The paradoxical position which Zamiatin assumes with regard to these fears is evident from the very first lines which describe the unearthing of the stone idol. Superficially, this incident is amusing. The discovery of such a rare object in the priest's threshing barn, in addition to later hints that he is not as orthodox in his religious practices as might be expected (i.e. his use of herbal medicine), alludes to the phenomenon of double-faith: the cult of Orthodox religion replaces the site of a pagan cult, but the belief in evil spirits remains.[48] There is much humour to be derived from the fact that such a rare and potentially interesting archaeological artefact should be dumped so carelessly on the side of the road.[49] For the peasant labourers, however, this discovery is no laughing matter. The Orthodox Church, which routinely denounced relics from Russia's pagan past as the work of the Devil, would have associated such stone idols with pre-Christian forms of sorcery, black magic, and 'spoiling'; indeed, the designation of this idol as a *nechist´* — 'Там — Никола себе Николай, а все-таки к нечисти надо с опаской: кабы какой вереды не вышло' (265) — refers to the term for harmful forces in the folk-religious imagination.[50] It is thus unsurprising that the labourers treat this artefact with a certain amount of care, and that, after dismissing the usefulness of a prayer to St Nicholas of Myra, a popular saint among the Russian folk and one widely invoked for special protection against evil spirits, they deposit it respectfully by the side of the road.[51] The point of view expressed here, however, is calculatingly ambiguous. The remark that this *nechist´* must be handled 'with caution' (s *opaskoi*), otherwise some 'harm' (*vereda*) might be caused, could belong to the implied narrator (direct free speech) or to the peasant labourers (indirect free speech). Furthermore, it is not clear which is the case even after the register of the language is taken into account.[52] There is further ambiguity in the statement that the idol is responsible for the hostility which subsequently arises between the two main protagonists: 'Через эту самую нечисть и пошла вражда между Иваном да Марьей' (265). Does this refer merely to the breaking of Mar´ia's axle, which gives rise to her anger and annoyance? Or is it more ominous? At this stage, the reader is justified only in assuming that Ivan himself, as someone directly employed by the priest, is one of the unidentified peasants who undertakes this operation, and is therefore potentially 'contaminated'.

The mention of potential harm in relation to the idol, and the fear it evokes among the labourers, establishes a degree of dramatic expectation on the part of the reader which seems ultimately fulfilled by the end of the story: the text concludes on a note of symbolic closure, since both Ivan's initial confrontation with Mar´ia, and his later death, occur while he is driving his cart and horse on a domestic errand. The scenes which connect these episodes, moreover, appear to pursue further the idea of long-term peril or danger. It is a *shishiga*, an evil demon believed to inhabit the barns of domestic farmsteads, which causes Mar´ia to look over her shoulder at Ivan while collecting water, thus giving him cause to suspect that she might be interested in him: 'Уж далеко отойдут, уж запутается между рыжих стволов белая баска

Марьина, тут-то и шишига толкнет' (266).[53] In addition, Mar´ia's
encounter with the sheat-fish on St Peter and Paul's Day, while clearly
orchestrated around a genuine fear of the fish's known predatoriness,
physical strength, and aggression, also alludes to the popular fear of
the evil spirit of the river (vodianoi), an unclean force intimately
associated in the peasant imagination with the danger of drowning.[54]
When, for example, Mar´ia suggests releasing the nets as a joke, her
friends express their nervousness about the depth of the water: 'Da tut
glyb´, omut´ia' (267).[55] Since it is afternoon and not evening — a
dangerous time for swimming as far as the folk were concerned —
Mar´ia decides that it is safe to enter the water and release the net
herself.[56] The agitation of her friends intensifies further when the dark,
whiskered form of the sheat-fish is spotted swimming lazily below the
surface — after all, this was a fish rumoured in certain quarters to be
the vodianoi's favourite mode of transport.[57] Mar´ia's friends urge her to
leave it alone, and express their fear that it will drag her underwater;
but her confidence and courage (or lack of superstitious fear) is such
that she attempts to catch it instead.[58] This is the reason, presumably,
why her success astounds both her friends and the local fishermen (her
instant reputation, and the excitement with which the feat is discussed
in the village, are otherwise rather difficult to explain). The fishermen
claim that the fish has been hit by a horse's hoof, and is perhaps sleepy,
but when Mar´ia leaps up and releases it they are shown to take a step
back in fear, a reaction which cannot be explained simply by its size
and strength. In the eyes of the girls, therefore, Mar´ia has challenged
the evil spirit which inhabits the rivers and waterways, and miraculously escaped retribution.[59]

Two subsequent passages involve animals which were also
associated in the folk imagination with the unclean force. According to
Chicherov, it was widely believed that the demons of the forests and
fields were at the height of their powers during the winter period.[60] St
Michael's Day was normally considered the time when these forces
came to prominence, possibly due to apocryphal legends which told
how the Archangel Michael brought all evil spirits into being when the
earth was first created. However, stories about the dangers of woods
and forests characterized the period from St Erofei's Day (4 October)
onwards.[61] This probably explains the episode that takes place on the
third day after the feast of St Cosmas and Damian in which a young
boy is bitten by a snake and dies from the poison. The snake is
described as a 'horrible demon' (omrak strashnyi), and thus positioned
implicitly within the category of evil spirit.[62] The language employed

here, moreover, echoes the use of the adjective *strashennyi* (267) in relation to the sheat-fish, and the use of the adverb *strashno* (267) in connection with the girls' terror of the river.[63] St Michael's Day, likewise, signalled the appearance of a number of predatory animals — in particular wolves — which were designated *nechisti* in the folk imagination. This is echoed in the priest's oft-repeated story about being attacked by wolves while returning home at night with geese for Christmas, a perilous journey during which he is forced to sacrifice them one by one in order to survive. In turn, this echoes the cautionary tales for travellers repeated during the dangerous 'wolf month' (*volchii mesiats*), which lasted from mid-November to mid-December.[64] Ivan sets off with a view to encountering these evil spirits so that he can have something to boast about later on. But because it is a bright night with the moon shining, he is not attacked as he returns home during the middle of the night, and makes it safely to the Unzha by midday.

For all the expressions of fear in the narrative, and the fact that Ivan dies at a time coinciding approximately with Christmas Eve (a dangerous time according to the Russian folk),[65] the cause of his death is mundane, if not banal — with the benefit of hindsight, it is clear that the author-narrator's flirtation with the fear of evil spirits is a further reversal of expectation in line with the pattern already established during the orchestration of events around Orthodox festivals. This subversion of expectation is where the tension between ostensible author and implied narrator is located, with the imaginative world of the protagonists fully conveyed, yet never fully shared. Furthermore, the employment of certain phallic objects in the narrative (the stone idol would have been sculpted in the shape of a phallus, and employed for the performance of fertility rituals) suggests a sly sense of humour. There is a lingering sense in which blame for the events should be attributed not so much to the pride of the central protagonists, but to the values which the community shares as a whole: propriety, conservatism, and stubbornness. The remark that the villagers themselves are calculating, and that there is nothing which escapes their attention, indicates the suffocating nature of this community, and continues a theme which is central to Zamiatin's description of provincial life in *Uezdnoe*.[66] A potential source of humiliation for Ivan lies in the fact that his initial rebuff and failure in his courtship of Mar´ia is the subject of public knowledge. His predicament is further compounded by the teasing and gossip which he suffers at the hands of the locals: 'Стали про них языки точить, стали их подзуживать — ну просто так, для потехи' (266). This is inflicted 'for a laugh', yet the fact that Ivan's death is prompted by a similar kind of teasing at the end of the story lends this deliberate mocking a more ominous quality. The dark joke of the narrative consists of the fact that the *nechist´* of the opening paragraph, rather than a genuinely demonic shaper of events, refers to the sexual imperatives which religious orthodoxy fears. It is a dark 'disease' and 'impurity' which, when released into a community which essentially fears and represses it, leads to a tragic denouement.

As a vision of Old Russia, 'Kriazhi' is essentially subversive. A pattern is established in Zamiatin's fiction whereby his provincial narrators, while poeticizing the exotic and primitive world of tiny communities on the peripheries of Russia's metropolitan consciousness, and taking unashamed artistic delight in obscure words and folk customs, give birth to fiction which emphasizes the deep frustration and oppression experienced by the people living in them. A similar paradox lies at the heart of 'Afrika'. This narrative, while evoking the beauty and strangeness of a White Sea coastal village, tells the tale of an unhappy fisherman obsessed with travelling to Africa in order to start a new and better life. Like Ivan, who is clearly one of the poorest members of an already poor community, the illiterate hero of 'Afrika' comes from the very lowest rungs of society. This focus on the ordinary and unsophisticated members of society as repositories of strong, unequivocal, and primitive urges is a characteristic feature of Zamiatin's rural prose. Furthermore, it is symptomatic of his world-view that the lives of these characters end tragically: social outcasts by birth, then by choice, they die before their desires for both sexual and spiritual fulfilment can be realized.

NOTES

1.   'Kriazhi' (I, 265–71) was first published in 1916 in the collection *Uezdnoe: Povesti i rasskazy* (*PZ*, 54). Subsequently, without authorization, it appeared in a special 1916 Easter edition of *Rech´*, the official newspaper of Russia's Constitutional Democrats (Kadets). Zamiatin refers to this embarrassing situation in a letter to Remizov dated 22 April/5 May 1916 from Newcastle-upon-Tyne. See 'Pis´ma E. I. Zamiatina A. M. Remizovu', ed. by V. V. Buznik, *Russkaia literatura*, 1992.1, 176–80 (p. 177). Henceforth, all references to 'Kriazhi' in the Neimanis edition in the text and notes will be given in parentheses without the volume number.

2.   'Молча, молятся за людей старицы-сосны в клобуках белых' (270). *Staritsa* refers more accurately to a very old woman (Dal´, IV, 317), but the religious connotations of the image — indicated by the cowls and prayers — are self-evident.

3.   For a description of this clearing process, and other place names which derive from it, see 'U chorta na kulichkakh' (1890), in Maksimov, XV, 61–67 (p. 64).

4.   'Старая там Русь, исконная, кондовая. С той поры как зачиналась земля Русская, там чуждых насельников не бывало. Там Русь сысстари на чистоте стоит — какова была при прадедах, такова хранится до наших дней.' See P. I. Mel´nikov (Andrei Pecherskii), *V*

lesakh, 2 vols (Moscow: Gosudarstvennoe izdatel´stvo khudozhestvennoi literatury, 1958), I, 14 (Book I, Chapter 1).

5. This expedition was undertaken in 1923 under the aegis of the Kostroma Academic Society. For the profile of the area, see Vas. Smirnov, 'Chort rodilsia', in *Tretii etnograficheskii sbornik*, Trudy Kostromskogo nauchnogo obshchestva po izucheniiu mestnogo kraia series, 29 (Kostroma: [n. pub.], 1923), pp. 17–20 (p. 17).

6. The description of Baryba is given by the lawyer Morgunov: '— Ты, брат, солидный очень, да и упористый, кряжистый. Тебя с толку не сбить' (I, 71). In *Sever*, the word is used as Kortoma helps his hired hands shift a pile of logs: 'Приплюснутый, медный, кряжистый напер — и крякнул венец: только пыль дымом' (I, 410).

7. *Norovistyi* derives from *norov*, a dialect variant of *nrav*, and means both 'stubborn' and 'attached to custom or convention'. See Dal´, II, 555.

8. Shane, p. 112.

9. In particular, see the woodcarvings of peasant types by the celebrated sculptor Sergei Konenkov in the first two decades of the twentieth century (Plate III). Zamiatin's knowledge of his work is revealed several years later in a letter to Aleksei Dikii, the actor and producer of *Blokha*: 'Коненков, это старое, исконное, кондовое, русское — русская сказка, и это основной тон' ('Perepiska', 290). For photographic reproductions of his sculptures, see *Sergei Konenkov* (Leningrad: Avrora, 1977).

10. See E. G. Mushchenko, V. P. Skobelev, and L. E. Kroichik, *Poetika skaza* (Voronezh: Izdatel´stvo Voronezhskogo Universiteta, 1978), pp. 175–77.

11. 'Таким образом весь год — триста шестьдесят пять дней — имеют каждый бесчисленное множество примет, и хотя эти приметы не имеют для вас, образованного читателя, никакого значения, даже смысла, но земледельческую народную мысль они достаточно-таки характеризуют.' See *Vlast´ zemli* (1882), in G. I. Uspenskii, *Polnoe sobranie sochinenii*, ed. by N. F. Bel´chikov, B. I. Bursov, and B. P. Koz´min, 14 vols ([Leningrad]: Akademiia nauk SSSR, 1949–54), VIII (1949), 7–121 (p. 39).

12. Among these epithets, two require further explanation: *konovod* derives from *kon*, meaning 'kitty', 'stake', 'bet', 'game', or 'round', and refers to the person who is always the first to initiate games and pranks during folk-religious festivals (Dal´, II, 154); and *zavodila* (*zavodilo* is presumably either local dialect or a typographical error on the part of the Neimanis editors) is a synonym for *zachinshchik* and *organizator* (*SRIa*, I, 504).

13. The sheat-fish, also known as the sheath-fish, is a species of predatory catfish (*Silurus glanis*) believed to be the largest kind of freshwater fish in European waters. Armed with an array of sharp teeth, it was not unknown for young sheat-fish to attack and drown children, as well as geese and ducks. See *ES*, XXX, 853–54.

14. 'Stoiat´— negasimuiu svechu', p. 118.

15. '— Эй, вы, заунженские! А ну-ко, по первопутку-то к нам?' (270). My emphasis.

16. See Shane, pp. 125–26; and Niqueux, p. 53.

17. Maksimov, XVII, 231–33.

18. *Poetika skaza*, p. 175.

19. In May 1920, for example, Boris Pil´niak wrote a draft short story entitled 'Ivan-da-Mar´ia', the title being retained for another story which eventually appeared in 1922. On the draft version, he made the following note: 'Иван-да-Марья — великорусское наше растение, некрасивое, шершавое, растет по полям, лесам и перелескам.' Jensen notes: 'As a title of a literary work it is rich in association: naturalness — commonness — Russia — a certain lyricism. However, the designation of the flower also contains the two Christian names that have stood for the typical Russian youth and maiden since the days of folk poetry. This extends the "typicalness" and also, via folk poetry, the lyricism.' See Peter Alberg Jensen, *Nature as Code: The Achievement of Boris Pilnjak: 1915–1924*, Institute of Slavonic Studies series (Copenhagen: Rosenkilde and Bagger, 1979), p. 156.

20. *V lesakh*, II, 283 (Book III, Chapter 1).

21. There exists a separate folkloric tradition in relation to this flower which takes the
     form of a number of folk lyric songs recorded in the Ukraine. These tell of a brother
     and sister whose incestuous but innocent love for each other leads to their becoming
     transformed respectively into the flower's blue and yellow petals. See A. Afanas´ev,
     Poeticheskie vozzreniia slavian na prirodu, 3 vols (Moscow: Soldatenkov, 1865–69; repr.
     Moscow: Indrik, 1994), II, 505–06. It is perhaps worth noting that Aleksei Tolstoi
     adapted these songs for a miniature fairy tale which was first published in 1910. See
     'Ivan da Mar´ia', in A. N. Tolstoi, *Polnoe sobranie sochinenii*, ed. by A. S. Miasnikov, A.
     N. Tikhonov, and L. I. Tolstoi, 15 vols (Moscow: Gosudarstvennoe izdatel´stvo
     khudozhestvennoi literatury, 1951–53), I (1951), 153–56.
22. *Narodnye liricheskie pesni*, p. 57.
23. Ibid., p. 15.
24. The symbolism of blond locks as an emblem of marital desirability is illustrated in the
     round dance song 'Kak za rechkoiu, kak za bystroiu', in which a young boy is asked
     to sell his locks but refuses because he needs them in order to attract a future wife.
     See ibid., pp. 194–95.
25. Worobec, p. 136.
26. Propp notes the popularity of songs about unrequited love: 'Чаще, чем о счастливой
     любви, поется о любви несчастливой. Несчастливая любовь вызвана препятствиями.
     Препятствия эти могут быть внутреннего характера, состоят в сложностях взаимных
     отношений, или внешнего — в той власти, которую над молодыми имеют старшие и
     весь уклад отстоявшейся традиционной патриархальной жизни. Тогда наступают
     тяжкие и трагические конфликты.' See *Narodnye liricheskie pesni*, pp. 15–16.
27. For the symbolic significance of this festival and the ways in which it was celebrated
     in the nineteenth century, see Maksimov, XVII, 185–87; Kalinskii, p. 141; Gromyko,
     p. 169; and Ermolov, pp. 355–60.
28. It is generally attested that drink is an important element of the St Peter and Paul's
     Day festivities. See *V lesakh*, II, 376–77 (Book III, Chapter 7).
29. Zamiatin's term for the round dance — *korogod* (268) — must be a dialect term.
     Regional variants on the more usual *khorovod* included *tanok*, *karagod*, and *ulitsa*. See
     Gromyko, p. 162.
30. In rural communities, this was the term given to the items of food which the young
     collected together for special festive occasions or feasts.
31. 'Kak po travke, po muravke' was recorded by Rimskii-Korsakov in the area of
     Tikhvinsk, Novgorod Province, and published in *Sto russkikh pesen dlia golosa s
     fortep´iano* (1877). For the reprinted text of the song, see *Narodnye liricheskie pesni*, p.
     193.
32. *V lesakh*, II, 379 (Book III, Chapter 7).
33. In post-Emancipation Russia, the exchange of gifts between a young man and woman
     was the first stage in a process which led initially to sexual intercourse, and then later
     to marriage. See Worobec, p. 142.
34. The noun *obrot´* referred to a certain type of bridle in which there was no bit between
     the teeth — hence the phrase *obrotat´ loshad´*, which referred to the placing of such a
     bridle on a horse, and the humorous expression *obrotat´ parnia*, which meant 'to
     marry' (Dal´, II, 616). Zamiatin had used the verb in this same, slang sense in
     'Poludennitsa (Kuny)' (the speaker here is the old witch, Petrovna): '— Коли дашь,
     девушка, одного божка — и я тебе снадобья дам такого, что с ним живо суженого
     своего обратаешь' (29).
35. 'Наране Петрова дня уехали мужики невод ставить на Лошадий остров, где поножь
     лошадиная каждый год' (267). Although obscure, *ponozh´* would seem to derive from
     pónozhi, the word given for chains and fetters, as well as ankle bracelets, placed on the
     legs, (Dal´, III, 287).
36. Maksimov, XVII, 228–30.
37. Zamiatin's awareness of the importance of this period in terms of matchmaking
     ceremonies, and his interest in the rituals and customs which took place from *Pokrov*

onwards, is indicated in the various notes he kept while travelling around Russia. See 'Iz bloknotov 1914–1928 godov' (1988), pp. 91–92. Here he refers to the first signs of snow (*zazimki*), and later to two of the rituals which take place as part of the betrothal process: the *zaplachka* is the colloquial expression for the bride's song which laments the fact that she is leaving her parents to join the family of her new husband; and the *posidka*, a northern expression, refers to the bridal party which takes place after the matchmaking negotiations have been concluded, but prior to the nuptials themselves. See Elizabeth A. Warner, *The Russian Folk Theatre* (The Hague: Mouton, 1977), p. 45. The location of the community in question is not directly indicated by Zamiatin, although it would appear to be somewhere in the North (he remarks, for example, that from September onwards the village community is swelled in numbers by the arrival of barge-haulers from St Petersburg). It is also worth noting that the last lines conjure up the isolation and deathly quiet of a rural village in winter in a manner very similar to the last section of 'Kriazhi': 'Отрезанность от мира, тишина деревни — когда падает снег.' See 'Iz bloknotov 1914–1928 godov' (1988), p. 91.

38.   See V. I. Chicherov, *Zimnii period russkogo narodnogo zemledel´cheskogo kalendaria: XVI–XIX vekov*, Trudy instituta etnografii im. N. N. Miklukho-Maklaia (new) series, 40 (Moscow: Akademiia nauk SSSR, 1957), pp. 48–49.

39.   Ibid., p. 50.

40.   The priest's knowledge of the healing powers of grasses hints at the possibility that he is considered the local *znakhar´* — in other words, a doctor capable of curing illnesses by means of herbal medicine.

41.   'Давняя сказочно-мифологическая традиция, говоря о змееборстве, сталкивала героя со змеем как с обладателем или похитителем женщины. [...] В сказках герой вел борьбу с мифическим чудовищем, чтобы создать семью' (V. P Anikin). Cited in *Byliny*, ed. by V. I. Kalugin (Moscow: Sovremennik, 1986), p. 179.

42.   Maksimov, XVII, 147–55.

43.   It may be relevant in this context that the two surviving drafts of 'Kriazhi' show the story to have been written in December. See IMLI, opis´ 1, ed. khr. 26 & 27.

44.   Chicherov, pp. 30–32.

45.   Ibid., p. 30. Additional portents include the following: 'Кузьма и Демьян — проводы осени, встреча зимы, первые морозы'; 'Кузьма-Демьян — Божий кузнец (— дороги и реки кует)'; 'Не заковать реку зим без Кузьмы-Демьяна'; and 'Демьянов путь — не путь, а только зимы перепутье.' See Ermolov, pp. 521–26 (p. 522).

46.   'Коли Кузьма Демьян с мостом, то Михайло с полумостом.' See also: 'Кузьма закует, а Михайло (8 Ноября) раскует (Михаиловские оттепели).' See ibid.

47.   Although *sviatki* are normally associated with Christmas Eve, for many peasants they signified the period of festivities from St Nicholas's Day (6 December) to Twelfth Night (6 January). See Maksimov, XVII, 3–27 (p. 3).

48.   It was common in rural Russia to attribute the skills of the local *znakhar´* in some measure to a collaboration with the 'unclean force'. See ibid., XVIII, 185.

49.   Stone idols made up only a small percentage of pagan idols generally, the majority being sculpted from wood. For further discussion and illustrations, see Rybakov, pp. 231–36.

50.   *Nechist´* possesses a range of connotations, and refers to uncleanliness, sickness, sexual disease, filth, and poisonous insects. See Dal´, II, 543. The context, however, suggests that it is a dialect variant either for *nechistaia sila*, which refers to the 'unclean force' of Russian folk belief, or *nechistyi*, a colloquial term for the Devil.

51.   For the popularity of St Nicholas of Myra, known in Russia as *Nikolai chudotvorets*, or more colloquially as *Nikola* and *Mikola*, see Ivanits, pp. 24–26.

52.   *Opaska* and *vereda* are colloquial (and in the latter case, probably regional) variations on *opasenie* and *vred* (Dal´, II, 677; & I, 260). The problem of the attribution of this 'speech' is compounded by the fact that the implied narrator also uses dialect terms, and therefore the vocabulary itself is not a reliable indication of point of view.

53.   For definitions of the *shishiga*, also known as the *kikimora*, see Zabylin, pp. 248–49.

54. It was widely believed among the peasantry that deep pools of water, whether ponds, rivers, or lakes, were the dwelling place of the *vodianoi*, a malevolent spirit which did not hesitate to drown those who trespassed through his watery kingdom. Fishermen were particularly prone to this superstition, and often threw back part of their catch into the river as a sacrifice. For further discussion, and the continuing relevance of this folk belief at the turn of the century, see Ivanits, pp. 70–74, & 182–85; and Maksimov, XVIII, 93–114.

55. *Glyb´* is a regional variant of *glubina* (Dal´, I, 356). *Omut´ia*, from *omut*, refers to deep pools or waters — hence the Russian proverb 'Devils breed in deep waters' ('В тихом омуте черти водятся').

56. 'Под вечер будь дело — бросили бы, а сейчас оно не так уж и страшно' (267). According to Russian folklore, the most dangerous time of the day to risk bathing was either at noon or after dark. See Ivanits, p. 72.

57. 'Хорошо осведомленные люди привычно не едят раков и голых рыб (в роде налимов и угрей), как любимых блюд на столе водяного, а также и сомовину за то, что на сомах вместо лошади ездят под водой эти черти.' See Maksimov, XVIII, 109. He describes the whiskered *som* as a 'river giant' (*rechnoi bogatyr´*) and 'roadside bandit' (*pridorozhnyi razboinik*) which loves to inhabit the same deep and root-bestrewn pools as the *vodianoi*. See ibid., p. 106.

58. 'Сом, сомяка! Батюшки, ну и страшенный! Ой, беги, Марья, в воду утянет' (267). The final three words are the standard way of expressing fear of drowning by a malevolent spirit.

59. A number of accounts tell how the bravura of a diver or swimmer angered the *vodianoi*. See Ivanits, p. 72.

60. Chicherov, p. 35.

61. Ibid., pp. 35–36; and Ivanits, p. 45.

62. Although given as a colloquial variant for *obmorok* (Dal´, II, 673), and thus referring to a faint or temporary loss of consciousness, *omrak* would seem in this context to derive from the verb 'to make dark or gloomy' (*omrachat´*, *omrachit´*), and thus refer to the 'unclean force'.

63. It is worth noting that this particular episode echoes the ethnographic report mentioned in note 5 of the present chapter about 'fire-breathing dragons'.

64. Chicherov, p. 37.

65. Dushechkina notes that 'if a person displays cowardice, ignorance, or recklessness, he or she pays with life or health, or loses a member of his or her family'. See Elena Dushechkina, 'Russian Calendar Prose: the Yuletide Story', *Elementa*, 1 (1993), 59–74 (p. 62).

66. The colloquial expression *na vedú* derives either from the verb meaning 'to possess information' (*vedat´*) or 'to know' (*vest´*).

CHAPTER 4

(THE NORTH)

AFRIKA

In a speech delivered on 11 February 1924 to celebrate the fortieth anniversary of Fedor Sologub's literary activity, Zamiatin elected to discuss the theme of dream-obsession and reality ('Fedor Sologub' (IV, 150–55)). He observed that Sologub's fiction was full of characters whose insatiable appetite for the transcendental led them to reject 'warts-and-all' reality in favour of shimmering visions of the beyond. Like Cervantes's Don Quixote de la Mancha, they were searchers on a quest for the unrealizable dream, deluded knights whose fierce attachment to their inner, private visions gave them a hypersensitive aversion to the truth — namely that their beloved 'Dulcinea del Toboso', a figure of unblemished purity, virtue, and nobility, was none other than the unremarkable peasant girl 'Aldonza' (ibid., 151). Unlike Cervantes, however, Sologub's love of humanity was simultaneously compassionate and ruthless. By having his characters die in sight of their goal, while sparing them the realization that this goal was essentially an illusion, Sologub displayed the medieval attitude of misericord: his art was a form of mercy-killing, a sword with which to put his wounded dreamers out of their misery (ibid., 152).

The short story 'Afrika', which Zamiatin published in issue no. 4/5 of the journal *Severnye zapiski* for 1916, conforms closely to the paradigm explored in the essay on Sologub.[1] Although it predates the speech by some eight years, the story's exploration of the twilight zone between dream and reality, and its use of a seemingly celestial female figure, associated symbolically with the colour white to imply the existence of a transcendental reality, to a great extent anticipates Zamiatin's reading of the eternal feminine theme as it appears in the work both of Sologub and the Symbolist poet Aleksandr Blok. The themes of dream-quest and Enchanted Lady feature regularly in his remarks about these two artists, and can ultimately be traced back, via a lecture on modern literature given at the People's University of Lebedian´ in September 1918, to a review of Blok's *Roza i krest* which appeared as early as 1914.[2] In terms of situation, image, and symbol, Zamiatin's northern tale shares much in common with Blok's quasi-mystical narratives: his *Stikhi o Prekrasnoi Dame* (1901–02), which embody spiritual aspirations in the form of a mysterious, beautiful woman; the self-parodying *Balaganchik* (1906), in which the lovelorn hero awaits with trepidation the arrival of his beloved Columbine, a mysterious and enigmatic figure dressed in white who is variously perceived in terms of an 'insubstantial ghost' and a 'girl from a distant shore', and is equated symbolically with Death; and *Roza i krest*, a courtly romance set in medieval times, the theme of which embodies idealized love, dream fantasy, and romantic quests to distant regions.[3] It is important in this context to note Africa's cult status among Symbolists as a romantic dreamscape and object of exotic fascination, primarily as a result of the trips undertaken there by Nikolai Gumilev from 1908 to 1913. His impressions were reflected in the three poems on African subjects in his first collection, *Romanticheskie tsvety* (1908), and the lyrics which he read at Viacheslav Ivanov's 'Tower' and published variously after 1912.[4] Indeed, the cult of travelling to exotic places, prompted in the case of Gumilev by the example of Rimbaud's celebrated voyage to Africa in the 1880s, had tempted other authors to undertake similar journeys — these included the poet and editor Vladimir Narbut, in whose journal *Novyi zhurnal dlia vsekh* Zamiatin had published his second short story, 'Devushka' (*PZ*, 54).[5] Of course, Zamiatin himself had travelled to Africa as early as 1905. The voyage there left him with a number of exotic impressions which he deemed worthy of recording in his 1929 autobiography. It is interesting to note, moreover, that the steamboat on which he sailed — the *Rossiia* — was the same one which took Gumilev to Egypt in September 1908.[6]

Despite these parallels with the concerns of the Symbolists, 'Afrika' is very much a turning point in Zamiatin's early period; it is a hybrid product which combines Symbolist paradigms with the stylistic conceits of literary populism. A similar experiment was being conducted in prose around this time by Ol'ga Forsh, a neorealist prose writer with whom Zamiatin was cómpared after the publication of *Uezdnoe* in 1913. Their shared objective, it seems, was to democratize the subject, manoeuvring it several notches down the social scale, away from the essentially aristocratic, courtly, and intellectual milieu into the very heartlands of the peasant imagination — in Cervantine terms, the equivalent of Sancho Panza swapping roles with Quixote himself. The result is a comic, parodic tension which automatically deflates the serious, somewhat abstract musings of the Symbolists. The very ordinariness of Zamiatin's male protagonist, an illiterate and inarticulate fisherman called Fedor Volkov who shares a hut with his faithful hunting dog until the day of his wedding, stands in hilarious contrast to the habitual medium of Symbolist reverie — the gaunt, decadent poet. Furthermore, unlike Blok's *Balaganchik*, which floats gently in the octane-filled ether of pure theatre, 'Afrika' is anchored securely to the topography of the northern Russian landscape and couched in the colloquial language and dialect of the settlements along the White Sea coast: this endows the text with a rough-and-ready feel against which the giddy transportation into dream can be effectively juxtaposed. Writers like Zamiatin and Forsh thus create a new type of *mechtatel´*, one of poor peasant extraction, whose tireless and comic pursuit of chimera reflects a general predisposition among the Russian *narod* towards belief in the magical and the supernatural. The poetics of neorealism dictated that these flights of fancy be expressed in terms of folk fantasy; and it is precisely as an example of post-Symbolist *lubok*, with the usual stylistic and ethnographic conceits, that I propose to examine 'Afrika' in this chapter.

In common with *Sever*, which forms the second part of Zamiatin's so-called 'northern trilogy', the narrative action of 'Afrika' takes place in a village situated along the western (Pomorian) shore of the White Sea, just south of the Arctic circle. Despite a degree of confusion regarding the actual dating of the story, it appears to have been written after a visit to the Pomor´e region in the summer of 1915.[7] Many years later, Zamiatin named the port of Kem´, the town of Soroka (now Belomorsk), and the famous Solovetskii Islands among the places he visited ('Zakulisy' (IV, 301)); this is confirmed by a number of letters to his wife during July and August 1915 which reveal that he stayed initially in Vologda and Archangel, and from there planned a three-day trip by steamboat to Soroka before returning to St Petersburg, presumably at the end of the month (*RN*, I, 191–92). Significantly, this was another area mentioned in his lectures at the House of Arts as the cradle of authentic Russian language ('O iazyke' (IV, 379)), possibly because of the large numbers of Old Believers who had settled there following the Schism in the Church during the seventeenth century.[8] Although a relatively remote region at the time of the First World War, it had already acquired something of a reputation among Slavophiles and Populists. Sergei Maksimov had spent a year in Kem´ on an official ethnographic mission sponsored by the Imperial Naval Ministry, and recorded his impressions in a long report entitled *God na Severe* (1859).[9] The area was also famous for the collections of traditional epic songs

recorded by P. N. Rybnikov and A. F. Gil´ferding in the 1860s and
1870s.[10] Ivan Bilibin, the graphic designer and illustrator, had spent
three brief summers in the North from 1902 to 1904 researching
wooden churches — on his return he produced a long article on
northern folk culture for Diagilev's journal *Mir iskusstva*, and offered
several of his paintings as designs for charity postcards (three were
landscape scenes from the Kem´ area itself).[11] And Mikhail Prishvin,
the agronomist-turned-novelist, had trekked along the Letnii and
Dvina shores of the White Sea coast and recorded his impressions in a
piece of ethnographic *belles-lettres* entitled *Za volshebnym kolobkom*,
which he published on his return in 1908.[12] Although Zamiatin was not
visiting this area voluntarily — it has been claimed that he was exiled
to Kem´ after the eruption of the 'Na kulichkakh' affair in 1914, but the
letters to his wife suggest that, on the contrary, he was contracted to
work there because of the war[13] — he would have been aware of this
strong cultural interest in the North. Remizov, his close friend and
collaborator at this time, boasted an extensive knowledge of northern
folk-religious culture: he had spent two years of his northern exile in
Vologda, and his earliest works drew on his experiences there.[14]
Zamiatin's later lectures at the House of Arts reveal an acquaintance
with the poetry of Nikolai Kliuev, a poet from the region of Olonets
renowned for his use of local dialect and sectarian spiritual songs ('O
iazyke' (IV, 380)). And his friendship with Prishvin, which developed
after their first meeting in the editorial offices of *Zavety* in 1913
('Zakulisy' (IV, 303)), indicates that he had might well have read *Za
volshebnym kolobkom* prior to his stay in Kem´. Certainly, both the
allusion to the magical *kolobok* at the beginning of Prishvin's narrative,
with its implicit warning of the dangers inherent in leaving the family
hearth, and the mention of Africa as an escape fantasy entertained by
the author as a young child (recalled as he crosses the White Sea by
boat), are strikingly germane to the theme of Zamiatin's tale.[15]

   'Afrika' is the tale of a simple man's fierce desire to reach Africa, a
place in which all his dreams for the future have been invested.
Structurally, the text is divided into four equal parts. The opening
chapter introduces the main protagonist, Fedor Volkov, an illiterate
fisherman with seal-like eyes, a crock-like head, and short, cropped
hair, who inhabits a small, isolated village called Keremet´ situated at
some point along the White Sea coast. The notion of travelling to Africa
is planted in his mind by a trio of well-heeled travellers — two
gentlemen and young girl — who arrive unexpectedly on a steamboat
and decide to stay the night before moving on the next day. For

Volkov, who is delegated to row them ashore and show them to their lodgings, they are exotic in every way. He is fascinated to hear them occasionally slipping into a foreign language, and concludes that they must be from abroad. Naively (they are presumably educated Russians from St Petersburg who switch occasionally into French), he asks them where they are from. They laugh, winking at each other, and reply that they are from Africa. Volkov is astonished: '— Из А-африки? Да неуж и по-нашему говорят?', he asks, to which they respond: '— Там, брат, на всех языках говорят...' (277). Volkov is impressed. He is even more impressed when, after having shown them to their lodgings — a cabin owned by a local man called Pimen — he sits down by the gate outside and overhears the young girl singing. It is a sad and enchanting melody, one which has a powerful impact on him, so powerful that after everyone has gone to bed, and the village is bathed in the surreal light of a northern white night, Volkov imagines that he has arisen and returned to the hut where the young girl is waiting for him by her bedroom window. In his dream (or is it real?), she leans out of the window and embraces him, clasping his head gently to her chest, and exuding as she does so a striking perfume. The next day, unsure of the true nature of this encounter, Volkov is initially suspicious when the girl invites him to visit her in Africa. Perhaps it does not exist, he thinks cautiously, suspecting that they are trying to make a fool of him. As he bends down to kiss her hand in parting, however, he thinks he recognizes the perfume from his dream: 'Нагнулся в низком поклоне Федор Волков и показалось: от руки — тот самый дух, который во сне...' (279). From this moment onwards he believes in Africa, and gives his word that he will come and visit her.

If the first part of this tale consists of a surreal vision, the second part witnesses Volkov trying to recapture the beauty and strangeness of his encounter in the circumstances of ordinary life. He experiences an uncanny sense of *déjà vu* one evening when he catches sight of Pimen's eldest daughter Iausta sobbing quietly at the very same window as the mysterious girl from abroad. Volkov is struck by the coincidence, and quite enchanted, since the light of the moon gives her a spectral beauty and grandeur far removed from her daily countenance. Iausta tells him that she is miserable and unhappy: she is past marrying age, and her father has been nagging her to find a husband so that he can marry off his two younger daughters. Volkov feels sorry for her — and again, as before, he finds himself consoling an unhappy young woman by the bedroom window of Pimen's *izba*. We are told that he courts her every night for much of the spring before deciding to propose marriage at the

beginning of summer. Daytime reality quickly intrudes into their
relationship, however. The previously shy and retiring Iausta, having
cleaned and tidied her new abode, ticks off her husband for forgetting
to wipe his boots when he enters — the magic spell of their courtship is
shattered. Volkov starts to disappear at night, wandering down to the
beach where he can be seen staring out to sea as if half-expecting the
visitors from abroad to return. Soon he is in trouble with his father-in-
law, who nags him to repair his severed relationship with his young
wife, or at least to spend his nights in bed with her at home for the sake
of marital propriety. This pressure estranges Volkov further from his
adopted family, and drives him to drink as the autumn nights begin to
draw in.

The extent of Volkov's unhappiness can be gauged by the
seriousness of his drink problem, which worsens as autumn turns to
winter. The third chapter opens with Volkov being locked up for his
own safety in the top-storey of a house, from which he tries to escape
by jumping out of a window into a snow-drift below. His miraculous
recovery from what can only be described as a failed suicide bid — he
is pulled out the next morning barely alive and spends the entire
winter in the local *bania* until he feels better — convinces him that he
must seek out his destiny and find the young girl, even though he is
now burdened by a heart condition: 'Только поехать до Африки', he
says to himself hopefully, 'там уж пойдет по-новому' (283). After a
midnight mass during the Feast of Prepolovenie, he approaches his
local priest for advice; but the ageing Father Seliverst, who is so fragile
that he falls asleep in the middle of their audience, regards his plan as
absurd. Later, however, by chance, Volkov encounters a monk who has
stopped over at Keremet´ to pick up volunteers for work in monastery
fields across the sea; in turn, he is referred to an experienced old whaler
named Indrik. An archetypal sea captain with black cap and grey
beard, Indrik hires hands for whaling expeditions from Sviatoi Nos (a
tiny peninsula at the point where the White Sea flows into the Barents
Sea). Indrik is renowned for his travels around the world and tales of
exotic adventures; indeed, Volkov recalls him vaguely from his
childhood, a time when his father worked as a harpoonist with Indrik,
and remembers above all his sad eyes and grave demeanour. Indrik not
only treats his inquiries respectfully, but confirms the existence of
Africa and tells him that he can easily reach it by steamboat.
Furthermore, he offers the excited Volkov the possibility of sailing with
him aboard his schooner as a harpoonist in order to pay for his journey:
two whales, and his long sought-after goal will finally be reached.

With much agitation and excitement, Volkov embarks on the fourth
and final leg of his journey. Indrik's schooner slips anchor and moves
slowly northwards into a strange world of mists and summer white
nights. To pass the time, Indrik tells Volkov stories about Africa: about
the bread-fruit which grows on trees, the elephants which trumpet into
the tropical air, and the flowers, the fragrance of which is so powerful
that once inhaled it can never be forgotten. The ship ploughs further
northwards. The all-pervasive mist makes it impossible to judge the
direction of the boat, while the white nights confuse the boundaries
between day and night, rendering imprecise the notion of passing time.
As reality itself becomes clouded, so Volkov's mind starts to become
confused and his dreams to lose their earlier vividness. He begins to
suspect that his earlier vision of the young girl may have been a deceit.
His weak heart pumping with excitement, he begins to feel dizzy the
moment he catches sight of the first whale, and temporarily blacks out
without remembering how he managed to harpoon it. After two days
tracking a second whale, during which time Volkov has been forced to
stand loyally at his cannon, he is on the verge of physical and mental
exhaustion. When the whale suddenly appears within range, and the
moment arrives to fire, the strain on his heart because of his nervous
agitation becomes unbearable. As the harpoon is released, hurtling
faster and faster towards its target, Volkov experiences heart seizure
and collapses at the prow of the schooner, dying just at the moment the
harpoon lodges harmlessly near the tail. The author-narrator observes
wryly: 'Есть Африка. Федор Волков доехал' (287); and with these words
the story is brought to a close.

On the level of realism, 'Afrika' fits squarely into the pattern of
poetic image-making established by Zamiatin's literary predecessors;
indeed, the topographical images of the North which these writers
offer are reflected to a striking degree in the seafaring *kolorit* of his own
northern tale. The *karbas*, for example, a fishing boat manufactured
solely in the Archangel delta, and widely employed by fishermen along
the White Sea coast, is mentioned by Maksimov in *God na Severe* — as
well as listing the various different types, he gives a detailed account of
its construction.[16] In addition, 'Afrika' shares a number of details with
Prishvin's *Za volshebnym kolobkom*: the dreamlike evocation of the white
nights (278); the poetic descriptions of ducks (ibid.) and jellyfish (286);
the fishing for salmon (this was the industry from which the *pomory*
made their living (278)); the reference to the capricious north-easterly
wind (*veter-polunochnik* (282)); and the presence of the indigenous
samoedy on the Kola Peninsula (284).[17] Prishvin reports the general level

of poverty in the area and its occasional dependence on outside supplies of basic foods;[18] this is paralleled in 'Afrika' by mention of the supplies of salt, flour, and sugar which are sometimes delivered by the steamboat (277). He also refers to the traditional distrust of outsiders on the part of the local inhabitants, echoed in Zamiatin's tale when the *pomory*, having received these supplies, turn back coastwards as soon as possible without indulging in pleasantries (ibid.).[19] Such hostility is explained by the isolation of the region and its historically sectarian allegiance.[20] Maksimov, for example, is introduced to a sectarian scriptural expert (*nachetchik*) during his stay in Kem´, and claims that it is not at all unusual to encounter such scholars even in the tiny communities outside the main towns.[21] It is unsurprising, therefore, that the fictional village of Keremet´ in 'Afrika' should also boast schismatics in its midst. Pimen, we learn, the father of Iausta, is the cousin of a *nachetchik dvoedanskii* (277) — in other words, a person well versed in the scriptures and a 'secret supporter of the Schism'.[22] This revelation not only buttresses the author-narrator's claim to intimate knowledge of the region, and underlines the impression of ethno-graphic authenticity, but also contributes to the development of his theme. For it is Volkov's clash with his father-in-law which supplies one of the vital dramatic conflicts in the plot, and causes him ultimately to consider leaving.

Old Believers were austere and disciplined people, with strict moral codes, strongly puritanical prejudices, and a firm adherence to pre-Petrine Russian tradition; indeed, they had a reputation for honesty, sobriety, cleanliness, and literacy (including women and children).[23] The description of Pimen confirms his allegiance to these values, but does so, strikingly, with negative connotations. His schismatic allegiance, aside from the family connection, is stressed on a number of occasions. The adjective *dvoedanskii* is used four times in Chapter Two, either in relation to himself or his *izba*. We are told that he does not attend evening mass at the local chapel, which would not have been permitted for a disciplined sectarian, but kneels instead to the ground by the rain-barrel outside his home and sings 'sweet' hymns to the Lord. His quayside cabin, in which the guests are billeted, is specifically described as 'ritually purified' or 'cleansed' (*chistyi* (277)). And he has a traditional attitude to the custom of marriage, being impatient to marry off his eldest daughter so that he can arrange the marriages of the younger two.[24] Pimen is renowned for his austerity and lack of charity — this is indicated by the treatment of his guard-dogs, which periodically slink away from the household due to lack of sufficient food; moreover, he himself is small and painfully thin, and has a tendency to nag and torment others.[25] First he nags his daughter Iausta for not being able to find a husband: 'Каждый вечер Пимен пилил Яусту, свою старшую' (280). Then he criticizes his son-in-law for slipping out at night when he should be at home with his wife, as marital propriety and God's Law dictate. Finally, when Volkov starts to drink out of unhappiness with his circumstances, Pimen unleashes a barrage of derogatory epithets — 'worthless beggar' (*rvan´ korishnevaia* (282)), 'parasite' (*zhivoglot* (282)), and 'miserable drunk' (*propoitsa gor´kaia* (282)) — which causes him to fly into a temper and threaten to leave for good. Indeed, it is Pimen's carping, compared to the persistent whining of a mosquito, which leads ultimately to Volkov's thoughts of departure.

Whether Volkov himself is a schismatic is not indicated in 'Afrika', but it is clear that Pimen is exploited as a crucial foil to his character, beliefs, and temperament.[26] His devotion to order and cleanliness, an attitude which Iausta has evidently inherited, is sharply and comically contrasted with Volkov's general slothfulness; and on two separate occasions, the latter's sluggishness and lack of wits is indicated by means of the disparaging epithets *leshii* and *lesheboinik*.[27] Pimen's autocratic dominance as male head of the household, reflected when Iausta meekly observes the traditional wedding custom of removing her husband's boots, is also juxtaposed to Volkov's more democratic and generous instincts.[28] As a secret worshipper, Pimen evidently enjoys a respectable status within the community — this is indicated by the fact that his cabin is chosen as a place for the three travellers to stay overnight. Conversely, it is hinted that Volkov is poor, disreputable, and something of a outcast. He is unable to read and write, a handicap which distinguishes him from the schismatic milieu generally. Furthermore, like his deceased father, he is a notorious drinker, one whose bouts of alcohol abuse cause moral censure on the part of the local community and lead to his being locked up in a tower for most of one winter. By employing the word *bobyl´* in relation to Volkov — 'У бобыля в избе — откуда порядку быть' (280) — a term which refers on one level to his status as a bachelor, but which also featured widely in the last century to connote a landless peasant whose situation was exacerbated by his lack of marital status, Zamiatin indicates his social isolation and lack of material wealth within a tightly-knit community (indeed, he has only been allowed to marry Iausta because Pimen is desperate to find her a husband).[29] It is instructive that Volkov, in order to pay for his trip to Sviatoi Nos, volunteers for harvest work (*pozhnia*

(283)) at a monastery across the sea. Furthermore, it is intriguing that Indrik's description of Africa towards the end of the story should be couched so precisely in a technical jargon which alludes specifically to the problems of farming in a hostile northern climate:

Хлеб такой в Африке этой, что ни камни не надо ворочать, ни палы пускать, ни бить колочь земляную копорюгой: растет себе хлеб на древах, сам по себе, без призору, рви, коли надо. (285)

This is presumably an allusion to Volkov's recent work at the monastery, and as such offers further proof of the author-narrator's familiarity with life in the North.[30] At the same time, however, it permits the reader a glimpse of Volkov as a social being, one whose reasons for quitting his village are as much material as spiritual. Indeed, his situation has its parallel in a short story by Ol'ga Forsh entitled 'Afrikanskii brat', apparently conceived at around the same time as 'Afrika', which features a peasant *bobyl´* whose dissatisfaction with his social and economic circumstances leads him also to seek a future in Africa.[31] This man is described as a *bobyl´* because he has been refused access to a plot of family land after the recent death of his wife. Furthermore, it is the future lure of an improvement in his social status as a result of travelling to Africa and helping missionaries administer to the indigenous poor which provides him with an alternative motivation — as he explains to his friends prior to his departure: 'Ни кола у меня ни двора, а там черному-то — ровно царь.'[32] Volkov's vision of meeting the young girl at night, and being embraced by her, can thus be read on one level as a dream about the desire for acceptance by one's social superiors; indeed, the entire narrative can be interpreted as a wish-fulfilment fantasy on the part of a poor peasant to overcome his humble status and join the ranks of the supposedly civilized, a fantasy which subsequently proves a tragic illusion.

Volkov's departure for Africa is an act of defiance against his community, one all the more touching because he does not know where it is or what exactly the future holds. If Pimen represents authority, convention, and propriety in terms of the community in which they live, then Volkov's rejection both of him and his daughter is nothing short of a rebellion. Through his obsession with the visitors from abroad, Volkov challenges the Old Believer's traditional distrust of all things foreign; yet his conflict with his community has a spiritual dimension which is no less important in explaining his impulse to leave. Volkov's desire to 'live anew', one with strongly Chekhovian overtones, is couched explicitly in terms of the spirit; indeed, he describes his quest in terms of a *zhelanie dushevnoe* (283) in his audience with Father Seliverst. Nevertheless, it must be distinguished from the ascetic impulses which govern Pimen's system of religious worship. It is symptomatic that whereas Pimen's dogs are ritually abused and starved in a manner which reflects their master's overriding concern with self-denial, Volkov's Iatoshka is given the freedom of the house until the day that Iausta arrives. Ironically, Pimen's treatment of his dogs, and their regular attempts to escape his charge, presage Volkov's later dissatisfaction with his new circumstances and his decision, ultimately, to leave — the final scene at the end of Chapter Two shows him snapping like a dog at his father-in-law, and nearly biting off his nose: 'Да перед носом у Пимена — хоп! — зубами как щелкнет. И еще бы вот столько — зацепил бы Пименов нос' (282). It is significant that the time of day when Volkov escapes domestic supervision occurs when Pimen is praying to the Lord outside his home while evening mass is being conducted in the local church. Furthermore, it becomes clear as the narrative progresses that Volkov's spiritual life resides exclusively in the form of fantasy — during his initial encounter with the young girl, in his courtship of Iausta, and in his nights spent out sleeping in the woods — and that this fantasy life lies at the heart of the story's symbolic structure. A kind of double-faith opposition is brought into play which permeates both Volkov's consciousness and the symbolic level of the text as a whole. Folk fantasy, superstition, and the apocryphal are juxtaposed with religious orthodoxy, the sacred, and the canonical, in what appears to be a statement about the true nature of spirituality for the typical peasant.

In the context of Volkov as peasant *mechtatel´*, a useful perspective may be gained by comparing 'Afrika' with another story by Forsh, this time 'Za zhar-ptitsei', which was first published in 1910.[33] This is the tale of a poor peasant's obsession with chimera, in this case taking the form of the exotic firebird of the Russian magic tale — a text which Benois and Stravinskii employed for their ballet of the same year — and a Persian princess from the realms of childhood fable (although not stated explicitly, this princess in all likelihood is Scheherazade).[34] Like Volkov, the main protagonist of Forsh's story is a peasant called Ivan Lapotok. He is a dreamer who gazes at the moon at night and confuses the world of fantasy with that of reality.[35] Forsh details first his obsession with a skilled seamstress, Steposha, whose celebrated embroidery designs intoxicate him with their exotic colours and motifs, reminding him of the magic tales which he was first told as a young child. He courts her, temporarily beguiled by her nocturnal appearance into thinking that she is the reincarnation of the fabulous Persian princess, and then later proposes to her. Her daylight appearance, however, causes him consternation and disappointment. Disillusioned by this encounter with mundane reality, he allows himself to become obsessed with a second love-object, a gypsy girl called Grun´ka, who arrives in the area at Shrovetide and also reminds him temporarily of his lost princess. This time it is her voice which enchants and beguiles him:

— Как завела Грунька голосом — заговорил он наконец, радуясь, что язык называет как раз то, что нужно, — как завела голосом, а мне вода вдруг нездешняя померещилась, зеленая... дно видать. А небо над водой си-и-нее, деревья белым цветут, кругом дух такой сладостный. А и где та страна я не знаю.[36]

In a dream sequence not entirely unlike the white night episode in 'Afrika', Ivan chases his beautiful singer through the fog-shrouded night, only to be told that it will cost him twenty-five roubles for the privilege of hearing her sing. By this stage, Forsh's peasant hero has sunk into such a trance that he nonchalantly kills his wife when she refuses to lend him the necessary money. Cruelly, Grun´ka accepts the money, but reneges on her initial promise.

Forsh's 'Za zhar-ptitsei' and Zamiatin's 'Afrika' share various details and motifs in common. The enchanted female voice, the exotic perfume, the 'heavenly world' (*nezdeshniaia strana*), the surreal subversion of daytime reality, and the treacherous female figure all point unambiguously to a shared artistic agenda. However, the vision of the *narod* which the two authors offer, one reflected very much in the characterization of the two central protagonists, must be sharply distinguished. Although both are poor and illiterate — Ivan's name, 'Lapotok', is the diminutive of the derogatory slang term *lapot´*, which means 'ignorant' or 'retarded' (*SRIa*, II, 164) — Zamiatin's protagonist is much gentler and far less prone to outbursts of frustrated, murderous aggression. According to Tamarchenko, Forsh's interest lay in high-lighting the paradoxical impulses in the Russian peasant soul, charac-terized on the one hand by a 'fundamental yearning for the beautiful', and on the other hand by an obsessive materialism; these come into conflict, giving rise to a tragic explosion of passions and disastrous consequences.[37] By contrast, Zamiatin stresses the naive, passive, and trusting nature of his peasant fisherman. Whereas Ivan Lapotok seeks the beauty of the fairy tale because it reminds him of the innocence and enchantment of childhood, Volkov is driven by the urge to understand a curious paradox — how a young girl, on the surface so happy and full of mirth, can produce such haunting, powerful, and melancholic music. His motivation is primarily emotional, spiritual, and artistic — hence the tragic irony that it is his heart which responds so vigorously to the emotional resonance of her song, and yet, simultaneously, is the instrument of his death. Volkov is more a victim of deception and external manipulation than any internal contradiction in his own personality. Indeed, while his natural gravitation towards the magical is undoubtedly one cause of his downfall, there is a sense in which he falls victim to supernatural forces far beyond his ken, forces which control human destiny and decide human fate.

Even a cursory reading of the text gives the impression that Fedor Volkov's life lies in the hands of powerful and mysterious forces. There is something enigmatic and ghostly about the characters who invite and encourage him to undertake his journey. Their arrival is an 'unusual event' (*proisshestvie neobychainoe* (277)). Furthermore, the author-narrator is deliberately vague about their identity, both in terms of their native language and their origins. The girl's nightdress, framed against the dark background of the hut window during the white night sequence, lends her a spectral aspect, an impression reinforced both by the general strangeness of the description itself and the deliberate punning on the word for perfume or fragrance (*dukh*), which can also mean spectre, spirit, or ghost (Dal', I, 503).[38] Indrik, moreover, the sea captain whose sad eyes see 'those things forbidden to ordinary mortals', seems to have prescient knowledge of Volkov's fate — he remains calm, even unaffected, when his newly-employed harpoonist collapses and dies at the prow of his boat (we note that he has taken a replacement along as a precaution (284)). It is worth remarking that all these characters are linked symbolically with the sea: the three travellers first arrive from over the sea; they are branded collectively *izzamorskie* (literally, 'from across the sea' (281)) by Iausta; Indrik is a sea captain with wide experience of travelling across the sea; and Volkov himself has to travel across the sea to Sviatoi Nos, the place where Indrik handpicks men to join him on his expeditions, in order to earn his passage. It is implied that people who have travelled widely across water belong to a different world, possessing a wisdom and tragic knowledge which is denied to the naive and childishly ignorant Volkov. Since his death takes place symbolically in the vicinity of water, it is tempting to look for evidence of the archetypal folk drowning text, as part of which an ordinary mortal is first enchanted, then lured to his death, by the hypnotic and haunting song of a female siren.

One hint that water functions symbolically in 'Afrika' occurs in the passage exactly halfway through the narrative which describes Volkov's father's penchant for 'swimming' (282) — a euphemism, we presume, for his habit of collapsing after too much alcohol and flailing his arms around drunkenly on the ground. We learn that Volkov himself has inherited this strange 'weakness', and shortly afterwards witness him diving out of a tall tower-room into a snow-drift and 'swimming all night' before being rescued, barely alive, the next morning. What is interesting about this fragment is the symbolic time-frame in which it appears. As I have already noted in Chapter 1 of this study, it occurs just prior to a reference to the Orthodox Festival of Prepolovenie, an event in the religious calendar which falls exactly halfway between Easter Sunday and Ascension Day. The Feast of Prepolovenie is one of the Orthodox Church's most ancient festivals, and was closely identified in the folk imagination with the mysterious and miraculous properties of water: priests conducted special blessings of rivers, streams, and springs in the vicinity, taking as their cue Jesus's words to the Pharisees during the Feast of the Tabernacle, which equated water with spiritual nourishment and salvation.[39] In certain areas of Russia, moreover, apocryphal legends emerged telling how the Virgin Mary was delivered from drowning as she tried to escape bandits by swimming across a river with the baby Jesus in her arms: according to this tradition, the Virgin Mary prays to her infant son to help her, and is miraculously blessed with a 'third hand' to help her swim to the other bank — hence the peasant expression for this festival, *preplavlenie*, which literally means 'a swimming across'.[40] Significantly, this term is echoed four times in the opening paragraphs of Chapter Three in the sense of 'to swim' (*plavat´*):

Покойный Федора Волкова отец китобоем плавал и был запивоха престрашный: месяца пил. В пьяном виде была у него повадка такая: плавать. В лужу, в проталину, в снеги — ухнет, куда попало, и ну — руками, ногами болтать, будто плавает.

И вот ведь чудно: оказалась повадка отцовская и у Федора Волкова. [...] В том сугробе целую ночь и проплавал. (282)

Interestingly, Volkov is described in the same fragment as seeking objects to grab for support with his hand as a result of his weak heart condition: 'Иной раз подкатится под сердце — только ищет Федор за что бы рукой ухватиться' (283). Moreover, the theme of the festival is echoed on two later occasions during the account of Volkov's harpooning expedition on Indrik's schooner in the sense of 'to sail' (*plyt´*): 'Неведомо куда плывут сквозь туман' (285); and later again: 'И в межени белой опять плыли, неведомо где, плыли неделю, и может — и две' (286).[41] The fact that the earlier swimming episode is linked symbolically with the idea of drinking — Volkov's father is described as a *zapivokha* (283) — also establishes an ironic parallel with the theme of the festival. It is perhaps this tale of divine intervention, possibly heard within the community, or in the church itself on the day of the festival (it is after midnight mass that he seeks an audience with the local priest), which prompts the gullible Volkov into believing that his own escape from the snow-drift must have been similarly miraculous, and that he must seek out his own destiny by sailing to Africa. Ironically, however, while offered a 'third hand' symbolically in the form of Captain Indrik, or perhaps the harpoon which will enable him to earn the money to pay for his voyage, Volkov's passage from one 'shore' to another is not guaranteed as safely or indeed as miraculously as the Virgin Mary's.[42]

This parodic and subversive orchestration of the plot around the folk-religious symbolism of certain Orthodox festivals is standard procedure in Zamiatin's provincial fiction: in 'Poludennitsa (Kuny)' and 'Kriazhi', as we have seen already, this is an important artistic device. In 'Afrika', however, the symbolic pattern spreads beyond the immediate textual vicinity. Both the Orthodox understanding of water in terms of spiritual nourishment, and the popular fear of water as an agent of death, inform the characterization of the two young women in the tale and blend subtly with the underlying themes of deceit and misrepresentation. Iausta, for example, is openly identified with the water-spirit (*rusalka*) of Russian folk tradition, a supernatural being traditionally understood as the soul of the 'unclean dead' who has returned to haunt the land of the living.[43] As with the Feast of Prepolovenie, the fragment which opens with Volkov encountering Iausta by the window of her father's cabin, and concludes with their nuptials, is organized stylistically around another fantasy of the folk imagination, this time the temptation-deceit-disaster theme of the *rusalka* folk fabulate. It is suggested initially, for example, that Volkov's attraction to Iausta derives from a trick of the moonlight which has the effect of magically transforming her into something enchanting and bewitching:

Да полно, Яуста ли это? У Яусты волосы — как рожь, а у этой — как вода морская, русальи, зеленые. Яуста — румяная, ражая, а эта — бледная с голубью, горькая. Или месяц весенний заневодил зеленесеребряной сетью ту, дневную? (279)[44]

The sea-green hair, the pale complexion, the unhappiness, the tears, and the hint of entrapment suggested by the 'nets' of the silvery-green moon are all archetypal *rusalka* motifs. Furthermore, on two subsequent occasions — as Volkov consoles Iausta during their initial courtship, and later on their wedding night — the adjectives *rusal´ii* and *rusal´naia* are used explicitly.[45] The symbolic time-frame of this passage establishes a similar parallel. It is indicative that the courting takes place during spring, the season in which the *rusalki* were believed to emerge from their ponds and rivers. Later, as the spring moon slowly begins to wane — the season is described as a 'shy young girl' (*devushka zastenchivaia* (280)) — so Iausta emerges from the realms of inhibition into the world of 'shameless' physical reality. The marriage of the young couple takes place as spring is replaced by summer, the time when the folk celebrated the *rusalki* leaving their ponds and rivers for the woods. Conforming to the *rusalka* theme, the enchantment of Volkov gives way later to a realization of deceit and his death by drowning, although in this case the drowning is treated with irony and assumes a symbolic, rather than literal dimension. For Volkov, the eternal *mechtatel´*, his young bride's magical appeal dissolves the moment she is revealed in daylight and imposes strict domestic discipline modelled on sectarian precepts; while his 'drowning' occurs when he dives out of the room in which he has been confined for the winter and 'swims all night' in a snow-drift, barely surviving until morning.

The importance of this fragment goes well beyond the courtship phase of Volkov's relationship with Iausta: it offers an intriguing, albeit retrospective reading of his earlier encounter with the young girl from Africa. It is made abundantly clear, both through symbolic juxtaposition (the identical time and place of the separate encounters) and explicit comment, that Iausta and the young girl are essentially doubles, the difference being that while one emerges from the twilight zone of folk fantasy to become Volkov's lawfully-wedded wife, the other remains shrouded in mystery — aloof, elusive, and unsullied.[46] Furthermore, contained within the description of the young girl from Africa is an analogous series of motifs which establishes her kinship with the treacherous water-spirit of folk mythology. She appears to Volkov on a spring night ('Noch´ svetlaia, maiskaia' (278)). She is associated with the element of water, not merely by virtue of her arrival from overseas by steamboat, but through her subtle symbolic link, via the colour white, with the crests of the incoming waves ('Na more begali beliaki' (277)). She is also associated with swings of mood, her paradoxical display of merriment and melancholy puzzling Volkov initially, but typical of the *rusalka*. And it is the intoxicating power of her voice, the instrument by which the mythical water-maiden lured her victims to their untimely deaths, which underpins the entire edifice of this sequence.[47] This reading of the opening sequence of the tale is confirmed when we come to consider other aspects of Volkov's encounter with the guests from overseas. His suspicion that the travellers might in fact be teasing him — 'Не потешаются ли они с Африкой с этой?' (279) — refers unsuspectingly to the malevolent activities of the *rusalka* (this often took the form of teasing and tormenting her victims prior to dragging them to their watery graves). Furthermore, the associative link between the girl and the sea, and the idea of playing a cruel joke on the hapless Volkov by inviting him to Africa, has been anticipated by the description of the ocean in terms of the 'teasing, turquoise tongues' which the sun paints on the surface of the water as it skims across the surface prior to his nocturnal vision.[48] The entire undercurrent of lying and deception which foreshadows the episode with Iausta receives its comic and ironic climax when Volkov accepts their offer and solemnly promises to visit them: 'Moe slovo — bezoblyzhnoe' (279), he says — literally, 'My word is my troth.'[49]

As we have seen already in 'Poludennitsa (Kuny)', the conceit of a female spirit allied symbolically with the element of water is not new in Zamiatin's prose fiction (to a certain extent, it also anticipates the characterization of Pelka in *Sever*). The topography and ethnographic conceit of 'Afrika', however, imply that this female spirit should be viewed more as a mermaid or siren figure — in other words, a spirit associated with the sea, rather than with rivers, ponds, or lakes. Fictional treatments of this theme, which describe the tragic love between mermaids and mortal men, were a common feature of both Romantic and Decadent/Symbolist fiction. H. G. Wells's *The Sea-Lady* (1902), which Zamiatin mentioned in his essay on Wells, is a striking case in point.[50] Furthermore, Blok's *Roza i krest* drew on Breton legends about sea fairies and sirens in connection with the sunken city of Ys, located just off the North-West coast of France.[51] Another influence may have been the intriguing, but by no means obscure, apocryphal legend which gave rise to the popular belief in Russia that mermaids hailed originally from Africa. According to the seventeenth-century *Skazanie o perekhode Chermnogo moria*, mermaids (*faraonki*) and mermen (*faraony*) were the souls of the soldiers, women, and children drowned in the Red Sea during the Israelite exodus from Egypt — hence the terms themselves, which derive from the Russian word for pharaoh.[52] If Zamiatin intended this allusion, it adds a doubly ironic and cruel twist

to the travellers' joke about coming from Africa and their invitation for
Volkov to join them. Such a reading, however, fits neatly the organization of the text around the symbolic function of 'crossings'. The
young girl becomes the ghost of a person who has died attempting to
cross a stretch of water — hence her unhappy song, which we assume
is a sad lament for her own past fate, as well as the fate of all those who
have drowned throughout the ages. The story about the crossing of the
Red Sea possesses parallels with the apocryphal legend of the Virgin
Mary identified with the Feast of Prepolovenie: both involve a watery
crossing (a *perekhod* across a sea juxtaposed with a *pereplavlenie* across a
river).[53] By arriving in Africa, therefore, a metaphorical 'land of the
dead' (indeed, the only place where all the languages of the world are
spoken), Volkov crosses the boundary symbolically separating this
world from the next, and joins the mysterious girl beyond the grave.

In defence of this reading, it should be pointed out that Zamiatin's
use of the mermaid *topos* may well have been modelled on the genuine
folk beliefs of the fishermen and whalers living along the White Sea
coast. According to Zelenin, a major authority on this subject, belief in
polymorphic beings was widespread among Russian folk generally,
irrespective of region or religious creed, and in his view this could be
witnessed by the popularity of wood carvings bearing mermaid
designs on the boards of peasant huts right across the country.[54] It is
well attested, moreover, that the inhabitants of the White Sea coast
were particularly prone to this type of double-faith due to the sea's
importance in their daily lives — indeed, it has been argued that folk
myths associated with the element of water survived in this region long
after they had lapsed elsewhere.[55] According to Bernshtam, the
Pomorians possessed a variation of their own on the Exodus theme,
believing that all the fishes and animals of the sea hailed originally
from 'Pharaoh's Army': since they were suspected of adopting certain
behavioural patterns, and of acting collectively, Pomorian whalers and
seamen imbued them with human characteristics and suspected them
of speaking a language of their own which humans could not
comprehend.[56] Bearing in mind the apocryphal origin of the mermaid
myth in Russian folklore — we recall that Pimen is the cousin of a
scriptural expert — there seems little reason to doubt that knowledge
and fear of mermaids was part and parcel of folk-religious mentality in
the fictional village of Keremet´.

This reading reinforces the impression gained previously in
connection with the Feast of Prepolovenie — namely that Fedor
Volkov's story is refracted through an authentically Russian seafaring

consciousness with solid roots in the ancient past and an imaginative view of the world which embraces sacred writing, apocrypha, and folk superstition. Such a poetic texture mirrors closely Zamiatin's insistence on narratorial authenticity. Yet at the same time the use of the mermaid *topos* and the pattern of sea imagery with which it is intimately linked offer an alternative, folk-based reading of Volkov's eventual fate. His death, rather than the accidental (and partly even comic) result of a heart attack brought on by over-excitement, becomes instead the tragic working-out of a fate which has been predetermined — indeed, it is this doom-laden feature of his condition generally which lends his journey a certain tragic pathos. Central to this reading is the symbolism of the sea. The ocean as the embodiment of wisdom, and its paradoxical role as life-giver, as well as life-destroyer, is a theme in literature as ancient as antiquity itself, and one which informs virtually all folk myths about dangerous women who emerge from its depths to seduce and tempt innocent mortals. This has a special resonance in a story about a fisherman sustained directly by the fruits of the ocean itself. It is an ironic reversal that a fisherman who himself uses nets in order to make a living (he takes his visitors out for a fishing trip the day after his dream, and is shown laying out his rope-bound set of hooks (*iarus* (278)) in order to catch salmon) should himself be caught in the 'silvery-green nets' of a mermaid. Additional pathos is gained from the Pomorian legend about the decimation of Pharaoh's Army: the language Volkov hears the travellers speak when he first meets them can be read as the 'language' of all the animals of the ocean, and therefore of the ocean itself. It is no coincidence that Volkov dies while trying to harpoon a whale which torments and teases the crew of Indrik's schooner for two days before finally coming within their sights; or that the jellyfish which explode into 'silvery-green, glittering stars' as Volkov leans over the side of the boat and stares into the water — an image which glances back to the silvery-green hair of Iausta's nocturnal transfiguration — lead him momentarily to mistake them for the life-giving flowers of Indrik's vision of Africa.[57] It is the ocean, and the sense of wonderment, enchantment, and danger which it arouses, which is 'Africa' according to the folk-religious conceit of the narrative.

The *real* Africa is described by Indrik, of course, yet even he is aware of Volkov's final destination. The stories and tales with which he sustains Volkov during their hunting expedition imply knowledge of mermaid legends; moreover, his crucial symbolic link to the young girl and her male companions has been emphasized and underpinned on several occasions earlier in the narrative. Indrik can be located within a second symbolic pattern — the never-setting sun, the white night, the eyes which never sleep, the sea, and the girl herself — which points unambiguously to approaching death. When Volkov walks along the row of huts during the dream sequence, for instance, he observes a white eider duck sleeping with its eyes open on a rock:

Идет мимо Ильдиного камня, а на камне белая гага спит — не шелохнется, спит — а глаза открыты, и все, белое, спит с глазами открытыми: улица изб явственных глазу до сучка последнего, вода в лещинках меж камней, на камне — белая гага. И страшно ступить погромче: снимется белая гага, совьется — улетит белая ночь, умолкнет девушка петь. (278)

The images in this passage, with their insistent repetitions of sound and shape, are peculiarly effective in conveying the uncanny quality of Volkov's dream. It is the open eyes of the duck, however, with their suggestion of sleepwalking and hypnotism, not to mention death itself, which supply the primary estrangement device. Significantly, the imagery of open eyes is employed in the story a second time to describe the summer nights as Volkov wanders off into the woods to escape his father-in-law:

Стал ночами пропадать Федор Волков. А ночи — страшные, зрячие: помер человек — а глаза открыты, глядят и все видят, чего живым видеть нелеть. (281)

Eyes are again identified symbolically with the sun and the white nights, yet their meaning in this instance has undergone a subtle metamorphosis — these eyes, blank and unsleeping, are those of the dead, which see things 'ordinary human beings are forbidden'. This phrase is twice picked up again later in conjunction with the eyes of Captain Indrik, each time with increasing emphasis: 'Все на свете Индрик видал: должно быть, и то видал, чего живым видеть нелеть' (285); and a few paragraphs later:

— Ну, Федор, тебе бы еще одного так-то, а там и в Африку с Богом, — говорил весело Индрик, а глаза грустные были, будто видали однажды, чего живым видеть нелеть: правду. (286)

Indrik, it seems, has travelled 'beyond the grave' and lived to tell the tale, rather in the manner of another character from Zamiatin's early provincial fiction, Marei in *Sever*, who survives a folk drowning at the hands of *rusalki* as a young child and is reputed to have seen the world 'on the other side of grave' (*tot svet*).[58] Indrik's eyes, which are repeatedly described as 'sad', and associated symbolically with the sea by means of their blue colour, tell a disquieting story. Like the young girl, however, he seems to hover like a ghost between an assertion of inevitable mortality and the possibility of resurrection and renewal; indeed, his stories about Africa, which evoke a mysterious, exotic paradise, reflect perfectly this ambiguity. The movement of the elephants which carry their riders off 'into the unknown' ('Завезет он тебя в страны неведомые' (285)) is echoed later when his schooner moves northward ('Неведомо куда плывут сквозь туман' (285)).[59] And he hints at the possibility of immortality by referring to the flowers in Africa in terms of their powerful fragrance and as a guarantee of everlasting life: 'Раз нюхнуть — и не оторвешься: потуда нюхать будешь, покуда не помрешь' (285). Since the fragrance of the flowers recalls the perfume of the young girl, these images seem to Volkov to authenticate his earlier vision. At the same time, we are reminded continually of the fate of Volkov's father. This is a character who functions very much as a model for his son, since he also worked as a harpoonist on Indrik's schooner, listened willingly to the sea captain's stories, drank heavily, 'swam', and yet is now dead. The fact that Volkov's father is deceased is a constant reminder of the fragility and precariousness of human existence.

It is intriguing in this context to note the etymological derivation of the word *indrik*, which refers to an animal intimately linked in Russian religious myth to the land of the dead. According to the *Golubinaia kniga*, a Flagellant spiritual song about the beginning of the world which was first recorded in the 1860s, the *indrik* is a huge beast which lives beneath Mount Zion and moves under the earth as the sun moves below the horizon at night.[60] Unsurprisingly, perhaps, this animal has been interpreted in some quarters as a mysterious, dark, and chthonic force. In his work on Slavic mythology, for example, Afanas´ev offered various interpretations of this image and linked the animal ultimately with mythological demons and serpents.[61] This reading was repeated by Remizov in his explanatory notes to *Posolon´*.[62] And it also forms the basis of Dutch scholar Joost van Baak's proposal that Captain Indrik is 'basically connected with the underworld and the realm of the dead'.[63] There is, however, a problem with this line of argument. As Afanas´ev admits, the wandering minstrels who performed the Flagellant song identified the *indrik* with the unicorn (in Russian, *inorog* or *edinorog*); and it hardly needs pointing out that this animal functions in Christian myth as a symbol of Christ, and thus of renewal and restoration, rather than of death (in Russia, as elsewhere, its horn was believed to possess miraculous healing and curative powers).[64] The lines in the song which describe the beast living under Mount Zion would seem to suggest sacred, rather than demonic origin. Furthermore, it is associated in the song with a number of animals and places which are sacred in the context of Christian religion, either because they feature in the life of Christ (such as the River Jordan, in which he was baptized), or because they are linked with Old Testament myths about Creation (such as the whale). The words of the song, *pace* van Baak, do not state that the animal is 'afraid' of the sun, only that it is symbolically linked to the sun because it moves under the earth during the night. More importantly, the text describes the *indrik* as the source of the world's water, and therefore of all earthly sustenance — all the different versions of the *Golubinaia kniga*, including those cited by Afanas´ev, repeatedly stress its nourishing and purifying powers.[65]

Leaving aside for a moment the ambiguity surrounding the symbolic meaning of this animal, it would seem entirely justified to attribute a mythic function to Indrik on the basis of his name and his inspirational importance to Volkov as a guide and pathfinder. Zamiatin's knowledge of sectarian spiritual songs from the North — he mentions them specifically in connection with Kliuev in 'O iazyke' (IV, 380) — and his habit of exploiting names for their allusive potential — see, for example, Kortoma in *Sever*[66] — make it impossible that Indrik's name was chosen haphazardly. A further argument in favour of identifying Zamiatin's sea captain with the unicorn of Christian myth is the tradition which traces the animal's origins to Africa and India (both continents are mentioned in relation to Indrik).[67] Another is the subtle semantic association between the location in which Indrik hires his sailors for whaling expeditions — Sviatoi Nos — and the sacred horn of the unicorn itself.[68] Twice, it should be noted, the word *nos* is employed in connection with the prow of Indrik's schooner.[69] Furthermore, like the *indrik* of the spiritual song, Zamiatin's sea captain is profoundly linked to the element of water: he is renowned for his travels overseas; he tells stories about the Indian Ocean; and his eyes are the same colour as the sea. In addition, via the images of open eyes, he is equated symbolically with the sun itself, even to the point where its dipping below the horizon at night and 'swimming' across the sea in Chapter One is imagistically analogous to the journey his schooner makes with Volkov on board. Indrik's reputed possession of knowledge, a fact stressed on several occasions during the course of the narrative, allies him strongly with a song purporting wisdom and profundity about the origins of the universe.

In view of the confusion surrounding the meaning of the *indrik* in the sectarian imagination — the Christian *edinorog* is a symbol of meekness, purity, and innocence, whereas in seventeenth century Russian alphabet books the *indrik* is depicted as a terrible beast[70] — it is probably advisable to focus on the motif common to most accounts, namely the miraculously curative properties of its horn. In many ways, Captain Indrik does indeed fulfil a restorative function in Volkov's life: he confirms the existence of Africa, tells him how he can get there, provides him with the means to pay for his passage, and keeps him sustained *en route* with exotic tales. It is indicative that Volkov's first encounter with Indrik is accompanied by a surge of strength and spontaneous outburst of joy: 'Крепился Федор Волков — крепился, да вдруг с радости загогочет лешим: гы-гы-гы-гы-ы-ы!' (284). It is also worth pointing out that the theme of renewed hope is symbolically associated with Christ's resurrection — Volkov is so exultant when Indrik confirms the existence of Africa that he wants to kiss him three times on the cheeks, a ritual act which was traditionally performed at Easter: 'Так Федор обрадовался, сейчас обхватил бы вот Индрика да трожды бы с ним, как на Пасху, и похристосовался' (284).[71] This underpins the general imagery of sustenance in the story and gives rise to a reading of Volkov's quest in terms of the search for a heavenly paradise. The central idea of the *Golubinaia kniga*, that the *indrik* is the source of all water, and thus of all nourishment, echoes the theme of spiritual sustenance as it applies to the Festival of Prepolovenie.[72] It is indicative, moreover, that initially Volkov is said to 'believe' in Africa as if it were an object of religious faith ('И поверил в Африку Федор Волков' (279)); and that his eyes are said to light up 'like candles dedicated to God' ('Только теплились свечкой Богу необидные его глазки' (286)) after he has earned one half of his passage. It is therefore the confirmation or subsequent denial of the promise which this sacred object holds for him which is the subject of the tale.

In his study of Zamiatin, Shane argues that the message of 'Afrika' is that 'men should die striving for their goals, rather than live to discover them to be false illusions'.[73] Approached from the folk-religious perspective, this message acquires layers of subtle ambiguities and paradoxes. The remark which closes the narrative — 'Есть Африка. Федор Волков доехал' (287) — is plainly ironic, since it implies that Africa is a symbolic, rather than a geographical destination. Because Volkov dies believing that his passage there has been financially secured (the second harpoon strikes its target just at the moment of his collapse and is harmlessly dislodged a few seconds later) Volkov

certainly 'arrives' in symbolic terms.[74] On the other hand, since this
'arrival' occurs at the moment of his death, Zamiatin points to a more
ominous implication. If Africa is a promise of renewal and a dream of
paradise, then the fact of Volkov's death suggests that it is an illusion
and a mendacious lie perpetrated on the innocent by those in
possession of the truth. The final section, with its sapping of confidence
in the revelatory power of dream, involves an imagistic echo which
links the action of inhaling Africa's immortal fragrances with Volkov's
actual collapse, and anticipates the revelation of a dark secret about
existence: human beings are mortal, and their dreams, which possess a
crucial, mobilizing force, are nevertheless unreliable.[75] From the folk
perspective, Volkov's encounter with a mermaid marks his tragic
destiny as a man permitted a glimpse of paradise for which he will
later pay a heavy price; while from a religious perspective, his glimpse
of a transcendent reality teases him with the prospect of eternal
salvation and an everlasting life which does not in reality exist. In both
cases, the illusion which Volkov takes to his grave resides in the naive
hope that the original vision can be recaptured and reexperienced — in
the words of a popular rhyme which Jakobson cites as a typical
example of the Russian magic tale's ethos: 'Не то чудо из чудес,/Что
мужик упал с небес,/А то чудо из чудес,/Как туда он влез.'[76]

'Afrika', it could be argued, is the most concise expression of
Zamiatin's *Weltanschauung*. His view of life as a ceaseless and tragic
struggle for the attainment of one's ideals is a fundamental paradigm
in his fiction, and one especially prevalent in the three tales set in the
Russian North. The trilogy is full of dreamers whose grandiose
schemes for improvement, whether for their own personal benefit or
for the benefit of the community at large, remain comically and
tragically unfeasible. In *Sever*, Marei's quest to bring illumination to his
sub-Arctic village by way of constructing a street light — a quest,
symbolically, for enlightenment in the wider sense — ends in failure.
While Tsybin's lifelong ambition in 'Ela' to secure a new 'bride' in the
shape of a Norwegian sloop is cruelly scuppered when a vicious storm
prevents him from reaching the safe haven of his coastal village. These
characters, all fishermen, are obsessive fantasists whose penchant for
solitary contemplation in the embrace of nature betrays similarities
with the Romantic tendency of *waldeinsamkeit*. Like those of Sologub,
Zamiatin's heroes die with their goals unrealized. It is axiomatic,
however, that the struggles of his fictional protagonists are neither
mocked nor depicted as futile. If 'Afrika' is a narrative about the
backwardness of Russia, the irresistible urge to escape the tedium of its

isolated provinces, and the attractive, albeit illusory, exoticism of travel abroad, then, paradoxically, it is also a poetic affirmation of inner spiritual vitality communicated with tremendous force through Zamiatin's lyrical explorations of the northern landscape, the stylization of regional dialect, and the fascination with its customs and belief in evil spirits.

NOTES

1. For publication details of 'Afrika', see *PZ*, 54. Henceforth, all references are to the version published in the Neimanis edition (I, 277–87), but without the volume number.
2. 'И Дульцинея — прекрасная и нежная, это воздух, мечта, которой Сологуб живет и которой нет на земле. Стихи Александра Блока — целые томы его стихов — об одном: о Незнакомке, о Прекрасной Даме, о Снежной Деве. И это в сущности то же самое, что Дульцинея Сологуба' ('Sovremennaia russkaia literatura' (IV, 351)). These remarks are already anticipated in the earlier review: 'После Андрея Белого читать Блока — все равно что из чадного балагана выйти в мрачную ночную тишь. Блок ясен и морозен, но в холодной дали плещутся неверно-ласковые звезды. И к ним, недостижимым, Блок устремляет свой путь: к Прекрасной Даме, которой — нет, которая — мечта, путь к которой — страданье: "Роза и Крест" — драма Блока в первом сборнике "Сирин" — о рыцарях, замках, певцах и турнирах, и все же драма эта — наша, близкая, русская. Драма зовет к страданью: нет радости выше страданья от любви к человеку. Это ли не русское? Уж что-что, а страдать мы умеем' ('Sirin. Sbornik pervyi i vtoroi' (IV, 498–99)).
3. For the three works in question, see A. A. Blok, *Sobranie sochinenii*, ed. by V. N. Orlov, A. A. Surkov, and K. I. Chukovskii, 8 vols (Moscow–Leningrad: Gosudarstvennoe izdatel´stvo khudozhestvennoi literatury, 1960–63), I (1960), 74–238; IV (1961), 7–21 (pp. 10, 11, & 12); & ibid., 168–246.
4. For a general discussion of the cult status of Africa at this time among the Symbolists, and its relevance for Gumilev's poetry, see Apollon Davidson, *Muza stranstvii Nikolaia Gumileva* (Moscow: Nauka, 1992).
5. Ibid., pp. 53 & 151–54.
6. Gumilev left Odessa on the *Rossiia* in September 1908 and his journey took him to Alexandria via Pireaus, Athens, Constantinople, and Cairo. See ibid., p. 45. Zamiatin, on the other hand, was travelling on the *Rossiia* to gain work experience as a student. He travelled from Odessa to Alexandria via Contantinople, Smyrna, Beirut, Jaffa (now Tel Aviv), Mount Athos, and Port Said (I, 28). The return journey brought him to Odessa in time to witness the 1905 Potemkin uprising, and his account of this uprising, 'Tri dnia', opens with the quintessentially African images of sand, camels, palms, and cacti (I, 130).
7. Zamiatin gave a reading of 'Afrika' to the editors of *Ezhemesiachnyi zhurnal* on 15/28 November 1915. See Zamiatin's letter to his wife dated 17/30 May 1916, in *RN*, I, 202–03 (note 2). The only other clue to the dating of the story consists of a brief fragment in Zamiatin's notebooks which clearly forms the basis for the description of Pimen which opens the second section of the story (it matches the text almost word for word). See Zamiatin, 'Iz bloknotov 1914–1928 godov' (1988), pp. 89–90.
8. According to one recent estimate, as much as half the population in these areas at the turn of the century may have been schismatic or sympathetic to the Old Believers. See T. A. Bernshtam, *Russkaia narodnaia kul´tura pomor´ia v XIX – nachale XX v.* (Leningrad: Nauka, 1983), p. 95. The *pomor* as authentic representative of the Russian *narod* is also mentioned by V. A. Keldysh in his introduction to a recently-published edition of

Zamiatin's prose fiction: 'И знаменательно, что рассказ ('Afrika' — PC) связан с темой русского Севера и что герой его — исконный северный житель, помор. Не впервые наши художники слова — напомним еще раз о Пришвине — искали здесь цельную народную душу.' See Evgenii Zamiatin, *Izbrannye proizvedeniia*, ed. by A. Iu. Galushkin, preface by V. B. Shklovskii, introduction by V. A. Keldysh (Moscow: Sovetskii pisatel', 1989), p. 16.

9. For the text of *God na Severe*, see Maksimov, VIII, 1–327; IX, 1–382; & X, 1–295. See also Catherine B. Clay, 'Russian Ethnographers in the Service of the Empire, 1856–62', *Slavic Review*, 54 (1995), 45–61.

10. *Pesni, sobrannye P. N. Rybnikovym*, ed. by A. E. Gruzinskii, 2nd edn, 3 vols (Moscow: Sotrudnik shkol, 1909–10); and *Onezhskie byliny zapisannye A. F. Gil'ferdingom letom 1871 goda*, ed. by M. K. Azadovskii, 3rd edn, 3 vols (Moscow–Leningrad: Akademiia nauk SSSR, 1938–40).

11. Bilibin travelled to the provinces of Vologda, Olonetsk, and Archangel under the auspices of the ethnographic division of the Russian Museum. His article 'Narodnoe tvorchestvo Russkogo Severa' appeared in *Mir iskusstva*, 1904.11, 303–18, and the postcard designs were issued by the St Eugenie Red Cross Society in 1905. There were ten postcards in all, three of which were modelled on scenes from the Kem´ area: number one, depicting a river in the Kem´ region; number five, depicting the small market town of Poduzhem´e, also in the Kem´ area; and number ten, which depicted a small cemetery in Kem´ itself. For information about Bilibin's trip to the North, see *Ivan Iakovlevich Bilibin*, ed. by S. V. Golynets (Leningrad: Khudozhnik RSFSR, 1970), p. 10. For details regarding the postcards, see the catalogue of Bilibin's work in ibid., p. 299.

12. M. M. Prishvin, *Sobranie sochinenii*, ed. by N. P. Smirnov, 6 vols (Moscow: Gosudarstvennoe izdatel'stvo khudozhestvennoi literatury, 1956–57), II (1956), 163–393. The title of the story refers to the famous 'Kolobok' folk tale, the equivalent of which in English culture is 'The Gingerbread Man'. For the text, see *Narodnye russkie skazki A. N. Afanas´eva*, ed. by L. G. Barag and N. V. Novikov, 3 vols (Moscow: Nauka, 1984–86), I (1984), 46–47.

13. See Lazarev, 'Vozvrashchenie Evgeniia Zamiatina', *Sovetskaia bibliografiia*, 1989.3, 53; and Oleg Mikhailov, 'Zamiatinskie torosy', *Slovo v mire knig*, 1989.11, 74–75 (p. 74). Zamiatin's letters to his wife, however, reveal that he undertook a number of expeditions within Russia during 1915, all of them connected with his professional duties as a marine engineer, and doubtless arising as a result of the ongoing war with Germany. The trip to the North would appear to be simply another of these expeditions. Indeed, the fact that he was looking for hotels in Archangel, and was free to travel around the area by steamboat, gives the lie to the idea that he was there under duress. See Zamiatin's letters to his wife dated 31 July/13 August, 1/14 August, 3/16 August, 6/19 August, and 8/21 August 1915 in *RN*, I, 191–92.

14. Greta N. Slobin, *Remizov's Fictions: 1900–1921* (Dekalb: Northern Illinois University Press, 1991), pp. 12–18. Among the intellectuals also exiled to the North at this time was the literary historian P. E. Shchegolev, a former student at Zamiatin's gymnasium in Voronezh. Zamiatin mentions him, and the warning of the school director not to get involved in radical politics, in his 1929 autobiography (I, 27). It is perhaps worth noting that Zamiatin graduated from the school in 1901, just two years after Shchegolev had been exiled to Vologda for his revolutionary activities.

15. *Za volshebnym kolobkom*, p. 244.

16. Maksimov, IX, 143–44. *Karbas* is a dialect term which reverses the more common *barkas*. For further details, see *ES*, XIV, 471.

17. *Za volshebnym kolobkom*, pp. 179, 176, 208, 191, 206, & 218, respectively.

18. 'Времена настали худые, семги все меньше, а подмоги все больше.' See ibid., p. 179.

19. 'Северные люди скупые на слова.' See ibid., p. 194.

20. Ibid., p. 169.

21.   Maksimov, IX, 87. Maksimov also draws attention to the predominance of Old
        Believers in the towns of Soroka and Kem´, and the villages which surround them:
        'Жители посада Сумы твердо стоят в православии, несмотря на то, что ближняя Сорока
        и все деревни по направлении к Кеми, сама Кемь и деревни по Корельскому берегу
        почти все и давно держатся раскола.' See ibid., p. 191.
22.   *Dvoedanskii* derives from the noun *dvoedanets*, meaning 'someone who pays two
        tributes'. Its special application to Old Believers originated in Siberia, where it
        referred to schismatics who were forced to pay a dual tribute to the authorities and
        the Orthodox Church from 1782 onwards — thus the verb *dvoedanit´* came to mean:
        'secretly to support the Schism' (Dal´, I, 419). That Zamiatin intended this meaning is
        confirmed in 'O iazyke'. Illustrating his technique of helping the reader grasp the
        meaning of exotic words, he writes: 'Давая читателю слово совершенно новое и
        незнакомое, надо преподносить его в таком виде, чтобы читателю было понятно, если
        не точное значение его, то во всяком случае — смысл. Если я говорю "двоединского
        (*sic*) начетчика племяш" — слово "начетчика" тотчас же ассоциируется с
        старообрядцами' (IV, 381). The error here in the spelling of *dvoedanskii* in the Neimanis
        edition is presumably either a typographical error or a mistake on the part of
        Zamiatin's wife (she was responsible for making the transcriptions of the lectures for
        publication).
23.   Bernshtam, p. 97.
24.   Gromyko, p. 123.
25.   'Пимен, племяш двоеданский — ростику маленького, тощий: такие всегда бывают
        зудливые, неотвязные' (280).
26.   It would certainly have been uncharacteristic for Volkov's marriage to take place in
        an Orthodox church, although increasingly this was being permitted at the turn of the
        century. This was especially true in the case of the *Pomorskoe soglasie*, an Old Believer
        sect which came into existence along the White Sea coast very soon after the Nikonian
        reforms of the seventeenth century. It was still strong at the turn of the century. See
        ES, XXIV, 504–06.
27.   These colloquial expressions, which derive from the term for the wood-demon (*leshii*)
        of Russian folk belief, are used by Iausta and Captain Indrik. The first instance occurs
        on page 281: '— Да где же это ты, лешебойник, ходисси … — днем голосила Яуста';
        and the second on page 287: '— Эка, эка! Леший сонный, ворон ему ловить.'
        Essentially, they refer to someone who is lazy and a good-for-nothing.
28.   The removal of a husband's boots was one of the most ancient customs practised by
        the *narod*, and served to symbolize the husband's expectation of submissiveness,
        servility, and humility on the part of his wife. See Zabylin, p. 177. Volkov, however, is
        embarrassed by this ritual, and interrupts it: 'Нагнулась Яуста, горькая, русальная,
        покорно сапог разобула Федору Волкову. Так покорно, что другого не дал ей снять
        Федор' (280).
29.   After the 1861 Act of Emancipation, the married couple became the primary labour
        unit within the commune. The term *bobyl´* thus came to refer to an unmarried man
        who, because of the particular laws dictating the organization of the typical peasant
        commune at that time, was unable to claim an allotment of land for himself. See
        Worobec, p. 119.
30.   Zamiatin may have picked up this specialist terminology from Prishvin. A
        professional agronomist before turning to writing, Prishvin devoted a considerable
        amount of time and space to the problem of farming in the North, especially in the
        ethnographic *ocherk* entitled *V kraiu nepuganykh ptits* (1907), which he wrote shortly
        after a trip to the Onega region in the Russian North. He records, for example, that
        the harsh climate and stony terrain made farming extremely difficult. A local peasant
        explains to him: '— Не пашем, а перешевеливаем камень'; and Prishvin later adds:
        'Такую землю за лето непременно нужно перешевелить раз пять, иначе ничего не
        родится.' Later still, in the same passage, Prishvin describes how the land is scorched
        in preparation for the next year's planting (the black ash which remains after the

burning is described as a *pal*): 'Ветер может разнести с холмика драгоценную черную золу, и вся работа пропадет даром. Потому-то нужно сейчас же принять за новую работу. Если камней мало, то можно прямо орать особой *паловой* сохой, с прямыми сошниками без *присоха*. Если же их много, землю нужно *косоровать*, разделывать ручным косым крюком, старинной *копорюгой*. Когда и эта тяжелая работа окончена, то пашня готова, и следующей весной можно сеять ячмень или репу.' All emphases in the original. See Prishvin, *Sobranie sochinenii*, II, 1–163 (pp. 83 & 86).

31. 'Afrikanskii brat' is taken from the fifth chapter of an unfinished novel which Forsh was writing between 1915 and 1916. It tells the story of a group of sectarians in St Petersburg, officially banned in 1894, who play host to German missionaries from Africa. Two of the story's protagonists resolve to accept their offer of a free trip to the continent in exchange for joining their ranks. In their general ignorance about Africa itself, and their naive belief in a better world elsewhere, there is a strong echo of Zamiatin's tale: 'Где была Африка, знали не все, но все, детски веруя, вдруг поняли, что именно там, в этой Африке, будет особенная, значительная жизнь, а они такие здесь бедные, серые люди, там, у черных, будут первыми нужными людьми.' See 'Afrikanskii brat', in Ol´ga Forsh, *Sobranie sochinenii*, ed. by M. Belousova, commentary by A. V. Tamarchenko, 8 vols (Moscow–Leningrad: Gosudarstvennoe izdatel´stvo khudo- zhestvennoi literatury, 1962–64), VI (1964), 243–57 (p. 256) (first publ. in *Krasnaia nov´*, 1922.5, 94–102).

32. Forsh, *Sobranie sochinenii*, VI, 256.

33. Ibid., 48–63 (first publ. in *Russkaia mysl´*, 1910.2, 95–105).

34. Scheherazade is the beautiful princess who tells the tales of the Arabian Nights in order to stave off a death sentence ordered by her husband. The popularity of this subject in Russian culture is the result in part of Rimskii-Korsakov's symphonic suite, *Shekherazada*, which was composed and first performed in 1888. It is worth noting that the publication of 'Za zhar-ptitsei' coincided with the première in Paris on 4/17 June 1910 of Diagilev's balletic version of the opera.

35. 'Za zhar-ptitsei', p. 58.

36. Ibid., p. 55.

37. Forsh, *Sobranie sochinenii*, VI, 607–45 (p. 613).

38. 'А руки у ней — так пахнули — только во сне так и может присниться' (278); and later: 'Нагнулся в низком поклоне Федор Волков и показалось: от руки — тот самый, тот самый дух, который во сне' (279).

39. The Feast of Prepolovenie coincides with the Jewish Feast of the Tabernacle and celebrates Jesus's words to the Pharisees as recorded in John 7. 37–38: 'If any man thirst, let him come unto me, and drink. He that believeth in me, as the scripture hath said, out of his belly shall flow rivers of living water.' Biblical scholars have interpreted this as an allusion to Isaiah 12. 2–3: 'Behold, God is my salvation; I will trust, and will not be afraid: for the Lord Jehovah is my strength and song; and he is become my salvation. Therefore with joy shall ye draw water out of the wells of salvation.' See *ES*, XXV, 69.

40. The apocryphal legend has been recounted as follows: '"Один раз гнались за Богородицей разбойники, а Она была с Младенцем на руках. Бежала, бежала Богородица, глядь — река. Она и бросилась в воду, разсчитывая, переплыть на другую сторону и спастись от погони. Но с Младенцем на руках плыть было бы трудно, потому что грести приходилось только одной рукой. Вот и взмолилась Богородица Своему Младенцу: 'Сын мой милый, дай ты мне третью руку, а то плыть мне невмоготы.' Младенец услышал молитву матери, и появилась у нее третья рука. Тогда уж плыть было легко, и Богородица благополучно достигла противоположного берега." Этим легендарным сказанием вполне объясняется, почему крестьяне всех великорусских губерний праздник Преполовение называют "Преплавлением" (от слова переплыть).' See Maksimov, XVII, 143. Dal´ also notes this popular association, citing the belief that 'V Prepolovenie Bogoroditsa Volgu pereplyla' (Dal´, III, 395).

41. These examples hark back to the initial image of the never-setting sun in the first chapter: 'Ночь светлая, майская. По-настоящему не садилось солнце, а так только принагнется, по морю поплывет' (278).

42. Zamiatin's symbolic switch from river bank to coastal shore is made possible by the flexibility of the word *bereg*. Indrik's schooner sets sail from the Murmansk Shore, known as the *Murmanskii bereg*. Furthermore, the word for 'shore' as it applies to those areas bordering the White Sea is also *bereg* in Russian: *Pomorskii bereg*, *Onezhskii bereg*, *Letnii bereg*, etc. It is indicative that Zamiatin uses *bereg* in the very first line of his story; he also uses the verb *bezhat´* twice in relation to the motion of boats — firstly, in the opening lines of the story: 'Как всегда, на взморье — к пароходу — с берега побежали карбаса' (277); and secondly in relation to Volkov's journey to Sviatoi Nos: 'А через две недели — на Мурманском бежал уж к Святому Носу' (284). This echoes the line 'bezhala, bezhala Bogoroditsa' in the apocryphal tale as recounted by Maksimov.

43. Ivanits, p. 78.

44. *Zeleneserebrianoi* should read *zeleno-serebrianoi* — for comparison, see the version of 'Afrika' as published in Evg. Zamiatin, *Sobranie sochinenii*, 4 vols (Moscow: Federatsiia, 1929), IV, 69–86 (p. 73).

45. 'Каждую ночь Федор Волков утешал горькую, с зелеными волосами, русальими, Яусту' (280); and later: 'Нагнулась Яуста, горькая, русальная, покорно сапог разобула Федору Волкову' (280).

46. Both encounters take place on a spring night outside Pimen's cabin, with the same emphasis on surreal sleight-of-hand: 'Как тогда — во сне или наяву — опять стоял Федор Волков у окна избы двоеданской, утешал горькую девушку' (279).

47. 'И дивно было: девушка, будто, веселая, а этак поет?
Век бы ее слушал, да поздно, уж: хочешь-не хочешь, время — спать' (278).
These lines echo reports that the *rusalka*'s voice is so intoxicating that those who fall under its hypnotic power are trapped 'for an eternity' (*na veki*). See Zelenin, pp. 168–69.

48. 'По-настоящему не садилось солнце, а так только принагнется, по морю поплывет и все море распишет золотыми выкружками, алыми закомаринами, лазоревыми лясами' (278). *Liasy*, used here poetically, refers more usually to jokes, teasing witticisms, and deceitful, cunning language (Dal´, II, 287).

49. *Bezoblyzhnyi* means 'truthful', 'accurate', and 'unfalse' (ibid., I, 67).

50. Herbert George Wells, *The Sea Lady* (London: Methuen, 1902). Zamiatin translates the title of this story as *Morskaia deva*, and refers to the use of *rusalki* in Wells's fiction in his essay 'Gerbert Uells' (IV, 198 & 211).

51. Gaetan, one of the key characters in the play, claims to have been brought up as a child by a sea-fairy. In Act II, Scene II, he alleges that the sound of the breaking waves is the evil Morgana, a sea-enchantress from Celtic myth and legend, combing her golden locks: 'За то же святой Гвеннолэ/Превратил ее в фею морскую.../И, когда шумит океан,/Влажным гребнем чешет злая Моргана/Золото бледных кудрей./Она поет, но голос ее/Печален, как плеск волны.' See *Roza i krest*, p. 197.

52. *Mifologicheskii slovar´*, ed. by E. M. Meletinskii (Moscow: Sovetskaia entsiklopediia, 1990), p. 554.

53. The possibility that the steamer on which the travellers arrive — in Russian, *parokhod* — could be an allusion to the title of the Old Testament legend — *perekhod* — is straining interpretational ingenuity too far. It should be pointed out, nonetheless, that Indrik mentions this word specifically in connection with travelling to Africa: '— Денег вот надо порядочно — тыща, а то и все полторы. На пароходе-то доехать до Африки ..: — глядел Индрик серьезно' (284).

54. Zelenin, p. 198.

55. Bernshtam, pp. 175 & 212.

56. 'Среди поморов существовало предание о том, что морские звери происходят от "фараонова войска", погибшего в море. [...] Морские звери, по мнению поморов,

обладают чувством коллективизма, собственным языком и вполне владеют приемами сопротивления человеку.' See ibid., p. 174.

57. 'По ночам возле шкуны неслись стаи медуз: ударится которая в борт — и засветит, и побежит дальше цветком зеленосеребряным. Только бы нагнуться — не тот ли самый? — а она уж потухла, нету: приснилась' (286).

58. *Sever* (I, 401).

59. His tales about elephants suggestively complete a circle of associations in Volkov's mind, beginning with a hazy childhood memory of the stories he used to tell his father, one of which describes an elephant running along and playing a silver trumpet: 'Все позабыл — вот одно Федору по сю пору запомнилось: бежит, будто, слон — в трубу трубит серебряную, а уж что это за труба такая — Бог весть' (283–84).

60. *Russian Folk Literature*, ed. by D. P. Costello and I. P. Foote, Oxford Russian Readers series (Oxford: Clarendon Press, 1967), pp. 173–77 (p. 175).

61. *Poeticheskie vozzreniia slavian na prirodu*, II, 553–55.

62. Aleksei Remizov, *Sochineniia*, 8 vols (St Petersburg: Shipovnik [I–VII], and Sirin [VIII], 1910–12; repr. Munich: Fink, 1971), VI (1911), 13–135 (p. 55, and the explanatory note on p. 254).

63. 'Visions of the North: Remarks on Russian Literary World-Pictures', in *Dutch Contributions to the Tenth International Congress of Slavists: Sofia: September 14–22 1988: Literature*, ed. by A. van Holk, Studies in Slavic Literature and Poetics series, 12 (Amsterdam: Rodopi, 1988), pp. 19–43 (p. 37). For the source of his information, van Baak cites Toporov. See his entry under the heading 'Mamont', in *Mify narodov mira*, ed. by S. A. Tokarev, 2 vols (Moscow: Sovetskaia entsiklopediia, 1980–82), II (1982), 96–97.

64. *Poeticheskie vozzreniia slavian na prirodu*, II, 556.

65. Ibid., p. 553.

66. The name Kortoma, which belongs to a merchant who believes firmly in the Western way of conducting business, derives in all probability from the noun *kortom*, meaning 'rent', 'loan', or 'speedy sale' (Dal´, II, 170).

67. *Mifologicheskii slovar´*, p. 204.

68. In northern dialect, Sviatoi Nos means 'Sacred Horn' or 'Sacred Point'. *Nos* in this context is a synonym for *mys*, which refers to a promontory or horn-shaped piece of land jutting sharply out into the sea; thus it is also a synonym for *rog* (horn), an archaic term used to denote a similar piece of land, as in the case of *Iarenskii Rog*, just north of Archangel, and *Olenii Rog*, which lies along the southern shore of the Kola Peninsula. See *SRIa*, II, 509; & III, 721, respectively. It is on a similar type of promontory — a wooded and waterlogged stretch of land called *Mysh´–navolok* (281) — that Volkov seeks nocturnal solace and waits for his guests to return.

69. 'Два дня стоял на носу Федор Волков, у пушки' (287); and later, after he has collapsed: 'Бежали, сломя голову, на нос, где возле пушки лежал Федор Волков' (287).

70. *Mifologicheskii slovar´*, p. 204.

71. Kalinskii, pp. 180–81. *Khristosovat´sia*, of course, derives from the Russian word for Christ (*Khristos*).

72. 'Тот самый дед Демьян, какой в суконной карпетке бутылку рома зятью в подарок вез. Да в пути раздавил и три дня прососал карпетку ромовую. Вот, будто, к карпетке к этой и приник Федор Волков и сосал: дрянь — и выплюнуть никак не может, беда!' (285).

73. Shane, p. 112.

74. 'Попал. Африка. Приникнуть теперь и не оторваться, покуда ...' (287). *Popast´* here is ambiguous, since it can refer either to the harpoon, meaning 'to strike home', or to Volkov himself collapsing at the prow of the boat. Earlier, for example, while about to harpoon the first whale, he thinks to himself: '— Ох, попаду. Ох, промахнусь ..."' (286). If the first meaning is inferred, then Volkov dies thinking that he has earned his passage to Africa; in the case of the second, however, Volkov dies without knowing whether he has struck home or not.

75. This phrase is used three times. Firstly, when Indrik describes Africa: 'Раз нюхнуть — и не оторвешься: потуда нюхать будешь, покуда не помрешь, вот дух какой ...' (285); secondly, when Volkov describes his dreams of the young girl: 'Да во сне известно, ничего не выходит: только руками она обовьет, как тогда, и не отрываться бы потуда, покуда не умрешь' (285); and thirdly, just as he collapses: 'Приникнуть теперь — и не оторваться, покуда ...' (287).

76. A. N. Afanas'ev, *Russian Fairy Tales*, trans. by Norbert Guterman, folkloristic commentary by Roman Jakobson (London: Routledge, [1946]), pp. 631–56 (p. 651).

CHAPTER 5

ZNAMENIE

Although 'Znamenie' was first published in 1918, and is therefore usually approached as a text which pertains to the post-revolutionary era, it was actually conceived at least twenty months previously, while Zamiatin was working in Britain. There are three versions of the text in IMLI. The first is dated 9/22 September 1916 (IMLI, opis´ 1, ed. khr. 39) — in other words, six months after his arrival on a shipbuilding contract at the Armstrong–Whitworth shipyards in Newcastle; and the two later versions (IMLI, opis´ 1, ed. khr. 40 & 41), while not dated, do not differ greatly from this version, or to the version published in the almanac *Mysl´* in 1918.[1] This suggests that the germ of the idea relates to the pre-revolutionary period, and not to the period after Zamiatin's return to Russia in September 1917. Furthermore, the various unfinished draft versions and notes preserved as a single item number in the archive (IMLI, opis´ 1, ed. khr. 42) give a fascinating insight into the process of composition and suggest that the inspiration for the story must certainly have pre-dated September 1916, if not the departure to Britain altogether in March 1916.[2]

If 'Afrika' is about a searcher who undertakes a spiritual quest in order to recapture an unearthly experience, 'Znamenie' is about a sceptic who seeks but ultimately fails to find salvation in religious faith. Despite the different origins of the two protagonists — Volkov, as we have seen, is an illiterate fisherman, while Seliverst, the main protagonist in 'Znamenie', is educated — the two stories can and should be viewed in tandem as emblematic of Zamiatin's *Weltanshauung* at this stage in his life. If Volkov is a dreamer in pursuit of visions and illusory chimera, then Seliverst is an 'insatiable soul' (*nesytaia dusha*) whose craving for truth and the revelatory power of the divine represents the condition of the authentic spiritual revolutionary. The tragic fate of this revolutionary consists in the fact that he cannot accept confirmation of a truth or the realization of an ideal because of a scepticism and eternal restlessness which renders all ideals and truths moribund once they have become proven. In embryonic form, this is the philosophical position of the rebellious Scythian which Zamiatin adopted later in relation to the October Revolution. 'Znamenie', however, reveals that this position was initially explored in relation to religion. It is highly likely that events in the personal sphere, in particular the death of his father in the early part of 1916, explain the sudden emergence of such a preoccupation at this point in his career (we will recall, perhaps, that his father was a priest). Furthermore, although the location of the narrative action in 'Znamenie' is not specific to any particular region of Russia, there are elements in the story which draw on his personal experience of the family home in Lebedian´ and his enforced stay there in 1906 after his release from a prison sentence for revolutionary activity. It will be argued that the attitude of revolt dramatized in this narrative, while it may have anticipated the revolutionary events of 1917 and the collapse of the Tsarist order, looks back in fact to the crisis in Zamiatin's relationship with his father and his conflict with the Church as a result of his political activities during the 1905 Revolution. Indeed, while the story attempts to explore a universal metaphysical predicament, it does so from a perspective which, while it may be applicable to the Russian intelligentsia as a whole, is in essence personal.

Although 'Znamenie' was written while Zamiatin was abroad, and thus at a time when his experiments in different narrative techniques would take his art in a new direction — away from literary populism towards the ornamental synthetism of his English satires — it must nevertheless be approached as a prototypical example of the early provincial fiction. Like the communities depicted in 'Poludennitsa (Kuny)', 'Kriazhi', and 'Afrika', the monastery in 'Znamenie' represents a traditional and conservative mode of being which is isolated and marginalized from the world at large. Zamiatin's *skaz* mask, moreover, while certainly more refined than in the earlier stories, is still the same blend of popular language and syntax, although there is an overt shift in emphasis towards the use of Old Russian archaisms and words deriving from ecclesiastical culture. A similar shift in emphasis can be witnessed in the imaginative world projected in the story. On the one hand, this reflects a general folk-religious world-view, and thus to a certain extent compares with the schismatic community depicted in 'Afrika'; but on the other hand there is a more spirited engagement with the doctrines and sacred writing of the Orthodox Church. This is reflected in the central role accorded to an icon of the Virgin Mary; the importance of hagiographic *topoi* in the structure of the plot; the use of biblical imagery; and the symbolic significance of the opening and closing images of the story, which describe a town reflected in the surface of a lake and the bells of its churches ringing as if from the invisible depths of the water. It will be argued that this last image is a covert reference to the apocalyptic Kitezh legend; thus it is one with a solid Populist pedigree and typical of the sort of *lubok*-style material which was infiltrating élite culture at the turn of the century.[3] Indeed, 'Znamenie' is concerned not merely with metaphysics *per se*, but also with religion as a cultural and ideological force which shaped the consciousness of the Russian *narod* right up until the Revolution.

'Znamenie' is set in a *skete* called Larivonova pustyn´, ostensibly situated on the shores of a lake deep in the heart of provincial Russia. This location is introduced by means of a brief lyrical passage in the opening paragraph which establishes the image of a secluded community lying reflected in the water. Life in this *skete* has continued peacefully and uninterruptedly for as long as its ageing gatekeeper Arsiusha can remember, an endless round of fasting and giddy prayer as Easter approaches. However, the submarine calm is rudely disrupted by the arrival of an outsider, an agitated and nervous young man called Seliverst, who appears mysteriously one spring evening and asks to be accepted into the community. Without giving any information about himself — Arsiusha's inquiry as to whether he comes 'in peace' is pointedly ignored — Seliverst is permitted to enter. Rumoured to be educated, he prays strangely before an ancient icon of the Virgin Mary, much to Arsiusha's pious indignation. He then asks to be installed in a cell whose previous occupant, a Holy Fool called Simeon, had consented to being chained to the wall of his cell, and ended his life eaten alive by rats. Seliverst, however, keeps a wick-lamp burning day and night to ward off the rodents, while himself maintaining an extremely ascetic regime: he remains in virtual isolation in this cell, emerging only for services; permits himself no cooked food of any kind; and accepts water only once a day. Despite the physical deterioration which this regime entails, it is strictly maintained. All that can be heard by the other monks outside the cell in the evenings and at nights is a muffled voice making bold, urgent, and persistent pleas.

The exact nature of Seliverst's torment becomes apparent after a personal interview with the Father Superior, Vedenei, who has been prompted to act by complaints from the monastery's elders. Father Vedenei is aware that the fires of spiritual faith have long since cooled in the fraternity, and that the monastery houses monks who abuse alcohol and take the Lord's name in vain. He is intrigued by Seliverst's routine of severe fasting and devout prayer, and wonders whether he might not be the person to rekindle the monastery's spiritual ardour.

During the course of their interview, however, the reader learns that
Seliverst's asceticism is the product of a desperate attempt to control
extreme sexual craving. After ushering the young monk into his office,
Vedenei points to a painting hanging on the wall which depicts a
Serpent of Debauchery (*Zmeevidnyi Blud* (381)). This consists of a
hundred-headed serpent, some of whose heads are sucking the breasts
of a woman, while others hover over her stomach and suck the hands
and eyes of a multitude of sinners. Seliverst recognizes himself as one
of these sinners — a gaunt, thin individual, into whose open mouth the
serpent is pouring a river of fire. Vedenei expresses sympathy, but then
remembers his position of authority and lectures him sternly on his
insolence, the sin of pride, and the petty temptations, and threatens to
send him out into the fields to work as a cowherd.

Rumours soon begin to spread locally about Seliverst's unusual
powers of devotion. The pilgrims who regularly visit the monastery in
order to seek blessing, having found that their usual intercessor,
Arsiusha, is now too old and frail to receive them, decide instead to
seek audience with Seliverst. The young monk is initially uncertain of
his power to give succour, but gains confidence after a summer service
in Larivon's old chapel, during which he is called upon to cure a
woman who has passed out because of the stifling heat. Seliverst
nervously places his hands on the woman's face, and his touch appears
to restore consciousness. Amazed, but not yet convinced that this is the
sign he has been seeking, Seliverst rushes back to his cell to continue
praying and firmly locks the door behind him. Later the same night, a
barn inside the monastery catches fire when a strong wind blows
embers over the monastery walls from the campfires in the fields
outside. A powerful blaze springs up which soon threatens to engulf
the little wooden chapel in which the service of the previous day had
taken place. Seliverst is called upon to produce a second miracle.
Standing with the icon of the Virgin Mary held aloft, and feeling a
surge of energy through his body, he makes the sign of the cross in
front of the fire; and as he does so, the fire seems to obey him, gradually reducing to smoke. Seliverst again rushes back to his cell and locks
the door. Everything has become dark and gloomy, and the wick-lamp
which provided his only safeguard from marauding rats has mysteriously become extinguished. At this moment of personal triumph,
paradoxically, Seliverst feels suddenly confused, empty, and disorien-
tated. His earlier strength seems suddenly sapped: 'Совершилось для
него первое в жизни величайшее чудо: и сразу же потухло, пусто' (387).
Fainting from fatigue, and suffering from strange hallucinations,

Seliverst contemplates leaving the *skete* quietly without being noticed. But it is too late — he has thrust a hand despairingly into the handcuffs chained to the wall, and therefore cannot escape. The next morning, he does not appear for morning mass. It is rumoured among the fraternity that a tall monk has been seen to enter the waters of the lake, which allegedly part to accept him, followed shortly afterwards by another figure, half-human and half-animal. It is also rumoured that his rat-infested body has been found in its cell, and that this is the reason that the entrance has been bricked over. All that is known for certain, however, is that both Seliverst and Arsiusha disappear from the monastery the day after the fire. The story ends with the image of the small town reflected in the surface of the lake, its bells tolling in the aquamarine depths.

Language, Topography, and Hagiography

In the opening lines alone, the reader encounters a number of expressions which fix the voice of the implied narrator as strongly folk-religious in orientation. The colloquial inflexion, for example, can be witnessed in the popular variants given for various ecclesiastical names (Larivon, Arsiusha, and Seliverst, instead of Ilarion, Arsenii, and Sil'vestr) and the expressions used to denote daily services (i.e. *povecherie, zautrenia, polunoshchnitsa*).[4] Elsewhere our attention is drawn to words which are exotic and derive for the most part from sacred literature: the title of the story itself, which means 'sign' or 'symbol' (*SRIa*, I, 616); *khlebar'*, an archaic term for 'baker' (Dal', III, 553); *trudnik*, an archaic expression for workers who work in monasteries without payment (ibid., III, 437); the rarely-encountered title of the icon, *Shir'shaia nebes* (literally, 'She who is wider than the heavens'), which refers to the Virgin Mary and can be found in menologies and Greek choral hymns (Srez., III, 1594);[5] the adjective employed in relation to the icon, *iavlennaia*, which refers to its miraculous origin and wonder-working properties (D'iachenko, 847); and the term given for the time when Seliverst arrives at the monastery — *Rusal'naia* — which is the archaic expression for Whitsuntide (i.e. the week before Trinity Sunday).[6] This language fixes the implied narrator as someone well versed in the sacred tradition, but also as someone intimately acquainted with the folk-religious imagination. Many of these terms, while certainly deriving from ecclesiastical literature, nevertheless also characterize the speech of the God-fearing *narod*: the expression *shir'shaia nebes*, for example, is encountered in the speech of one of the

characters in 'Sem´ s polovinoi'.[7] By means of this language, therefore,
the implied narrator draws the reader immediately into the world of
the folk-religious mind, a world in which the miracles and legends of
the past are revered as revelatory and true. The plot of 'Znamenie' is
thus seen to unfold against a broad, historical canvas, one which
engages in a poetic dialogue with the Orthodox culture, language, and
imagination of the pre-Petrine era.

The topographical setting of the narrative further underlines this
dialogue. The monastery functions typically in literature as a sanctuary
or refuge. The word *pustyn´*, however, with its etymological roots
drawn from the adjective *pustoi*, meaning 'deserted' or 'empty', has a
specific connotation in Russian Orthodox culture. This is the term for a
monastery, cloister, or *skete* positioned in an area of great seclusion and
isolated from the concerns of the non-contemplative world; as a rule,
the word refers to the decision of a particular anchorite at some point
in the past to reject urban civilization and to seek spiritual perfection in
the wilderness. It is clear from the first draft version of 'Znamenie' that
Larivonova pustyn´ was envisaged initially as a fictional location
which combined and drew upon Zamiatin's knowledge or recollections
of a number of famous and ancient Russian monasteries. On the top of
the title page, for example, we encounter a list of names — Optina,
Sarovskaia, Valaamskaia, Solovetskaia (IMLI, opis´ 1, ed. khr. 39, p. 1)
— which refer to four well-known hermitages in Russia. The first was
famous as a place of spiritual contemplation in the nineteenth century:
it had been visited both by Dostoevskii and Tolstoi.[8] The second was
famous for the celebrated mystic Serafim of Sarov (formally canonized
in 1903), and had been visited by Zamiatin in his youth.[9] The
topography of the Valaam monastery, situated in the North on the
shores of Lake Ladoga, is similar to the monastery in 'Znamenie': it is
surrounded by a number of *sketes*, one of which was dedicated to the
anchorite Aleksandr Svirskii, whose grave was situated next to the cave
in which he found salvation (*ES*, V, 395–96). And the Solovetskii
monastery (Solovki), which was famous for its resistance to the
Nikonian reforms of the seventeenth century, was one of the areas
visited by Zamiatin during his trip to the North in 1915 ('Zakulisy' (IV,
30)). It is clear from the narrative that the *skete* in 'Znamenie' has also
grown up around an anchorite — Larivon — and therefore conforms to
this general type. Its age, however, is difficult to determine. The word
kinoviia (381) suggests that it is a primitive type of cloister, while the
decaying wooden chapel in which Larivon is said to have prayed, and
which is made out of logs, dates his ascetic ordeal from the late

seventeenth to the early eighteenth century at the very earliest (unless they were rebuilt, wooden churches tended not to last for very long on account of the process of decay).[10] This would seem to be confirmed by the mention of Larivon's skullcap, which is obviously in a state of reasonable preservation, since the visiting pilgrims are allowed to place it on their heads 'in order to acquire Understanding' ('Chtoby v razum voiti' (382)).

The topographical setting is important in the sense that it complements the structuring of the narrative around a series of hagiographic *topoi*. By entering a *skete*, living in the isolation of his cell, and subjecting himself to rigorous fasting, Seliverst follows a mode of practice established by Christ during his forty days in the wilderness (*pustyn*´), and adopted as a model of asceticism by the early Christian fathers in the Egyptian and Palestinian deserts. It is symptomatic of this paradigm that, as Christ was tempted from fasting and spiritual contemplation by Satan (Mark 1. 13; Luke 4. 2), so the early Christian ascetics were forced to withstand demonic intervention on their road to true salvation. It is a conventional *topos* in the hagiographic tradition, illustrated forcefully by the example of St Martinian (f.d. 13 February) — the saint invoked by the Russian *narod* for protection against carnal desire — that this temptation takes the form of Woman; indeed, the extreme solutions devised by such anchorites in order to contain their lust bear eloquent testimony to the heroic nature of their battle with Sin. St Martinian, for example, walked on hot coals in order to avoid temptation (*ZVS*, 103–04); while St John the Sufferer (f.d. 18 July), so called because of his heroic battle against the temptations of the flesh in the twelfth-century Kievan Cave Monastery, starved himself, wore heavy chains around his body, and eventually buried himself up to the neck in earth (ibid., 392–93).

If Seliverst's situation conforms to this sacred model, however, it must be stressed that he arrives in the *skete* without faith, or at least at the point of a crisis in his faith. His urgent appeals to the Mother of God, and the mention in the description of the icon of her dark-blue pallium (*sinii pokrov* (379)), emblematic of her role as the protectress of sinners at the Last Judgement, indicate that he is a penitent seeking salvation, or someone whose faith has seriously lapsed.[11] In earlier versions of the narrative, this lack of faith is explicit: Seliverst responds to the inquiries of the Father Superior by saying that he prays 'in order to believe' (IMLI, opis´ 1, ed. khr. 39, p. 2); and earlier still, as he enters the monastery, Arsiusha has asked him not if he comes 'in peace', but whether he comes 'with belief' (ibid., p. 1). In the published version, there is a much stronger emphasis on the carnal nature of his sin. The painting in Vedenei's office, the title of which in the third version was *Zmeevidnyi grekh* (IMLI, opis´ 1, ed. khr. 42, p. 5), now bears the title *Zmeevidnyi blud*, with its specific connotations of lechery, debauchery, and adultery (Srez., I, 117). Furthermore, his dietary regime of bread and water is the traditional means by which to combat the capacity for sinful thought.[12] However, as in the reworkings of the hagiographic genre by anticlerical writers — I am thinking of Flaubert's *La Tentation de saint Antoine* (1874), Anatole France's *Thaïs* (1891), and Tolstoi's 'Otets Sergii' (1898) — Zamiatin invokes this model of piety and self-denial mainly in order to subvert it. It is a paradoxical reversal that at the moment of success, after the enactment of two miracles which testify to his extraordinary powers, and offer proof of divine existence, Seliverst experiences only despair, anguish, and immeasurable fatigue. The story undeniably ends on a note of failure; and the problem which needs to be addressed is the cause of this failure and the meaning of Seliverst's dissatisfaction and despair.

Insatiability: The Paradigms of Judas Iscariot and the Wandering Jew

The paradox of seeking an ideal, but rejecting that ideal once it has been attained, lies at the heart of Zamiatin's vision of the authentic spiritual revolutionary. In his 1924 essay on Sologub, for example, he talked about the existential condition of modern man in terms of eternal restlessness (IV, 150–55). Moreover, in his discussion of 'Alchushchii i zhazhdushchii', a short story which Sologub published in 1908, he outlined the concept of the *nesytaia dusha* — literally, the 'insatiable' or 'greedy' soul:

Путь этот — трагический путь Агасфера, путь в Дамаск Сологубовского рыцаря Ромуальда из Турени, путь тех вечно несытых душ, о которых поют в чистый четверг на страстной. [...] Великий и тяжкий их рок в том, что их не удовлетворит никакой достигнутый Дамаск: всякое достижение, всякое воплощение убивает для них настоящий Дамаск, для них нет ничего страшнее оседлости, стен. (ibid., 151)

As Zamiatin correctly indicates, the expression *nesytaia dusha* derives from a song sung on Maundy Thursday (*Chistyi chetverg*): the relevant lines, as illustrated by the Fasting Triodion (*Triod´ postnaia*), refer specifically to the treachery of Judas and warn of the dangers of greed and ingratitude.[13] It is clear from the fragment above, however, that Zamiatin's understanding of Judas's motives was more complex than the conventional Orthodox view. Moreover, to a certain extent his comments reflect the treatment of the theme by writers writing in the preceding decade. In 'Iuda Iskariot', for example, the short story by Leonid Andreev which caused something of a scandal at the time it was published in 1907, Judas is depicted as the most intelligent and knowledgeable of the disciples. Furthermore, although a duplicitous, unattractive, and ambiguous figure, his betrayal is presented as an act of fanatical love, rather than of treachery: he is motivated by a desire to seek a sign of God's existence, to test the powers of divine deliverance, and thus to force Jesus to accomplish his divine mission on earth. His suicide, therefore, as well as the product of anguished remorse and disappointment that God has not intervened to save His Son from the cross, is an act of fidelity to the memory of Christ's agony, and as such illustrates his desire to share with him the anguish of self-sacrifice.[14] A similar interpretation of the Judas theme is offered by Remizov at more or less the same time. His stylized medieval mystery play, 'Tragediia o Iude printse iskariotskom' (1908), and the accompanying poem 'Iuda predatel" (1908), were based on a number of apocryphal legends and spiritual songs published in the second half of the nineteenth century. Here also, as in Andreev, we glimpse a more complex set of motives than those usually attributed to Judas. As witnessed in a key confrontation between Judas and Pilate, the former explains that his role is to take upon himself the 'final and most awesome sin' so that the road to salvation for the rest of humanity (as represented by Jesus) can finally be forged.[15] The act of betrayal which he commits consciously, therefore, is an admission of his understanding that the drama which is about to be enacted is part of God's overall design.

Irrespective of whether Zamiatin's characterization of the *nesytaia dusha* is appropriate to Sologub's short story, it would seem from his essay that the Judas paradigm for him meant the demand for evidence that Jesus was the Son of God: he is 'greedy', not in the sense that he seeks financial reward for an act of betrayal, but that he is not content with the argument that belief requires humility, submission, and faith. This is relevant for 'Znamenie' because it characterizes Seliverst's intellectual dilemma and his demand for a sign in order to believe. Both in the draft and final versions of the narrative, he is identified with Judas and the *nesytaia dusha*. In the first version, for example, after observing his breathlessness and the nervous movement of his fingers, the ageing gatekeeper Arsiusha reminds him of the song sung during Passion Week: '— Ты брат, попомни, как про Иуду-то на страстной поется: несытая душа' (IMLI, opis´ 1, ed. khr. 39, p. 2). In the published version, although the direct reference to Judas has been omitted, the reference to the Maundy Thursday song remains: '— Попомни, брат, на Страстной-то поется: несытая душа' (378). Furthermore, Arsiusha's warning, which comes shortly after the references to Easter and fasting in the opening paragraph, is part of a nexus organized around images of hungering and craving, but with the usual spiritual connotations subverted or at least compromised. The crucial exchange takes place in front of the painting hanging in Father Vedenei's office. The title — *alchba* — which derives from the archaic verb *alkat´*, and thus means 'craving' (D´iachenko, 872), features frequently in the Gospels, but usually with a spiritual, rather than physical connotation. In the Sermon on the Mount, for example, Christ promises salvation to all those who 'hunger and thirst after the truth, for they shall be satiated' (Matthew 5. 6). In Russian translation, this reads: 'Блаженны алчущие и жаждущие правды, ибо они насытятся' — hence the title of Sologub's short story, which alludes directly to this sermon. Here it is the desperate thirst for the miraculous on the part of the crusaders in the Syrian desert which results in their salvation; whereas it is the scepticism and rationality of Romuald of Turenne, who sees that their visions are empty chimera, which result in his death.[16] Sologub's narrative bears testament to the power of (irrational) mind over (rational) matter. By contrast, the *alchba* in 'Znamenie' involves an ambiguous conflation of spiritual and bodily imperatives. Seliverst 'hungers' physically in the sense that he experiences powerful carnal desires; but it is with this same hunger that he demands a sign in order to believe:

— Так, отче, алчу я. Огонь меня снедает, невозможного алчу, знамения молю — чтобы поверить, знамения требую... (381)

By confessing that he seeks a sign in order to believe, Seliverst pleads guilty to the psychological reflex against which Christ himself specifically warned — as he says to the Pharisees: 'An evil and adulterous generation seeketh after a sign' (Matthew, 12. 39). Yet while Seliverst's situation parallels that of Judas in that he seeks proof of God's existence, 'Znamenie' explores the idea of a spiritual thirst so powerful that it cannot be satiated, even by evidence of miraculous powers.

The second paradigm which Zamiatin invokes in his essay on Sologub is the fate of the Wandering Jew — as we can see in the above fragment, the situation of Knight Romuald of Turenne in 'Alchushchii i zhazhdushchii' is compared to the tragic fate of Ahasuerus (in Russian, *Agasfer*). According to legend, Ahasuerus refused Jesus the possibility of respite on the road to Golgotha, as a result of which he was denied the peace of the grave and condemned to eternal wandering until the Second Coming.[17] In Zamiatin's understanding, no doubt influenced by Romantic treatments of the subject, the Jew is envisaged as a rebel and sinner whose sceptical intelligence makes him the embodiment of rationality and religious doubt.[18] He refers variously to the legend of Ahasuerus in his essays of this period, and its importance to him as a paradigm for the ceaseless searching of the authentic revolutionary must be strongly emphasized. In 'Skify li?', for example, he invokes the tragic condition of the Jew in the context of the freedom-loving Scythian:

Удел подлинного скифа — тернии побежденных; его исповедание — еретичество; судьба его — судьба Агасфера; работа его — не для ближнего, но для дальнего. (IV, 504)

Later in this same manifesto, he writes of 'defeat' and 'martyrdom' in the earthly sphere, and the 'eternal reaching out, but never reaching' of the spiritual revolutionary:

Поражение, мученичество в земном плане — победа в плане высшем, идейном. Победа на земле — неминуемое поражение в другом, высшем плане. Третьего — для подлинного скифа, для духовного революционера, для романтика — нет. Вечное достигание — и никогда достижение. Вечное агасферово странствование. (IV, 512)

There can be little doubting the appeal of this Romantic gloss on the legend within the specific context of post-1917 cultural politics. The curse of the Wandering Jew provided Zamiatin with a ready-made model with which to articulate his scepticism vis-à-vis the possibility, or even desirability, of a paradise on earth, and his refusal to accept that struggle ceased because of the notional attainment of an ideal. In 'Skify li?', Ahasuerus represents the sceptic who cannot accept the victory of an idea in any sphere of human activity: he is the restless seeker, the tragic and solitary incarnation of the principle of eternal forward movement, and someone whose experience of the different epochs of history means that he can view the rise and fall of societies, and the seismic shifts in political events, with a level-headed and rational objectivity.[19]

Although 'Znamenie' predates the remarks in 'Skify li?', there are strong hints that Seliverst's revolt is an early fictional exploration of the Ahasuerus paradigm. The fact of his seeking respite in a monastery is a *topos* in various adaptations of the legend; indeed, not only does it parallel the very first version of the legend in the English language, an account in the Middle Ages by a monk called Roger Wendover, but also, no doubt coincidentally, it bears a close resemblance to an adaptation penned pseudonymously by a friend of Lord Byron's.[20] The characterization of Seliverst in 'Znamenie' employs various physical and psychological traits with which the legendary figure is usually associated. It is symptomatic, for example, that in an early draft he is given the Jewish name of Veniamin (IMLI, opis´ 1, ed. khr. 42). His piercing gaze — a Romantic leitmotif which features in Vasilii Zhukovskii's unfinished narrative poem on the same subject[21] — is illustrated when Arsiusha asks angrily whether he seeks to 'penetrate' (*proburavit´* (379)) the eyes of the Virgin Mary depicted in the icon. His lean, wiry, and gaunt physiognomy, his exceptional height (this is mentioned on three separate occasions), the aura of mystery which surrounds him from the moment he arrives (he is known as the *neznaemyi monakh* or 'unknown monk'), the implication that he may have been wandering for some time (he is described as tanned), the fact that he is an outsider who avoids contact with the larger community within the monastery, and his taciturn manner are all suggestive.[22]

Unlike earlier meditations on this subject in Russian literature — see, for example, Kiukhel´beker's *Agasfer* (written from 1832 to 1846) — Zamiatin is uninterested in the subject as an opportunity to revisit the momentous historical events of the past, and thus to poeticize the Jew's longevity and world-weary wisdom.[23] Rather, as does Zhukovskii, he concentrates on his tragic metaphysical situation in the present. Zhukovskii's Ahasuerus comes to realize that only through acceptance of the faith, and the hope therefore that at some point there may be an end to his terrible suffering, can his fate be endured — once crazy with anger at the unjustness of his punishment, he now wanders the world with resigned acceptance and practises as much as possible the precepts of Jesus.[24] In 'Znamenie', we may surmise, Seliverst's arrival at the monastery betokens a similar realization. His recognition of himself in the painting as a sinner whose belly is *endlessly* filled with fire ('Bez kontsa poglashchaia ogon´' (381)) mirrors the Romantic conception of Ahasuerus as an eternal rebel whose fate is never to find rest or peace. Furthermore, it is interesting that the moment of truth for Seliverst occurs at a moment identified symbolically in the narrative with the Last Judgement: 'Странный красный день, как день последнего судилища' (386). His fate, however, unlike the character of Zhukovskii's poem, suggests that even the revelation of divine presence in the world, and by implication the prospect of eternal peace, will not bring an end to his suffering. This is implied by the imagery at the beginning and end of the narrative, with its insinuation of continuity and circularity, rather than linear disruption. Seliverst's arrival at the monastery is described initially in terms of the waters of the lake parting to let him enter: 'Разверзлась перед Селиверстом зеленая глубь' (379); and the same image is employed to describe his departure from the monastery after his 'death': 'Voda pered nim rasstupilas'' (388). This suggests that while Seliverst dies in a corporeal sense, on the symbolic or fabular plane his soul rises from the dead and continues his struggle in an endlessly repeated drama of his desperate attempt and failure to find Christ. His fate, indeed, acquires a universal and semi-mythic pathos. Like the biblical Cain, who becomes a fugitive and wanderer as a result of slaying his brother; and Sisyphus, condemned by the gods eternally to roll the same boulder up the side of a mountain; and Prometheus, the Titan, who teaches men the secret of fire and is chained eternally to the side of a mountain as punishment, Seliverst is a metaphor for humanity punished divinely by the Fall and destined to continue the search for salvation.

Flesh and Spirit: Russian Orthodox Models of Piety

The paradigms of Judas Iscariot and Ahasuerus are universal ones. Both are figures punished for their lack of faith in the truth that Christ represents, and their tragic dilemmas are crucial to Zamiatin's polemic. A related, but more Russian-specific element involves the models of piety celebrated by the Orthodox Church and embodied in the characters of Larivon, Arsiusha, and Simeon: together these men represent the ascetic ideal, the powers of prophecy and presentiment, and the native tradition of the Holy Fool. Seliverst is directly juxtaposed to these figures, and yet at the same time usurps their fictional space in terms of their achievement (he emulates Larivon's working of miracles), their function within the monastery (he assumes Arsiusha's role as intercessor), or their physical territory (he inhabits Simeon's cell in the basement of the tower). On one level, the point of these juxtapositions lies in Zamiatin's desire to collapse all sense of space and time: the archaic stylization of the narrative contributes to the sense that the historical past coexists with the present and provides models of behaviour still relevant to the dilemma of the main protagonist. At the same time, these figures are also all associated with the problem of the complicated relationship between the spirit and the flesh. If the Judas and Ahasuerus subjects are exploited to dramatize Seliverst's quest to understand the meaning of Christ's martyrdom, the paradigms of the ascetic, visionary, and Holy Fool are part of

Zamiatin's rejection of the Orthodox doctrine that the spirit and flesh are indivisible and dependent on each other. This is further poeticized by the spatial organization of the text into the world which exists outside the monastery (the sinful and profane world, as represented by the pilgrims) and the world which exists within the monastery (the sacred and contemplative world, as represented by the elders), both of which compete for Seliverst's attention. Even as he seeks to identify himself with each of these models of behaviour, his pride and the ambiguous sources of his spiritual powers conspire to defeat him in the end.

Arsiusha is a central figure in the text in the sense that he symbolizes the waning powers of Christianity. He is a model of Orthodox propriety, fierce in his love of the icon of the Virgin Mary, humble in prayer, and generous in the blessings he gives to pilgrims. Furthermore, his status as elder (*starets*) evokes a particularly Russian notion of spirituality. These were cloistered men and women who gave spiritual direction to thousands of pilgrims and provided by their lives of prayer a linking force between human beings and God — hence their designation as 'intercessors' (*zastupniki*), and thus their symbolic link with the Virgin Mary. As someone with the gift of foresight — *prozorlivets* (383) means 'prophet' (D'iachenko, 507) — Arsiusha is a saintly figure. It is suggested, nevertheless, that his physical weakness owing to his advanced years has led to a corresponding decline in his powers. When Father Vedenei considers the condition of the monastery, for example, he recognizes that the wilderness has depleted the spiritual resources of the fraternity, and compares the once sturdy and strong Arsiusha to a mouldy oak tree which is covered in moss and virtually on the point of collapse:

Хорошо знал Веденей: под зеленый гул пустынских колоколов лениво его людишки живут, и винопийцы есть и суесловы, а главное — ни в ком огня нет, духом оскудела пустынь. Старец Арсюша? Да и тот обомшал уж, и аки дуб трухлявый: притронуться страшно. (381)

This same image is employed later when Arsiusha is compared to the old chapel standing in memory of the hermit Larivon:

А служили нынче в старой церкви — еще батюшка Ларивон в ней маливался — бревенчатая и такая какая-то вроде старца Арсюши: ласковая, квелая, к земле пригнулась, затянуло мохом бревна. (383)

Crucially, however, the juxtaposition of physical with spiritual decline becomes more ambiguous as the narrative progresses. If Arsiusha is a moss-covered oak tree on the point of collapse, the strict dietary regime which Seliverst imposes upon himself causes his face to pale like the shoots of a vegetable grown in the dark ('Овощной росток, проросший в погребе' (380)). Initially, if Seliverst seems strong and vigorous, and comes to replace Arsiusha as an intercessor because of the latter's old age, after the miracle his mental exertions and physical deprivations have clearly taken their toll. In the final chapter, it is his immeasurable fatigue which causes the hallucinatory and confusing visions: his sense of dimension has become surreal; he seems to be suffering from double vision; and he is behaving irrationally (how else to explain the act of forcing his hand frustratedly into Simeon's handcuffs?). Thus if Seliverst appears initially to represent a force which will regenerate the Christian faith, his defeat suggests that asceticism is counter-productive. The 'giddiness' mentioned joyfully at the beginning of the story in relation to the Easter celebrations — 'Постом истомиться на повечериях, заутрениях, полунощницах' (378) — has by the end of the story received its gruesome and ironic culmination.

In common with his unorthodox manner of prayer, which is too proud and fierce for the liking of Arsiusha, Seliverst's claim to saintly status is unconventional from the Orthodox point of view. The ambiguity of his position is reinforced, moreover, by the parallels drawn between himself and Simeon Pokhabnyi, the 'fool for Christ's sake'. Seliverst's request to be located in Simeon's cell is significant in light of the dual status traditionally accorded the Holy Fool. By common consent, the *iurodivyi* was a self-appointed social outcast who voluntarily turned his back on conventional modes of behaviour and deliberately denied himself physical comfort in the name of his folly. In certain cases, moreover, on account of their ascetic feats, willingness to share the lives of the poor, powers of prophecy, and ability to perform miraculous cures, Holy Fools had been officially canonized by the Church (*PPS*, II, 2394). At the same time, however, the feigned madness and unnerving displays of indecency which sometimes accompanied their acts of folly — *pokhabnyi* refers to displays of obscenity and vulgarity (Dal´, III, 365) — tended to blur the distinction between the sacred and profane source of their powers. This made the question of sanctification a thorny one. The problem for the Orthodox Church consisted in trying to define the boundary which separated divinely inspired madness (i.e. the attempt to emulate Christ's 'folly' in allowing himself to be crucified) and ordinary insanity or mental instability, which in medieval times was viewed as a form of demonic possession.[25]

The name of the *iurodivyi* in 'Znamenie' may well be an allusion to the eccentric visionary of the sixth century, Simeon Salos (f.d. 21 July), whose folly included such obscene displays as defecating in public, entering the female quarters of public baths in the nude, and revealing his genitalia before the wives of tavern-owners (his holy feat or *podvig* consisted of the attainment of 'bodilessness', i.e. the sensation that he consisted only of the spirit and not bodily matter).[26] Since this name may also be a pun on the Greek word for sign (*semeion*), and thus an echo of the meaning of the title, the memory of Simeon occupies a central place in the text's symbolism. It would seem, for example, that Seliverst's request to be placed in his cell is motivated primarily by its association with *pokhabshchina*, not because he wishes his actions to be perceived in terms of *iurodstvo*; his proud and insolent prayers to the Virgin Mary are in any case the very antithesis of the Fool's customary humility in relation to the sacred objects of the Orthodox Church. Furthermore, he demonstrates nothing of the confusing behaviour of the *iurodivyi*, with its apparent lack of logic and subversion of public norms. On the other hand, the fate of Simeon, which echoes that of Simeon Salos in that it testifies to the achievement of bodilessness (presumably he no longer felt physical pain, and thus felt able to martyr himself in imitation of Christ) is clearly relevant for a monk who is seeking to extinguish within himself the temptations of the flesh. This is perhaps the meaning of his deliberate choice of cell. The way in which Seliverst's death, albeit accidental, parallels that of his predecessor is obvious. Furthermore, it is significant that in the sequences after the miracle particular attention is drawn to the physical sensations which Seliverst experiences and the sense in which his mind and body seem to have become divorced from each other. On the one hand, he appears to feel the weight of physical matter more intensely — his hands are described in terms of 'mountains' which he is incapable of moving. Yet at the same time Zamiatin describes how one part of him is going to arise and leave the monastery, while the other, still chained to the wall, rests his head on the window of his cell and awaits the onset of dawn. This anticipates the split perspective of the final paragraphs — the eyewitness accounts of the monks (rumour, fantasy) balanced by the insinuation of the truth (the dead body has been found and the entrance to the cell bricked over) — but also testifies symbolically to the separation of the body and soul, and thus, ironically, to a form of bodilessness.

The reaction of the monastic authorities in bricking up his cell suggests that Seliverst's achievement is not one to be emulated or formally offered as a model of piety. Furthermore, the suspicion that his powers derive from profane, rather than sacred, forces receives confirmation in the depiction of Seliverst's relationship with the pilgrims. These pilgrims constitute a sinful and all-suffering crowd whose very presence and need of healing inspire Seliverst with the confidence to perform his duties. On the first occasion that their need for blessing is granted, he notices the strength emanating from their eyes:

И было у них в глазах такое крепкое, неодолимое, катило на Селиверста, как морская волна, взметывало его вверх, и знал он твердо: невозможное — возможно, и чуял: близко уже, и ничего не было страшно. (383)

Later, on the threshold of healing the woman who has fainted in chapel, it is their eyes which again catch his attention:

Как малую песчинку — с утра вихрем подняло Селиверста и несло, ближе и ближе, все мелькало, не слышал, не видел: только одни громадные, вечные глаза, вобравшие в себя скорбь тысяч глаз. […] Тишина, и сотни глаз — на него, Селиверста. (384)

And later still, as he stands with the icon aloft to protect the old church from the fire, he looks over his shoulder towards the onlookers and feels a wave of incredible power surging through his body:

Последний раз оглянулся Селиверст: обступили кругом глаза. Зачерпнул оттуда — из глаз, неистовая волна хлестнула снизу, от сердца — к рукам. (386)

The eyes of the pilgrims are deliberately juxtaposed with the eyes of the icon — 'Икона древняя, явленная — одни глаза, громадные' (379) — and thus represent a domain which lies outside the precinct of the monastery. This is further emphasized by the fact that it is the embers from the campfires outside the monastery which originally cause the conflagration, and the fact that there is an implicit identification between the hundred-headed serpent of the painting ('Змий — зеленый, как яспис, стоглавый' (381)) and the hundred-voice crowd (*stogolosyi gul* (387)) as it stands and watches the conflagration. The pilgrims are also associated symbolically with the colour red; indeed, the conflagration scene marks the culmination of a radical shift in the use of colour symbolism, away from the blue of the Virgin's pallium and the blue-green waters of the lake (emblems of peace, calm, and tranquillity) towards the red associated with the hunger which keeps Seliverst alive and the destructive force of the fire. The wick-lamp which burns in his cell is a 'red eye' (*krasnyi glaz* (380)) (this image can also be juxtaposed with the eyes of the icon). The crowd during the conflagration is said to move apart 'like the Red Sea' (*Chermnym morem* (386)). The fire which threatens to destroy the chapel is described in terms of its 'red tongue' (*krasnyi iazyk* (387)). Even Father Vedenei's beard, which has earlier been described as grey, but with a greenish tinge, is reddened by the raging fire.

Zamiatin's use of fire imagery illustrates well his strategy of subverting images which derive from sacred literature. In the books of the Old and New Testaments, for example, fire represents the presence and manifestation of the divine spirit. Jehovah appears to Moses in the form of a burning bush which is not consumed by the flames (Exodus 3. 2); the Word of God is described in terms of a flame (Jeremiah 23. 29); the prophet Elijah ascends to Heaven in a chariot of fire (II Kings 2. 11); God's angels are compared to fire (Psalms 104. 4); the Holy Ghost, metaphorically depicted in the shape of a dove, descends at Pentecost and speaks to the apostles with tongues of fire (The Acts 2. 1–4); it is foretold that the end of the world will be accompanied by a destructive conflagration (II Corinthians 3. 10–11); and that the Second Coming will occur in the midst of fire (I Thessalonians 1.8). These images give rise to the idea of the 'sacred flame' (*sviashchennyi ogon´*), a metaphor for the faith in general. At the same time, paradoxically, this flame is also juxtaposed with the conventional flame of sexual desire. In hagiographic literature, for example, fire is a cleansing force which quenches the burning temptations of the flesh. In the *vita* of St Martinian, as we have seen, the saint walks on hot coals in order to control his carnal desires. In the *Zhitie protopopa Avvakuma, im samim napisannoe*, the archpriest holds his hand over three candle flames during the erotic confessions of a young woman so that the pain will distract him from sexual arousal.[27] And the miraculous powers of the Holy Virgin in relation to fire underlie the symbolism of the Icon of the Virgin Mary of the Burning Bush (*Ikona Presviatoi Bogoroditsy Neopalimoi Kupiny*), which is celebrated by the Orthodox Church on 4 September. This derives from sacred songs which compare the preservation of her virginity during the conception and birth of Jesus Christ with the burning bush of Exodus: she is impregnated by the sacred flame, but does not 'burn' (in other words, she is 'unconsumed', and thus remains chaste). Moreover, the symbolism of this festival gave rise to the belief prevalent in Russia that the Virgin could be invoked as a protectress against fires — hence the practice among the folk of walking around burning buildings holding the icon aloft in the hope of extinguishing the flames.[28]

If there is a clear distinction in the Orthodox imagination between the sacred flame of divine will and the flame of carnal desire, in 'Znamenie' this distinction is blurred. Initially, when Father Vedenei contemplates the state of the monastery under his supervision, fire is equated explicitly with the Orthodox faith: 'Ни в ком огня нет, духом оскудела пустынь' (381). This idea has been anticipated earlier by the metaphorical comparison between the flames of the monastery candles during all-night mass and the scarlet-coloured fern-flower (*paporotnik* (379)), a flower which blooms twice a year and was associated in the folk-religious imagination with the resurrected spirit of Christ.[29] As the narrative progresses, these images are subject to a delicate subversion. This is initiated by the description of Seliverst's carnal desire in terms of a 'river of fire' (*ognennaia reka* (381)), and then developed further by means of the 'inextinguishable fire' (*negasimyi ogon´* (387)) which burns in his wick-lamp. Symbolically, the fire which threatens to destroy the monastery is the very same fire which consumes Seliverst internally. In a reversal of the earlier *paporotnik* metaphor, the 'fiery seed' of the wind creates a mass of hungry, dazzling flowers which swiftly burst into bloom: 'Бил, гудел, сеял огненное семя — секунду цвели жадные, жаркие цветы' (386); and the flames, which had earlier been described in terms of 'fiery doves' (*ognennye golubi* (386)) — an allusion to the symbolism of Pentecost — are now described as 'little devils': 'А быстрые бесенята суетятся уже в соседнем корпусе' (386). By miraculously dousing the flames, therefore, Seliverst simultaneously extinguishes the life-force which has protected him from death in the shape of the wick-lamp: 'Негасимый огонь в лападке загас' (387). We can only conclude that it is the fire of fornication which is the source of his miraculous powers, and one which religious faith cannot replace.

The Kitezh Paradigm

The appearance of Ahasuerus was traditionally associated with imminent disaster and impending doom. There are eschatological currents running through 'Znamenie' — underlined by mention of the Last Judgement in the final chapter and the symbolism of the fire which threatens to destroy Larivon's chapel — which bear witness to an apocalyptic sense of ending and suggest that Seliverst's struggle can be read as a universal paradigm with ramifications for the Russian intelligentsia as a whole.

Crucial in this context is the symbolism of the opening paragraph, with its description of a town/monastery reflected in the waters of a lake and the pealing of bells as if from under the surface of the water; this is an image made all the more striking by virtue of the privileged place it occupies both at the beginning and the end of the narrative. For the reader well-versed in folk-religious culture, this is instantly recognizable as an allusion to the legend of the holy city of Kitezh, one very much in vogue among neo-Populists in the latter part of the nineteenth and early twentieth centuries. This legend recounts the story of a beautiful and holy city on the shores of a lake which miraculously disappears, thanks to divine intervention, at the moment when it is about to be sacked by invading Tatar hordes.[30] Although these events purportedly took place in the twelfth century, the legend in its written form, *Kniga glagolemaia Kitezhskim letopistsem*, dates from the second half of the eighteenth century and is thought to have been modelled on the writings of monks driven out of their monasteries for sectarian allegiances in 1713. Komarovich, for example, suggests that the author belonged to the radical Old Believer sect known as the 'runners' (*beguny*), members of which were regularly encountered on the shores of the lake during the summer months. He speculates that they visited the area annually as part of their allegiance to the Old Faith, and their conviction that the rule of the 'Antichrist' would be short-lived. Furthermore, he argues that Kitezh — known popularly as the 'invisible' or 'heavenly' city (*nevidimyi, nezdeshnii grad*) — served as a guiding beacon during their years of wandering, hunger, and persecution; indeed, like the New Jerusalem, it was an earthly paradise and place of refuge which would reappear after the Second Coming.[31]

After publication of the Kitezh chronicle in 1862, the legend acquired a richness and complexity which went far beyond its symbolism in the minds of the *beguny*. The visits of ethnographers and intellectuals to the site where the city was supposed to have stood (Lake Svetloiar, Nizhnii Novgorod province); the recording of local folklore around the shores of the lake where the *beguny* lived in earth dugouts; the growth of a Kitezh cult which witnessed hordes of pilgrims, both Orthodox and Old Believer, visiting the area every year on Midsummer Night's Eve in order to catch the ringing of its bells; and the adaptations of the legend in the work of writers, poets, painters, and composers in the second half of the nineteenth and the first decades of the twentieth centuries added a multitude of additional layers to its meaning.[32] For Orthodox believers, the city came to represent Kievan Rus' saved by divine intervention in order to protect its cultural identity and spiritual purity in the face of a barbaric invasion. This developed into a general metaphor for spiritual withdrawal in the face of violence, anarchy, and revolt, and was frequently employed by intellectuals of various political persuasions and philosophical inclinations in the context of disasters which threatened Orthodox Christian values. Remizov and Maksimilian Voloshin, for example, drew on the Kitezh legend to describe the destruction wrought by war and revolution in 1917.[33] More recently, it has been invoked as a metaphor for the practice of internal emigration during the Stalinist terror of the 1930s and 40s.[34]

It is unlikely that Zamiatin was acquainted with the written version of the legend. Nevertheless, his use of the reflection motif and the tolling of bells suggests the influence of certain ethnographic belletrists and novelists, in particular Mel´nikov-Pecherskii, Vladimir Korolenko, and Prishvin.[35] The reflection of its towers and battlements in the surface of the lake, and the sound of its bells pealing softly beneath the surface of the water, were Kitezh's most celebrated leitmotifs, yet their origins are traceable, not to the Kitezh chronicle as such, but rather to local folklore as poetically transcribed by Mel´nikov-Pecherskii in his novel V lesakh. The opening paragraph, for example, offers a lyrical vision of the city as if glimpsed for real:

Преданья о Батыевом разгроме там свежи. Укажут и тропу 'Батыеву' и место невидимого града Китежа на озере Светлом Яре. Цел тот город до сих пор — с белокаменными стенами, златоверхими церквами, с честными монастырями, с княженецкими узорчатыми теремами, с боярскими каменными палатами, с рубленными из кондового, негниющего леса домами. Цел град, но невидим. Не видать грешным людям славного Китежа. Скрылся он чудесно, божьим повеленьем. [...] И досел тот град невидим стоит — откроется перед страшным Христовым судилищем. А на озере Светлом Яре, тихим летним вечером, виднеются отраженные в воде стены, церкви, монастыри, терема княженецкие, хоромы боярские, дворы посадских людей. И слышится по ночам глухой, заунывный звон колоколов.[36]

The notion that this city is invisible, and can be seen and heard only by the righteous, derives from the folklore which Mel´nikov-Pecherskii heard on the shores of Lake Svetloiar and then later wove into his novel as a matter of ethnographic record. The section of the novel dedicated to the legend depicts a pilgrimage to Lake Svetloiar, during which the characters encounter not only a number of sectarians who have settled in the area as hermits, but also a number of stories which relate how local people had found their way to the city at the bottom of the lake after they had died.[37] This poetic recreation influences a number of subsequent treatments, most famously the opera by Rimskii-Korsakov, in which the tolling bells are a key musical leitmotif. Furthermore, the existence of the folk beliefs which Mel´nikov-Pecherskii incorporates into his novel is subsequently confirmed by the accounts of Populist writers who visit the lake as part of their exploration of Russian folk-religious culture. Korolenko undertakes a trip to Lake Svetloiar in the summer of 1890, and reports the belief that only the righteous can hear the tolling of the bells.[38] He also records the conviction that some people had even managed to reach a monastery at the bottom of the lake — it allegedly marked the entrance to the holy city — and repeats almost verbatim a tale along these lines as recounted to him by a local fisherman.[39] While sceptical generally about the truth of these claims, Korolenko nevertheless evokes the magical spell which the eerie calm of the lake seems to cast over him. In his description, it is a location seemingly removed from the real world, and one which embraces two spheres of being — the authentic, but invisible, and the inauthentic, but visible — which intermingle and flow into each other.

The Kitezh legend was by no means the only Russian legend involving sunken cities and tolling bells.[40] There are compelling reasons, nevertheless, for supposing that it is this particular legend which forms the basis for the central image in 'Znamenie'. The city is mentioned explicitly in *Uezdnoe* (I, 72), which suggests that Zamiatin must have been acquainted with it at least by 1913. Furthermore, an unfinished fragment bearing the title 'Monastyr'' among his papers in the Bakhmetev archive incorporates an image of an 'invisible' and 'heavenly' city which echoes unmistakeably the popular conception of Kitezh:

На низеньком лугу, пьющем воду из Волгу — странный, весь ярко-белый, нездешний, неземной городок. И поют на усладу всему миру — колокола: тихим, низким, глубоким, умиротворенным звоном, будто не здесь, наверху, а под водой, в невидимом граде этот звон, прошел через дремотно-зеленую глубь, оттого такой тишиной, таким миром полон.[41]

As we can see, this fragment echoes closely the description of Kitezh in Mel´nikov-Pecherskii. Significantly, the tolling bells are later described in terms of their soft pealing (*malinovyi zvon*), a quality which echoes both the description in *V lesakh* and the subtitle of Rimskii-Korsakov's opera.[42] In addition, Zamiatin indicates the geographical location of this town through the mention of goods hawked at a fair to celebrate the monastery's altar-day — combs from Yaroslavl, honey-cakes from Kineshma, and carved wooden artefacts (*iskusnye baklushi*) from Dievo Gorodishche.[43] This places the town along a stretch of the Volga, possibly between Yaroslavl and Kineshma, in an area closely linked with the composition of the legend in its written form and later

propagation.[44] It is not inconceivable that 'Monastyr'' is a poetic description of Gorodets, a town which lies on a bend of the Volga just
north of Nizhnii Novgorod and features in the legend as Kitezh's 'twin-
town' (in the chronicle, it is known as 'Malyi Kitezh').[45] This suggests
either that Zamiatin had 'overheard' the legend while on his many
trips up and down the Volga, or possibly came into contact with it via
the itinerant monks who used to visit his home in his childhood
(*strannik*, for example, the term used by Strizhev, is a common
synonym for *begun*).[46]

Although there is no way of dating this unfinished manuscript, and
no extratextual evidence linking 'Monastyr'' with 'Znamenie' as such,
the title and the cross-echoing of these central images suggests that the
latter is the final crystallization of ideas first explored tentatively in the
former: the peace and calm of the opening scenes; the comparison of
the white-walled monastery with a town beneath the surface of the
water; the tolling of the bells from the green depths; and the goods sold
at the altar-day fair are identical in both. It is clear, nevertheless, that
certain important modifications have been introduced. The location of
the monastery in 'Znamenie', for example, is no longer specific to any
particular region: this is witnessed by the fact that the goods sold at the
fair, while identical to those in 'Monastyr'', are no longer associated
with particular towns along the Volga.[47] On the other hand, the substi-
tution of the Volga for a deep blue lake links the narrative more
directly to the legend — the reference to its depth ('Ozero — glubokoe,
goluboe' (378)) and radiance ('Ozero bylo iasnoe, svetloe' (388)) are
telling in this regard. More significantly, perhaps, 'Znamenie' introduces a reflection motif which is actually absent in 'Monastyr'' (the
bells, while appearing to toll beneath the surface of the Volga, belong to
an 'invisible city' which is hidden to the naked eye); indeed, the
opening description in 'Znamenie' bears a closer resemblance in this
respect to Mel'nikov-Pecherskii's *V lesakh*, although it is complicated by
the problem of narrative point of view (is this picture given to the
reader objectively by the author-narrator, or is it a vision entertained by
Arsiusha, the gate-keeper?). The central importance of this opening
passage and its attendant motifs can be witnessed by the fact that they
are integrated carefully into the main framework of the narrative: the
tolling of the bells is mentioned no fewer than six times during the
course of the story, as are the green depths of the lake.

In *Uezdnoe*, Kitezh functions as a symbol of provincial Russia's
religious conservatism and isolation from the revolutionary events of
1905. Timosha, the bar-room philosopher with liberal sympathies,

notes gloomily that all the excitement in 'Babylonian' St Petersburg is unlikely to reach his own town:

— Не-ет, до нас не дойдет, — говорил Тимоша уныло. — Куды там. Мы вроде, как во град-Китеже на дне озера живем: ничегошеньки у нас не слыхать, над головой вода мутная да сонная. А на верху-то все полыхает, в набат бьют. (I, 72)

This nineteenth chapter of Zamiatin's tale is vital to an appreciation of the way in which the Kitezh legend functions in 'Znamenie'. The subtle shift in narratorial perspective from a description of the view above the lake at the very beginning ('И у самой воды, на мху изумрудном' (378)) to the experience of living underwater midway through the first paragraph ('И так хорошо, тихо жить отделенным от мира зеленой глубью' (378)) signals clearly the coexistence of two parallel spheres in the story, one of which exists on the realistic plane (above the water), and the other on the symbolic plane (below the water). The monastery in 'Znamenie', however, occupies both dimensions simultaneously. On the realistic plane, the lake exists adjacent to the monastery. The elders congregate by the side of the lake in the evenings, see the stars reflected in the surface of the water, and strain to catch the sounds of pealing bells and singing (380). The pilgrims rest by the side of the lake and listen to the deep rumblings of the bells (382). And the monks sit by the lake on the morning after Seliverst's death and from there witness the sight of his ghost entering the water, followed shortly afterwards by a figure who would appear to be Arsiusha. But the monastery also exists in the symbolic dimension in the sense that the ensuing drama seems to take place below the surface of the water: the waters of the lake are said to move apart to admit Seliverst when he first enters the monastery (379); his arrival is described in terms of a stone which causes ripples to expand outwards across the surface of the lake (379); and Vedenei is a *podvodnyi tsar´* (380) who runs the monastic community as if it was his own underwater kingdom (the draft versions confirm the suspicion that his name puns on *vodianoi*, the folk term for the spirit-king of the water). As in Korolenko's description of Lake Svetloiar, these parallel spheres intermingle and flow into one another. The description of the monastery as a 'fairy tale town' (378)) implies that it is a fiction, but one which possesses its own reality in the realms of the folk-religious imagination.[48] The temporal perspective reinforces this sense of duality. This is a fantastic realm which seems to lie outside time, one in which the age-old rituals of life in the monastery, such as the baking of bread, the milking of cows, the collection of alms, and the fasting prior to the celebration of Easter have all remained unchanged into the present day.

The vision presented in this opening paragraph involves something of a reversal of the usual sectarian conception of Kitezh, with its emphasis on a backward-looking but essentially utopian vision. If sceptical themselves about the truthfulness of the legend, but reflecting the apocalyptic fantasies of the sectarians with whom they have come into contact, the accounts of Mel´nikov-Pecherskii, Korolenko, and Prishvin present Kitezh as an earthly paradise which exists not in the present, but in the future, after the end of history and the Second Coming.[49] 'Znamenie', by contrast, offers no such utopian vision: Vedenei's comment about the laziness of the monks and their lack of spiritual stamina suggests otherwise. Neither is the monastery a lost or invisible world which can only be perceived by the righteous — on the contrary, although envisaged as existing in a parallel dimension, it is a visible world which is tangible to all who seek a refuge for the purposes of spiritual contemplation. In essence, the monastery in Zamiatin's tale is a metaphor for a pre-Petrine version of Holy Russia which has survived into modern times with its values and mode of consciousness more or less intact, even if its faith is waning; as such, it is an extension of the conceit which informs the earlier provincial narratives. Like Kitezh, but for different reasons, it is a place which faces destruction and desecration from the pagan world outside its borders.[50] Furthermore, if the holy city symbolizes the divine protection of cultural and spiritual values in the face of external invasion, Larivonova pustyn´ in Zamiatin's story functions as a metaphor for Orthodox withdrawal from the modern world beyond its boundaries.[51] Like Seliverst, the reader is drawn into the confines of this world and enters a symbolic zone in which the apocalyptic events of Russian history are constantly replayed in the popular imagination.

If we view the world of Larivonova pustyn´ as a microcosm of Rus´, the conflagration which threatens its core values also assumes a universal dimension. Seliverst represents that sinful, sexual, rebellious, 'Babylonian' force which threatens to destroy the foundations of Ortho-dox Russia for ever. Arsiusha's guarded response to his arrival ('С чем, брат, приходишь? С миром ли?' (378)); the remark that the gatekeeper is afraid of 'rebellious people' and seeks refuge in the forest to escape them (ibid.); the image of the stone causing ripples across the surface of the lake (379); and the complaint by the elders that Seliverst's method of praying is causing disagreements and disputes among the elders of the monastery ('Только смута и свара завелась по всей киновии' (381)) are symptomatic of the challenge which his arrival presents to the community. Paradoxically, the narrative charts the gradual neutralization of this challenge. 'Znamenie' describes the emptiness which results when complete disengagement from the world of the flesh is achieved. This is a story about the draining of that quintessentially modern life-force — sexual desire — and the failure to find an equivalent force to replace it. Vedenei's words about the isolation of the monastery having drained the 'fires of the spirit' are here subject to ironic reversal, since it is the spirit of rebellion which is sapped by ascetic practice. If Arsiusha perceives Seliverst as a new 'Messiah' (after the first miracle he rings his handbell and invites the pilgrims with him to Jerusalem), and if he becomes symbolically associated with the 'invisible city' by virtue of the rumours which circulate concerning his posthumous fate (it is interesting that Arsiusha, whose body is never found, joins him in the waters of the lake), the psychological truth which lies behind the formation of the legend is disturbing.

The Private Paradigm

Seliverst's designation as a rebel is crucial in terms of the private experience which informs the general metaphysical concerns of Zamiatin's tale. To a certain extent this is a story about Zamiatin's own relationship to Kitezh and the religious fantasies which lie at the core of its imaginative world. The evocation of the legend in the specific context of the 1905 revolution in *Uezdnoe*, and the explicit parallel drawn between the holy city and rural, conservative Russia, suggest that, despite the prognosticatory dimension of the title, the focus of the concerns in 'Znamenie' has its roots in the past, and that it relates to the strained relationship with Zamiatin's mother and father as a result of his revolutionary inclinations at the time.

Zamiatin's renewed interest in this subject, as I have suggested earlier, was probably triggered by the death of his father in the early part of 1916. The (approximate) date of his death is confirmed by a letter from Zamiatin to his wife dated 20–21 December 1925, written ostensibly in response to the death of his mother:

Странно, что все вышло так же, как с моим отцом: так же — в тот же день, в субботу — заболела, в тот же день — в пятницу — конец, и так же — в воскресенье — приехал я, на несколько часов позже, чем нужно.

[...] Я попал сюда уже в состоянии 'окамененного нечувствия' — может быть, к счастью — а, может, после будет хуже. Когда я приехал при тех же обстоятельствах в 16-ом году, мне было страшнее — хотя мать я любил больше отца. (*RN*, I, 295)

The tone of his remarks in relation to his father's death is confirmed by reports, based on later conversations with his sister Aleksandra, about the conflict between father and son as a result of his arrest and incarceration in 1905; this led to their mutual estrangement in subsequent years.[52] In a letter to Liudmila dated 22 April/6 May 1906, Zamiatin referred to his father's view of these activities as 'harmful', both for himself and for society at large (*RN*, I, 31). It would seem that Zamiatin viewed these events in terms of the passing away of the old world and the onset of the new. In a letter dated 9/22 May 1906, he compared the disintegration of his family to the dramatic conflict at the heart of Chekhov's *Diadia Vania* and *Vishnevyi sad* (ibid., 35); and in an earlier letter dated 26 March/8 April 1906, he contrasted the heady days of revolution with the inert, 'stony' reality which greeted him during his first days of freedom in Lebedian´:

Спокойно катится по небу солнце и лениво спать ложится — страстей, страданий сильных оно не видит: под ним Спокойствие, покачиваясь, дремлет, глаза закрывши; бредет старуха вековая Покорность, дряхлою походкой и крадется чуть слышными шагами Вера в черном одеяньи и опытной рукой страданья заглушает в людях... и жизнь — коварно убивая смелость, гордость.

Опять один я, среди чужих, холодных стен. И камни серые тюрьмы мне ближе были: за камнями страдали люди там, как люди, камни говорили, а здесь... как камни, люди говорят, и за людьми — глухие, неподвижные, холодные мне видны камни... (ibid., 14)

This passage is a ghostly anticipation of the opening passage of 'Znamenie' and the images of frailty associated with Arsiusha. Furthermore, aside from the general parallels between Lebedian´ and Larivonova pustyn´ intimated in this correspondence, there are echoes of Zamiatin's circumstances in the drafts and final version of the text. The theme of betrayal associated with the figure of Judas, for example, has an obvious resonance in the private sphere, and it is interesting to note in this context that in the very first draft of 'Znamenie' the Jewish name Veniamin, rather than Seliverst, was preferred for the main protagonist (this means 'favourite son' in Hebrew).[53] It is also noteworthy that the church in which Zamiatin's father served was also dedicated to the pallium (*pokrov*) of the Virgin Mary; this means that the whole poetics of intercession, with its subtext of sinners seeking repentence, is potentially identified with home. The confession scene between Vedenei and Seliverst, in which the latter refers to the former as 'father' ('— Tak, otche, alchu ia' (381)), and the former refers to the latter as 'my poor, poor child' ('— Bednoe ty moe chadushko, bednoe!' (ibid.)), is thus lent a pathos beyond the customary mode of address between Father Superior and monk. Furthermore, there is evidence on the basis of Zamiatin's notebooks that the legend of the Wandering Jew (the term used in this context is *vechnyi zhid*) was associated with an eccentric character from his youth who had escaped from home as a teenager (he is called Larivon, but most likely this is a coincidence).[54] These facts hint strongly at the possibility that the torment experienced by Seliverst in relation to the question of religious belief has its roots in the complex set of emotions, not to mention terror, which Zamiatin admitted to having experienced when confronted with his father's death.

The letters from this period, while testifying to a sense of alienation and emptiness, offer evidence of Zamiatin's continued commitment to his revolutionary ideals. 'Znamenie', by contrast, suggests that his views had developed in a confusing and ambiguous direction, perhaps under the pressure of his father's death. While the failure to accept the sign as a sufficient condition of belief testifies to Zamiatin's continued loyalty to the position of restless seeker, the stylization of the text, like so many of the early provincial stories, betrays a secret admiration for Orthodox culture in its historical guise. As already indicated in Chapter 1, Zamiatin's dilemma to a certain extent parallels that of the main protagonist (Senia) in 'Neputevyi', a character who is also 'divided in two', although he later dies on the barricades in support of revolt. This ambiguity or division is a far cry from the blatantly satirical approach employed in *Uezdnoe* — here the monks are presented as cruel, grotesque caricatures with no appetite for life beyond the crudely physical and material — but reinforces the general impression of the early provincial period as one in which Zamiatin struggles to clarify his position vis-à-vis Orthodox religion, rejecting the ideology, but respecting the form in which it had entered Russian culture. It is only a short step from 'Znamenie' to the *chudesa* or hagiographic parodies, the aesthetic paradox of which is located in the tension between the formal style (ecclesiastical and archaic) and the content (subversive). As we will see in the next chapter, the first drafts for 'O sviatom grekhe Zenitsy-devy. Slovo pokhval'noe' probably pre-date the writing of 'Znamenie'. In both cases the increasing influence of Remizov on Zamiatin's literary development from about 1915 onwards can be detected. His stylizations of medieval folk-religious materials pioneered a means of linguistic stylization which Zamiatin found amenable for other, blasphemous purposes; indeed, whereas Remizov is largely celebratory in his treatment of these materials, Zamiatin's approach is essentially flippant and parodistic.

NOTES

1. 'Znamenie' (I, 378–88) was first published in the journal *Mysl´* in 1918, along with the essay 'Skify li?' (*PZ*, 54). Henceforth, all references will be to the Neimanis edition, but without the volume number.

2. Among these early versions is an unfinished short story entitled 'Sem´ s polovinoi' (IMLI, opis´ 1, ed. khr. 42, p. 6). Although undated, this clearly belongs to the fiction of the provincial period — in other words, the period prior to Zamiatin's departure to Britain. Another version of this story, also undated, is found in the Bakhmetev archive at the University of Columbia. See Evgenii Zamiatin, 'Nezakonchennoe', pp. 124–26.

3. The cult status of the legend, its religious symbolism, its popularity among certain artists, and its relevance for 'Znamenie' will be examined during the course of this chapter.

4. N. A. Petrovskii, *Slovar´ russkikh lichnykh imen* (Moscow: Russkie slovari, 1996), pp. 63, 147, & 255, respectively. For the terms referring to the services, see Dal´, III, 143; I, 657; & III, 252, respectively.

5. *Shir´shaia* would appear to be the archaic comparative of the adjective *shirokii*, and thus means 'wider' (from the Greek *platutera*). See Srez., III, 1594 (nota bene: the information is given here under *shirii*). Its generic relation to the Virgin Mary's pallium can be demonstrated with reference to one of the very earliest acathists of the Orthodox Church, the sixth song (*ikos*) of which includes the chant: 'Радуйся, Покрове миру, ширший облака.' This was composed in the first half of the seventh century AD by Deacon Georgii Pisidiiskii, and was the first acathist to be accepted as part of the Orthodox liturgy by Sergius, the patriarch of Constantinople. See 'Akafist preblago-slavennoi vladychitse nashei bogoroditse i prisnodeve Marii, gl. 8', in *Molitvy i pesnopeniia Pravoslavnogo Molitvoslova*, translations and commentary by Nikolai Nakhimov (St Petersburg: Sinodal´naia tipografiia, 1912; repr. Moscow: Donskoi Monastyr´, 1994), pp. 188–200 (p. 193). This suggests that the icon described in 'Znamenie' might be dedicated to the Virgin Mary's pallium or cloak (according to Kondakov, the acathist betrays the growing influence of the cult of the Virgin Mary and her pallium in the temple of Blachernae in Constantinople). On the other hand, the Greek term from which the Church Slavonic comparative is derived suggests that the icon might conform either to the 'Virgin Platutera' or 'Orans' type — the most significant figurative element of which consists of the depiction of the Holy Virgin with her hands outstretched — or the 'Znamenie'/'Velikaia Panagiia' type, which similarly depicts the Virgin with hands outstretched, but with a circular image of Jesus Emmanuel hanging like a medallion in front of her chest (this icon prophesises the birth of Christ). On the basis of the text alone, it is not clear which is the case. For detailed background discussion, see N. P. Kondakov, *Ikonografiia Bogomateri*, 2 vols (St Petersburg: Tipografiia Imperatorskoi Akademii nauk, 1914–15), II (1915), 96–123.

6. Kalinskii, pp. 189–93.

7. Here it is explicitly associated with the Holy Virgin : '— Ах ты, горе мое горькое, да что же это за страм такой! Мать Пресвятая, ширьшая небеси, Пет-Павел.' See Zamiatin, 'Nezakonchennoe', p. 124.

8. Ziolkowski, pp. 14–15.

9. 'Iz perepiski s rodnymi', p. 116n.

10. George Heard Hamilton, *The Art and Architecture of Russia* (New Haven: Yale University Press, 1954), p. 164.

11. The symbolism of the Virgin Mary's pallium, which is celebrated by the Orthodox Church on 1 October (hence the name given to the festival, *Pokrov*), derives from the *vita* of St Andrew, a 'fool for Christ's sake' (*iurodivyi Khrista radi*) living in the tenth century. According to this Life, St Andrew has a vision in which he sees the Virgin Mary and her pallium floating in the air above a group of assembled pilgrims in the temple at Blachernae, as if protecting them. It then disappears from view, along with

the Holy Mother, shortly afterwards. For an account of this miracle cited from the menologies, see Kondakov, II, 96–97.

12. The reasons for fasting are given by St Theodosius from the Kievan Cave Monastery: 'И еще надо воздерживаться от обильной пищи, ибо от многоядения и пития безмерного возрастают лукавые, от возросших же помыслов случается грех.' For the sake of clarity, I have given here Likhachev's modern Russian translation of the original. See *PVL* (6582), 217.

13. See Chapter V, 'Iz triodi postnoi', in *Molitvy i pesnopeniia Pravoslavnogo Molitvoslova*, pp. 68–106 (p. 86).

14. See Leonid Andreev, *Sobranie sochinenii*, ed. by I. G. Andreeva, Iu. N. Verchenko, and V. N. Chuvakov, 6 vols (Moscow: Gosudarstvennoe izdatel'stvo khudozhestvennoi literatury, 1990–96), II (1990), 210–64. For further details regarding the reception of the story, and the views expressed at the time by, among others, Zinaida Gippius, Vasilii Rozanov, Leon Trotskii, and Maksimilian Voloshin, see the commentary in ibid., pp. 530–34.

15. Remizov, *Sochineniia*, VIII (1912), 91–184 (p. 168). For further discussion of the use of apocryphal sources in his play, see E. R. Manouelian, 'Judas: apocryphal legend into symbolist drama', *Slavic and East European Journal*, 37 (1993), 44–66. It is worth noting in this regard that Remizov's play, while originally intended to be performed in 1909, was postponed due to the death of the actress, Vera Komissarzhevskaia, in whose theatre it was due to be premièred. Instead it was first performed on the sixth anniversary of her death on 10/23 February 1916 (in other words, just prior to Zamiatin's trip abroad to Great Britain), and was reviewed, among others, by Vladislav Khodasevich in *Utro Rossii*. See the commentary to his '"Prokliatyi prints" A. Remizova', in Vladislav Khodasevich, *Sobranie sochinenii*, ed. by John Malmstad and Robert Hughes (Ann Arbor: Ardis, 1983–), II (1990), 509.

16. Fedor Sologub, *Rasskazy* (Berkeley: Berkeley Slavic Specialties, 1979), pp. 305–14.

17. For discussion of the origins of this legend, and its enormous appeal in West European literature since medieval times, see *Mifologicheskii slovar'*, p. 18; and *ES*, VII, 700–01.

18. For further discussion, see the chapter entitled 'Bienheureuse malédiction: Ahasvérus or le temps de la révolte', in Marie-France Rouart, *Le Mythe du Juif errant* ([Paris]: [José Corti], 1988), pp. 111–88.

19. It is worth noting that in other essays from this period he employs the paradigm in relation to writing. Il´ia Erenburg, for example, is characterized as opting for the most difficult artistic route of all — that of 'all-encroaching scepticism' — which is symbolized by the fate of Ahasuerus ('Erenburg' (IV, 577)). And in his article on the Serapion Brothers, he compares Slonimskii's search for identity and experimentation in different artistic forms with the condition of the Wandering Jew ('Serapionovy brat´ia' (IV, 535)).

20. *Mifologicheskii slovar'*, p. 18. In John Galt's *The Wandering Jew: Or the Travels and Observations of Hareach the Prolonged*, the Jew arrives at Mount Athos. Surly, unsociable, and highly irreligious, he cannot be persuaded to pay attention to the orderly life of the monastery, and in fact is suddenly overcome by an acute attack of demonic hysteria which leaves him with the pale and haggard look of a man exhausted by a great struggle. He dies, and is buried, but his body disappears during the night. See George K. Anderson, *The Legend of the Wandering Jew* (Providence: Brown University Press, 1965), pp. 148–49.

21. *Stranstvuiushchii zhid* (written 1851–52), in V. A. Zhukovskii, *Polnoe sobranie sochinenii*, 3 vols (Moscow: Marks, 1906), II, 474–93 (p. 477). For the piercing gaze as a Romantic leitmotif, see Anderson, pp. 177–79.

22. Seliverst's refusal to talk to the other monks in the monastery is indicated on three separate occasions: 'Молча отдавал встречным из братий поклон, и все запахивался, торопился скорее в келью' (380); 'Молча стоял Селиверст у дверей' (381); and, in the

words of the monks themselves to the pilgrims: '— И с нами ни с кем не разговаривает: куда уж ему с нами, грешными' (382).

23. V. K. Kiukhel'beker, *Izbrannye proizvedeniia v dvukh tomakh*, ed. by N. V. Korolevaia (Moscow–Leningrad: Sovetskii pisatel', 1967), I, 76–138.

24. *Stranstvuiushii zhid*, pp. 488–89.

25. For further discussion, see Harriet Murav-Lavigne, *Scandalous Folly: The Discourse of 'Iurodstvo' in the Works of Dostoevsky* (Ann Arbor: Ardis, 1985), pp. 1–59.

26. 'Zhizn' i deianiia avvy Simeona, Iurodivogo Khrista radi, zapisannye Leontiem, episkopom Neapolia Kritskogo', in *Vizantiiskie legendy*, ed. and trans. into modern Russian by S. V. Poliakova, 2nd edn (Moscow: Ladomir, 1994), pp. 53–83 (pp. 69–70). It is worth recalling in this context the obscene Holy Fool who, according to Zamiatin's memoirs, used to participate in religious processions in Lebedian'. See 'Avtobiografiia' (written 1931), p. 12.

27. For a further discussion of this episode, see Ziolkowski, p. 234.

28. Kalinskii, p. 27. For the origin of the symbolism of this idea in the hymns and teachings of the early Christian fathers, see *Bibleiskaia entsiklopediia*, compiled by Arkhimandrite Nikifor (Moscow: Snegirova, 1891; repr. Moscow: Terra, 1990), p. 416.

29. 'Шла всенощная, бедная, будняя. Редкие свечи — цветы папоротника в купальскую ночь' (379). The *paporotnik* or fern-flower was renowned for its fiery colour and symbolic associations with lightning, flaming tongues of fire, and the sun. According to the folk-religious tradition, it burst into brief and brilliant bloom twice a year in the middle of the night: its colour was so intense that the eye was completely dazzled and all surrounding darkness temporarily dispelled. The two occasions on which it was rumoured to bloom were Easter Sunday and the Eve of St John (23 June). See Afanas'ev, *Poeticheskie vozzreniia slavian na prirodu*, II, 379–80.

30. For the text of the chronicle with a modern translation, see *Pamiatniki literatury drevnei rusi: XIII vek*, ed. by L. A. Dmitrieva and D. S. Likhachev, Pamiatniki literatury drevnei rusi series, 3 (Moscow: Gosudarstvennoe izdatel'stvo khudozhestvennoi literatury, 1981), pp. 211–27. For speculation as to the identity of the authors, see V. L. Komarovich, *Kitezhskaia legenda*, Monuments of Early Russian Literature series, 5 (Moscow: Akademiia nauk SSSR, 1936; repr. Berkeley: Berkeley Slavic Specialties, 1982), pp. 23–48.

31. Ibid., pp. 37–40

32. Space does not permit a detailed list of the numerous occasions on which the Kitezh legend appears in the work of Russian artists at the turn of the century. Aside from the ethnographic treatments in the work of Mel'nikov-Pecherskii, Vladimir Korolenko, and Prishvin, which will be discussed in due course, it is worth mentioning Rimskii-Korsakov's celebrated opera, *Skazanie o nevidimom grade Kitezhe i deve Fevronii*, which was premièred in St Petersburg in February 1907.

33. See the poem entitled 'Kitezh' (written August 1919), in Maksimilian Voloshin, *Stikhotvoreniia v dvukh tomakh*, ed. by B. A. Filippov, G. P. Struve, and N. A. Struve (Paris: YMCA, 1982), I, 233–35; and the sermon/lament entitled 'Slovo o pogibeli Russkoi Zemli', in Aleksei Remizov, *Ognennaia Rossiia* (Revel: Bibliofil, 1921), pp. 10–24 (p. 20) (first publ. in *Skify*, II (1918)).

34. V. Turbin, 'Kitezhane. Iz zapisok russkogo intelligenta', in *Pogruzhenie v triasinu: Anatomiia zastoia*, ed. by T. A. Notkina (Moscow: Progress, 1991), pp. 346–70.

35. *V lesakh* (Book IV, Chapter 2). Korolenko's account of his travels to the lake forms the second chapter of a lengthy account of his wanderings entitled *V pustynnykh mestakh* (1890). See V. G. Korolenko, *Sobranie sochinenii*, ed. by S. V. Korolenko and N. V. Korolenko-Liakhovich, 10 vols (Moscow: Gosudarstvennoe izdatel'stvo khudo-zhestvennoi literatury, 1953–56), III (1954), 110–208 (pp. 128–43). Prishvin's account of his visit to the lake, an ethnographic report entitled 'Svetloe ozero', was first published in 1909 under the title 'U sten grada nevidimogo'. See Prishvin, *Sobranie sochinenii*, II (1956), 395–475.

36. *V lesakh*, I, 5 (Book I, Chapter 1).

37. Ibid., II, 287–314 (Book IV, Chapter 1).
38. Korolenko, p. 131.
39. The stories about people having reached Kitezh take the form of a tale told to him by a local fisherman. This man tells him a story from his youth about an Old Believer who claims one day to have been blessed by a vision of the holy city and to have been able to hear its bells tolling at the bottom of the lake. Interpreting this as a sign that he is soon to be summoned there, he stops eating and drinking, and sells his beehives, his hut, and all his worldly belongings. The fisherman claims to have seen the old man later in the presence of two mysterious monks; the next day he simply disappears. It is rumoured in the local village that he was later seen in a boat in the middle of the lake with these two monks —the fisherman therefore believes that he was being taken to Kitezh. As he explains to Korolenko: '— На дне тоже самое монастырь. И на самой середке главны ворота.' See ibid., pp. 137–40.
40. The Kostroma Academic Society claimed to have discovered several such legends in areas immediately bordering Svetloiar, many of them deriving from historical events of the past. See Vas. Smirnov, 'Potonuvshie kolokola', in *Tretii etnograficheskii sbornik*, pp. 1–4.
41. Evgenii Zamiatin, 'Iz literaturnogo naslediia', p. 77.
42. Ibid. One of the *beguny* in Mel′nikov-Pecherskii's novel describes the bells as follows: '— И егда приидет час блаженным утреню во граде Китеже пети, услышите звон серебряных колоколов... Густой звон, малиновый — век слушай, не наслушаешься...' See *V lesakh*, II, 302 (Book IV, Chapter 2). For the subtitle of the opera, see L. Danilevich, *Poslednie opery N. A. Rimskogo-Korsakova* (Moscow: Gosudarstvennoe muzykal′noe izdatel′stvo, 1961), p. 174.
43. Zamiatin, 'Iz literaturnogo naslediia', p. 77. For a sense of the location, including the specific location of Dievo Gorodishche in relation to the Upper Volga, see *Bol′shoi vsemirnyi nastol′nyi atlas Marksa* (St Petersburg: Marks, 1905), illustration nos. 20 & 21.
44. The later and most complete version of the chronicle hails from Yaroslavl, while the village of Sopelki, which lies on the south bank of the Volga only a few miles southeast of Dievo Gorodishche, was the birthplace of the *beguny* and thus, in all likelihood, the chronicle itself. See Komarovich, pp. 39–41.
45. Ibid., p. 22.
46. 'Iz perepiski s rodnymi', 116n.
47. 'Гребенки, пряники, красные баклуши' (383). In the first version of the story, however, Zamiatin had preserved the geographical specificity of the items, but in two cases substituted the names of different (and obscure) towns — here he refers to combs from Iaropol′, cakes from Kropivensk, and wooden artefacts from Dievo Gorodischche. See IMLI, opis′ 1, ed. khr. 39, p. 3. In actual fact, Dievo Gorodischche and the artefacts associated with it are the sole explicit link between 'Monastyr′' and 'Znamenie'.
48. Prishvin, p. 426.
49. The *Povest′ i vzyskanie o grade sokrovennom Kitezhe* is mentioned by all three writers, although it is universally recognized as an Old Believer fiction. In Mel′nikov-Pecherskii's novel, for example, the fictional character Vasilii Borisovich confronts the elderly monk reading excerpts from the *Povest′* and corrects him on a point of historical accuracy. See *V lesakh*, II, 289–90 (Book IV, Chapter 2). Prishvin meets a local scholar living in the village of Shadrino, only two versts away from the lake, who presents him with a copy of the Kitezh Chronicle and also informs him that the legend is historically inaccurate. See Prishvin, pp. 429–30.
50. The fact that Batu Khan razed the city to the ground is mentioned in the original chronicle: 'И после того разорения запустели города те, малый Китеж, что на берегу Волги стоит, и Большой, что на берегу озера Светлояра.' See 'Legenda o grade Kitezhe', p. 219.
51. It is interesting to note that the Kitezh chronicler also uses *miatezhnyi* in the context of historical upheaval: 'И сей град Большой Китеж невидим стал и оберегаем рукою

божиею, — так под конец века нашего многомятежного и слез достойного покрыл Господ тот град дланию своею.' See ibid., p. 225.

52. 'Iz perepiski s rodnymi', p. 115.
53. Petrovskii, p. 82.
54. This is an anecdote which clearly dates from after the Revolution, yet the way in which it is recounted suggests that Zamiatin was aware of this man's existence well beforehand. See Zamiatin, 'Iz bloknotov 1914–1928 godov' (1989), pp. 133–34.

CHAPTER 6

THE *CHUDESA* OR MIRACLE STORIES

Introduction

'O sviatom grekhe Zenitsy-devy. Slovo pokhval´noe' (1917), 'O tom, kak istselen byl otrok Erazm' (1922), and 'O chude, proisshedshem v Pepel´nuiu Sredu' (1926) were published together for the first time only in 1989 — it is here, strikingly, that they appear under the collective heading of *chudesa* or 'stories of the miraculous'.[1] This title is significant and at the same time misleading. In sacred writing, the term *chudo* refers to an account of a miracle performed by a righteous figure of the Orthodox Church — it may appear as a fragment within a longer narrative, or independently, and therefore belongs formally to the loose and amorphous tradition better known as hagiography.[2] Since, however, Zamiatin's stories assume the guises of ecclesiastical narratives in order to subvert and undermine their Christian message, it would be better to define them as mock-hagiography or parodies in the hagiographic style, i.e. as 'miracle stories' in inverted commas. On the one hand, they exploit the stock themes (*topoi*) of saintly biography, and combine the dual elements of laudation and edification which characterize and unite the various sub-genres of hagiographic literature;[3] while on the other hand, they are counterfeit texts and neo-fabulist forgeries, the *jouissance* of which, to borrow briefly from Barthes, consists of gradually stripping away the impression of authenticity to reveal the underlying burlesque and carnivalesque intent.[4] Furthermore, as will be made clear in this chapter, their polemical target is not only the moral teaching of the Church. These are allegorical satires aimed at specific events in the ideological and cultural arena, ones which don the mask of the monastic chronicler as a screening device with which to communicate provocative, controversial, and politically sensitive messages.

Consideration of 'Pepel´naia Sreda' is excluded from the analysis which follows. This is because the action is located not in Russia as such, but in some indeterminate country in Central Europe. More importantly, while obviously exploiting themes and *topoi* from the hagiographic tradition, and thus conforming to the notion of mock-hagiography, it is not a stylization or linguistic performance in the manner of the two earlier *chudesa*, and does not seek to create the illusion of an author whose narrative purports to have been written at some point in the distant past; for this reason, it cannot be considered a 'stylization of Rus´' in the strict sense.[5] By contrast, the archaic stylization of 'Zenitsa-deva' and 'Otrok Erazm' is their defining formal characteristic, and provides the main source of estrangement for the modern reader. Indeed, like some of the stories of the early provincial period, such as 'Pravda istinnaia' (1916), they are explicit *skaz* narratives in the sense that their alleged authorship derives from a persona explicitly not identified in the first instance with Zamiatin himself. In the sense, moreover, that they are laughter texts with roots in the Bakhtinian notion of the carnivalesque — in his work on Rabelais, for example, Bakhtin included parodies of sacred genres as belonging to the carnival sphere[6] — they belong to a category in Zamiatin's prose fiction which is aimed at the subversion of public mores. It is indicative that neither work could be published in a mainstream outlet, and that publication, while possible because of a temporary and (as it later proved) short-lived liberalization in censorship, brought Zamiatin into conflict with the new authorities and led to his condemnation as a 'counter-revolutionary' and oppositional figure. 'Zenitsa-deva', for example, was published in *Delo naroda*, the official organ of the SRs, which was subject to persistent harassment throughout 1917 and 1918, and eventually forced to close down in 1919; while 'Otrok Erazm' appeared courtesy of Zinovii Grzhebin's émigré-based Petropolis publishing house, one of the few semi-autonomous outlets for independent and free-thinking writers in the early 1920s (it was eventually forced to shut down in 1923), but in a print-run of only one thousand copies.

The first section of this chapter is devoted to providing a literary context for these parodies. Attention will be drawn to the interest generally in saints' Lives in the work of Russian writers in the nineteenth and early twentieth centuries, in particular in the writings of Aleksei Remizov, a close associate and collaborator of Zamiatin's at this stage in his literary career. Remizov's stylizations of folk-religious material, both in terms of language and form, establish a vitally important precedent for Zamiatin, and probably explain his interest in the potential of archaic material from 1915 onwards. The conceit of ecclesiastical authenticity, bolstered by the use of archaic lexicon, syntax, and grammar, will be the subject of detailed examination.

Moreover, I will be seeking to identify the aesthetic impact of such texts in the context of the literary norms prevailing at the beginning of the twentieth century. As parodies which assume blasphemous disguises, and as allegorical satires which offer concealed commentaries on contemporary political and cultural events, they will be approached as a modern form of *skomoroshina*, or clowning, which paves the way for the dramatic conceit of the later *Blokha*. They are quintessential illustrations of the growing ecleticism of Zamiatin's writing, and usher in a new phase in his career characterized by increasing frivolity and whimsy.

Background

The use of saints' Lives as literary sources enjoyed something of a vogue in the latter half of the nineteenth century, attracting writers as diverse as Dostoevskii, Tolstoi, Leskov, A. K. Tolstoi, and Dmitrii Merezhkovskii, to name but a few.[7] On the whole, these authors were concerned more with the value of the Christian message contained in the Lives, and their relevance for modern-day humanity, than with their literary form or style. It was common to borrow individual episodes from well-known *vitae*, to model fictional characters on celebrated saintly types, to adapt a particular *vita* for a modern, secular audience, and to rework entire narratives for polemical, sometimes anti-ecclesiastical purposes. It is rare, on the other hand, to find these authors imitating the style and language of their hagiographic source. For the most part, the *topoi* of sacred biography are transferred unmodified to a modern setting, and the language remains recognizably contemporary, even in those cases, such as Leskov's adaptations of the Greek Synaxarion (in Russian, *Prolog*), where the action of the narrative takes place in antiquity.[8]

Only at the beginning of the twentieth century does this purely thematic emphasis undergo significant and radical revision. This is most evident in the work of Remizov, whose stylizations of archaic folk-religious narratives are concentrated primarily in the period from 1907 to 1917. They include such pre-war collections as *Limonar'* (1907), the title of which is borrowed from a thirteenth-century Byzantine patristic miscellany by John Moschus (*ES*, XVII, 691–92); *Paraleipomenon* (1912), which takes its title from the two apocryphal books of the Old Testament after Kings (ibid., XXI, 763); *Tsep' zlataia* (1913), the title of which refers to a fifteenth-century miscellany of homiletic literature, i.e. *Zlataia tsep'* (ibid., XII, 600–01); *Podorozhie* (1913), which adopts the anecdotal form of the paterikon and contains several stories narrated by fictitious monastic personae; the two war collections *Za sviatuiu Rus´: Dumy o rodnoi zemle* (1915) and *Ukrepa: Slovo k russkoi zemle o zemle rodnoi, tainostiakh zemnykh i sud´be* (1916); and finally the lament for the destruction of Old Russia at the hands of war and revolution, *Slovo o pogibeli Russkoi Zemli* (1917). Analysis of these collections reveals an eclectic body of work which relies on a wide range of folk-religious sources: spiritual songs, apocrypha, menological collections, Byzantine patristic miscellanies, the Synaxarion, sermons, and various hagiographic sub-genres.[9]

Remizov's experiments in this field constitute a massive restatement of Orthodox Russia's cultural and literary heritage. However, it is primarily the unorthodox religiosity of the folk which he seeks to communicate in these stories, rather than the elevated pieties and dogmas of the official Church. His interest in the apocryphal, marginalized, and heretical — strikingly illustrated in his pornographic aetiological tale *Chto est´ tabak* (1908), but also evident in his unorthodox treatment of biblical subjects and motifs — has given rise to the idea of him as essentially a transgressional and ambiguous figure. Greta Slobin, for example, describes him as a modern-day merryman or *skomorokh* who rejected all forms of religious and secular authority.[10] Certainly, the private inauguration in 1908 of Obezvelvolpal, a mock-literary society dedicated to anarchy and the exploration of sexual taboos, might be said to offer strong evidence in support of this view. In a number of miniature texts which accompanied the public declaration of this society, Remizov championed the idea of authorship as a form of *skomoroshina* aimed at official hypocrisy and mendacity — as he loftily declared: 'Ложь всегда будет ложью, а лицемерие всегда будет лицемерием, чем бы они ни прикрывались.'[11] It is indicative of the close relationship between Remizov and Zamiatin during this period that Zamiatin was co-opted into Obezvelvolpal under the title of 'Zamutius, Bishop of the Apes' in 1919. This is the title under which he responds to Remizov's *skomorokh* manifesto with a pseudo-ecclesiastical laughter text of his own — also entitled 'Tulumbas' (III, 72–74) — which was published in the same journal as Remizov's miniature, and thus declarative in intent.[12] It is further noteworthy that Zamiatin, as one of the editors at the Alkonost publishing house, must have been involved in the reprinting of *Chto est´ tabak* in 1920 as part of a collection of Remizov short stories. This was a blatantly provocative act, since the story in question was clearly offensive even to the new revolutionary sensibility, and the title of the collection, *Zavetnye skazy*, alluded specifically to Afanas´ev's bawdy Russian folk tales, which even in the supposedly heady days of sexual licentiousness after the October Revolution were still deemed unsuitable for publication.[13]

If the period from 1915 to 1920 marks the high point in the artistic collaboration between Remizov and Zamiatin, it is more than likely that the experiments of the former in the field of historical stylization to a certain extent explain the latter's remarks on ecclesiastical literature and language in 'O iazyke', his lecture at the House of Arts. These are intriguing, not only for the light they shed on his writing techniques generally (the language of the early stories, as we have seen, is also characterized by a mixture of the archaic, ecclesiastical, and vernacular), but also for the range of sources with which he was familiar, some of them directly relevant for his own *chudesa*. In this lecture, Zamiatin recommended a number of antique materials with which, in his view, the modern writer should be acquainted: these included various examples of medieval ecclesiastical literature, apocrypha, acathists, and menologies or *chet'i minei* (readings from the Lives of saints, arranged according to the calendar month), in particular those compiled by the Old Believers (IV, 379). He also drew attention to the deforming of church books and menologies of various kinds during the reign of Peter the Great — according to Zamiatin, this took the form of replacing old words with new ones, the purging of primitive and vulgar expressions, and the censoring of love episodes and miracles which, while 'enchanting', were deemed either fanciful or absurd (ibid., 379). He blamed this phenomenon on the 'positivist spirit' prevailing at the time, in all likelihood a reference to the *Reading Menaea* of Metropolitan Dmitrii of Rostov, which was compiled in the latter half of the seventeenth and the beginning of the eighteenth centuries on the basis of Western (Bollandist) sources.[14] Zamiatin's insistence that this literature be read in the original suggests that, like Remizov, he was acquainted with unexpurgated versions. Furthermore, like Remizov, whom he characterized later in the lecture as a celebrated specialist in the field of schismatic literature (IV, 380), his privileging of the pre-Petrine over the post-Petrine, and his championing of the older, purer forms of the language, suggested a conservative writer whose brand of modernism, paradoxically, consisted of a renewal of the linguistic present through retrieval of its past.

It has been suggested on the basis of their linguistic texture that the folk-religious stylizations of Remizov and Zamiatin constitute a novel form of *ostranenie*. Lampl, for example, argues that their use of anachronistic and obsolete word-forms not only expanded the norms of modern Russian, but ruptured them altogether.[15] In so far as this strategy complements the *skaz* stylizations of the early provincial period, it is possible to view the *chudesa* as a particular brand of literary populism; indeed, as we have seen already, Eikhenbaum mentioned the biographies of the saints (*zhitiia*) and monastic chronicles (*letopisi*) in his definition of *lubok*.[16] The conceit of Zamiatin's *chudesa* depends firstly on the notion that the folk-religious imagination is characterized by a belief in the miraculous; secondly, that the *topos* of the miracle in saints' Lives had caused certain commentators to treat the genre of saintly biography as a form of fabular fiction, rather than the edificatory treatment of historical fact;[17] and thirdly that there were popular brands of hagiography — for example, the sermons read out during church services and the abbreviated versions of Lives offered by the menologies — which were intended for mass consumption and thus less elevated, rhetorical, and sophisticated than the narratives produced for monastic or clerical readers. In this context, it is useful to bear in mind that cheap, accessible, and largely abridged versions of the Lives of popular saints were being distributed in the countryside and sold at markets and fairs with great success at the turn of the century.[18]

The approach which emphasizes the aesthetic impact of the *chudesa* in terms of *ostranenie* is all well and good; it does, however, ignore the vital element of the carnivalesque in these stories and their essentially comic ambitions. One of the key differences between Zamiatin and Remizov, for example, lies in their respective attitudes to the Orthdox literary heritage and the manner in which they manipulate their sacred material. For all his transgressions and occasional straying into the field of pornography, Remizov is celebratory in his reworking of sacred models. His stylized adaptations, with their poetic exploration of archaic language and mixture of high and low genres, constitute a genuine renewal of form and language on the part of a literary modernist; indeed rarely, apart from *Chto est' tabak*, does he seek to provoke through parody or blasphemy (few of his works are laughter texts in the strictly Bakhtinian sense, and almost none encountered hostility from the censors). The novelty of Zamiatin's parodies, by contrast, lay in his carnivalesque sense of playfulness and the blatant incongruity between the elevated ecclesiastical tone of the narrative and the occasionally obscene content. While it is clear that he derived pleasure from the archaic language of Old Russian, in particular those words which had become obsolete, or the meaning of which had changed subtly over the centuries, he was suspicious of the eternal truths of Orthodox religion and sought to undermine them. His 'miracle tales' mock not only the hagiographic tradition, but also the very saints themselves, their spiritual achievement, and the fantasies of the miraculous which constitute the unofficial fabrication of their legends. They are blasphemous in the sense that they ridicule the sacred objects of Christian veneration, in particular the cult of the Virgin Mary. Furthermore, while relatively tasteful in comparison with such extreme works as *Chto est´ tabak*, they are vulgar and bawdy in the sense that they incorporate sexually explicit material into what is usually considered a puritanical and prudish mode of discourse. In short, much more so than Remizov, Zamiatin's mock versions of this genre deserve the epithet *skomoroshina*.

'Zenitsa-deva'

The plot of 'Zenitsa-deva' appears simple and straightforward. The author records the tale of a beautiful young girl who decides to sacrifice that which is most precious — her virginity — in order to save her country from oppression at the hands of a barbaric and ruthless foreign warlord. After a brief opening declamation, in which the author praises the 'saintly sin' of the Precious Virgin, and explains that by succumbing to a sin of the flesh she succeeds in saving her soul, the reader learns of a miraculous healing which took place while the virgin was still a young girl. While drinking a bowl of water from her father's cistern, she accidentally swallows a tiny snake — this swells up inside her stomach and gives her the appearance of being pregnant. After the unsuccessful attempts of local sages to rid her of this unwanted incumbent, the girl turns to a Gothic miracle-worker called Ulfil who makes a mysterious sign and succeeds in banishing it. The young girl is sufficiently impressed by this miracle to adopt the commandments of his faith: she devotes her life to the poor, and refuses marriage, preferring to lead a life of virtuous chastity. When the land is invaded by the barbaric Erman, however, her first thoughts are with the women and young girls taken prisoner and tortured by his hot-blooded warriors. Seeking Erman in person, she brokers a deal whereby her body is offered in exchange for a cessation of brutalities. For thirty days there is an armistice and the nation rejoices. Erman becomes frustrated by her lack of ardour, however. Cruelly rebuffed, he reneges on his agreement, subjects her to terrible tortures, and imprisons her in the cistern from which she first contracted the mysterious illness in her youth. For three days and nights she prays for divine intervention, during which time earthquakes and storms ravage the country, and frighten the invading Goths into fleeing. It is recorded that her terrible wounds miraculously heal and that she dies a number of years later, revered and honoured by a grateful nation.

Before proceeding to interpret the narrative content of 'Zenitsa-deva', and to assess its polemical and allegorical strategies, it is crucial to stress that there are problems relating to the dating of the text which vitally affect our reception of it. This is particularly important in view of the suspicion that Zamiatin may be satirizing events in the political sphere (although clearly set in antiquity, the mention of a conflict between Teutonic and Slavic tribes alone is suggestive in the context of the First World War). Furthermore, the archaic stylization of the text gives rise to problems of comprehension. Not only is there evidence that Zamiatin made a number of mistakes himself in relation to the meanings of certain archaic words, but there are several errors and inconsistencies in the versions of the text hitherto published for which the editors must ultimately be held responsible. It is ironic, bearing in mind the ecclesiastical conceit of the narrative, that none of these versions matches the four draft variants preserved in IMLI, and thus that there is at present no 'canonical' version of 'Zenitsa-deva'. None of the articles devoted to the *chudesa* hitherto has paid any attention to this aspect of the text.[19] Yet these problems must be resolved before proper consideration can be given to the aesthetic qualities of 'Zenitsa-deva' and its various literary strategies.

'Zenitsa-deva' was first published on 15/28 October 1917 in the SR newspaper *Delo naroda*. All the available evidence, however, suggests that it was conceived and written prior to Zamiatin's departure for Great Britain in March 1916. The first mention of the story occurs in a letter dated 22 April/5 May 1916 from Zamiatin to Remizov while still in Newcastle; the manner in which he refers to the narrative suggests that Remizov is in possession of a manuscript and has been requested to find a publisher.[20] This would seem to be confirmed by the next reference to the story in a letter to his wife dated 28 April/11 May 1916, in which he refers to a 'proof' (*RN*, I, 200). In the absence of more detailed information, we can only speculate about the reasons for the extended delay in publication. Nevertheless, it seems to have been responsible for the incorrect dating of the four draft variants of 'Zenitsa-deva' in the Zamiatin archive (IMLI, opis´ 1, ed. khr. 58, 59, 60, & 61). For reasons which are still obscure, these were all initially dated 1918. Later, however, presumably in recognition of the actual date of publication, the date was crossed out and replaced with 1917, this in spite of the fact that the fourth version is typewritten and conforms to the new orthography (Lunacharskii's decree took effect from 1 January 1918). A similar confusion has accompanied the reprinted versions of the story. The Neimanis edition dates the story from 1917, yet the version published differs markedly from the text in *Delo naroda* (since the Neimanis version does not accord with any of the draft variants preserved in IMLI, its provenance must be considered something of a mystery). The Galushkin edition, which is reprinted from the text in *Delo naroda*, but (unfortunately) modernizes the orthography, dates the story to 1916. It should be clear from the evidence cited above that 'Zenitsa-deva' was written at some point prior to March 1916. Furthermore, the existence of so many draft variants of the text, and the very minor discrepancies between them, suggest perhaps that the difficulties involved in the stylization forced Zamiatin to accept certain adjustments, either at the behest of Remizov or the editors at *Delo naroda*, prior to the story being ready for publication.

Since the *Delo naroda* version as reprinted by Galushkin is the most authoritative available, and accords closely to drafts 60 and 61 in the archive, it will form the basis for the reading of the text which follows. It is clear, nevertheless, that certain minor errors and inconsistencies have arisen as a result of the archaic stylization of the language. These relate not only to the spellings of certain words, but also to their meaning, and it is not always clear to whom the blame should be attributed. Where an alternative and correct version is given in the drafts, it can only be assumed that the editors at *Delo naroda* or Galushkin are at fault; whereas if the drafts contain the same errors, it must be assumed that Zamiatin himself is responsible.

In the former category, we should include the sentence which tells of the virgin's response to her incarceration: 'Три дня с молитвой и терпением добриим' (530, line 38). The last word here should read *dobliim*, the archaic term for 'courageous' and 'brave' (Srez., I, 673), since *dobrii* does not make sense in this context (the drafts are unanimous on this point, and the phrase *doblee terpenie* appears in a list of archaic expressions which Zamiatin noted down prior to writing the story).[21] A further mistake or oversight arises in relation to the number of years lived before the virgin's death: 'И так лет В̃ пребывала, и уже преклонна днями была, образ же юной девы имела все тот же' (531, lines 1–3). This has been indicated according to the Byzantine practice of using letters from the alphabet — the letter В̃, however, which signifies the number two, appears extremely unlikely in the context (it is worth noting that draft variants 59, 60, and 61 all give the letter И̃ (i.e. eight), whereas the Neimanis version (III, 67) gives the letter М̃ (i.e. forty)). Lastly, there is an inconsistency in the spelling of the adjective meaning

'Hellenian': 'Изваяно же на камени том словесы эллинскими, и словен-
скими, и готскими' (531, lines 12–13). As we can see here, Galushkin has
presented us with the modern spelling (эллинский), which does not
derive from the *Delo naroda* version, and is the form preferred in the
(modernized) draft variant 61; whereas the pre-revolutionary draft
version 59 gives the archaic spelling (еллинский), which would be more
appropriate in view of the stylistic conceit.

In the latter category of error, we should also include Zamiatin's
intriguing use of the adjective *nevostiagnovennyi* in relation to Erman's
complaint about the young virgin's lack of ardour: '— Пошто от
страстей невостягновенна ты?' (530, line 23). This would appear to owe
its origin to the archaic *vostiagnut´*, which means 'to bridle', but is the
exact reverse of the meaning implied by the context (Erman is clearly
not accusing the girl of 'unbridled' passion, but of frigidity).[22] The
presence of this same word in drafts 59 and 60, and its absence in 61,
suggests that the error may have been pointed out to Zamiatin at some
point after the text was published, and for this reason was subsequently removed (it is possible, perhaps, that he was confusing this
word with *nevstiagnovennyi*, which means 'unrepentant' and
'desperate' (D´iachenko, 341)).

The presence of these errors is by no means crucial, but they are
indicative of the hazards encountered by the reader when dealing with
this type of stylization. Many of the archaic forms employed can be
traced to the ecclesiastical documents of the early medieval period
which Zamiatin recommended to his students of creative writing in 'O
iazyke'. In this lecture, for example, he describes 'Zenitsa-deva' as an
'experiment' in which he sought to create the illusion of an early
medieval text:

'Зеница дева' — трудный, но удавшийся эксперимент стилизации языка: вещь
написана отнюдь не по-древнеславянски, но создает иллюзию.[23]

In general, Zamiatin is careful to facilitate the reader's task and make
the language accessible and comprehensible. Some of the forms he
incorporates, for example, can be traced easily from their modern
Russian derivations (the following are given with these spellings in
Sreznevskii): *zlatyi* (528, line 6); *okrugnii* (ibid., line 17); *tselit´* (ibid.,
line 21); *rekovat´* (ibid., line 24); *sazhda* (ibid., line 28); *povedat´* (529, line 31);
skvernennik (530, line 28); *oplenenie* (ibid., line 46); *umertvie* (531, line 5);
and *slovenskii* (ibid., line 13). Others, while archaic and ecclesiastical in
origin, were still part of the folk-religious lexicon at the turn of the
century (the following can all be found in Dal´): *otverstyi* (528, line 2);

kudesnik (ibid., line 16); *volshba* (ibid., line 18); *tokmo* (= *tol'ko*) (ibid., line 30); *viashche* (= *bol'she*) (ibid., line 31); *ud* (= *chlen, chast' tela*) (529, line 21); *divii* (ibid., line 37); *brashno* (= *pishche, sned'*) (ibid., line 42); *zloumnyi* (530, line 34); *trus* (= *zemletriasenie, grom*) (ibid., line 40); and *chut'* (531, line 5). The *jouissance* of the narrative, however, relies to a certain extent on words which were either obsolete at the time of writing, or the meaning of which had altered subtly over the preceding centuries. It is precisely this type of word which indicates Zamiatin's enormous debt to medieval ecclesiastical sources and his desire to resurrect the old in the service of the new.

Without access to a dictionary of early medieval Russian, or a specialist knowledge of medieval ecclesiastical literature, it is likely that the following words would have posed difficulties (the literary sources cited here are not unique in their employment of these words, and are indicative only of their archaic origin). *Otrozhdennyi* (528, line 6), for example, derives from the Greek *patrogennitos* (literally, a 'begetting from the father'), and appears to have been borrowed from the text of a sacred song of praise (*kanon*) sung at Easter (D'iachenko, 397). *Ves'* (528, line 1; & 530, line 42), which means 'village' (*derevnia*) or 'settlement' (*selenie*), can be found in the eleventh to thirteenth century Nikonian chronicle (*SRIa XI*, II, 122). *Lepota* (528, line 36; & 529, line 41), a synonym of *krasota*, features in the *Sinaiskii paterik*, an eleventh-century patirikon, as well as Epiphanius the Wise's fourteenth-century *Zhitie Stefana Permskogo* (*SRIa XI*, VIII, 209). *Brakoneiskusnyi* (529, line 10), which means 'virginal', and derives from the Russian noun for marriage (*brak*) and the adjective meaning 'without experience' (*neiskusnyi*), occurs in an eleventh-century *Triod' postnaia* or prayer book (*SRIa XI*, I, 165), as well as certain acathists.[24] *Liashcha mochenaia* (529, line 47), a genus of lentil (*aqua maceratus*), appears in the thirteenth-century *Skitskii paterik* (*SRIa XI*, VIII, 351). *Steblie* (530, line 5), *pace* Rogachevskaia, who mistakes this noun for a neologism, means 'straw' or 'stalk' (in modern Russian, *stebel'*), and occurs in Ilarion's eleventh-century *Slovo o zakone i blagodati* (Srez., III, 583). And *liute* (530, line 6), meaning 'woe' (in modern Russian, *gore*), can be found in the *Povest' vremennykh let* (*PVL*(6523), 62).

Those words, the archaic spelling of which initially renders them difficult to identify with their modern equivalents, should also be added to this list of obsolete items. For example, *skarpiia* (528, line 14; & 530, line 41) is one of three archaic spellings for 'scorpion' (in modern Russian, *skorpion*) — it appears with this spelling in the *Izbornik Sviatoslavov*, a translation into Church Slavonic of an eleventh-century patristic miscellany compiled by John the Deacon (Srez., III, 366). *Pelyn´* (530, line 6), the archaic spelling of *polyn´*, and thus meaning 'wormwood' or 'poison', occurs in the twelfth-century *Slovo Daniila Zatochnika* (*SRIa XI*, XIV, 14). Finally *inii* (530, line 37), the archaic spelling for *inei* (i.e. hoarfrost), occurs in a thirteenth-century *Irmologion* or book of sung prayer (Srez., I, 1100).

A related problem consists of words, the archaic sense of which differs subtly from the modern. *Prel´shchat´*, for instance, the verb which appears in the sentence 'Кудесники стали прельщать его кознями пестрых словес' (528, line 22), here means 'to trick' or 'deceive' (Srez., II, 1661–62). *Pestryi*, in the same sentence, means 'cunning' or 'sly', rather than its modern sense of 'motley' or 'varied'.[25] *Nerazumnyi* (529, line 19), which means 'devoid of reason' or 'stupid' in modern Russian, is employed in the archaic sense of 'unclear' (*neiasnyi*) or 'incomprehensible' (*neponiatnyi*) (Srez., II, 422). The word employed to describe Erman's residence, *khlevina* (529, line 34), which means 'barn' in modern Russian (Dal´, IV, 553), could refer in antiquity to a house, cell, fortified bank, trench, rampart, or dugout (D´iachenko, 789). The noun *ozloblenie* used by the young virgin ('— Тленное телесе озлобление оскорбит меня только здесь' (530, line 15)), rather than deriving from the modern verb meaning 'to embitter' (*ozlobliat´*), possesses the archaic nuance of 'suffering' (*stradanie*) and 'torture' (*muchenie*) (Srez., II, 637). Lastly *poklonnyi* (531, line 2), an adjective which derives from the noun *poklon*, is here employed in the archaic sense of 'bowed' or 'bent' (with age), rather than the modern sense of 'humble' (*pokornyi*) (D´iachenko, 446).

'Zenitsa-deva' is a fascinating *exercice du style* for the reader and scholar alike. The tracing of certain archaic words and the fixing of their meaning has its own peculiar pleasures, not least of which is the encounter with the language in its old and antiquated forms. As we will see, the narrative is a burlesque parody in so far as it exploits an archaic generic form and linguistic register for the purpose of subversion; it is a carnivalized or laughter text in the Bakhtinian understanding, the comic effect of which relies on the subtle puncturing of an elaborate illusion of solemnity and stylistic authenticity. Furthermore, much in the manner of Saltykov-Shchedrin's celebrated *Istoriia odnogo goroda* (1869), a 'found document' purportedly dating from the early eighteenth century, this stylistic mantle conceals a polemical and satirical attack on various doctrines and attitudes associated with the Orthodox Church, not merely in the sphere of personal morality, but also in the wider public and political arena. In essence, the

hagiographic conceit is a literary 'Trojan horse' by means of which
Zamiatin can mock Orthodox models of saintliness and virtue, the role
of princely saints in protecting the nation from catastrophe and
invasion, and Christian apologetics on the subject of war. The obvious
relevance of these themes in the context of the First World War gives
rise to the suspicion that the narrative seeks to subvert not only a series
of patriotic ideological positions, but also their expropriation and abuse
by artists in support of the war effort. It will be argued here that the
echoes of contemporary events in 'Zenitsa-deva' relate both to the
sphere of canonization as an instrument of imperial policy and the
unsuccessful military prosecution of the war with Germany. Indeed,
while the position which Zamiatin adopts in relation to these events
may be broadly defined as pacifist, the flippancy of 'Zenitsa-deva' and
its whimsical treatment of the subject of war borders on literary
anarchism. The result is a multi-layered and complex text which can be
approached from a variety of different angles.

(i)   Orthodox models of saintliness: the conceit of authenticity

The title of 'Zenitsa-deva' (*slovo pokhval´noe*) refers to the encomiastic
sermon, a liturgical address in the ornate style with roots going back to
the early Christian Church and the Greek funeral oration.[26] The
primary function of this sermon was to praise an outstanding person,
whether a martyr or non-martyr, whose piety, devotion to God, and
miraculous powers were deemed worthy of veneration. Composition
was associated with the day on which this person was buried, the
anniversary of his or her death, or the ceremony during which his or
her relics were examined officially as evidence of saintliness.[27] It was
common for the encomiastic sermon to precede the longer *vita*, and
thus it formed part of the campaign by means of which an outstanding
person venerated by a local church or Christian fraternity could be
promoted for canonization.[28] It has been observed, moreover, that the
vita and encomiastic sermon have a number of traits in common, these
being defined in terms of their shared 'disposition of themes'.[29] The
encomiastic sermon must therefore be distinguished from the simple
eulogy or panegyric (also a *pokhval´noe slovo*) which usually appeared at
the end of a saint's Life, but differed from the sermon in that it was not
a chronologically driven account, but a rhetorical enumeration of qualities and accomplishments.[30] The fact that Zamiatin conceived his story
initially in the form of a *vita* — the title of draft variant 59 is 'Zhitie i
konchina sviataia Zenitsy-devy' — indicates his awareness of the

stylistic affinities between the biographical account and the encomiastic sermon. Moreover, his awareness of the liturgical function of the sermon is suggested by the fact that he rejected two draft variants (58 and 60) in which the ostensible author reveals himself to be a monk who has witnessed the events in question.[31] While this would have lent his literary account a sense of immediacy and authenticity, it assumes an audience of clerical or lay *readers* (more typical of the *vita*), rather than congregational *listeners* (more typical of the *pokhval´noe slovo*).

By means of the title given to the ostensible author, Zamiatin establishes a level of literary expectation on the part of the reader. This initial impression of authenticity is then consolidated through careful development of the plot and the characterization of the main female protagonist. Her virginity and martyrdom (*muchenie*) are obviously crucial elements in this conceit. Several leitmotifs employed in relation to the Precious Virgin echo *topoi* in the legends (*passiones*) of the virgin-martyrs.[32] Her name alludes both to the Virgin Mary — in the Life of her parents, for example, she is described as the 'apple of their eye' (*zenitsa oka*) — and a number of female martyrs for whom *deva* is part of their name.[33] Like the majority of these women, she is blessed with great beauty and parents of noble stock. Like St Irina (f.d. 5 May), she is converted to the faith as a young girl and experiences a prophetic sign in relation to her conversion (*ZVS*, 233–34). Like St Tat´iana (f.d. 12 January), she devotes herself in her youth to charitable work on behalf of the poor and destitute (ibid., 30). Like St Barbara (f.d. 4 December), and many others, she rejects the possibility of marriage with a wealthy suitor in order not to compromise her faith (ibid., 680–82). Like all the virgin-martyrs, she suffers vicious reprisals at the hands of an evil figure of authority because of her refusal to renounce her faith — as in the case of St Agnes (f.d. 21 January) and St Catherine (f.d. 24 November), these reprisals are motivated by the refusal of an explicitly sexual proposition by a person in a position of authority, or a member of his family (either a son or relation) (ibid., 53–54; & 658–59). Like St Agatha (f.d. 5 February), whose severed breasts are a subject of Renaissance painting, she survives these tortures and her wounds heal miraculously by themselves.[34] Again like St Irina, her ordeal involves being thrown into a pit of snakes which leave her unharmed (*ZVS*, 234). Again like St Agatha, her martyrdom is accompanied by divine intervention in the form of a natural catastrophe (in both cases an earthquake).[35] And again like St Irina, she senses in advance the time of her death (*ZVS*, 234).

If the *passio* provides Zamiatin with a skeletal framework on which to hang his mock-encomiastic sermon, it is clear that he has introduced two variations on the martyrdom theme. The first (minor) variation consists of the fact that the Precious Virgin does not die directly at the hands of her tormentor. While this might at first glance appear a reversal of conventional expectation, the Life of St Irina provides a precedent for the martyr who does not die as a result of her terrible wounds, but lives on until her natural death at some unspecified point later (*ZVS*, 234). It is important to recognize in this context that although it is true that the vast majority of male and female martyrs did die as a result of their terrible persecutions, the Christian concept of martyrdom referred to the great, but not necessarily fatal, suffering endured on behalf of one's faith.

The second departure from the *passio* consists of the theme of foreign invasion. This is a subject more readily associated with the Lives of Old Russian saintly princes and princesses, and their importance as defenders of nation and faith.[36] Although, as we will see, Zamiatin sets out to question patriotic notions of bravery and piety in the context of foreign aggression, he incorporates several of the stock elements of the *kniazheskoe zhitie* as part of his hagiographic conceit. The nobility *topos*, for example, is established by means of the description of the virgin's family: she has a 'wealthy' and 'most upstanding' father, and possesses a 'crown' (*venets*), metaphorically speaking, from birth. The *topos* of prayer for divine assistance is paralleled by the prayers she undertakes during her brief period of incarceration. The miracle *topos*, proof of the divine assistance she seeks, takes the form of the terrible storms and earthquakes which cause the invading Goths to flee in disarray. The rhetorical depiction of the enemy as a satanic force is echoed in the chronicler's description of Erman as an 'architect of evil' (*zlu izobretnik* (529, line 12)), and his warriors as 'lawless' and 'barbaric' (ibid., lines 18–19). Lastly, a premium is placed on the virtues of wisdom, courage, and protective concern for the populace as a whole, rather than on individual salvation. There are various royal figures from this Russian tradition, both male and female, with whom Zamiatin's female protagonist can be directly compared. Like Vladimir, the king who brought Christianity to the Eastern Slavs, it is the miraculous restoration of her health which makes her see the light (*PVL*(6496), 49–54). Like the anonymous chronicler of the Life of Dmitrii Donskoi, who famously defeated invading Tatar hordes at the Battle of Kulikovo, the author has recourse to natural similes in order to convey the physical characteristics of his heroine — the young virgin's beauty is compared to spring flowers (528, lines 35–36), whereas Dmitrii is compared in stature to the Lebanese cedar and in blossoming health to the fig tree.[37] Like St Ol´ga, the queen who sacked Constantinople in the tenth century and became the first Russian pagan to convert to Christianity, her body does not succumb to mortal decay, but instead retains a sweet-smelling perfume and radiance (*PVL*(6477), 32–33).[38] Finally, there is the small number of holy women (only seventeen in all), virtually all of them royal, who are venerated by the Russian Orthodox Church as models of Christian femininity; many were associated in the public mind with times of civil and international strife, and many were allegedly the sources of miracles which protected their localities from invasion, disease, and fire.[39]

The third element in Zamiatin's conceit of authenticity lies in the sphere of the historical framework. If the female protagonist herself and the events which relate directly to her are obviously fictional, the conflict described in the narrative and two of the main characters are loosely based on fact. Ulfil, for example, appears to have been modelled on Wulfila (AD 311–76), the bishop of the Visigoths celebrated for his translation of the New Testament into runic script — his name is Vul´fila or Ul´fila in Russian (*ES*, XIII, 453–55). Whereas the name of 'Erman-tsar´' would appear to have been taken from the ruthless fourth-century warlord, encountered variously in the chronicles of this period as Ermenrikh, Germanrikh, and Hermanarikh (the name *Ermanarikh* appears in a note which Zamiatin penned on the back of what appears to be — because aborted — the very first version of the opening paragraphs), who invaded neighbouring Slavic and non-Slavic tribes during the establishment of his Ostrogoth kingdom. He reigned from AD 350–70, and his kingdom, as accurately indicated by the anonymous chronicler in 'Zenitsa-deva', stretched from the Baltic Sea (*Variazhskoe more*) to the Black Sea (*Surovskoe more*).[40] Lastly, all the Slavic and Finnish tribes mentioned in the narrative — the Radimichians, Dulebians, Drevlianians, Severians, Polianians, Merians, Vesians, and Chud — are genuine and feature in the 'pre-historical' section of the *Povest´ vremennykh let* (*PVL*, 10).[41]

(ii)   Orthodox models of saintliness: the subversion

Despite the elaborate veneer of authenticity, the deviant nature of Zamiatin's stylization quickly becomes apparent. The purported historical context, for example, contains an inbuilt absurdity, since the conversion of Zamiatin's heroine pre-dates the first recorded conversion of a pagan Russian (St Ol´ga) by some five hundred years. Furthermore, had he stuck with the conceit of a monastic chronicler who has witnessed the events in question, his sermon would pre-date the *Povest´ vremennykh let* by some seven hundred years, and thus enjoy the reputation of Orthodox Russia's first literary document. Even as it stands, the document is clearly apocryphal (the author is 'hidden', and it is not clear whether Zamiatin contributed his name to the piece when it was first published in *Delo naroda*).

This author's unorthodox treatment of his theme gives further cause for suspicion. His inability or reluctance to expand on the faith to which the virgin converts is curious and diverges markedly from standard practice. The euphemistic reference to the 'true faith' (*vera istinnaia* (528, line 31)) suggests that it must be Christianity, yet the ignorance of the sign made by Ulfil (patently the sign of the cross) is baffling. This can be appreciated more fully if we compare the account of the miracle in 'Zenitsa-deva' with the similarly miraculous healing which precedes Vladimir's conversion in the *Povest´ vremennykh let*; here the reference to the God of the Christian faith is explicit (*PVL*(6496), 49–54). Further unorthodoxies are revealed in the treatment of the marriage *topos* — rather than announce herself a 'bride of Christ' (the usual reason given for the refusal of marriage), Zamiatin's protagonist states that she is a 'bride of the poor': 'Убогих невеста я, но не ваша' (529, line 8). This strikes an unconventional note, and is heightened by the use of certain risqué images in later passages. The scene in which Erman licks the virgin's severed nipples is a grotesque variation on the *topos* in the legends of the virgin-martyrs. Furthermore, the anonymous chronicler's references to the Radimichian women being 'flayed with bull-whips', and their 'tender parts' flamed by 'torches', is too sexually suggestive for the conventional hagiographer, whose prose style was characterized by sobriety, puritanism, and a certain colourlessness of tone.

These elements in 'Zenitsa-deva' constitute a puncturing of the elaborate edifice of authenticity which has been constructed around the text; indeed, the perception of a playful, blasphemous authorial persona behind the anonymous chronicler becomes stronger when we examine the two scenes which constitute a major reversal and subversion of the virgin-martyr *passio*. The first of these scenes consists of the episode in the virgin's youth. This would appear to have been modelled on a legend from the Life of St Simeon the Stylite in which the pillar saint is called upon to cure a woman who has swallowed a serpent while drinking a glass of water at night. The original contains little in the way of sexual innuendo: the author mentions only that the snake grows inside the womb until it has become quite large; that she seeks guidance from the saint because the local doctors are unable to cure her; and that the snake is miraculously expelled after the saint advises the woman to drink a cup of water from a local source.[42] In 'Zenitsa-deva', by contrast, this incident is reworked into an allegory of pubescent liminality. The insinuation that the virgin is 'pregnant' (*plodna* (528, line 16)) suggests not only that she has reached adulthood, and is thus capable of conceiving (Srez., II, 968), but that, symbolically, she has lost her virginity. In the sense that this event is prognosticatory, it conforms to hagiographic type. On the other hand, because the event itself clearly involves corruption at the hands of an evil force (symbolized by the 'tiny' serpent), and anticipates the later loss of her prized virginity, it reverses the usual paradigm. Furthermore, it provides a comic realization of the Orthodox doctrine, known as *pokhotenie oches*, i.e. that sin can penetrate the soul by means of the eyes. The identification of celibacy with eyes and openings generally is suggested firstly by the virgin's name (*zenitsa* combines the image of the pupil — i.e. an opening onto the retina — with the purity of the Virgin Mary). But the swallowing incident pursues this identification much further, and with consciously blasphemous effect. The mouth (the means by which the serpent enters her body) becomes associated with the vulva (the point of Erman's 'invasion' of her body, and the means through which a woman becomes pregnant), and these by extension are identified with the eye (the pupil, mouth, and vulva are all openings which are circular in shape and protected by an external screen). In retrospect, the 'door to salvation' mentioned in the opening lines ('Дверь отверста для всех, она же и дверь во спасение' (528, lines 1–2)) assumes an ambiguous and preposterous character: on the one hand, it is clearly an allusion to Christ's metaphorical representation of himself as a 'door' for sinners seeking to enter the Kingdom of Heaven (John 10. 6); but on the other hand, reinforced by the eye-mouth-vulva imagery discussed above, it is a symbolic representation of the girl's hymen (a metaphorical 'door' which 'opens' onto the vulva and similarly leads to the young girl's salvation). Paradoxically, Zamiatin's Precious Virgin enters the Kingdom of Heaven by herself being entered.

If the first scene reveals a blasphemous author at play, the second scene is the focal point for a polemic on the meaning of virtue in circumstances of duress. It is an axiom in the legends of the virgin-martyrs that they refuse to renounce their faith; for them celibacy is an absolute virtue which may not be compromised under any circumstances. The act of sacrifice on the part of the female protagonist in 'Zenitsa-deva' thus constitutes a significant reversal of this *topos*. Moreover, the subversive nature of the compromise is enhanced by the fact that this act is not undertaken in order to protect fellow Christians (which would make it more acceptable), but for the benefit of pagan Slavs who are being persecuted, not for their faith, but for their ethnic identity. As the title and opening paragraph suggest, the virgin's claim to saintly status rests on a notion which is oxymoronic, i.e. that of 'sacred sin':

Жены и девы да не презирают естества своего, мучения, ибо дверь отверста для всех, она же и дверь во спасение. Так и Зеница-дева, мучительному греху свое тело предавши, тем душу спасла есть. (528, lines 1–4)

The crux of the argument appears to be that a sin committed for the benefit of the persecuted is an act of sacrifice akin to martyrdom, and thus will it be judged in Heaven — as the virgin herself proclaims in her initial exchange with Erman:

Тленное телесе озлобление оскорбит меня только здесь, а там телесное нечестие в честь мне будет, ибо гонимых ради то сотворила. (530, lines 15–18)

This idea is further developed during her second exchange with Erman, in which she argues that the body and soul are separate entities (the first may be mortal, but the second is immortal):

Тело мое, если хочешь, можешь взять, ибо оно есть тлен, душу же нет скверненник: душа нерастленна есть. (530, lines 27–28)

The fact that the virgin is able to engage in the act of copulation while remaining indifferent to the act itself — Erman asks why she joins him on his bed like an 'insensible stone' (*kamenie nechuvstvennoe* (530, line 24)), and later describes her purity in terms of frost ('Chistota iniia viashche i snega!' (530, line 37)) — proves her argument that the body can function independently of the spirit (a comic case, perhaps, of mind over matter).

This philosophy strikes at the heart of the *passio* and the cult of the Virgin Mary, both of which encapsulate the Orthodox Christian view of celibacy as an ideal. The uncompromising stance of the virgin-martyr, which leads to her extinction, has been replaced here by a practical compromise which offers a chance of survival, not only for the martyr herself, but for the wider community of women and children to which

she belongs. Zamiatin appears to be conducting an argument about the
conditions in which the committing of a 'sin' may be justified in moral
terms. At the heart of this argument, inevitably, lies the Christian
doctrine of forgiveness. Christ's parable of the two moneylenders, for
example, states that the greater the sin, the greater the forgiveness of
that sin.[43] This is the edificatory message at the heart of the Lives of
penitent whores, many of whom achieve sainthood despite a wicked
and sinful past. It is also the message of those sacred legends, such as
the legend of Aza from the Greek Synaxarion, in which good people,
having found themselves in desperate straits on account of their
altruism, are forced to sin by circumstance (Leskov's adaptation of this
legend in 1888 — 'Prekrasnaia Aza' — opens with a line from Peter the
Apostle, i.e. 'Love covers a multitude of sins').[44] One might also include
in this category the Old Testament stories in which sinful means are
permitted to justify pious ends. Abraham, for example, allows his wife
to enter into sexual relations with the Pharoah in order to protect
himself from assassination (Genesis 12. 11–20). Lot is prepared to
sacrifice the virginity of his daughters in order to protect the identity of
the angels staying at his house (Genesis 19. 4–11). Sarah and Rachel
encourage their husbands to have sexual relations with their servants
because they themselves are infertile (Genesis 16. 1–4, 30. 3–8). And in
the apocryphal tale of Judith, the female protagonist of the title is
prepared to lie with her enemy, eat non-kosher food, and drink wine in
order to facilitate his murder, thus saving her village from almost
certain destruction at the hands of his besieging armies.

As Lebedev points out, the Orthodox position in relation to this kind
of sin at the turn of the century was by no means unambiguous;
moreover, as he rightly observes, in most of the above cases the
readiness to sin is not tested in practice.[45] Where that sin does take
place, as in the case of the penitent whores, it is committed prior to the
act of conversion and is accompanied by sincere repentance for past
deeds (the case of Mary of Egypt, as we will see later, demonstrates
how the magnitude of the sin bears a direct relation to, and is
subsequently atoned by, superhuman feats of ascetic contemplation in
the desert). Indeed, only in the case of Judith do these circumstances
not apply. On the contrary, commentators commend the wisdom and
justice of her act of murder, and her story is frequently cited in support
of the doctrine that violent means justify peaceful ends if undertaken in
defence of religious values and the survival of a God-fearing nation.

It is highly likely that Zamiatin conceived his narrative as a direct
attack on the kind of ethical position adopted in Judith. Not only was

the subject a commonplace in the world of post-Renaissance art (in her recent discussion of decapitation motifs in the painting of this period, Julia Kristeva ranks this tale alongside the story of Salome and John the Baptist in terms of popularity and importance),[46] but Serov's operatic treatment of the subject, first staged in 1864, had been successfully revived with Fedor Shaliapin in the role of Holofernes in Moscow and St Petersburg from the turn of the century onwards — indeed, its fiftieth anniversary had been publicly celebrated in 1914, and such was its popularity, and that of Diagilev's balletic version of the third act, that it was repeatedly staged both before and during the war, and provoked a number of responses in the literature of the immediate pre-war period (in particular, see Nikolai Gumilev's poem 'Iudif'', published in the twelfth issue of *Novaia zhizn'* for 1914).[47] There are obvious parallels between the two narratives in terms of the dramatic situation (a female 'combatant' takes on a male adversary) and the larger context (catastrophe brought about by brutal foreign invasion). In both accounts the heroines are devout, celibate, and models of religious propriety. They are motivated by the desire to save their compatriots. They bravely take the initiative by crossing into the territory of the enemy (this, incidentally, is a *topos* which Zamiatin's tale shares with Flaubert's *Salammbô*, and it is noteworthy that he discusses this novel in the context of archaic stylization in 'O iazyke' (IV, 375)). Their beauty is a crucial factor in gaining the confidence of their male opponent. They are prepared to sin in order to gain their objectives. And they are subsequently celebrated by their compatriots for their courage, daring, and wisdom. Further and specific echoes of the biblical narrative can be found in the description of Erman's tent — like that of Holofernes (Judith 10. 21), it is decorated with silver and precious stones (529, line 27) — and in the words used by him during his initial audience (529, lines 42–43), which are intended to put his female guest at her ease (cf.: Judith 11. 1).

Zamiatin's travesty of Judith depends on the distinction which must be drawn between the policy of active resistance and that of appeasement in the face of evil. The Old Testament tale is generally interpreted as an exaltation of national and religious patriotism. A crucial argument in the narrative takes place when Judith opposes the city elders of Bethulia on the grounds that they are prepared to sacrifice the values which the community deems sacrosanct in the interests of survival; she considers this a betrayal of their belief in divine providence, and the significance of her mission lies in the demonstration that providence can occur through natural means, rather than through miraculous intervention. The essence of Judith's character lies in her aggression and determination: she is the 'saint who murdered for her people', a 'warrior' and *'femme fatale'* rolled into one, who reveals herself in her dealings with Holofernes as a shameless flatterer, a boldfaced liar, and a ruthless assassin.[48] Kristeva, following Freud, views her act as a symbolic form of male castration.[49] By contrast, while certainly proactive in the sense that she seeks out her oppressor, Zamiatin's virgin exhibits no aggressive tendencies and is the embodiment of self-sacrifice and negotiation. Unlike Judith, she is not narrowly identified with any particular nation or ethnic group; her faith is supra-national, a fact emphasized by the information that three different languages are carved into her epitaph, one of them being Gothic, the language of her enemy, and another being Greek, the international language of the early Christian faith. Furthermore, although she may be acting on behalf of the broad community of Slavs under the Gothic yoke, it is primarily the poor who welcome her timely intervention: 'И славили сирые все Зеницу-деву' (530, line 21). In terms of her faith, the settlement with Erman constitutes a moral surrender akin to the proposal of the elders in Bethulia to sue for peace. Zamiatin appears to be arguing, therefore, that courage and wisdom are moral virtues which lie less in the sphere of military prowess and valour on the battlefield than in the recognition of defeat when it occurs and the necessity of negotiation for the survival of the vulnerable. If the sacrifice of the Precious Virgin is unsuccessful in the long term, it does at least succeed in ensuring peace for thirty days. Moreover, the rightness of her decision is given divine approval through the mechanism of miracle and her eventual success, via prayer, in banishing the invaders. Her physical defilement (the invasion of Slav territory undertaken by Erman has its analogy in his sexual 'invasion' of her body) indeed becomes inconsequential and is seen as a necessary and morally unimportant sacrifice.

(iii) Orthodox models of saintliness: the modern context and the comic absurd

If 'Zenitsa-deva' seeks to promote a reorientation of Christian prerogatives towards the interests of peace and survival, the modern context of war prevailing at the time when it was first conceived, and the patriotic climate of opinion which prevailed among the Russian intelligentsia in the first two years of the war, add a further dimension to its polemical and parodic strategies. It is clear that Zamiatin was watching political events closely at this time. In a letter to his wife dated 12/25 July 1914, for example, he reports a conversation on a train with a general about the ongoing strikes in St Petersburg and the recent assassination attempt on Rasputin (*RN*, I, 176–77 (p. 177)). In other letters, moreover, he reveals openly his concern, if not contempt, for the wave of hurrah-style patriotism which was sweeping the country in the opening months of the war. In a letter to his wife dated 25 July/8 August 1914, he notes the recent attempt on the part of the authorities to pressure the editors of *Rech´*, the Kadet newspaper, into a more patriotic line (ibid., 179–80 (p. 179)). In the same letter, he reveals that he excluded himself from the general flag-waving, portrait-carrying, and cheering which had taken place in Lebedian´ the previous day (apparently, he had stayed at home and continued with his writing (ibid., p. 179)). And in a letter dated 8–9/21–22 November 1914, he expresses his anger and indignation that the editor of *Otechestvo*, a newly established journal which was encouraging patriotic literature on the part of its contributors (many of them — including Remizov — were among his friends) had published his name as a future contributor (ibid., 181–82 (p. 182)).[50] We recognize from these reports the stance of a sceptic who refuses to be influenced by the momentary enthusiasms and prejudices of the crowd. That Zamiatin was proud of his independent stance is confirmed in an angry letter written to Lunacharskii after the war was over.[51] Furthermore, the sardonic remarks aimed at the patriotic and vulgarly anti-German poems of Nikolai Kliuev, Fedor Sologub, and the Futurists in his post-October essays — in particular, see 'Skify li?' (IV, 511) and 'Ia boius´' (IV, 253–54) — suggest that he was contemptuous of writers who abandoned their radical and pacifist views at a moment's notice once the country was at war.

It should be obvious that 'Zenitsa-deva' is the literary expression of these dissenting views, and that this explains its delayed publication. It must be stressed, however, that its polemical strategy has several potential targets in its sights. One of these targets, suggested by the archaic stylization of the tale, is the patriotic tradition in Russian literature generally. A second target is undoubtedly those writers who had drawn on that tradition in the service of the war effort. This has recently been the subject of detailed investigation which does not need to be rehearsed here.[52] It is interesting, nevertheless, to note the frequency with which the saintly models of the past were invoked as a mode of historical parallel by writers who were essentially justifying Russia's participation in the war against Germany. In the work of these artists, for example, war was defended as the highest form of Christian self-sacrifice. The suffering of the Slavs (both Poles and Russians) was described in terms of a heroic martyrdom (this was associated symbolically with Christ's crucifixion, and in some cases with the early Christian martyrs). Appeals were made to the saints who traditionally protected Russia from calamity (St Nicholas and St George). Memories were evoked of the icons of the Virgin Mary which, according to legend, delivered glorious and miraculous victories on the battlefield. The Prussian army was demonized in terms of barbaric Huns, Vandals, and Tatars. Kaiser Wilhelm was frequently compared to the barbarian warlords of the past (Attila the Hun), and in one instance to the King Nebuchadnezzar, Holofernes's commander-in-chief. The glorious victories of the past, such as the Battle of Kulikovo, were invoked in order to rally the troops. Tsar Nicholas was eulogized as the protector of the nation and the Christian faith along the model of the saintly princes. And the question of Russian war aims in relation to the recapture of Constantinople was viewed in terms of Orthodox Russia's Byzantine heritage.[53]

While not uniformly guilty of chauvinism and xenophobia, the writers who indulged in such representations were seeking to restate the Orthodox concept of Holy Russia as the embodiment of superior moral and spiritual values. Remizov, one of the writers whose work does not fall within the scope of Hellman's study, is an illustrative example of this tendency. His stories of this period, published initially in journals and newspapers (mostly in *Otechestvo* and *Rech´*), and subsequently in individual collections, avoid the kind of vulgarly anti-German sentiment of his contemporaries, but draw nevertheless on the Orthodox and heroic literary tradition. His short story 'Svet neoborimyi', for example, takes as its subject the legendary blinding of invading Mongols by a Kostroma merchant holding aloft an icon of the Virgin Mary; while 'Chervlenyi shchit' seeks to summon up the warrior spirit of the past by juxtaposing (fictitious) excerpts from letters written by soldiers at the front with lines from *Slovo o polku Igoreve*.[54] His second collection, while orientated much more towards the folk tale, also employs Orthodox religious symbolism. 'Nikolin zavet', for example, first published in *Otechestvo*, is a story about a peasant whose three sons are conscripted into the army and who is blessed by St Nicholas and told that everyone must suffer for the good of their country. 'Za Russkuiu zemliu', first published in *Rech´*, is about a young woman who prays at the entrance of a church dedicated to the Icon of the Virgin Mary of the Sign in order that her husband may not die at the front (according to legend, this is the icon which was reputed to save armies and besieged cities from invasion).[55] While clearly supporting the war in these short stories, Remizov does not attempt to conceal its tragedy. Nevertheless, as illustrated by the opening story of the sequence, 'Stradnoi Rossii', which is written in the style of an ancient lament, and punctuated by the sound of tolling bells which signal that Holy Russia is in danger and that 'Christ has arisen', his call for sacrifice is based on the conviction that Orthodox spiritual values are at risk, but worth defending.[56] Undeniably, there is a sentimentality and pathos in these works, and an absence of ironic distance, which lends support to the view that Remizov was putting his literary skills into the service of what Lampl has called Tsarist 'war psychology'.[57]

In direct contrast to this kind of writing, Zamiatin's choice of stylization and his subversion of genre clearly possesses a parodic value: his choice of archaic model is therefore not a celebration of tradition, but rather a debunking of that tradition. The presence of ironic distance, something which Remizov's stylizations clearly lack, opens up a tension or disjunction between past and present which is exploited for both comic and absurd effect. The language of the dialogue, for example, as witnessed in the virgin's first question to Erman ('— Почто воинам своим не претишь, о беззаконниче, муками мучити жен?' (528, line 39–40)) sounds stilted and comic to the modern ear — the grammar (i.e. use of the vocative) is archaic, the syntax is convoluted, and the register does not quite achieve the (presumably desired) elevated tone (a similar effect is achieved in modern English by deliberately slipping into Shakespearian English, or punning on those words which used to be pronounced with an 's', such as 'Sire', but printed with what appears to be an 'f'). This ironic distance also negatively affects the credibility of the miracles themselves. The breasts which are miraculously restored to health, the Goths who flee before an advancing army of snakes, vipers, and scorpions, and the bodies which do not putrefy after death — all are outlandish and absurd to a modern imagination now conditioned to read the narrative as mock, even anti-hagiography. The modern reader will no doubt also find amusing the incident from the virgin's youth, the comedy of which relies on per-verse sexual innuendo (the 'tiny serpent' which causes her to become 'pregnant' makes it sound as if she has swallowed a spermatozoon). One is forced to the conclusion that the choice of archaic stylization itself, rather than an exercise in *ostranenie*, is in fact an exercise in the absurd. For by resorting to such a device, Zamiatin draws attention to the absurdity of drawing on the heroic tradition of the past as means of seeking succour in the present.

Another comic aspect of 'Zenitsa-deva' concerns its veiled allusions to the events of the present, events which loomed large at the time when Zamiatin came to compose his narrative (it is mainly for this reason that a correct dating of 'Zenitsa-deva' is so important). This lends support to the view that his tale is an allegorical satire which has been projected into antiquity as a means to disguise its contemporary relevance. The events in question relate to a number of scandals which engulfed the royal family during the course of 1915: these concerned official attempts to circumvent the Holy Synod in the sphere of canonization, the unsuccessful prosecution of the war by the Imperial Army, and popular suspicions that there was a pro-German peace party gathered around the figure of the Empress which was conspiring to sign a separate peace treaty in breach of Russia's obligations to the Entente.

The first scandal involved the attempted canonization of a holy figure from the Siberian town of Tobol´sk, Rasputin's birthplace, which gathered momentum during the summer and autumn of 1915.[58] On 15/28 June, Bishop Varnava of Tobol´sk and the local townspeople petitioned the Holy Synod for the canonization of Ioann Maksimovich, a pious theological scholar who had died exactly two hundred years previously. Suspecting Varnava of manoeuvring for promotion, and finding his association with Rasputin distasteful, the Synod demanded proof that miracles had occurred at Ioann's grave, and that his body had been preserved from mortal decay (it was known from an earlier examination of his grave that his body had indeed decayed, and thus it was hoped that such a demand would put an early end to the matter). In the face of this resistance, Varnava turned for support via his ally Rasputin and the Empress Aleksandra Fedorovna to the Tsar himself, arguing that recognition would greatly increase the popularity of the Orthodox Church at a time when religious belief generally was on the wane. On the instructions of the Empress, and in flat contradiction of the official position of the Synod, Varnava was given permission in September to sing laudation, this being the first stage towards full canonization (it was recorded that for several days no thunder was heard above the town — proof, supposedly, that the heavens were rejoicing in the imperial decision). Prior to this celebration, however, Rasputin's machinations were exposed. Censorship restrictions were lifted so that newspapers could attack him publicly; indeed, a series of exposés entitled 'Zhitie startsa Rasputina' appeared in *Birzhevye vedomosti* on 17/30 and 18/31 August.[59] This added fuel to the faction-fighting around the throne, and within the Orthodox Church as a whole, so much so that it apparently became the talking point of the whole country. By 15/28 September, the ensuing power struggle had forced the resignation of the Holy Synod's director-general, Aleksandr Samarin, this being followed two days later by strikes in several large factories. Representatives in the Duma delivered public denunciations of Rasputin's meddling in state affairs, and the scandal quickly developed into a political crisis of serious proportions.[60]

A parallel reason for this state of crisis was the disastrous failure of the military campaign against the Germans. This had forced Nicholas himself to assume control of the High Command in August 1915, but he could do nothing to reverse the general loss of confidence in the Imperial Army's prosecution of the war. 'Zenitsa-deva' was conceived at a time when the Russian and German armies were in a position of stalemate. Nevertheless, a successful German offensive over the summer had led to the loss of large parts of Poland, as well as territory along the Baltic corridor. One by-product of this state of affairs, universally commented upon at the time, and later the subject of an official commission of inquiry by the Kerenskii government, was the almost pathological desire on the part of the population to seek a scapegoat for the defeats — hence what became known as the 'Legend of the Separate Peace'.[61] From the very beginning of the war, rumours had been circulating in the capital to the effect that pro-German elements within the establishment were seeking to negotiate a peace treaty with the enemy in repudiation of Russia's treaty obligations with the Entente.[62] The finger of suspicion was initially pointed at the Empress, since she was of German descent and known to have tried publicly to halt the drift to war during the diplomatic manoeuvrings in the summer of 1914 (one historian has described her as 'the sole force for peace' at this time).[63] Worse still, her close links with Rasputin, a figure generally mistrusted by the population at large and also known to have opposed the war (a superstitious man, he was convinced that it would eventually lead to the end of the Romanov dynasty), were public knowledge at this time. With the benefit of hindsight, buttressed by the examination of her correspondence with the Tsar by the Kerenskii commission, it appears that rumours about the Empress's involvement were without foundation. They were widely believed at the time, however, and this gave rise to a popular lack of confidence in her loyalty to the Russian state. The manoeuvrings of the so-called 'German Party' around the throne, and rumours concerning the impending resignations of certain ministers, and their replacement by politicians suspected of being pro-German, or at least more likely to take an appeasing stance towards the enemy, were reported throughout August, September, and October.[64] Indeed, it has been argued that the political crisis triggered by the canonization scandal, combined with the hostility towards the 'pro-German' Empress and her associate Rasputin, sowed the seeds for a popular revolt which would eventually unseat the monarchy itself.[65]

An allegorical reading of 'Zenitsa-deva' depends on a number of allusions, both general and specific, which relate to these events and the person at their centre, the Empress Aleksandra Fedorovna. The healing of the main protagonist by a German miracle-worker, her desire to seek an armistice, and the popular confusion as to the nature of her faith (her epitaph, as we have noted, is written partly in the language of the enemy) allude generally to the fact of the Empress's German descent, her known opposition to the war, and the rumours about her pro-German sympathies. The hagiographic conceit of the narrative may be read as an ironic commentary on the policy of canonization in general, but clearly it has a resonance in relation to the scandal of 1915: both the *topos* of perishability (the body of the Precious Virgin does not putrefy) and the *topos* of the miraculous thunderstorms (the Goths are frightened into fleeing by the outbreak of severe storms) echo the controversial circumstances surrounding the attempted canonization of Ioann Maksimovich by the people of Tobol'sk. It is conceivable, moreover, bearing in mind the title of draft 59 of 'Zenitsa-deva' (this was the variant which played with the conceit of the *vita*), that the story was triggered by the articles about Rasputin in *Birzhevye vedomosti*. The difference, of course, lies in the fact that while the newspaper columnist was seeking to attack the scandalous way in which Rasputin's 'life' deviated from the saintly norm, it was clearly Zamiatin's intention to accentuate and 'celebrate' that deviation (bearing in mind Rasputin's rumoured proclivities at this time, the fact that the deviation is sexual in 'Zenitsa-deva' is also suggestive).

This potential identification is reinforced by a number of specific allusions which relate to the Empress's position as monarch and to certain events which relate to her actual life. Zamiatin hints at the aristocratic bearing of his fictional female protagonist in a number of subtle ways. The title of the tale, for example, and the modelling of the narrative in part on the *kniazheskoe zhitie*, give rise to the suspicion that it is a royal female figure who is the object of veneration: as we have seen already, very few women had been canonized by the Orthodox Church, but nearly all were royal, and one of them had been canonized as recently as 1908.[66] Within the pre-Christian conceit of the narrative, moreover, it is clear that the Precious Virgin belongs to the ruling caste. This is indicated by the information about her father, who is wealthy and clearly a figure of authority (in one unfinished draft variant, he is described as a *voenachal'nik* or warrior leader (IMLI, opis´1, ed. khr. 59, p. 10)). The fact that she enjoys privileged protection when the invasion takes place (a hiding place has been dug for her in the ground (529, lines 23–24)), and the fact that she is later buried in a *kurgan* or barrow (531, line 11), a place usually only reserved for the pagan aristocracy, reinforces this sense of her special status. A further hint lies in the description of her hair in terms of a golden *venets*: 'Волосы же имела, как венец златый отрожденный, из злата червлена' (528, lines 6–7). This could be a wreath, laurel, or halo, and thus function as an indication of her saintly status and the immortality that will be accorded to her in heaven. The use of the adjective *otrozhdennyi*, however, a word which, as we have seen, means 'a begetting from the father', suggests that it refers to a crown inherited as a result of one's birth. That this *venets* confers authority on the virgin is confirmed by the scene in which she seeks an audience with the enemy leader: the guards, noticing her great beauty and the 'golden crown' (*zlatyi venets*) which adorns her head, decide to let her enter. This suggests that they recognize her as a person of distinction.

Other details in 'Zenitsa-deva' allude indirectly to actual occurrences in the life of the Empress and her general appearance. Her hair, for example, was genuinely a flaming red-gold colour.[67] Furthermore, the curious episode of the small serpent which swells up in the virgin's womb may well have its origins in a real-life incident which was widely known about in the capital, albeit in the form of rumour. I am referring here to the phantom pregnancy experienced by the Empress in the spring of 1902, while she and her husband were awaiting the birth of an heir to the throne. This followed several months of consultation with an assorted group of mystics and faith-healers, among them a quack French doctor called Monsieur Philippe, whose medical 'expertise' included occult medicine, sorcery, fortune-telling, mesmerism, and somnambulism (being of a strong mystical bent herself, the Empress was impressed by his purported ability to select the sex of an embryo 'through the most transcendental practices of hermetic medicine, astronomy and psychurgy', a skill which obviously failed him in his moment of need).[68] This episode receives its analogy in 'Zenitsa-deva' with the references to the protagonist's appearance of pregnancy ('Budto byla ta plodna' (528, line 16)), and the many 'sages' (*kudesniki*) from far and wide who are invited to cure her. Further

echoes of the real life of the Empress can be found in the virgin's
devotion to the poor, the hungry, the peasants, and the 'wandering
beggars' (*kaliki perekhozhie* (528, lines 32–33)) — the imperial couple's
trust in the wisdom and goodness of the common folk, the performing
of charity work as part of their public duties, and the Empress's
concern for the soldiers conscripted into the Imperial Army were
public knowledge at this time (she visited several military hospitals
during the opening months of the war, for instance, and set up a
committee under the presidency of Prince Nikolai Golitsyn to look after
the interests of Russian prisoners of war).[69]

'Zenitsa-deva', the composition of which coincided approximately
with the declaration of the Zimmerwald Manifesto in 1916, is a striking
illustration of Zamiatin's stated philosophy of following the path of
greatest resistance. Based on a fantasy of the popular imagination (the
supposed manoeuvrings of the pro-German peace party constitute
what nowadays would be called an 'urban myth'), it is a celebration of
unorthodoxy which maintains a delicate balance between seriousness
of intent and outright whimsy. On the one hand, we encounter a
polemic with patriotic/heroic cultural stereotypes and moral
absolutism; on the other hand, we are faced with a carnivalesque
parody which, even while it expresses support for the idea of peace via
patient diplomacy, portrays the nature of that diplomacy with such
comic and grotesque hyperbole that it could hardly be deemed
persuasive (the idea that the virgin has to sleep with an enemy so ugly
that no one dares look him in the face totally undermines the seriousness of her sacrifice). Even as allegory, the text teeters on the farcical,
since the support for the (supposed) initiatives of the Empress is
expressed in a form so offensive that she herself, a God-fearing woman
with delicate sensibilities, would no doubt have found it repugnant.
Similarly, one cannot imagine many of Zamiatin's readers reacting
sympathetically to a narrative which seems to treat the war itself with
such frivolity (Erman's reference to the Radimichians living off lentils
(529, lines 46–47) is hardly amusing in the light of the general
deprivations suffered by the civilian population at the time). In short,
like the *skomorokh* who frequently abuses his audience while at the
same time ridiculing those in authority, Zamiatin's parody verges on
literary nihilism.

'Otrok Erazm'

Zamiatin's second experiment in the hagiographic style, 'Otrok Erazm', was first published four years after the October Revolution.[70] By this time, he was a formal member of Obezvelvolpal, and therefore officially dedicated to the practice of the carnivalesque. The different political situation after 1917, however, meant that narratives of this kind were received within a new ideological context, one in which, ostensibly, the pre-revolutionary hierarchy of values had been turned upside down. The official promotion of atheism, witnessed by the widespread circulation of agitprop films ridiculing the practices of the Orthodox Church — the future Cinema-Eye theorist Dziga Vertov, for example, launched his career in 1919 with a film showing the inspection of Sergii Radonezhskii's relics (contrary to pious expectation, the lid of the coffin was opened to reveal a few bones and fragments of cloth)[71] —, meant that the parodying of sacred genres and the blasphemous treatment of religious subjects were no longer considered subversive or taboo. Paradoxically, however, the new Soviet authorities were puritanical as far as sexual matters were concerned. Furthermore, although various manifestations of popular street culture did survive into the 1920s, the official attitude towards the carnival itself was one of suspicion, if not outright hostility: it was regarded as a crude and vulgar form of mass entertainment which required careful adaptation and 'purification' in order to prove useful.[72] Publication of sexually risqué material therefore put artists on a collision course with the new orthodoxy. It is symptomatic that while both Zamiatin and Remizov found outlets for their more impious and sexually explicit narratives at this time — witness the reissuing of *Chto est´ tabak* in 1920 — by doing so they incurred the wrath of officialdom and found themselves condemned as counter-revolutionaries. Their joint arrest in 1919, prompted by their alleged links with the Left SRs, then Remizov's self-imposed exile in 1921 and Zamiatin's second arrest in 1922 (this prompted the start of a number of attempts to be allowed to emigrate during the mid-1920s) is adequate illustration of the delicacy of their situation in the immediate aftermath of revolution, and the degree to which their work was deemed provocative and unacceptable by those in authority.

The paradox inherent in this new situation is illustrated with a certain degree of ironic wit in Zamiatin's 'Tulumbas' (III, 72–74), his response to Remizov's declaration of subversive intent in his Obezvelvolpal manifesto. In its disguised attack on the saintly model of asceticism, 'Tulumbas' provides a convenient bridge between 'Zenitsa-deva' and 'Otrok Erazm'. The irony, however, lies in the fact that while it consists of a mock defence of the body-hating and pleasure-denying attitudes of the early Christian sects, and thus ostensibly parodies the genre of the Christian epistle, it is also aimed at the grim realities of war communism and the puritanical zealotry of the Bolsheviks. Life in these new conditions is mocked as a form of monastic rigour in which all pleasures of the flesh are denied and the inhabitants of the community are subjected to permanent fasting. Zamiatin's mouthpiece, Bishop Zamutius, alludes to the shortage of soap, clothes, food, alcohol, and tobacco (here, by referring to 'Savrasius's loathsome, gigantic member' ('Savrasieva merzkogo udishcha' (III, 73)), he manages a concealed reference to Remizov's *Chto est´ tabak*). Zamutius also alludes to the fact that, much in the manner of the early Church, the Bolsheviks had promoted their own 'saints' whose icons adorned the walls of every monastic cell and place of worship. The new culture of conformity and intolerance of difference is compared to the early Church's condemnation of heretical sects — indeed, reflecting the development of the dualistic model in early Christian theology, all deviations from the norm are considered the work of the 'Devil', and thus a threat to the health of the community at large. Zamutius concludes his narrative with a paradoxical and flagrantly absurd piece of philosophizing in which he suggests that the heart should rejoice at the general lack of rejoicing, since those that rejoice in this world will be lamenting in the next, while those who grieve in this world will be rejoicing in the next; this, he solemnly proclaims, is surely the essence of authentic monastic existence (*zhitie*).

The analogy which 'Tulumbas' seeks to establish suggests that 'Otrok Erazm' be approached with a certain degree of caution. Like 'Tulumbas', it is a coded text which, while challenging the attitudes of the Orthodox Church, and thus functioning as a continuation of the polemic launched in 'Zenitsa-deva', also satirizes certain aspects of the new reality. Zamiatin's argument that the revolutionary movement, despite its professed atheism, bears many resemblances to early Christian utopianism (belief in the possibility of a paradise in heaven simply being replaced by belief in the possibility of a paradise on earth), is pursued in a number of narratives written at this time which resort to a coded means of expression in order to deceive the censors. The historical pageant play *Ogni sv. Dominika* (II, 243–81), published in 1921 as part of the World of Literature's grandiose project for educating the masses, attacks the ideological conformity and repressive mentality of the Bolsheviks in the immediate aftermath of revolution, and compares the spirit of persecution and dogmatism to the Inquisition. 'Tserkov' bozhiia' (III, 94–95), a parable for 'grown-up children' dating from 1920, tells the tale of a 'new church' built with money extracted through murder and robbery. And *My*, which employs the Dostoevskian paradigm of the Grand Inquisitor, satirizes the utopian tendencies of the new regime's supporters as evidenced in the work of the Proletkul't poets.[73] Zamiatin's idea of the artist as a heretic, one of his central contributions to the cultural polemics of the 1920s, his identification with the rebellious Lucifer of the Romantic tradition, and his discussion of entropy in terms of the historical experience of the Christian Church is part of his warning to the new authorities that freedom of speech and thought is the only guarantee of a vibrant, dynamic, and self-confident society.

Although it was published for the first time in 1922, the first draft of 'Otrok Erazm' dates from August 1920 (IMLI, opis' 1, ed. khr. 70) — in other words, while Zamiatin was teaching creative writing skills at the House of Arts. That he intended this narrative as a forgery in the style of 'Zenitsa-deva' is evident from the design of the original edition. Printed according to the pre-revolutionary orthography, and graced with sketches by the painter and illustrator Boris Kustodiev (these took the form of inset pictures and frames across the top and bottom of each page), the pamphlet might be said to resemble the chapbook or *lubok* versions of the Lives which had become widely available at the turn of the century. Furthermore, the title of the edition, both in its initial rendering on the cover page ('O tom, kak istselen byl otrok Erazm'), and the much longer version given on the inner page just prior to the text proper ('O blazhennom startse Pamve nereste, o narochitoi premudrosti ego, o mnogikh proisshedshikh chudesnykh znameniiakh, i o tom, kak byl istselen inok Erazm'), echoes strongly the titles of certain stories about holy monks and their miraculous deeds which constitute the earliest redactions of the *Kievo-Pecherskii paterik*, the first natively inspired patristic miscellany in Russian literature.[74] The episodic nature of these stories is reflected in the fact that 'Otrok Erazm' itself is not a full biography or *vita* in the conventional hagiographic sense. There is, however, an edificatory and laudatory motive for its composition. As the reader learns at the very end, the ostensible author, a scribe called Innokentii, has been given permission by Pamva to record his story for the 'edification' of the monastic authorities:

И лишь я, недостойный схимник, Иннокентий, с благословения мудрого старца записал все к назиданию и руководству игуменов нашей обители. (474)

The designation of Pamva in the title as a 'blessed elder' (*blazhennyi starets*), a conventional indication of his saintliness, suggests that Innokentii's narrative may well provide the basis for a fully-fledged biographical account in which Pamva's wisdom and miraculous healing powers will be recorded for posterity. With its dual focus and fixed axis in the teacher-pupil relationship, 'Otrok Erazm' thus models itself loosely on the type of hagiographic text in which the theme of guidance is central — see, for example, the eleventh-century *Zhitie Feodosii*, which forms the opening section of the paterikon of the Kievan Cave Monastery mentioned above.[75] It is also worth noting that this collection in its later redactions contains an account of the Life of the icon painter St Alypius (f.d. 17 August), a saint celebrated in Russia for the miraculous appearance of an angel which descended into his cell and painted an icon while he was incapacitated by illness, and thus unable to fulfil an important commission.[76] In Zamiatin's story, as we have come to expect, the usual edificatory paradigm has been parodied: it is the teacher, not the pupil, who acquires the necessary wisdom; and, as we shall see, the lesson learnt is an unorthodox, if not sacrilegious, one.

'Otrok Erazm' charts the passage from innocence to experience of a young novice under the wise and experienced tutelage of a pious elder. The main subject appears to concern the temptations of the flesh. Pamva, the saintly head of a monastic community, is renowned for his ability to perform miracles of various kinds, including the ability to cure women of long-standing infertility. He himself brings the young Erasmus into the world by miraculously curing his mother, but demands in return that the boy enter the monastery as soon as he is old enough. Erasmus proves to be an extraordinary child. Already on the day his parents bring him to be consecrated, there are signs that he will be a troublesome addition to the fraternity: as Pamva welcomes him, two doves alight on a gravestone nearby and indulge in amorous frolicking. The meaning of this sign is not lost on the blessed elder; indeed, he tells his young novice that the devils are already casting their nets for him, but that they seek only 'precious quarry' (464). The innocent Erasmus turns out to possess many talents, one of which is his voice. Compared to a mountain stream which tumbles from great heights and fertilizes the barren wastes below, his reading of Song of Songs possesses a powerfully erotic charge which excites his audience, causing their breath to quicken and their cheeks to flame (465). The subversive power of this gift is not lost on the saintly Pamva; as a precaution, therefore, he isolates the young man in a cell of his own, and entrusts him with the task of painting an icon of St Mary of Egypt in the hope that the Life of the penitent whore will provide him with a proper understanding of the evils of the flesh. Unfortunately, however, his plan goes awry. Erasmus is ignorant of the female form, and thus unable to depict the naked harlot correctly. Frustrated, he prays to the saint for a vision which will reveal to him the secrets of the flesh and, miraculously, his prayers are answered. Like a shimmering apparition, St Mary herself appears and reveals to him, one by one, the four secrets which her body possesses. Erasmus is aroused by this lesson in biology, and cannot help but express his ecstasy in the icon painting itself. Taking advantage of Pamva's temporary absence from the monastery on important business, Erasmus exhibits his painting to the other monks. The erotic force of the work is simply too much for them. Their pent-up sexual frustration explodes, and Pamva returns to find the entire monastery engaged in impious activities with the local womenfolk. The blessed elder prays that they may be saved, and as he does so, a voice speaks to him, saying: 'Спусти стрелу, и слабнет тетива, и уже не будет более смертоносен лук' (474). Pamva interprets this message as an instruction from God to initiate Erasmus into the fourth and final secret of the female body, thus satisfying his desire to know the truth, and at the same time releasing him from sexual frustration. The stratagem is successful. Erasmus is no longer visited by demonic visions, and his painting of holy figures ceases to possess its impious force. To all intents and purposes, therefore, he is healed.

In so far as 'Otrok Erazm' celebrates the acquisition of sexual knowledge — in this sense it might be viewed as a reversal of the Paradise myth (it is significant that Erasmus paints a golden fruit at the feet of the young Mary of Egypt as she awaits her sexual encounters with the men of Alexandria) — it must be considered one of Zamiatin's most irreverent pieces of whimsy. Gor´kii's reproach that he considered the narrative a 'vulgar joke' (*grubaia shutka*) unwittingly draws attention to its sense of carnivalesque playfulness, while at the same time providing an excellent illustration of the puritanical tendencies of those in authority. Indeed, Gor´kii's references in the same letter to Anatole France and Aleksei Remizov as the guilty parties who have clearly spawned such unpalatable and tasteless offspring showed that his negative reaction was a matter of personal taste, not literary judgement.[77] Certainly, while not as explicit or grotesque in its use of imagery, Zamiatin's resort to a fictitious authorial persona and fairy tale (monastic) setting is strongly reminiscent of *Chto est´ tabak*. Furthermore, in its deliberate subversion of the Lives, and its combination of

libertinage and *gauloiserie,* his short story owes much to the anticlerical
stylizations and hagiographic forgeries of Anatole France at the turn of
the century (Zamiatin's obvious familiarity with much of France's
writing is indicated initially in his 1924 obituary for the journal
Sovremennyi zapad (IV, 195–96), and confirmed in his 1929 autobiography (I, 27), where he mentions his youthful passion for both Gogol´
and France).[78] Other precursors worth mentioning in this context are
Pushkin's *Gavriiliada* (written 1821), a scandalous and blasphemous
account of the Annunciation which was published for the first time
legally in Russia only in 1918;[79] and Afanas´ev's collection of bawdy
folk tales which, while still only available in émigré editions at this
time, was certainly in the possession of other lecturers at the House of
Arts (Viktor Shklovskii, for example, had analysed certain images from
this collection in his 1917 essay 'Iskusstvo kak priem', and it is
interesting to note, in view of the archery metaphor with which 'Otrok
Erazm' concludes, that he had also discussed the bow and arrow as a
euphemism for the private parts in Russian *byliny*).[80]

While the treatment of sexual material in the work of these authors
varies considerably in terms of explicitness and crudity, the narratives
in question are all blasphemous and obscene from the point of the view
of the Church. 'Otrok Erazm', for example, while relatively tasteful by
modern standards, was still provocative in terms of the public
sensibilities of the day, and far more subversive in this regard than the
earlier 'Zenitsa-deva'. Kustodiev's sketches, which Zamiatin compared
favourably in terms of their subtlety to the explicit illustrations which
accompanied the original publication of *Chto est´ tabak,* nevertheless
incorporate depictions of female breasts and pubic hair.[81] On closer
inspection, moreover, it becomes clear that many of the seemingly
innocent depictions of flowers and stamina which accompany the
opening page are in fact representations of female pudenda and
erections (see Plate IV). This identification is made more explicit in the
illustration on page thirty-five; and there is a second erection, barely
disguised in the shape of a tree, in the vicinity of the women lying
prostrate on the ground in the illustration on page eleven (see Plate V).
The text itself contains several direct references to what Bakhtin terms
the 'lower bodily world'. The cloud which Pamva summons above the
assembled monks after Erasmus's reading of Song of Songs rains down
a thick, milky substance which one can only assume is semen (466) — it
possesses an 'unpleasant' (*smradnyi*) aroma, and a similarly sticky
substance, likened by the author to 'resinous dew', drips onto the
monastery roof as the narrative moves towards its climax (472). On his

first encounter with Mary, Erasmus experiences an erection and is
forced to adjust his clothing in order to conceal his agitation — this is
described in terms of a stalk filled with 'spring juice', straining tensely
towards the sun (468–69). During the same encounter, as he explores
the breasts of the young virgin with increasing excitement, he feels the
life suddenly draining out of him — a reference, presumably, to a
premature ejaculation. As in Zamiatin's private correspondence with
his wife, the female genitals are described poetically in terms of a two-
petalled flower, and he refers to their aroma, which Erasmus detects as
he first kisses Mary's legs (see Plate VI);[82] and at a later juncture in the
narrative, Erasmus is described as 'drinking' from the fourth secret in
his dreams (473). The act of copulation is described at the culminating
point of the narrative:

И увидел, как совлек Еразм с нежного тела одежду и, вновь коснувшись трех первых
тайн, со стенанием погрузился в последнюю.
    И погрузилось солнце в воды озера за обителью, и на невинной белой одежде
стены проступило красное, как кровь, пятно. (474)

Although metaphorical and poetic, the detail of the rupturing of the
virgin's hymen (indicated by the red stain on the white wall) might
well be deemed crude, rather than delicate.

    Like 'Lovets chelovekov', which recounts the seduction of a respec-
table suburban housewife against the background of an increasingly
frenzied and eroticized London landscape (Nelson's Column is described in the opening paragraphs in terms of a phallus), 'Otrok Erazm'
charts the building up of sexual tension and the eventual explosion and
release of that tension; indeed, the structural dynamic of the narrative
as a whole has its analogy in the three stages of the male orgasm, i.e.
erection–ejaculation–detumescence. Carnivalesque subversion is thus
the organizing structural principle of the text. It is mirrored in the
battle between the forces of piety, represented by the saintly Pamva,
and the forces of impiety, represented by the demons (*besy*) which at
key moments of disruption are described in terms of their 'games'
(*igry*), 'intrigues' (*koznia*), and 'laughter' (*smekh*) — all of them modes of
behaviour associated with the carnival. Anticipating the ideas of
Barthes, who characterizes the act of reading as one which is essentially
erotic, the *jouissance* of 'Otrok Erazm' consists of an elaborate striptease:
as Mary is gradually divested of her garments, and revealed in all her
naked splendour, so the illusion of ecclesiastical authenticity is laid
bare and the author-joker or *skomorokh* revealed to the reader. The
erotic adaptation of the Life of St Mary of Egypt; the teasing out of the

latent erotic potential of Song of Songs; the subversion of imagery from
the Bible; and the inappropriate references to the Old Testament and
Gospels are part of a deliberate policy of titillation which makes a
mockery of the text's supposed provenance. A pagan sensibility is
revealed which not only mocks the pious ambitions of the ostensible
author, but undermines his authority over the text itself. The narrative
is thus Janus-faced: on the one hand, it strives for an impression of
decorum and decency; while on the other hand we see between the
lines a subtle process of deconstruction at work which negates the
value of this respectability and turns it upside down.

(i)   Orthodox models of saintliness: the conceit of authenticity

Although printed according to the pre-revolutionary orthography, a
fact which seems especially provocative in view of the attempt to
modernize the orthography in January 1918 (this was also true of the
reprinted version of *Chto est' tabak*), the linguistic stylization of 'Otrok
Erazm' is less radical than 'Zenitsa-deva'. The syntax, clearly, is ecclesiastical and poetic, but for the most part the grammar is modern and the
number of obsolete words and archaic spellings has been pruned. It is
noteworthy that *steblie* (463 & 469), *lepota* (466), and *brakoneiskusnyi*
(ibid.) have been pressed into service directly from 'Zenitsa-deva'. Elsewhere, we encounter *lozhesna* (463), meaning 'loins' (D´iachenko, 286);
tshchanie (467), meaning 'endeavour' (D´iachenko, 740–41); *miatisia*
(473), meaning 'to suffer' or 'grieve' (D´iachenko, 325); and *mzda* (471),
meaning 'reward' or 'payment' (D´iachenko, 305). All were exotic
anachronisms in the context of modern Russian usage at this time. A
particularly interesting archaism is the word *razzhenie* (471), which
means 'fire' or 'burning desire', and appears with exactly the same
spelling in the celebrated *Zhitie Protopopa Avvakuma, im samim napisannoe* (*SRIa XI*, XXI, 130). Here it refers to the carnal thoughts which the
archpriest seeks to extinguish by placing his hands over a candle flame;
whereas in 'Otrok Erazm' it is employed in the context of the Life of St
Mary of Egypt as a scurrilous euphemism for the male erection.

Along with a number of references to sacred texts — the
Pentecostarion (*Tsvetnik*), patristic miscellanies (*izborniki otecheskie*), and
menologies (*chet´i minei*) (465) — the author draws on a number of
images and themes taken directly from the Bible. The miraculous circumstances of Erasmus's birth, for example, identify him symbolically
with a number of holy figures born after their parents experience the
humiliation of infertility. These include Isaac (Genesis 21. 2), Samuel

(II Samuel 1. 1–20), John the Baptist (Luke 1. 5–25), and the Virgin Mary, whose Immaculate Conception, deriving originally from the apocryphal *Protoevangelium of James*, is described in the menological account of the Lives of her parents Joachim and Anne (like Erasmus, we should note, Mary was consecrated to the service of the Lord when she reached sufficient age).[83] Much of the imagery associated with Erasmus is modelled on the Old Testament Song of Songs. The flowers which are sprinkled on the ground to celebrate Trinity Sunday (464); the description of his eyes in terms of wells of deep water (464); the depiction of his voice in terms of a mountain stream which descends into a green valley (465); and the sweetness of Mary's voice, which penetrates his heart 'like a sword', all find their echo in this most sacred, and yet at the same time most erotic of religious texts. There are references to the creation of woman from the rib of Adam (463 (cf. Genesis 2. 21)) and to the Gospel account of 'doubting' Thomas (469), the apostle who was reluctant to accept the resurrection of Christ until after he had touched his body with his own hands (John 20. 25). Zamiatin also incorporates the Old Testament legend of Samson, although in 'Otrok Erazm' this has been wickedly parodied: his loss of hair, which extends to the pubic area, makes him 'doubly naked' (471); and whereas the biblical Samson is locked in chains because of his physical strength, Zamiatin's Samson is restrained because of his powerful libido.

Both the main protagonists are endowed with saintly characteristics and associated with hagiographic *topoi*. The name of Zamiatin's novice — from the Greek *erasmios*, meaning 'charming' or 'delightful' — belongs to various saints of the Orthodox tradition, one of whom (f.d. February 24) served in the Kievan Cave Monastery (*ZVS*, 120). Moreover, the *topos* of parental infertility identifies him not only with the above-mentioned biblical figures, but also with Euthymius the Great (f.d. 20 January) and the popular Alexis, 'Man of God' (f.d. 17 March), both of them Eastern saints.[84] The special gifts which Erasmus possesses from his youth are variations on a common theme. Furthermore, the visitation or vision *topos*, which takes the form of his encounter with the young virgin, echoes the various visions of the Virgin Mary entertained by righteous figures of the early Church (see, for example, the above-mentioned Lives of Erasmus and Aleksis, 'Man of God'), and also the temptation *topos* in the Lives of the early Christian Fathers, according to which the Devil assumes the guise of a woman and appears before the righteous figure in order to tempt him into sin — this *topos* is mentioned specifically by Zamiatin in

connection with 'Otrok Erazm' in his obituary of Kustodiev ('Vstrechi s
B. M. Kustodievym' (IV, 169)). Pamva, whose name means 'shepherd to
all', is thus identified with a fourth-century saint (f.d. 18 July)
venerated for his great piety and wisdom (*ZVS*, 392). An episode in his
vita involves an encounter with a woman dressed in fine garments who
is renowned for tempting men into evil; on meeting this woman, he
sheds tears, stating his desire 'to take care of his soul as well as this
woman has taken care of her body' (ibid.) Furthermore, his wonder-
working power as a 'spawner' (this is presumably the meaning of his
sobriquet *Pamva-nerest´* in the title) echoes the life of the martyr-saint
and miracle-worker Ipatius (f.d. 31 March), the saint invoked by the
Russian folk against the curse of sterility and childlessness.[85]

(ii) Orthodox models of saintliness: the subversion

One of the central elements in Zamiatin's parodic strategy lies in the
blasphemous subversion of the Life of St Mary of Egypt, a seventh-
century hagiographic account written in Greek and (it would appear
mistakenly) attributed to the pen of Bishop Sophronius of Jerusalem; it
is this version which forms the basis of the entry in Dmitrii of Rostov's
Reading Menaea and the Russian *Prolog* for 1 April. Sophronius's
account opens with a brief introduction about the fantastic nature of his
story, in which he appeals to the reader's belief in the miraculous. This
is succeeded by a brief description of the source of his story, a monk
called Zosima from a monastery in Palestine. We learn that Zosima is a
good man and pious believer, unflagging in his praise of God, and
occasionally rewarded with divine visions. Tormented, nevertheless,
by the thought that he has reached a state of perfection, and therefore
has no need of further instruction, Zosima decides to leave his
monastery and withdraw into the Egyptian desert. There he comes
across a naked woman who first appears to him in the guise of a ghost
hovering several inches above the ground in the moonlight. Zosima is
intrigued by this apparition, and begs to hear her story. Mary tells of
her misspent youth in the city of Alexandria, and how she became a
harlot because of a burning and insatiable sexual hunger:

Коротко скажу, чтобы ты узнал, как похотлива я была и как падка до наслажденья: 17
лет, да простишь ты мне это, я торговала собой и, клянусь, не ради корысти, ибо
часто отказывалась, когда мне предлагали плату. Поступала я так, безвозмездно
совершая то, чего мне хотелось, чтобы привлечь к себе большее число желающих. Не
думай, что я не брала денег, потому что была богата: мне приходилось просить
подаяние или прясть, но я была одержима ненасытной и неудержимой страстью
пятнать себя грязью.[86]

Her conversion is a particularly dramatic one. Driven by curiosity, she decides one day to accompany a group of pilgrims travelling to Jerusalem for the Festival of the Exaltation of the Holy Cross, many of whom she seduces during the voyage. Having arrived at the church, however, she is prevented from crossing the threshold by an invisible force, and is then immediately overwhelmed by a sense of contrition for past deeds. She breaks down, weeping, and prays to the Virgin Mary that her sins may be forgiven. The next morning she is able to enter the church and venerate the cross; and as she does so a voice speaks to her telling her that in order to find eternal peace from her inner torment she must cross the river Jordan into the desert. There she spends the next forty-seven years, living on a diet of bread and water, until found by the pious monk.

An unorthodox model of repentance, Mary was nevertheless extremely popular in Russia. As Ziolkowski points out, along with the story of Aleksis, 'Man of God', her legend captured the imagination of several Russian writers in the nineteenth and early twentieth centuries, including Remizov, who adapted the story twice prior to 1917, although using different sources in each case.[87] Unlike these adaptations, however, Zamiatin's narrative subverts the central edificatory message. The *vita* account, while providing the broad thematic framework, is transformed through an act of creative imagination and fantasy into a provocative, eroticized, and visual narrative. Indeed, a triangular tension arises by virtue of the juxtaposition between the menological account, the visions which the young Erasmus experiences under its pressure, and his subsequent icon depiction, which draws on both simultaneously.

In both the *vita* and 'Otrok Erazm', for example, Mary is presented as the instrument of a divine message, the meaning of which is eagerly sought by the protagonists concerned. The nature of that message, however, and the lesson which can be learnt from it, are radically at odds. In Sophronius's account, Mary tells the story of her youth in a tone of voice which reveals her anguish and deep-rooted regret. While this account is certainly dramatic, and depends for its effect on the sheer force of her lust and the scale of her depravity (she emphasizes the vast numbers of youths whom she seduced, and expresses amazement that the bowels of the earth did not swallow her up in retribution), it is balanced by the extraordinary feat of penitence represented by her wandering in the desert. She is celebrated as a shining example of humility and modesty, the like of which Zosima can never hope to emulate.

In 'Otrok Erazm', by constrast, the eroticism of Mary's adolescent years, and the hunger for sexual experience which it expresses, is held constantly before the eyes. She appears before Erasmus, not scorched from the desert sun and aged after nearly fifty years of desolate wandering, but dressed alluringly in shimmering clothing. Likewise, the concealment of nakedness which characterizes the menological account (Mary is embarrassed by her lack of clothing and asks Zosima to lend her his cloak so that she can hide her femininity from view) has been replaced by the revealing of nakedness (Erasmus divests Mary of her clothing in order to divine the secrets of the flesh). Ironically, his initial depiction of the saint in his icon, which stresses her androgyny because he does not know the secrets of the female form, is actually faithful to the original, since Zosima is unable to tell whether Mary is a man or a woman when he first encounters her. But under the pressure of his own fantasies, and encouraged by Pamva to investigate those aspects of the female anatomy which define femininity, Erasmus introduces motifs into his painting which are absent in the Menaea. The young girl's breasts are accentuated (Pamva perceives two nipples glowing dimly beneath her clothing); her pudenda are depicted in the form of a two-petalled flower; the antics of her youth are portrayed in the form of a sumptuous bedroom in which the young girl awaits a queue of sexually aroused young men; and the lending of the cloak becomes a scene which reveals an embarrassed state of excitement on the part of Zosima (this is shown in Kustodiev's illustration on page thirty-one of the Berlin edition). In short, the figure of Mary as she first appears before Zosima is obliterated completely. Furthermore, the motifs of heat and desert have been reversed. In the *vita* account, the heat has charred the skin of the penitent whore and to all intents and purposes de-sexualized her; whereas in 'Otrok Erazm', the heat is associated with the fires of sexual arousal (the young men of Alexandria and the monks in the monastery are equipped with 'red-hot swords' with which they are ready to fall on an unspecified enemy).

If not for this blasphemous subversion of a sacred text, and the generally impious spirit of his narrative, Zamiatin's celebration of sexual love might be positioned within a semi-respectable philosophical tradition, especially prevalent at the turn of the century, which sought to approach the mysteries of sexuality from a mystical point of view. In his treatise on the meaning of love, for example, the philosopher and poet Vladimir Solov´ev drew on Song of Songs in support of his view that sexual love was the only force capable of transforming the physical nature of man into something of spiritual value.[88] The writings of Vasilii Rozanov, moreover, the chief 'phallus-bearer' in Obezvelvolpal, also demonstrate how the boundaries between the sacred and profane could become obscured in the first two decades of the twentieth century. Zamiatin's tale, however, pursues this argument beyond the realms of the acceptable. In 'Otrok Erazm', the demonic and divine are merged into one, and knowledge of the sexually forbidden is presented as a vital element in the creative process. Pamva's suspicions regarding the true sources of Erasmus's talent, and his uncertainty as to the origin of the visions which he experiences in his cell, give rise to the possibility of demonic influence. The 'flowers of evil' which blossom at the height of the sexual excess are indicative of this influence (they also echo the title of Baudelaire's *Fleurs du mal*, Zamiatin's favourite collection of poetry); so, too, are the words which guide the blessed elder to his solution. The blasphemous nature of this advice can best be appreciated by comparing it with the source from which it is most likely to have derived. In 'Gora. Egipetskaia povest'' (1890), Leskov's adapation of a Synaxarion legend, a very similar metaphor, attributed to the Egyptian king Amasis, is employed as an argument against the practice of strict asceticism. The speaker, a merchant called Zeno who has previously struck out his eye in order to resist the sexual provocations of a female pagan, believes that religious faith is best demonstrated at crucial, testing moments, rather than on a continual ritualistic basis:

Тетива на луке слаба, пока на нее не наложат стрелу и рукой ее не натянут. Когда же нужно, чтобы она напряглась, она напряжется и сильно ударит; но если ее постоянно тянут и держат в напряжении, она истончает и сила ее ослабеет.[89]

Zamiatin has transformed this argument into a metaphor with bawdy implications. Paradoxically, it is the release of this 'sinning' arrow (a metaphor for ejaculation) which reduces the sexual tension of the young monk and neutralizes the dangerous impact of his art. Zamiatin seems to be arguing that the forbidden is dangerous precisely because it is forbidden; indeed, although this is given a pseudo-religious justification in Pamva's words at the end of the story — 'Ничто в мире не творится без изволения Творца, даже и грех, и все ко благу' (474) — it is essentially an exhortation to blaspheme.

Because the combination of restraint, tension, and release applies to many spheres of human experience, this bow-and-arrow metaphor can be read on several levels. Undeniably, a central preoccupation of 'Otrok Erazm' is the mystery of the creative process and the degree to which art should or should not be placed under official control. In so far as

Zamiatin's tale depicts an artist in the process of creation, it is essentially a metafiction and displays all the hallmarks of the archetypal *mise–en–abîme*. Erasmus's impulse to encode his own experience into the subject of his painting, thereby reshaping his material into an original vision, finds its analogy in the devices employed by Zamiatin himself as the real author who stands behind the ecclesiastical chronicler; indeed, as Erasmus unconsciously subverts the didactic message of the *Reading Menaea*, so Zamiatin distorts the Life of St Mary of Egypt and compromises the piety of Innokentii's account. The implicit identification of the author-creator with his own fictional protagonist is humorously laid bare in 'Zhitie Blokhi' (1929), an account of the conception and staging of *Blokha* which parodied not only the tradition of the Lives, but also Zamiatin's own forgeries in the hagiographic style (see Plate VII).[90] Furthermore, comparing 'Otrok Erazm' with the earlier 'Tulumbas', it is clear that this is a parable about the relationship of art not only to religious, but also to secular authority. In his attempt to protect Erasmus from 'devilish' influences, and to ensure that his dangerous gift does not infect those around him, Pamva is surely executing the task mockingly recommended by Zamutius, the Humble Bishop of the Apes, to his fellow brethren, namely to nurture talent for certain purposes only, while at the same time endeavouring to neutralize any potentially menacing impact.

The setting of his tale in a monastery, and the fact that its composition coincided with the period when Zamiatin was teaching young writers the art of creative writing in the Petrograd House of Arts, has crucial resonances for 'Otrok Erazm' as a coded text. In his response to Zamiatin's 'Ia boius´', an essay which expressed his fears concerning the future direction of literature under the Revolution (it was published by the House of Arts in 1921 (*PZ*, 54)), Anatolii Lunacharskii referred to the House of Arts as a 'Petersburg literary monastery', and criticized the 'unrepentent hermits' who inhabited it.[91] Furthermore, the symbolic role of Pamva as 'feeder' and 'protector', and the exploration of the teacher-pupil relationship, has several analogies in the circumstances prevailing at the time, in particular with the role played by Gor´kii in establishing and patronizing various organizations with a view to keeping literature alive during the terrible conditions of war communism. As a person who benefited from Gor´kii's largesse both in the professional and private sphere (Gor´kii was instrumental in 1919 in finding alternative accommodation for his mother after her house had been repossessed by the authorities), Zamiatin was in a better position than most to appreciate this new reality.[92] From 1918 to 1920, for example, he was working as an editor at the Union of Practitioners of Imaginative Literature and the World Literature Publishing House;[93] and at roughly the same time, between 1919 and 1921, he was actively employed in translation studios and, along with other literary luminaries, giving lectures on the techniques of creative writing at the House of Arts in Petrograd.[94] In his allegorical treatments of this period, such as his comic 'history' of the World of Literature publishing venture, Zamiatin describes these activities in terms of a 'blossoming' and 'bearing of fruit' against a background of (sexual) barrenness and sterility (it is symptomatic that the coded words used for the production of literature in this piece — 'labour' (*trud*), 'fruit' (*plod*), and 'barrenness' (*besplodie*) (III, 334)) — are echoed in 'Otrok Erazm').[95] Gor´kii, whose code-name in the text is Augustus, is the regent who makes this all possible. In his 1936 obituary, Zamiatin referred to Gor´kii as the 'literary archpriest' of Soviet literature, a term which Gor´kii had used jokingly about himself in describing his role as a purveyor of taste and 'intercessor' on behalf of needy authors and families ('M. Gor´kii' (IV, 191)). In this same article he also describes Gor´kii's over-protective attitude towards the Serapion Brothers in terms of a chicken fussing over her brood (ibid., 192) — a metaphor which had earlier figured in 'Otrok Erazm' in relation to Pamva (469). The idea of Zamiatin as an impious contaminator of innocent minds, an idea which drew on the analogy of the demons in hagiographic literature who tempted saints from the path of true piety, featured in his discussion of Kustodiev's designs for the Berlin edition of his story ('Vstrechi s B. M. Kustodievym' (IV, 169)); this suggests perhaps that the teacher-pupil paradigm in 'Otrok Erazm' may have its analogy in the situation prevailing at the House of Arts itself, one which later became renowned because of the battle fought for influence over the future direction of Soviet literature.

Although the Serapion Brothers as a literary circle was not officially inaugurated until February 1921 — that is to say, six months after the first draft of 'Otrok Erazm' — Zamiatin had been teaching four of its future members (Lev Lunts, Nikolai Nikitin, Mikhail Zoshchenko, and Mikhail Slonimskii) since December 1919, i.e. from the moment the studio was launched.[96] The relative influence of Gor´kii and Zamiatin on these aspiring writers was a subject of some conflict at the time, and has subsequently become a matter for scholarly dispute now that its significance for the future course of Soviet literature has been recognized. It would be exaggerating matters to claim, however, as some have done, that the conflict over the development of these young writers was hostile and bitter. Gor´kii guarded his acolytes jealously, and wrote an enthusiastic preface to the first Serapion almanach in the summer of 1921. It is no secret, moreover, that he was regarded as a teacher, master, and even prophet by some in the group. Zamiatin, however, took an entirely different view of the matter. His own review of the almanach, written in 1922, argued that, with the exception of Konstantin Fedin, the Serapions had clearly rejected the realistic approach of their mentor in favour of a more radical and experimental neorealism ('Serapionovy brat´ia' (IV, 535)). In his obituary, moreover, he insinuated that their great respect for Gor´kii owed more to his wisdom and knowledge of life than to any intrinsic interest in him as a practising artist ('M. Gor´kii' (IV, 192)). Whatever individual members of the group might have said to the contrary — Nikitin, for instance, rejected Zamiatin's influence in a private letter to Voronskii, but this denial is undermined by other pieces of evidence to the contrary[97] — the very conceit of their circle suggested Zamiatin's baleful influence, since the Hoffmann tale from which the name derived tells of a young man calling himself 'Priest Serapion' whose mind is hostage to such brilliant fancies that he imagines himself to be an anchorite martyred in the fourth century.[98] The battle with Gor´kii, if 'battle' is the correct word, was fought over the realistic and fantastic tendencies in the work of the Serapions, with Gor´kii favouring the former, and Zamiatin promoting the latter. Although Gor´kii encouraged these writers to read Zamiatin, and admitted that he had written 'much that was truthful' in his 1922 review, it was primarily the early fiction which he recommended to them, rather than the ornamental stories of the middle period.[99] Indeed, the early 1920s found him increasingly irritated by the supposed coldness and mechanical qualities which he found in Zamiatin's work, especially in the works of literary fantasy, such as 'Rasskaz o samom glavnom' (1924), and later, when it was published in the émigré journal *Volia naroda*, the novel *My*.[100] More than this, he seemed personally offended by the whimsical tendencies in some of Zamiatin's output. Writing to A. I. Tikhonov in 1924, after 'Otrok Erazm' had been reprinted in the fourth issue of *Russkii sovremennik*, he claimed to see nothing of literary merit in it.[101] Furthermore, Zamiatin's mocking comparison of the World Literature project with the building of the Towers of Babylon also caused him consternation:

Мало понятна мне ирония Замятина по поводу 'Вавилонских башен'. Я думаю, что именно к построению таковых и сводится вся суть культурной деятельности человека.[102]

The offended tone seems out of proportion to the nature of the offence, and suggests perhaps that Gor'kii had recognized himself as the nominal target in each case.

Read from this perspective, 'Otrok Erazm' becomes a laughter text in the manner of several works written by Zamiatin in the early 1920s. These texts were typified by the employment of private allusions and in-jokes, either because they were intended for an initiated audience who would appreciate them as such, or as a strategic ploy with which to deceive the censors. An early example of this kind of narrative, as we have seen already, was the humorous history of the World Literature project: the artists, writers, and philosophers who feature in this account were given codenames which would have been incomprehensible to the non-initiated.[103] A second example was the aforementioned 'Zhitie Blokhi', which was written for an evening of parody organized by the Physico-Geographical Association (FIGA). A self-referential narrative, this relied on a number of private jokes and allusions to real people involved in the production of culture and the staging of the play. Both narratives were intended for internal consumption only, not primarily for publication. This situation receives its paradoxical culmination in the final pages of 'Otrok Erazm', where it is stated that although the text has been written for the purposes of instruction, it is only the elders who are allowed access to it, not the ordinary monks.[104] A disjunction is thus set up between those who can be trusted with certain types of information and those who cannot. Implicitly, this is a reference to the situation of publishers under conditions of harsh censorship (they are permitted to read subversive manuscripts, but not necessarily allowed to publish them), and thus by extension to the situation of artists (they are allowed to produce their subversive works, but no one is allowed to read them).

NOTES

1. Zamiatin, *Izbrannye proizvedeniia*, pp. 528–31, 531–40, & 540–46, respectively. Henceforth, for the sake of simplicity, I shall refer to these texts as 'Zenitsa-deva', 'Otrok Erazm', and 'Pepel'naia Sreda'. For reasons which will be explained in due course, all page and line references to 'Zenitsa-deva' will be based on this version, rather than on the text published by Neimanis. Page references to 'Otrok Erazm', however, are taken from the Neimanis version (I, 463–74), but without the volume number.

2. Hagiography has been defined as an account in either verse or prose which describes the lives, deaths, or miracles of saints. For a discussion of the genre which stresses its diversity, see Alexandra Hennessey Olsen, '"De Historiis Sanctorum": A Generic Study of Hagiography', *Genre*, 13 (1980), 407–29 (p. 424).

3. For the dual objectives of hagiography, the first devotional (to honour the saint), and the second instructive (to explain to the hearer or reader the significance for Christian

truth of the saint and his or her life), see Alison Goddard Elliott, *Roads to Paradise: Reading the Lives of the Early Saints* (Hanover, NH: University Press of New England, 1987), p. 3.

4. Roland Barthes, *The Pleasure of the Text*, trans. by Richard Miller (Oxford: Blackwell, 1990), p. 14.

5. For a discussion of this story within the context of the demonic tradition, see my own 'Playing Devil's Advocate: Paradox and Parody in Zamiatin's "Ash Wednesday"', in *Russian Literature and its Demons*, ed. by Pamela Davidson (New York: Berghahn), 1999, pp. 441–72.

6. *Rabelais and His World*, trans. by Hélène Iswolsky (Bloomington: Indiana University Press, 1984), pp. 13–15.

7. For further discussion, see Ziolkowski, *Hagiography and Modern Russian Literature*, pp. 3–33.

8. Leskov's reworking of the legends in the Greek Synaxarion have been discussed in terms of their 'unmarked' (*nichtmarkierten*) and 'neutral' (*neutralen*) prose. See Horst Lampl, 'Altrussisch-kirchenslawische Stilisierung bei Remizov und Zamjatin', in *Wiener slavistisches Jahrbuch*, 21 (1975), 131–45 (p. 132).

9. See ibid., pp. 131–41; and M. V. Koz´menko, '"Limonar´" kak opyt rekonstruktsii russkoi narodnoi very', in *Aleksei Remizov: Issledovaniia i materialy*, ed. by A. M. Gracheva (St Petersburg: Izdatel´stvo 'Dmitrii Bulanin', 1994), pp. 26–32.

10. Slobin, pp. 34–35.

11. For a detailed discussion of the history of Obezvelvolpal, see S. S. Grechishkin, 'Arkhiv Remizova', in *Ezhegodnik rukopisnogo otdela Pushkinskogo Doma na 1975 god*, ed. by M. P. Alekseev and others (Leningrad: Nauka, 1977), pp. 20–44. 'Tulumbas' was first published in 1919 in the first issue of *Zapiski mechtatelei*. See *Bibliographie des oeuvres de Alexis Remizov*, p. 134. Three further texts — 'Kaftan Petra Velikogo', 'Obezvelvolpal', and 'Manifest' — are also linked to the establishment of the anarchic society, but were published alongside 'Tulumbas' for the first time only in 1922. See Aleksei Remizov, *AKHRU: Povest´ Peterburgskaia* (Berlin: Grzhebin, 1922), pp. 48–49, 49–50, & 50–51, respectively. For the citation in question, see 'Manifest', in ibid., p. 50.

12. It is not known when exactly Zamiatin was co-opted into the Order, but Remizov first mentions his title in connection with a series of arrests made by the Cheka in February 1919 of artistic figures believed to be sympathetic to the Left SRs. See Aleksei Remizov, *Vzvikhrennaia Rus´* (Paris: Tair, 1927; repr. Moscow: Sovetskii pisatel´, 1991), p. 377. For further information about this incident generally, see Shane, p. 17. Zamiatin's 'Tulumbas' was first published in 1922 in issue no. 2–3 of *Zapiski mechtatelei* (PZ, 54).

13. *Bibliographie des oeuvres de Alexis Remizov*, p. 53. Zamiatin's editorial activities after the Revolution are outlined in Shane, p. 41. For further discussion of censorship attitudes towards Afanas´ev's folk tales at this time, see B. Uspenskii, '"Zavetnye skazki" A. N. Afanas´eva', in *Anti-mir russkoi kul´tury*, ed. by N. Bogomolov (Moscow: Ladomir, 1996), pp. 143–64 (pp. 144–45).

14. Dmitrii compiled his *Reading Menaea* from 1685 to 1705 on the basis of two sources: the *Vitae Sanctorum Orientis et Occidentis*, a Latin adaptation of the Greek versions of the Lives as undertaken by Simeon Metaphrastes; and the *Acta Sanctorum*, which were compiled by the Bollandists, a society of Jesuit scholars who pioneered the 'systematic critical' and scientific approach to the legends of the saints, and whose aesthetic inclinations were profoundly hostile to all unverifiable facts, especially miracles. See Georges Florovsky, *Puti russkogo bogosloviia*, 2nd edn (Paris: YMCA, 1981), pp. 54–55.

15. 'Stylization functions principally on the basis of its "quality of being different", against the background of an expected contemporary linguistic norm (which at the turn of the century can be equated with the traditional narrative language of Realism).' My translation from the German. See Lampl, p. 131.

16. 'Leskov i literaturnoe narodnichestvo', p. 12.

17. It has been suggested, for example, that the legends of the saints are essentially spiritual fables intended to delight the simple-minded and fill them with awe and reverence. See Olsen, p. 409.
18. Ziolkowski, p. 23.
19. Anna Gildner, 'Stylizacje na gatunki staroruskie v twórczosci Eugeniusza Zamiatina', *Slavia Orientalis*, 37 (1988), 103–09; Ekaterina Rogachevskaia, 'Zamyatin's Чудеса and the Medieval Russian Tradition: Certain Aspects', *Essays in Poetics*, 21 (1996), 79–92; and Andrei Lebedev, '"Sviatoi grekh" Zenitsy Devy, ili chto mog chitat´ inok Erazm', in *Novoe o Zamiatine*, pp. 36–55.
20. 'Pis´ma E. I. Zamiatina A. M. Remizovu', p. 178.
21. Two of the draft versions (IMLI, opis´ 1, ed. khr. 59, p. 4; & ed. khr. 60, p. 4) give s *terpeniem dobliim*. The phrase *doblee terpenie* (underlined) also appears in a list of phrases and expressions which Zamiatin noted down on the reverse side of the final paragraph of draft variant 59. These phrases, many of which can be found in the text itself, suggest that as part of his preparations for writing the story Zamiatin read examples of medieval literature and simply noted down those words or sentences which he found potentially useful. See IMLI, opis´ 1, ed. khr. 59, p. 5.
22. D´iachenko (97) cites Psalms 31. 9 here as an example of archaic usage: 'Uzdoiu cheliusti ikh vostiagneshi' (Authorized Version: 'Be ye not as the horse or as the mule, which have no understanding: *whose trappings must be bit and bridle to hold them in*'). My emphasis.
23. 'O iazyke', as published in 'Tekhnika khudozhestvennoi prozy', p. 81.
24. 'Akafist preblagoslovennoi vladychitse', p. 190.
25. *Lukavyi* and *khitryi* are frequently cited as archaic equivalents for *pestryi* (Srez., II, 1778). It is worth drawing attention to the fact that the example given here by Sreznevskii — 'Не прельщай мене козьни пестрых словес' — matches exactly the phrase used by Zamiatin in 'Zenitsa-deva'.
26. Julia Alissandratos, *Medieval Slavic and Patristic Eulogies* (Florence: Sansoni, 1982), pp. 1–3.
27. V. O. Kliuchevskii, *Drevnerusskie Zhitiia Sviatykh kak istoricheskii istochnik* (Moscow: Tipografiia Gracheva, 1871; repr. Farnborough, England: Greg International, 1969), pp. 110–12.
28. Alissandratos, p. 90.
29. Ibid., p. 89.
30. Norman W. Ingham, 'The Limits of Secular Biography in Medieval Slavic Literature, Particularly Old Russian', in *American Contributions to the Sixth International Congress of Slavists, Prague, 1968, August 7–13: Vol. II: Literary Contributions*, ed. by William E. Harkins, Slavistic Printings and Reprintings Series, 81 (The Hague: Mouton, 1968), pp. 181–99 (pp. 189–90).
31. Each contains in the opening paragraph a statement from this author: 'Аз же, мних недостойный, увидеть сподобился тайну сию пречудную, и еще постиг, написать' (IMLI, opis´ 1, ed. khr. 58, p. 1); and in the later draft: 'Аз же, мних недостойный, увидеть сподобился пречудную тайну сию, и то, что постиг, записать' (IMLI, opis´ 1, ed. khr. 60, p. 1). There is also an unfinished fragment, attached to item number 59, which actually names this monk: 'Аз же, Глеб недостойный, сподобился написать все то, что постиг' (IMLI, opis´ 1, ed. khr. 59, p. 10).
32. For a discussion of the *passio* in terms of its narrative structure and *topoi*, see Elliot, pp. 16–17.
33. 'Zhitie sviatykh i pravednykh bogoots Iaokima i Anny', in *Zhitiia Sviatykh na russkom iazyke izlozhennye po rukovodstvu Chet´ikh–minei sv. Dimitriia Rostovskogo s dopolneniiami iz Prologa*, 12 vols (Moscow: Sinodal´naia tipografiia, 1903–11), I (1903), 185–92 (p. 191). For examples of the virgin-martyrs whose name is accompanied by the epithet *deva*, see Evfrasiia deva (f.d. 19 January); Favsta deva (f.d. 6 February); deva Dorofeia (f.d. 6 February); Glikeriia deva (f.d. 13 May); Feodora deva (f.d. 27 May); Feodosiia deva (f.d. 29 May); Fevroniia deva (f.d. 25 June); and Sira deva (f.d.

24 August). Brief accounts of their Lives are given in *ZSV*, 49, 88, 252–53, 277, 281–82, 338, & 470–71, respectively.

34. For a brief summary of the Life of St Agatha, see *The Golden Legend of Jacobus de Voragine*, pp. 157–61. Agatha is often depicted in art carrying her breasts on a dish (the resemblance of the shape of breasts to bells led to her adoption as a patron saint of bell-founders). See *The Penguin Dictionary of Saints*, ed. by Donald Attwater, 2nd edn (London: Penguin, 1983), p. 32. For a general discussion of breast-mutilation as a *topos* in the *passiones*, see Thomas J. Heffernan, *Sacred Biography: Saints and Their Biographers in the Middle Ages* (New York: Oxford University Press 1988), p. 283. It may be worth noting that the reworking of this *topos* had also appeared in the work of the post-Symbolist poet Sergei Gorodetskii. See his 'Mucheniia sv. Iustiny' (1912), in Sergei Gorodetskii, *Stikhi* (Moscow: Gosudarstvennoe izdatel´stvo khudozhestvennoi literatury, 1964), pp. 124–25.

35. *The Golden Legend of Jacobus de Voragine*, p. 159.

36. Norman W. Ingham, 'Genre Characteristics of the Kievan Lives of Princes in Slavic and European Perspective', in *American Contributions to the Ninth International Congress of Slavists, Kiev, September 1983: Vol. II: Literature, Poetics, History*, ed. by Paul Debreczeny (Columbus, OH: Slavica, 1983), pp. 223–37.

37. 'Slovo o zhitii i o prestavlenii velikogo kniazia Dmitriia Ivanovicha, Tsaria russkogo', in *Pamiatniki literatury drevnei rusi: XIV – seredina XV veka* (Moscow: Gosudarstvennoe izdatel´stvo khudozhestvennoi literatury, 1981), pp. 208–29 (p. 208).

38. This was a standard litmus test of saintliness in the Orthodox Church, and the ritual of relic inspection (*otkrytie moshchei*) continued well into the early twentieth century. Interestingly, Zamiatin himself mentions the ritual in a letter to his wife dated 28 July/11 August 1914 in which he refers to the bell-ringing in his home town which accompanied the opening of the grave of Archbishop Pitirim of Tambov (*RN*, I, 180–81 (p. 180)). This was presumably the initial stage in a planned process of canonization.

39. For further information and discussion, see A. Trofimov, *Sviatye zheny Rusi* (Moscow: Entsiklopediia russkikh dereven´, 1993).

40. See George Vernadsky and Michael Karpovich, *A History of Russia* (New Haven: Yale University Press, 1943), pp. 119–20. The note in question — 'Ерманарих завоевал северян, полян, древлян, радимичей, вятичей' — appears on the reverse side of an unfinished introduction to the story which is attached to the draft version preserved in item 59 (IMLI, opis´ 1, ed. khr. 59, p. 10).

41. Zamiatin's misspelling of the adjective 'Radimichian' — twice in the text he refers to the tribe as 'Rodimichian' (*rodimichskii* (528, line 17; & 529, line 14)) — must be deliberate (the previous note demonstrates that he knew the correct spelling). Because the Radimichians were essentially a Polish tribe (*PVL*, 10), he may have done this in order to establish a means of identification for the modern Russian reader with the idea of the homeland (*rodina*) and kinship (*rodnoi*).

42. 'Zhizn´ i deianiia blazhennogo Simeona Stolpnika', in *Vizantiiskie legendy*, pp. 25–36 (p. 29).

43. See Luke 7. 41–50. The parable of the two moneylenders is also discussed in Lebedev, pp. 48–49.

44. 'Liubov´ pokryvaet mnozhestvo grekho´.' See 'Prekrasnaia Aza', in Leskov, *Sobranie sochinenii*, VIII (1958), 291–302 (p. 291).

45. Lebedev, p. 53.

46. Julia Kristeva, *Visions capitales* (Paris: Réunion des Musées nationaux, 1998), pp. 84–85.

47. Aleksandr Serov's *Iudif´*, an opera in five acts, was one of a number of works performed by the Moscow Private Opera as part of the huge nationalist revival at the turn of the century. The sets were designed by Valentin Serov, and the première of the balletic production took place in St Petersburg's Mariinskii Theatre on 13/26 November 1912. See Lynn Garafola, *Diagilev's Ballets Russes* (New York: Oxford University Press, 1989), pp. 15–16, & 389. The revived opera, with Fedor Shaliapin in

the lead, was still being performed during the first and second decades of the twentieth century. The fiftieth anniversary was celebrated by Valentin Serov in a short article for the Kadet newspaper *Rech'* on 19 January/1 February 1914, and performances were still being staged as late as 1916. See *Letopis' zhizni i tvorchestva F. I. Shaliapina*, ed. by Iu. Kotliarov and V. Garmash, 2 vols, 2nd edn (Leningrad: Muzyka, 1989), II, 75, 94, 95, 113, & 116. For the text of Gumilev's 'Iudif'', see Nikolai Gumilev, *Sobranie sochinenii*, ed. by G. P. Struve and B. A. Filippov (Washington: Kamkin, 1962–), I (1962), 227–28. It is perhaps also worth mentioning D. W. Griffith's first full-length feature film, *Judith of Bethulia*, which was released in 1913. Although this film never reached Russia, Zamiatin may have seen it in Berlin during his trip to Germany in April 1914. For further details, see William Rothman, *The "I" of the Camera* (Cambridge: Cambridge University Press, 1988), pp. 18–30.

48. *Judith*, introduction and commentary by Carey A. Moore, Anchor Bible series, 40 (New York: Doubleday, 1985), pp. 62 & 65.

49. Kristeva, p. 85. Freud's discussion of the apocryphal tale arises in the context of his interest in Friedrich Hebbel's *Judith*, a dramatic version of the Old Testament subject first staged in 1840. See 'The Taboo of Virginity' (1918), in Sigmund Freud, *Standard Edition*, trans. and under the general editorship of James Strachey, 24 vols (London: The Hogarth Press, 1953–74), XI (1957), 191–208 (pp. 207–08).

50. The announcement had apparently been made in the very first issue of *Otechestvo* on 2/15 November 1914. Despite the fact that no works of Zamiatin's ever appeared in the journal, the editors continued to announce his future participation in the issues which came out in the latter part of 1914 and the opening months of 1915. See *RN*, I, 182 (note 1).

51. 'Otvet A. V. Lunacharskomy', in Zamiatin, *Ia boius'*, pp. 239–40 (p. 240).

52. For a detailed discussion of this literature, and in particular the attitude of Symbolist writers and poets to the war, see Ben Hellman, *The Poets of Hope and Despair: The Russian Symbolists in War and Revolution (1914–1918)* (Helsinki: Institute for Russian and East European Studies, 1995).

53. See Hellman, pp. 27–190 (esp. pp. 67, 73, 77, 84–102, 111–18, 132–38, & 184–90).

54. *Za sviatuiu Rus'* (St Petersburg: Otechestvo, 1915), pp. 43–45, & 53, respectively.

55. 'Nikolin zavet' and 'Za Russkuiu zemliu', in *Ukrepa: Slovo k russkoi zemle o zemle rodnoi, tainostiakh zemnykh i sud'be* (Petrograd: Tipografiia Sirius, 1916), pp. 12–13, & 35–37 respectively.

56. Ibid., p. 13.

57. Lampl, p. 140.

58. The following account of these events is based on the information given in Joseph T. Fuhrmann, *Rasputin: A Life* (New York: Praeger, 1990), pp. 128–39.

59. Ibid., p. 131.

60. The political importance of canonization as an instrument of domestic policy in Russia before the war, in particular the importance of Serafim of Sarov's canonization in 1903, is discussed in Robert L. Nichols, 'The Friends of God: Nicholas II and Alexandra at the Canonization of Serafim of Sarov, July 1903', in *Religious and Secular Forces in Late Tsarist Russia*, ed. by Charles E. Timberlake (Seattle: University of Washington Press, 1992), pp. 206–29.

61. For a detailed discussion of the background to this episode, see the chapter entitled 'Tsaritsa — "Nemka"', in S. P. Mel'gunov, *Legenda o separatnom mire* (Paris: [n. pub.], 1957), pp. 81–95.

62. The historian W. Bruce Lincoln, while dismissing these rumours as false, nevertheless confirms their widespread popularity. As he writes: 'Almost three-quarters of a century has now passed since the Great War's first winter, and not a shred of evidence has ever been found to implicate the Empress Aleksandra in any plot against her adopted homeland. That Russians high and low believed she had done so was a tragedy made all the more profound because it was partly of her own making.'

See W. Bruce Lincoln, *Passage Through Armageddon: The Russians in War and Revolution* (New York: Simon & Schuster, 1986), p. 97.

63. Fuhrmann, p. 110.
64. An article entitled 'Opiat´ Rasputin' appeared on 17/30 August 1915 in Suvorin's right-wing *Vechernoe vremia*: the monk was here accused of enjoying the patronage of the 'German party', and of having conducted propaganda in favour of a peace treaty. *Birzhevye vedomosti* reported rumours about the impending resignation of Interior Minister S. D. Sazonov and his replacement by I. L. Goremykin in October 1915. See Mel´gunov, p. 82.
65. Fuhrmann, p. 138.
66. Princess Anna Kashinskaia (f.d. 12 July and 2 October) died in 1368. Her relics were inspected in 1649 and later believed to have been responsible for a number of miracles, including the saving of the town of Kashin from the plague in the eighteenth century and the Napoleonic invasion in 1812. After a lengthy campaign on the part of the townspeople, the authorities finally agreed to her canonization in July 1908. This ceremony attracted more than one hundred thousand pilgrims (the population of the town itself was only eight thousand people). It was attended by the sister of the Tsarina, Elizaveta Fedorovna, and it is worth noting that a temple dedicated to Anna's memory was erected on Sampson´evskii Prospekt in the Vyborg district of St Petersburg in 1910. See Trofimov, pp. 77–92 (pp. 84–88).
67. Bruce Lincoln, p. 28.
68. For a fuller account of this episode, see Fuhrmann, pp. 19–20. A slightly different version, but one which nevertheless confirms the bizarre circumstances surrounding the event, is given in *The Fall of the Romanoffs*, a scandal-mongering account of the fall of the Imperial Family published anonymously in 1918. According to the author, believed to have been a well-connected aristocrat on the fringes of the court, the French doctor insinuated to the Empress under hypnosis that she would shortly conceive an infant of the male sex. A short while later the Empress felt herself to be pregnant, and a male heir was expected for June 1902. Nothing happened, however, and a specialist later pronounced the Empress to have been suffering from an 'illusion'. See *The Fall of the Romanoffs*, introduction by Alan Wood (London: Herbert Jenkins, 1918; repr. Cambridge: Ian Faulkner, 1992), p. 13.
69. Fuhrmann, p. 117.
70. Zamiatin, *O tom, kak istselen byl otrok Erazm*, with illustrations by Boris Kustodiev (Berlin: Petropolis, 1922; repr. Moscow: Kniga, 1989).
71. Mark Le Fanu, *The Cinema of Andrei Tarkovsky* (London: BFI, 1987), p. 34n.
72. In particular, see the views of Anatolii Lunacharskii, the Minister of Enlightenment, as cited in Catriona Kelly, *The Russian Carnival Puppet Theatre* (Cambridge: Cambridge University Press, 1990), p. 185.
73. For the biblical symbolism of *My*, see R. A. Gregg, 'Two Adams and Eve in the Crystal Palace: Dostoevsky, the Bible, and "We"', *Slavic Review*, 24 (1965), 680–87.
74. *Izbornik: Povesti drevnei rusi*, ed. with commentary by D. S. Likhachev, L. A. Dmitrieva, and N. V. Ponyrko (Moscow: Gosudarstvennoe izdatel´stvo khudozhestvennoi literatury, 1986), pp. 107–30.
75. 'Zhitie prepodobnogo, bogonosnogo ottsa nashego Feodosiia, igumena Pecherskogo', in *Kievo-Pecherskii paterik*, trans. by E. Poselianin (Moscow: [n. pub.], 1900; repr. Moscow: Izdatel´stvo imeni sviatitelia Ignatiia Stavropol´skogo, 1996), pp. 55–118.
76. Ibid., pp. 219–28. It is worth noting that this paterikon includes a separate fragment entitled 'Ob ikonnom ukrashenii', which relates to the establishment of a community of icon-painters within the monastery. See ibid., pp. 156–65.
77. See Gor´kii's letter to Tikhonov dated 23 October 1924, cited in Primochkina, p. 151.
78. For a more detailed discussion of this aspect of France's work, see Dushan Bresky, *The Art of Anatole France* (The Hague: Mouton, 1969), pp. 159–78.
79. 'Zametki o Gavriiliade', in M. P. Alekseev, *Pushkin* (Leningrad: Nauka, 1972), pp. 281–325 (p. 284).

80. Viktor Shklovskii, *Gamburgskii schet: Stat´i – Vospominaniia – Esse* (Moscow: Sovetskii pisatel´, 1990), pp. 58–72 (pp. 69–70).

81. There were only three illustrations in all, but they must be judged grossly indecent on the grounds that all of them show male genitalia (two of the pictures show erect penises), and the title page depicts an explicit act of fornication in a bathouse. See Aleksei Remizov, *Chto est´ tabak* (St Petersburg: Troinitskii, 1908), title page, p. 5, & p. 33.

82. The imagery in these episodes is strongly reminiscent of the language used to describe the act of cunnilingus in a letter to his future wife: 'Я очень тихо поцелую тебя сначала в волосы: а потом, когда ты немного раскроешься, — в твою розовую женскую тайну, с ее странным и милым мне запахом, с ее непонятными ощущениями, с ее милым бесстыдством и жадностью какого-то цветка.' See Zamiatin's letter to Liudmila Usova dated 12/25 July 1911, in *RN*, I, 90.

83. 'Zhitie sviatykh i pravednykh bogootets Ioakima i Anny', p. 187.

84. Ziolkowski, p. 166.

85. Kalinskii, p. 109.

86. 'Zhitie Marii Egipetskoi, byvshei bludnitsy, chestno podvizavsheisia v Iordanskoi pustyne', in *Vizantiiskie legendy*, pp. 84–98 (p. 90).

87. 'Mariia Egipetskaia' (1907), in Remizov, *Sochineniia*, VII (1912), 45–46; and 'Mariia Egipetskaia' (written 1915), in Aleksei Remizov, *Trava-Murava* (Berlin: Efron, 1922), pp. 39–45. For the popularity of the legend and adaptations in the work of Boris Almazov, Elizaveta Shakhova, and Fedor Dostoevskii, see Ziolkowski, pp. 73–80.

88. *Sobranie sochinenii V. S. Solov´eva*, ed. by S. M. Solov´ev and E. L. Radlov, 2nd edn, 9 vols (St Petersburg: Prosveshchenie, [n.d.]), VI, 356–418 (p. 376).

89. N. S. Leskov, *Sobranie sochinenii*, VIII, 303–89 (p. 389). For the original source, see Ziolkowski, p. 102 (note 69).

90. The full title is 'Zhitie Blokhi, zapisannoe Evgeniem Zamiatinym ot dnia chudesnogo ee rozhdeniia i do priskorbnoi konchiny, a takzhe svoeruchnoe B. M. Kustodieva izobrazhenie mnogikh proisshestvii i lits' (II, 507–18).

91. Cited in Galushkin's commentary to 'Otvet A. V. Lunacharskomu'. See Zamiatin, *Ia boius´*, p. 330.

92. Gor´kii's intervention on behalf of Zamiatin's mother took the form of a telegram dated 25 March 1919 to the Union of Worker and Peasant Deputies in Lebedian´. It is cited and discussed in Primochkina, p. 150.

93. For a discussion of the role of the World Literature Publishing House, and its importance as the sole source of subsistence for the vast majority of its employees (something which Gor´kii himself remarked upon in a letter to Lunacharskii), see Troitskii's introduction to Zamiatin, 'Kratkaia istoriia "Vsemirnoi Literatury" ot osnovaniia i do sego dnia' (III, 329).

94. Shane, p. 26.

95. '— Отныне муж твой уже не будет подобен пахарю, возделывающему песок, и труд его принесет плоды' (463).

96. Shane, pp. 36–37.

97. See his letter to Voronskii dated 29 December 1922, cited in Primochkina, p. 155. For comparison, however, see Nikitin's letter to Zamiatin dated 30 September 1920 in anticipation of the new term: 'Нетерпеливо дожидаюсь начала занятий с Вами. Я чувствую ту огромнейшую пользу, которую они мне принесли — и не знаю, чем смогу Вас за это отблагодарить. Из слепого Вы меня сделали зрячим. Буквально!'. Cited by Galushkin in Zamiatin, *Ia boius´*, p. 303.

98. For further information regarding the emergence of this group of writers, and the reason for choosing this name, see *The Serapion Brothers*, ed. with an introduction by Gary Kern and Christopher Collins (Ann Arbor: Ardis, 1975), pp. xii–xiii. For Hoffmann's story in English, see 'The story of Serapion', in *Great Short Stories of the World*, ed. by B. H. Clark and M. Lieber (London: Heinemann, 1926), pp. 256–65.

99. Gor´kii's letter to Kaverin dated 13 December 1923, cited in *Gor´kii i sovetskie pisateli: Neizdannaia perepiska*, Literaturnoe nasledstvo series, 70 (Moscow: Izdatel´stvo Akademii nauk SSSR: 1963), pp. 177–80 (p. 178).
100. Primochkina, pp. 152–56.
101. Gor´kii's letter to Tikhonov dated 23 October 1924, cited in ibid., p. 151.
102. Ibid., pp. 151–52.
103. For a guide to these code names, see 'Kratkaia istoriia' (III, 331–33).
104. The foreword to 'Zhitie Blokhi' states that the text is intended only for a 'small group of friends' (II, 507); and 'Kratkaia istoriia', according to Troitskii, was also written for 'internal use' only (III, 333).

CHAPTER 7

BLOKHA AND FOLK THEATRE

The conceit of the writer as modern-day *skomorokh*, as we have seen in
the previous chapter, was first proposed by Aleksei Remizov in the
small pieces accompanying the formal inauguration of Obezvelvolpal.
In the opening miniature of the sequence — the title, 'Tulumbas', refers
to the Turkish drum banged by itinerant players as they moved from
village to village — the conceit is outlined as follows:

В страдный год жизни — в смуту, разбой и пропад — когда, казалось, земля
разверзается, готовая поглотить тебя с твоим отчаянием —
    в минуты горчайшей народной беды и обиды выступали вперед на Руси
скоморохи.
    Звенели на дурацких шапках бубенчики, гудел тулумбас, пищали дудки, лихо
разливался соловей —
        скоморохи люди вежливые,
        скоморохи люди почестливые.
С широким поклоном всему народу под звон, гуд и писк шли скоморохи по русской
земле,
    а за ними катила волна — русская правда. [...]
    Без обиды для всех —
    на потеху — посмех
Все смеются, князь смеется и поп в воротник ухмыляется —
        скоморохи люди вежливые,
        скоморохи люди почестливые.[1]

The 'politeness' and 'respectability' of Remizov's *skomorokh*, while
certainly a standard catchphrase, is pure obfuscation. To anyone
familiar with the historical figure of the minstrel-buffoon, and his
persecution as a subversive mocker of the ruling establishment, this
was nothing less than a declaration of artistic non-conformity and inde-
pendence vis-à-vis the new authorities.[2] As stated in 'Obezvelvolpal',
the third part of the declaration, the aim of the society was the 'free
expression of anarchy'.[3] Furthermore, as cited in the previous chapter,
the fourth part, 'Manifest', committed the artist to the exposing of
mendacity and hypocrisy 'however it might be dressed up'.[4] His
championing of carnival-style jocularity in a time of such evident strife
and revolutionary chaos was doubtless a brave step (made no less

brave by the fact that the declaration was issued in emigration). But it was an early indication of the forms literature would take in the hands of certain independently minded and freethinking writers in the 1920s — mocking and whimsical, their fiction would challenge official orthodoxy by virtue of its seeming lack of seriousness.

Zamiatin's pseudonym in Obezvelvolpal was Bishop Zamutius. Deriving from the verb *mutit'*, and thus carrying connotations of dirtiness, impurity, and devilishness (the archaic sense of the verb *zamutit'*, for example, was 'to sow discord' or 'to obfuscate' (*SRIa*, I, 547), while a *mutnaia molitva* was an impious prayer (D'iachenko, 320)), it indicated his commitment to deviance, defiance, and subversive humour. Zamiatin's carnivalesque predisposition was illustrated by a number of laughter texts in the post-revolutionary period, some of them satirical, some of them merely jocular. The four Theta tales ('Skazki pro Fitu' (III, 101–10)), possibly the first attempt to lampoon the Bolshevik leader Vladimir Lenin in literature, were published in October and November 1917 in *Delo naroda*. These were followed shortly afterwards by 'Tulumbas', Zamiatin's response to Remizov's Obezvelvolpal manifesto; the coded 'history' of the World of Literature publishing venture ('Kratkaia istoriia "Vsemirnoi Literatury" ot osnov-aniia i do sego dnia' (written 1921–24) (III, 334–47)); the Panoptikum section of the journal *Russkii sovremennik* ('Tetrad' primechanii i myslei Onufriia Zueva' (IV, 77–92)), penned by Zamiatin himself and his co-editor Kornei Chukovskii; and the 'epitaphs' and greetings delivered at various gatherings of writers and satirical societies ('Burime' (written 1924) (III, 353); 'Privetstvie ot mestkoma pokoinykh pisatelei' (written 1927) (III, 356–57); and 'Epitafii 1929 goda' (III, 354–55)). As we have seen in the previous chapter, the playful impiety of the hagiographic parodies had their analogy in the anarchic, sometimes obscene, and anticlerical antics for which itinerant players acquired their reputation in pre-Petrine Russia.[5] Furthermore, one could also include in this category the bawdy 'Nadezhnoe mesto' (IV, 48–50), a *skaz* stylization which employs the 'red-haired devil' (*ryzhii chert*) of the Russian street carnival tradition as part of its irreligious and Boccaccio-style conceit.[6] Indeed, it has been argued that as officially approved art became increasingly pompous and prescriptive, so Zamiatin's commitment to 'buffoonery' (*skomoroshina*) became more and more marked.[7]

Zamiatin's interest in the carnival acquired its most forceful expression in *Blokha*, an adaptation for stage of Leskov's 'Skáz o tul'skom kosom Levshe i o stal'noi blokhe' (1881).[8] This was premiered in Moscow in February 1925, and moved one year later to Leningrad.

Zamiatin envisaged the play as a stylization in the form of a play by itinerant fools (*skomorosh´ia igra*); and significantly, in a pre-production letter to the actor-director Aleksei Dikii, he signed himself 'Your merryman' (*Vash khaldei*), as if in recognition of the fact that, like the masked entertainers who introduced the play on stage, he was, as author, the 'jester' who improvised the entire spectacle from behind the scenes ('Perepiska', 302). As an experiment in dramatized *skaz* which exploited folk materials, popular language, and a masked form of narration, *Blokha* can be said to be a 'stylization of Rus´' in the manner of the early fiction. At the same time, it represented an interesting development away from the neorealistic principles outlined in Zamiatin's lectures at the House of Arts. In his discussion of modern narrative techniques, as we saw in the opening chapter of this study, Zamiatin talked about the writer as an actor and his work as a kind of 'play' (*igra*) ('O iazyke' (IV, 374)). Moreover, the neorealist writer entered into the consciousness and imaginative world of his fictional protagonists in much the same way the method-actor entered into the role of his or her adopted character in the realistic theatre of Stanislavskii (ibid., 375). *Blokha*, however, is a stylized form of theatre in which the 'illusion' of reality is no longer sought. It is metatheatrical in the manner of street theatre and openly parades its formal devices; as a result, the relationship between the author and his 'players' is not disguised at all, but 'laid bare' for the audience to see. Yet it would be wrong on this basis to suggest that *Blokha* is all about formal trickery and games-playing at the expense of serious content. As a carnivalized text which celebrates the Old Russia of Zamiatin's youth, and in particular his reading of Leskov, it is a fitting epitaph to the tendency of ventriloquism in his prose fiction, and shows the degree to which he had progressed beyond the harsh and unsympathetic vision of provincial life as portrayed in *Uezdnoe*.

Only six months separate the writing of the last hagiographic parody, 'Pepel´naia Sreda', and the beginning of preparatory work on *Blokha*. As a writer, journalist, and critic, Zamiatin had frequently displayed knowledge of popular street entertainment. In his 1914 review of two *Sirin* volumes, for instance, he had evoked the dismal wintry picture of an organ-grinder and his 'urchin-contortionist' companion to convey the narrative clumsiness of Belyi's novel *Peterburg*; this marked the beginning of an extended metaphor in which two of the most popular fairground attractions — the peep-show (*raek*) and 'smoke-filled showbooth' (*chadnyi balagan*) — were evoked ('Sirin. Tom pervyi i vtoroi' (IV, 497, & 498–99)). In his prose fiction, by contrast, the

dramatic rituals and games of the rural community, and the commercial fairgound as it related to the celebration of Orthodox feast days
in the rural areas and small towns of provincial Russia, are celebrated
as colourful and exotic occasions. In 'Kuny' (written 1914–16), as we
have seen already, the centrepiece of the action consists of a round
dance game (*khorovodnaia igra*) with gestures, mimes, and actions
which, technically, belong to the world of folk theatre. Another
example of such theatre is the ritual of 'ploughing to ward off death'
(*opakhivanie ot smerti*), mentioned briefly in the 1915 short story
'Starshina' (I, 261).[9] The commercial fairground, with its various goods
hawked at colourful stalls, is forcefully evoked in 'Kuny' (33–34),
'Kriazhi' (268), and 'Znamenie' (383). The descriptions include such
edible items as honey, nuts, poppy-seed cakes (*makovniki*), biscuits
baked in the shape of goat figurines (*kozuli*), treacle-cakes (*prianiki*), and
spice-cakes (*zhamki*); and such games for children as the carved toys
(*baklushi*), small boxes made out of birchwood (*berestianye korobki*), slate
boards (*aspidnye doski*), and whistles made out of clay. In 'Rus'', the
short story inspired by Kustodiev's *lubok*-style portraits of Russian folk
'types', there is a vivid depiction of a small-town fair during the Feast
of Epiphany, with its *balagan* theatre, balloons, stalls, and carousels (II,
47). These were archetypal features of the fairground in nineteenth-
and early twentieth-century Imperial Russia.[10] Furthermore, Zamiatin's
interest in popular street culture was not restricted to Russia. In
Ostrovitiane, the satirical tale based on his stay in Great Britain, key
scenes take place at a vaudeville theatre and at a boxing match (I, 305–
09; & 316–21); while in 'Lovets chelovekov', also based on his stay in
Britain, a Punch and Judy Show is mentioned during a lazy summer's
afternoon on Hampstead Heath (it is Punch who slyly encourages
those in the park to indulge in sexual misdemeanours as news of the
Zeppelins over the North Sea hits the news-stands (ibid., 357)).

As with other aspects of folk-religious culture in Zamiatin's prose
fiction, these examples serve primarily as *kolorit* and testify to the
authenticity of his implied narrators and their familiarity with
provincial life. *Blokha*, however, operates in a different and more
sophisticated manner. The play does more than simply exploit the
visual and verbal material of street culture; rather, it borrows some of
the formal devices of folk theatre as part of its dramatic conceit. The
stylization (*uslovnost´*) of the showbooth tradition, along with the mask-
changing and improvisation of the Italian commedia dell'arte, the
doggerel of the peep-show operator (*raeshnik*), and the absurd farce of
the pantomime and vaudeville traditions are integrating elements in

the play's dramatic structure; indeed, combined with Kustodiev's bright and colourful stage designs, which were also modelled on *balagan* theatre, these devices lend the play a strongly *lubok* flavour. According to Iurii Annenkov, a close friend and collaborator at the time when the play was being conceived, it was Zamiatin himself who initially defined his experiment in terms of 'dramatized *skaz*'.[11] Annenkov's perception of the play's originality, and his view that it was far more radical than anything attempted earlier in the theatre, has received its echo in the observations of various scholars on the subject. Since Vinogradov's early observations on the formal conceit of the spectacle, it has become a commonplace to discuss *Blokha* in terms of *skaz* — indeed, Douglas Clayton claims that 'the effect achieved by Zamiatin in this play (as in some of his early prose) is much more complete and convincing than that of Leskov'.[12] These views notwithstanding, however, there has been little sustained analysis of the folk sources from which Zamiatin drew his inspiration, or any sense of the play as a dramatic event. Neither has there been any focus on the play's merits as a literary text in its own right, and as an example of Zamiatin's changing attitudes towards the provincial Russia of his early fiction. His overwhelming preoccupation with the formal and comic potential of the *skomorosh'ia igra*, expressed so vividly in his letters to Dikii, and the source of much subsequent debate, has distracted attention from the thematic content and the relevance of this content as far as Zamiatin himself was concerned. It is these neglected aspects of the stage adaptation, along with a detailed examination of the Russian sources which he consulted, and his attitudes towards them as examples of folk culture, which constitute the central focus of this chapter.

It is not known exactly when Zamiatin accepted the offer to adapt 'Levsha' for the stage — it is known only that he did so after Aleksei Tolstoi had declined, claiming ignorance of the peep-show and the traditions of street theatre.[13] The first explicit reference to *Blokha* occurs in a letter dated 3 February 1924 from Zamiatin to Viktor Kliucharev, director of repertoire at the Second Studio of the Moscow Art Theatre; this is obviously a response to an earlier, formal invitation ('Perepiska', 281–85). Yet there is also a letter from Zamiatin to his wife dated October 1923 which suggests that the idea may have arisen within the context of discussions concerning the stage adaptation of *Ostrovitiane* (*RN*, I, 260–62 (p. 261)). In 'Zakulisy' (IV, 302), Zamiatin claimed that the play took four months to gestate, but only five weeks to write, a time-span more or less confirmed by his letters to Dikii. It should be pointed out, however, that the process of conception and execution was far from smooth. After an initial exchange of views in March about how the story should be adapted, there was a gap of approximately two months, at the end of which Dikii called for a version of the play 'even if only in draft form' ('Perepiska', 296). This suggests that the play had not been completed, even in draft form, more than two months after the original deadline set by Kliucharev in his letter of 18 January (ibid., 285 (note 1)). Work on the rehearsals did not commence until October, yet in the very same month Dikii asks for Act IV to be seriously revised because it is unacceptable in its present form and, in his view, requires the reintroduction of the merrymen (ibid., 297). This problem is resolved by the end of the month (ibid., 298–300). Nevertheless, additional material is still being supplied as late as December: this included the merryman's prologue in Act I; the doggerel of the peep-show operator at the beginning of Act II; the proposal to double up the first merryman as the Dutch Doctor-Apothecary and the English Chemist-Mechanic in the final act; and the decision to have the play end on an upbeat note (Levsha and Masha, the hero and heroine, leaving the stage arm in arm) ('Perepiska', 314–17). After a last-minute flurry of activity concerning the posters, programmes, and the kind of cape to be presented by the Tsar to Levsha in Act IV, the play finally opened at the Second Studio of the Moscow Art Theatre (MKhAT–2) on 11 February 1925.

Although the lack of agreement between Zamiatin and Dikii in their early letters is significant, and has attracted scholarly interest, their difference of opinion has been somewhat exaggerated. It is commonly held, for instance, that Zamiatin's conception differed fundamentally from his director's; and that while the former stuck tenaciously to his guns, invoking in his defence the legendary dispute between the Italian playwrights Carlo Gozzi and Carlo Goldoni, the latter bowed to his will without resistance.[14] Strictly speaking, the correspondence does not support such an argument. Leaving aside the decision to rearrange the material purely for dramatic purposes, on which both men were in accord, the fundamental disagreement arose out of the relative importance they attached to the form of the play, as opposed to its content. Zamiatin was more interested in Leskov's tale from the formal point of view as an illustration of the Russian *skazka*;[15] while Dikii was more preoccupied with what he saw as its content, i.e. as a tragi-comic tale about 'the fate of the Russian genius'. This led to initial disagreement about the approach which should be adopted from the dramatic point of view. Zamiatin insisted that the comic stylization of the play required an upbeat ending:

Первая и главная причина — кончить минором — не в духе народной сказки и народной комедии. [...] Там минор возможен только в середине, в конце он разрешается мажором: добродетель объязательно торжествует. [...] И другая причина — неожиданный трагический конец не воспримется зрителем. [...] Хорошо, когда трагический корень прорастает сквозь весь сюжет сперва незаметно, потом вырывается наружу, взрывая все. А ведь тут корень сюжета — комический со самого начала (и у Лескова). Такой конец, такой трагический прирост возможен в рассказе, но не в пьесе. [...] (Да и в рассказе у Лескова это звучит чуть-чуть неверно). ('Perepiska', 291–92)

Dikii, on the other hand, wanted to end the play on a minor note to reflect the pathos of the original:

Мы должны заострить, усилить его главную мысль, а главная мысль Лескова — не сказка, а мысль сказки — судьба русского гения. Пусть будет конец лесковский выпадать из сказки, несколько снижать общий тон в минор, но это, и именно это, делает произведение ценным (смерть Левши). (ibid., 294)

What seems to happen during the course of their correspondence is that some sort of compromise is cobbled together. After Dikii's second letter of 'before' 1 March 1924, in which he confesses himself appalled by the overly formal and upbeat emphasis of Zamiatin's outline ('Perepiska', 293–95), there is a conspicuous silence lasting two months, a silence partly excused by Zamiatin's involvement in the launching of *Russkii sovremennik*. This alone, however, by no means explains his total lack of response to the issues which Dikii has raised previously. Undoubtedly, and frustratingly, since there is no correspondence to chart the subsequent refinement of Zamiatin's initial ideas, this is the period during which vital artistic decisions were taken. In his letter dated 30 October, for example, we learn that Zamiatin has deliberately left out the merrymen from Act IV in order to tone down the playful and comic elements, and to allow the underlying seriousness of the themes to peep through ('Perepiska', 299). Furthermore, the conclusion of the play underwent several alterations — from the unambiguously happy ending in the draft outline, in which Levsha is handsomely rewarded for his inventiveness and can now afford to marry Masha (ibid., 284), to the death-and-resurrection scene in the final version, according to which Levsha is killed by the police but is miraculously resurrected by a magical stove (387). This offers proof, surely, that Zamiatin accepted Dikii's reservations, and was endeavouring to correct the imbalance, even if now, ironically, it is Dikii who is pointing out the inconsistent treatment of the merrymen and calling for their reinstatement in the final act.

Although Zamiatin and Dikii agreed from the outset that the play should be an adaptation which could depart from Leskov if dramatically required, it is obvious that the latter had doubts about the inclusion of the merrymen as a metatheatrical device. Both seemed to agree that the play should take a non-realistic form. Initially, in fact, Dikii insisted that he was quite happy with this conception of the play. He writes: 'Главное в "пьесе" — сказ, былина, легенда, миф. Народный!' ('Perepiska', 285). Furthermore, in his letter dated from 'before' 1 March, he writes enthusiastically: 'Сказка — да! Это при всех вариантах. Это при всех возможностях остается. Это форма. Это объязательно. Это и интересно, и нужно, и выгодно' (ibid., 294). What concerns Dikii is the danger that the 'fun and games' will negatively affect the tone of the production and compromise his tragic ambitions. Stressing that the magic tale elements should affect only the form of the play rather than its content, he failed to grasp, as Zamiatin evidently did, that the two were inextricably linked and could not be disassociated. It is noteworthy, however, that little flesh had been given to the concept of the merrymen during these initial explorations. The outlines given in Zamiatin's letters of 3 February 1924 (to Kliucharev) and 22 February 1924 (to Dikii) contain detailed scenic considerations, but the presence of the merrymen is indicated only in Act I, in which they perform a play on the subject of the 'Dog-King and his son Peregud' ('Perepiska', 282). At this stage there is little hint of the practical form these meta-theatrical devices will take during the rest of the play, and no sense in which they will be allowed to dominate proceedings. This is curious in view of the position which Zamiatin adopts in his first letter to Dikii dated 22 February. Here he states that only the relativistic style of folk comedy and *balagan* can fully convey the flavour of Leskov's story, thus the adaptation should be modelled on the plays of itinerant fools, the devices of which would be periodically laid bare during the course of the spectacle. The three merrymen, modelled on the commedia figures of Pantalone, Tartaglia, and Brighella, would appear as if by accident in Act I, but would remain an organic part of the play from that moment onwards — they would wear masks and assume the roles of several characters, at various points changing their costumes in full view of the audience ('Perepiska', 290–91). Furthermore, the rest of the cast would consist of non-realistic, fantasy figures: the Tsar, for example, should not be modelled on the historical Nicholas I, but on such fairy-tale prototypes as Saltan and Dodon (ibid., 281). Presumably, Zamiatin was referring here to Rimskii-Korsakov's operatic versions of Pushkin's *Skazka o tsare Saltane* (1831) and *Skazka o zolotom petushke* (1834), the first of which had been banned by the Tsarist censors, but revived in the post-revolutionary period, and the second of which had also been produced by Diagilev in a balletic version as part of his Ballets Russes season in Paris in 1914.[16]

At some point during this correspondence, possibly between the end of February and the beginning of May, Zamiatin undertook some rigorous research into the history of folk drama. The final script, as I have indicated, was the product of a four-month gestation period during which Zamiatin saturated himself in a range of materials pertaining to the epoch he wished to evoke. In 'Zakulisy', for example, he mentions traditional folk comedies, *skazki*, the plays of Gozzi and Goldoni, *balagan* posters, *lubok* engravings, and the books of Dmitrii Rovinskii (IV, 302).[17] Parallel sources amplify this information further. A letter from Dikii to Zamiatin dated 5 January 1925 refers him to Leifert's *Balagany* (1922) with a view to acquiring ideas about original showbooth posters ('Perepiska', 333). The essay 'Narodnyi teatr' (1927), moreover, reveals an additional range of sources which go well beyond those mentioned later in 'Zakulisy'. Here he mentions various forms of folk theatre, some with roots stretching back centuries in Russian culture: the Iarilo festival; wedding ceremonies; pagan funeral feasts (*trizna*); the plays of the *skomorokhi*; the medieval Furnace Play (*peshchnoe deistvo*, not *peshchernoe deistvo*, as misprinted in Neimanis (IV, 424));[18] the Petrushka puppet-theatre; the folk comedy *Tsar´ Maksimilian;* and the *balagan* repertoire of Leifert, Malafeev, and Berg as performed during the Shrovetide and Easter carnivals of the previous century (ibid., 424 & 426). It seems that the merrymen, known as the Chaldeans (*Khaldei*), were taken from Adam Olearius's account of seventeenth-century Muscovy life: Zamiatin quotes a fragment which describes the Chaldeans with honey-soaked beards letting off fireworks and setting fire to the beards of peasant onlookers in the period between Christmas and Epiphany (ibid., 429). From this essay it would appear that he also consulted Vsevolodskii-Gerngross's researches into the history of the wedding ceremony ritual, and was clearly aware of recent attempts to revive this ritual for the modern stage (ibid., 426). He refers also to *Komediia o khrabrom voine Anike*, versions of which had been published by Onchukov and others (ibid); and in a lecture given at the State Institute of Art History (GIII) in Leningrad in 1926, he furnished one further example from the sphere of traditional folk theatre — *Anika i*

Smert´ — as well as two comedies from the itinerant players' repertoire in the North, i.e. *O bogatom goste Terent´ishche* and *O Fome i Ereme*.[19]

Zamiatin's attitude towards these materials was plainly discerning. Far from incorporating them indiscriminately into his dramatic presentation of Leskov, or eulogizing them romantically and naively in the manner of the Slavophiles, he was careful to assess their utility for the professional artist concerned with an impression of dynamism, vitality, and vigour. In his essay, for example, he drew an important distinction between the 'Theatre for the People' movement (*Teatr dlia naroda*), which he characterized as an élitist movement patronized by the royal family to encourage theatre-going among the lower classes in the pre-revolutionary era (but having nothing in common with their actual tastes, language, and culture), and 'Folk Theatre' (*Narodnyi teatr*), which he described as the idiosyncratic forms of theatre which had been developed over centuries by the lower classes themselves primarily for their own entertainment (IV, 424). He observed that, unlike other areas of folk culture, such as music, sculpture, and oral literature, modern artists had largely avoided this area of experience, exploiting only the themes of folk theatre rather than its forms or devices (ibid., 424–25). In his view, the only exceptions to this rule were Remizov's *Rusal´nye deistva* which, because they had been written and performed before the Revolution, belonged 'in the museum'; and Kurochkin's comedy for puppets, *Prints Lutonia* (1872), which he found 'clumsy and crude' (ibid., 425).[20] This lack of interest was explained in terms of the intrinsic weaknesses of Russian folk theatre generally:

Если без всякого благочестия, без умилительной слезы (слезы всегда мешают видеть) подойти к нашему народному театру вплотную, то мы увидим, что в большой части — это наименее совершенная, наименее зрелая из всех форм народного творчества. (ibid., 425)

Furthermore, he argued that ritual theatre, undeniably the richest and most pure form of folk theatre, with roots stretching back to pagan times, was locked into religious forms so outmoded and obsolete that it would be impossible to breathe new life into them for a modern audience (ibid., 425–26). He was more impressed with the Petrushka puppet-theatre, which had managed to adapt itself successfully to new revolutionary conditions, even if professional playwrights themselves had been slow to appreciate its formal potential;[21] and he also expressed a strong interest in the Shrovetide and Easter showbooth tradition, which frequently skirted the boundaries of good taste and incorporated all kinds of genre material, ranging from romantic drama through to the harlequinade and peep-show. Sadly, in his view, previous attempts to adapt this kind of material for élite audiences had been undertaken not by playwrights, but by 'hacks' (*dramadely*), and thus with indifferent results (ibid., 426–27). A similar proviso applied to such comedies as *Tsar´ Maksimilian*, which Remizov had presented in a modern version in 1912: Zamiatin believed that contemporary audiences had long outgrown the original text of this comedy, which was, in any case, 'banal and impoverished' (ibid., 427). He believed that the professional artist in the modern era was obliged to eliminate all the 'cheap debris' of folk theatre, and to combine its forms and methods with a new subject — in his own words:

Нужно другое: руду народного театра пропустить через машину профессиональной обработки, нужно отсеять весь налипший в царской казарме, в кабаке мусор, нужно использовать не темы, а формы и методы народного театра, спаяв их с новым сюжетом. (ibid., 427)

In his view, it was the unexpected twists, anachronisms, and relativism of folk theatre which were its most valuable assets:

Мне казалось наиболее подходящим назвать 'Блоху' *игрой:* истинный народный театр — это, конечно, театр не реалистический, а условный от начала до конца, это именно — *игра*, дающая полный простор фантазии, оправдывающая любые чудеса, неожиданности, анахронизмы. (ibid., 428; all emphases in the original)

Bearing in mind the programmatic nature of this essay, it is curious that Zamiatin overlooks the dramatic experiments of the previous two decades as far as stylized theatre was concerned. He cannot have been ignorant of the fact that *Blokha* followed a period of intense artistic experimentation which witnessed a veritable craze for commedia dell'arte techniques in the theatrical world, ranging from Meierkhol´d's production of Blok's *Balaganchik* in 1906 to Vakhtangov's magnificent production of Gozzi's *Turandot* in the Third Studio of the Moscow Art Theatre in 1922. (It was from this production, in all probability, that Zamiatin borrowed his ideas for the mask-changing merrymen.)[22] It was disingenuous in the extreme to claim that artists had made little use of the formal devices of showbooth theatre. On the contrary, relativistic devices, metatheatre, improvisation, and masks had been employed consistently throughout this period, both in the sphere of Symbolist and avant-garde theatre — witness, for example, Meierkhol´d's programmatic essays 'Uslovnyi teatr' (1907) and 'Balagan' (1912) — and in such well-known cabarets as *Letuchaia mysh´*, *Brodiachaia sobaka*, and *Krivoe zerkalo*. The devices of Italian street theatre were also vital to the attempt to establish a popular Soviet theatre after the Revolution, for example, in Radlov's Red Harlequinades and the Petrograd Free Comedy Theatre. Four commedia-style productions ran concurrently in the theatres of Petrograd alone in 1922, and if anything represented the zenith of an avant-garde wave which subsequently fell foul of a popular reaction against élitist experiments. Almost uniformly, however, as Douglas Clayton has pointed out, these experiments were based on foreign (Italian or French) models. He writes:

The intellectual élite, who had appropriated the *balagan*, had preferred by and large to use foreign motifs and sources, rather than building directly on the Petrushka tradition.[23]

Benois's denunciation of Meierkhol´d's 1910 production of Molière's *Dom Juan* as *nariadnyi balagan* (farce in fancy dress) — a pun, of course, on the expression *narodnyi balagan* (folk theatre) — is particularly pertinent in this regard.[24] By contrast, despite his reservations about the 'cheap debris' of folk drama, Zamiatin aimed for a kind of lumpen authenticity which would give force to the word *balagan* as a term of opprobrium for any manifestation of disorder, scandal, or farce. It was not so much the gaiety of the spectacle which constituted its novelty — this had certainly been presented before to the public — rather it was the crude, primitive, and coarse flavour of the play, which stemmed exclusively from its use of popular language and genuinely Russian folk sources.

Blokha was probably the first attempt to reproduce an authentic *balagan* experience for a theatre-going audience, the composition of which had been swelled and subtly altered by the inclusion of a newly literate urban mass. Great care was taken with this particular aspect of the play's stylization. The poster, designed by Kustodiev in red and black ink, was deliberately modelled on *balagan* originals in the possession of Leifert, whose father had been the proprietor of a famous fairground showbooth in St Petersburg during the late nineteenth century (see Plate VIII).[25] The audience which arrived for the first night performance was greeted with a programme also closely modelled on *balagan* prototypes — this contained the obligatory *stishok* on the front page, which Zamiatin had insisted upon at the very last minute, the proud boast that 'thousands' of scientific gadgets and inventions would be on display, and ironic witticisms to accompany the descriptions of the scene settings.[26] Employing a device first used in *Balaganchik*, the producers arranged for the stage curtain to be raised only to reveal a second curtain behind it which had been designed by

Kustodiev in *balagan* style — this was decorated with enormous, brightly coloured floral patterns, and projected onto it by means of a magic lantern was a magnified image of a flea.[27] Additional fairground props were positioned just in front of this curtain and took the form of two booths selling tickets for the performance, separate posters carrying pictures of 'The Flea' and the author of the play (i.e. Zamiatin), and noticeboards advertising such typical *balagan* freak shows as 'Katia — the Educated Pig' and 'The Miracle-Woman with a Beard'.[28]

The purpose of these devices was to prepare the audience psychologically for the stylized nature of the spectacle which ensued. This took the form anticipated in Zamiatin's early letters to Dikii, with borrowings from various aspects of folk theatre. The first merryman, dressed in the outfit of a peep-show operator, entered the stage before the lifting of the second curtain to present the play in the form of a prologue (for a *lubok* version of this fairground scene, see Plate IX). His remarks, delivered in the *raeshnik*'s traditional style of doggerel, contained references to his Chaldean pedigree, his birth out of wedlock (he has never clapped eyes on his father), and his father's profession as a *koza* (according to Rovinskii, a young boy disguised in a mummer's mask who served as an assistant alongside the itinerant owner of a performing bear).[29] The introduction of the other two merrymen during this speech was followed by several costume changes in full view of the audience. The first was undertaken in Act I as the leading merryman donned a false beard and spectacles in order to play the Dutch Doctor-Apothecary, a stock figure of the puppet-theatre repertoire and one renowned for his quack cures and ignorance of medical science. The magic trick which he performs for the benefit of the Tsar involves restoring a 120-year-old woman, Malafevna, to the first flush of youth; it is strongly reminiscent of a famous eighteenth-century *lubok* picture, and the content of his speech mimics the traditional ditty beneath the engraving.[30] Cross-purpose dialogue, another device typical of the puppet-theatre, was employed twice in the opening exchange between the Tsar and Malafevna.[31] At the beginning of Act II, the first merryman produced a peep-show, together with a small *balagan* curtain, and invited the local townspeople to look at a famous *lubok* engraving of Platov, the feared Don Cossack commander. The second merryman, who had previously played the Imperial Messenger Boy, and not the Tsar (as announced in the Prologue), took the role of Masha's father, the wealthy Tula merchant. In Act IV, moreover, the first merryman simultaneously assumed the role of the Dutch Doctor-Apothecary and the English Chemist-Mechanic. For the 'triumphant' conclusion (the brutal death and miraculous resurrection of the hero), Zamiatin employed the device of reification; this was also borrowed from the puppet-theatre, and had been effectively exploited in *Balaganchik* and the Diagilev–Stravinskii ballet *Petrushka*.[32]

True to the expectation aroused in the programme, the choice of stage-design, costumes, and props was flagrantly inspired by the showbooth. It is difficult perhaps to communicate this aspect of *Blokha* without having witnessed the actual production. The flavour of the spectacle, nevertheless, can be gauged by the detailed discussions in the Zamiatin–Dikii–Kustodiev correspondence, Dikii's later recollections of the initial performances in his memoirs, the contemporaneous reports of audience reaction to the play, and the publication of Kustodiev's set designs and costumes (these were devised under Zamiatin's supervision and later exhibited in Paris).[33] Visually, it seems, the guiding aesthetic principle was the *lubok* engraving: this was the reason given by Dikii for his decision at a dangerously late stage in the proceedings to replace the first choice set designer, Nikolai Krymov, with an artist more comfortable with the *faux-naïf* style required.[34] All three sets — St Petersburg, England, and Tula — were presented as if through the prism of the peasant imagination; as indicated by Kustodiev's instructions to the artists carrying out the work on the spot, they were eye-catchingly bright and colourful, with a hint of 'showbooth-style tastelessness' (*balagannaia aliapovatost´*), but nothing excessive ('Perepiska', 335). The court in Act I was envisaged as a blend of French and Nizhnii Novgorod imperial styles — everything was daubed in red, yellow, and green, and fantastically large in terms of scale: Kustodiev's sketches show huge palm trees growing from vases with handles, their branches hanging with pears, portraits on the walls of the Tsar's 'closest relatives' (the Turkish and Chinese emperors), and a modern stall with a crowd selling beer and crayfish right in front of the audience.[35] The Tula set consisted of a simple backcloth of sky and clouds, three brightly painted green hills, a crooked *izba* with smoke coming out of the chimney, two large wooden birds sitting on a tree, a small church, a fence, and a large sign saying: 'Tula'.[36] England was envisaged as a form of mechanized Hell, with screeching machines, samovar-shaped chimneys, massive cogwheels, seats which gave off electric sparks, a Russian-style tavern with pot-bellied teapots carried aloft by black waiters, and a dazzlingly clean water closet (*nuzhnoe mesto*), along with thermometer, flowers for fragrance and general *bon ton*, and an umbrella in case the weather turned nasty (the presence of this particular prop, insisted upon by Dikii in spite of the protests from Zamiatin and Kustodiev on account of its supposed vulgarity, was symptomatic of the somewhat risqué nature of the spectacle).[37] The dimensions of the other props were similarly comic and outlandish. One suggestion for Act I envisaged the Tsar's throne as the size of a child's stool ('Perepiska', 317). For the character of the Watchdog-General, Kustodiev planned a tiny hut the size of a dog's kennel which would boast an incongruously large bell that would be rung vigorously in order to announce the arrival of important persons, but would produce only a pathetic tinkling sound (ibid.). In the first scene, as described in the final stage instructions (345), the Tsar is offered an enormous, two-yard-long tray with apples the size of watermelons and grapes the size of apples. The church in Tula was only waist-high. The *melkoskop* (microscope) took the form of a massively large telescope which was almost half the size of the stage itself and had to be carried aloft on the shoulders of several generals.[38] The *buremetr* (barometer) consisted of a wooden bucket of water in which floated a semi-circular piece of wood with a large javelin embedded in it.[39] The horses ridden by the Don Cossacks were painted plywood figures about one-and-a-half yards long with bast manes and tails. They were designed to look as dashing as possible, but were obviously absurd and undermined Platov's claim to imperial gravitas ('Perepiska', 320). The Cossack sleigh, moreover, which was also made of plywood, was so small that it was virtually impossible for anybody to get in it (ibid., 329).

As far as the costumes were concerned, these were bright and festive, with an element of grotesque exaggeration and cartoon-style absurdity. Kisel´vrode was given a false nose made out of cardboard which he removed only to look at the flea through the massive microscope in Act IV ('Perepiska', 327). Furthermore, photographs of the production show him made up as a clown.[40] The generals, dressed in outrageous and fantastic outfits, were so ancient that they appeared to be disintegrating physically on stage (this was realized metaphorically — particles of sand periodically seeped from their clothing and formed little heaps on the floor which were then swept away by a janitor employed especially for the purpose).[41] The Tsar was given fake, larger-than-life epaulettes, a crown which was so huge that it sat on his ears, shoes which were too large for him, and an absurd military uniform ('Perepiska', 327). The merryman playing the English Chemist-Mechanic had a large top hat and oversized pocket from which dangled a grotesquely large pipe (the same character is depicted smoking this pipe in the poster).[42] The English Meria looked like a striptease dancer: she was swamped in furs, with gloves covering her entire arms, and was envisaged as a kind of NEP or pre-revolutionary bourgeois type, with recognizably Russian features.[43] The merrymen were not actually masked in the style of the commedia dell'arte, but wore Russian-style fools' caps with bells dangling from the front and cloaks emblazoned with stars which they removed when changing roles; their bottom halves remained the same throughout the performance, enabling them to execute quick changes of costume while still on stage ('Perepiska', 327). The intention was to make quite clear to the audience that these roles were being played by the same three actors, although in the end only four costume changes actually took place on stage.

It is clear from Dikii's later memoirs that the *balagan* stylization represented a considerable challenge to the actors, but that it was an experience which they nevertheless valued and thoroughly enjoyed. Trained like himself in the Stanislavskian tradition of method-acting, they found themselves forced to learn the art of improvisation, a technique deriving from the commedia dell'arte, in order to enter fully into the play's spirit of mischief. After paying tribute to the way in which Kustodiev's designs helped orientate the actors towards the required acting style, Dikii then described their preparations:

Актеров правды, актеров школы переживания нужно было 'развязать', приохотить к сценическому озорству, научить 'балаганить', сохраняя верность 'истине страстей' в шутейных, скоморошьих обстоятельствах народной комедии. […] Я разрешал им на репетициях дурачиться, нарушать привычные 'синтаксические' интонации, играть запятую как точку, импровизировать, потому что знал, что линия правды чувств ими уже проложена, логика действий усвоена, внутренний мир образов познан в его индивидуальной сути.[44]

It is clear from these and other remarks on this subject that the performance was a collaborative effort between director and actor. Furthermore, the great emphasis placed on improvisation suggests that, like most folk culture, the relationship between the 'text' and its performance was an extremely fluid one, with lines being changed and stunts pulled which may have radically departed from the original script. A sense of *Blokha* as 'performance' is given in Dikii's memoirs — here we are presented with a lively and exuberant account of how *balagan* theory was realized in practice — and it is symptomatic that few of these recollections bear any resemblance to the text published either in 1926 or 1929. He recalls, for example, the comic, folksy figure of Popov (playing the Tsar), with his small stomach, protruding bottom, and brand new galoshes, which he placed in a corner and waited to see whether they would stand upright or not; the generals turning their bottoms suggestively towards the audience while peering into the microscope in Act IV; the rowdy entrance of the Cossacks in

Act II — described as a massive *intermediia* in its own right — during which a wooden crow was shot off the roof of the church and leapt upwards into the air, squawking, but without flapping its wings; the negro waiter in London who cleaned the table so vigorously with his cloth that sparks flew from it; the English stool which, when sat upon, caused an electric bulb to go on and off in the background; the 'spiral of sweat' released when the Cossacks removed the roof of the gun-smiths' hut, causing everyone present to collapse, asphyxiated, to the floor; and the toilet, which flushed all by itself with a noisy and deafening roar. In his view, this was the kind of 'saucy' and 'racy' improvisation which frequently skirted the bounds of the acceptable and constituted the very essence of folk comedy.[45]

Many of the critics who reviewed *Blokha* were impressed by the visual strength of the spectacle and conceded that the stylization had been a great success. Zamiatin was praised for his borrowing of *balagan*-style devices; Kustodiev was congratulated for his costumes and set-designs; and the actors were applauded for their cabaret-style mode of acting.[46] The play also proved extremely popular with audiences. Within a month of opening, as reported in a letter by Dikii, the early reviews had aroused curiosity and given rise to sharply increased attendances ('Perepiska', 351). With some minor changes, *Blokha* was transferred to Leningrad and premièred on 25 November 1926 at the Bolshoi Dramatic Theatre: the artistic director this time was Nikolai Monakhov, but the set designs and costumes were again sup-plied by Kustodiev. This production also played to packed audiences — Annenkov calculates that there were at least three thousand performances in Moscow and Leningrad alone[47] — after which it was taken on a tour of the major provincial cities. *Blokha* continued to run at the Second Studio of the Moscow Art Theatre until 1930. It was taken off temporarily at this time in order to introduce fresh material (supplied by Zamiatin during the winter of 1930–31), after which the play was ready to reappear for the next autumn season.[48] As well as proving popular with audiences, the staging of *Blokha* provoked a great deal of interest on the part of certain academics. A general discussion of the spectacle took place at the State Institute of Art History (GIII) on 20 November 1926, just prior to the Leningrad première, with the partici-pation of Zamiatin, Boris Eikhenbaum, the literary historian B. M. Engel´gardt, and the Formalist linguist V. V. Vinogradov. Vinogradov later expanded his contribution into a lecture, 'Teoriia dramaticheskoi rechi', which he delivered at the State Academy of Artistic Studies on 20 January 1928;[49] while Zamiatin's talk, entitled 'Moia rabota nad

"Blokhoi"', formed the basis for the later 'Narodnyi teatr' — this was published in a special pamphlet issued to coincide with the Leningrad production, along with an important essay by Eikhenbaum ('Leskov i literaturnoe narodnichestvo'), and smaller pieces by Kustodiev, Leifert, and Monakhov.[50] Such was the play's immediate popularity that the satirical Physiogeocentric Association held a specially organized Flea Evening in December 1926, resulting in the publication of a humorous account of the play's conception and reception, 'Zhitie Blokhi' (1929), which was penned by Zamiatin and accompanied by illustrations from Kustodiev. An English translation of the play was undertaken by Zinaida Vengerova, possibly with a view to facilitating productions of the play in Anglophone countries (in his 1931 autobiography, written just prior to his exile, Zamiatin mentioned one in New York by an English director called A. Coates).[51]

Despite its popular appeal, there have always been reservations about *Blokha* as a meaningful piece of dramatic craftsmanship. Broadly speaking, these may be divided into two camps. Contemporary Soviet critics, while saluting the stylization of the spectacle, nevertheless grumbled that this was not 'proletarian art' and had little to say about contemporary society. They objected to the light-hearted and flippant way in which the era of Tsarist rule had been treated, criticized the characterization of the Tula peasants as 'alien' to contemporary rural reality, and were wary of a stylization which relied so blatantly on the norms of pre-revolutionary folk culture. The Western perspective, in some quarters, has been no less patronizing or dismissive. Unconsciously echoing the reservations of early Soviet critics, Douglas Clayton has described *Blokha* as a 'cute exercise in theatrical virtuosity' which did not respond 'in any profound way to the issues either of the theatre or of its age'.[52] It has also been condemned as 'long-winded and literary in manner'— its language is 'irritatingly pseudo-folksy', and as a 'supposedly fairground text [it] would have stood a good chance of being booed out of any self-respecting *balagan*'.[53]

Such views, while obviously not shared by the audiences of the day, are excessively harsh. *Blokha* was certainly not *engagé* in the manner of, say, Maiakovskii's *Klop* (1928), but herein lay the nature of its challenge to the theatre of the 1920s. It might be argued, for example, that the flippancy, whimsy, and gaiety constituted a large raspberry blown in the face of official puritanism and ideological seriousness. One of the satirical lyrics written for the Flea Evening, for example, was aimed at V. I. Ekskuzovich, the director of the Academic Theatre in Leningrad who sat on Zamiatin's play for more than a year before deciding not to stage it, and it nicely captures this sense of official unease:

> Понравилось мне представление.
> И вот — почему,
> Никак не пойму.
> Прямо обидно
> И перед коллегами стыдно.
> Никаких серьезных задач —
> Насекомое прыгает вскачь,
> Туда и обратно, —
> А смотреть приятно.[54]

In 'Zhitie Blokhi', moreover, Zamiatin himself mocked reviewers who tried to endow his stage adaptation with a gravitas to which it simply did not aspire (in *Zhizn´ iskusstva*, for example, a reviewer had tried to make a case for reading the play as a sustained meditation on the problems of modern industrialization).[55]

If audiences enjoyed *Blokha*, it was because it created its own watertight capsule in which, apart from the occasional topical aside, the realia of Soviet life and ideological norms could not intrude. There can be little doubt that the *balagan* mode of stylization was an important instrument in achieving this effect. The comic, fairy-tale version of Tsarist autocracy, as Soviet critics were not slow to appreciate, was controversial in terms of official Marxist propaganda; and even if the gaiety of the spectacle became muted towards the end, and a note of tragic pathos began to push its way to the surface, the re-emergence of Levsha from the magic stove brought the stylized nature of the play firmly back to the forefront of attention. To suggest, as Kelly does, that this spectacle was not as spontaneous or amusing as the authentic *balagan* is to ignore firstly the dramatic exigencies which Zamiatin was forced to confront in his attempt to adapt Leskov's story for stage, and secondly the enthusiastic response of audiences (who else, after all, judges the spontaneity of a spectacle and the authenticity of the language?).[56] There can also be little doubt, finally, that the exploitation of the carnival tradition and the skirting of the boundaries of good taste ran counter to the attempt by the authorities to expropriate and sanitize 'vulgar' street culture for agitprop purposes. Infused with the spirit of the carnival, with its satirical humour and anti-bourgeois mischief-making, *Blokha* was a celebration of art as fun-making. There are several instances, such as the song in the first act about the Tsar scratching 'vzad, i vpered' (a reference, presumably, to his bottom and genitals (345)), Malafevna's joke about going to bed with her cat (350), and the 'cure for fleas' which involves smearing the naked body with honey (350), where the humour is ribald, risqué, and straight out of the carnival grandad's repertoire. This is also not to ignore the occasional descent into bad language — Platov uses the expression *sukin syn* in Act III (367) — or the lavatorial humour (the decision to include the water closet may have been inspired by the desire to replicate something of the outrage caused by Marcel Duchamp's infamous *objet trouvé*, the urinal, when it was exhibited at the Society of Independent Artists in New York in 1917). Indeed, it can only be imagined to what extent the level of sauciness was further amplified during the actual performance as a result of the actors' freedom to improvise.

At the same time, the view of *Blokha* as an exercise in theatrical virtuosity with no relevance to the issues of the age must also be vigorously resisted. The Formalist interest in the play — illustrated by Eikhenbaum's essay on literary populism and Vinogradov's lecture on dramatic speech — places it within the evolving history of *skaz* in Russian culture and the expropriation and adaptation of folk culture by successive generations of élite. The fact that this phenomenon was crudely interrupted with the arrival of Socialist Realism does not diminish its importance or relevance in any way. Indeed, while it is clear with the benefit of hindsight that Zamiatin's programme for a truly popular theatre was destined to failure, or rather, that the Soviet state would promote its own, inauthentic folklore for propaganda purposes from the 1930s onwards, his remarks about the expropriation of folk culture in the spheres of music, painting, literature, sculpture, and theatre remain valid as far as the period of literary populism is concerned. Interestingly, the play's nationalistic underpinnings, and the degree to which they challenged the official ideology of the time (i.e. the preference for internationalism and the downgrading of all things 'Russian' in favour of all things 'Soviet') were noted and remarked upon by émigré reviewers, who did not have to contend with censorship.[57] Lunacharskii, for instance, is alleged to have remarked cryptically that *Blokha* marked the death knell of Constructivism.[58] Moreover, Dikii observed in his memoirs that the play had restored a sense of spectacle and rich colloquial speech to the theatre.[59] It is ironic, of course, bearing in mind the fact that the folk-religious edifice of Old Russia had more or less crumbled under the impact of civil war, revolution, and famine (it would later be destroyed almost completely by the anti-Orthodox campaigns and collectivization), that Zamiatin should take it upon himself to celebrate its persistence and project its resurrection and reification. The stove, which has the ability to restore youth to the ageing body, can be read as a metaphor for the artistic processes at work in *Blokha* (it is significant, for example, that in 'Narodnyi teatr' he uses the term *omolozhenie* (IV, 426) to describe the way in which professional artists had adapted and renewed folk theatrical forms for modern audiences). This can be seen perhaps as the one serious point of *Blokha:* that although buried by revolution and civil war — Zamiatin refers to Old Russia as a *pokoinitsa* in his article on Kustodiev ('Vstrechi s B. M. Kustodievym' (IV, 147)) — Rus´ would resurface because its traditions were deep-rooted and vital. His play was an expression of optimism, albeit a naive one, that Russian folk culture would not be swept away completely by a new wave of technological revolution.

Clearly the relationship between Zamiatin's play and Leskov's original is the vehicle by means of which many of these themes, and the problem of dramatized *skaz*, are explored. The choice of title, while possibly inspired by Musorgskii's 'Flea Song' — in other words, his setting to music of Goethe's 'Song of Mephistopheles in Auerbach's Cave' —, and doubtless intended to give the play a satirical edge, reinforces nevertheless its essentially parasitic status. As Keenan has observed, Zamiatin exploited the Leskov tale in much the same way peripatetic players performed the stock repertoire of popular theatre, with the pleasure and enjoyment of the spectators deriving from how the artist would reinterpret and refashion familiar material each time.[60]

At the same time, however, Zamiatin did not leave this 'familiar material' completely intact. He altered the dynamic of the plot, and introduced a number of themes which were absent in Leskov but very much germane to his own artistic concerns. *Blokha* can be compared to a number of works — for example, 'Elektrichestvo' (1918) and *Sever* — in which the superstitious peasant comes into contact with the world of enlightened rationality and technological progress, often with tragi-comic results. The character of Levsha bears more of a resemblance to the disreputable and illiterate Fedor Volkov in 'Afrika' than to the prototype in Leskov's original; indeed, it is symptomatic that both men belong to a schismatic community, and that the same disparaging epithet — *rvan´ korichnevaia* — is employed in relation to them both.[61] Similarly, Zamiatin's treatment of the English subject in *Blokha* differs significantly from Leskov's, reflecting as it did his own (unhappy) experience of living there and the theme of orderliness and mechanization as present in his two English satires and stage adaptation of *Ostrovitiane* (*Obshchestvo pochetnykh zvonarei* was staged for the first time in Leningrad's Mikhailovskii Theatre in November of the same year). The mocking of the British obsession with punctuality (compare, for example, Vicar Dewly's timetable for public and private functions in *Ostrovitiane* (I, 294) and *Obshchestvo pochetnykh zvonarei* (II, 285) with the constant checking of watches in Act III of *Blokha*); the use of the striptease as emblematic of modern sexual decadence (Didi, the *femme fatale* in *Ostrovitiane*, removes her clothing behind a screen in the theatre (I, 308), while in Act III of *Blokha* the English Meria is prepared to perform her *golaia tekhnika* in front of Levsha (377)); the joking about mechanized forms of human behaviour (Campbell is described as a tractor in *Ostrovitanie* (I, 295), while the English Meria, her name punning on the Russian verb for 'to measure' (*merit'*), moves and sings mechanically like a clockwork doll); and the use of English realia which would perhaps have been exotic to Soviet audiences (the setting fire to puddings, the decoration of the water closet etc.) are part of Zamiatin's deep contempt for and yet fascination with the English middle-class obsession with order and cleanliness. As someone who knew English well, and who himself had been sick, miserable, and unhappy in Britain until rescued by his wife, Zamiatin was ideally suited to appreciate the pathos of the Russian artisan stranded abroad and desperate to return home.[62] It suggests not only that the theme of Leskov's tale was one close to his heart, but that, as Matskin has rightly observed, *Blokha* was an exercise in co-authorship, not merely adaptation.[63]

When Leskov first published 'Levsha' in Aksakov's journal *Rus´*, he was plunged into immediate controversy, both in terms of his attitude towards the backwardness of Russia and the folk source on which the tale was allegedly based.[64] He claimed initially that the story was based on an authentic armoury legend which expressed the pride of Russian masters in the trade of the gunsmith. The epilogue, for example, described the tale as a 'legend of antiquity' (*predan´ie stariny*) and a 'popular fantasy' (*narodnaia fantaziia*). Piqued, however, by the tendency to overlook his own artistic contribution, Leskov subsequently issued a note of clarification in which he stressed that the story was not the product of folk fantasy after all, but rather the invention of his own imagination. It turned out that the only authentic folk element in the story derived from a witticism or *pribautka*: 'Англичане из стали блоху сделали, а наши туляки ее подковали да им назад отослали.'[65] It is now generally accepted that Leskov's initial claim about the armoury legend was false, and that such a legend never in fact existed. Furthermore, it is clear that the narrator of his tale is not the authentic Tula raconteur of the popular imagination. While 'Levsha' conforms to the idea of *skaz* in the sense that the telling of the tale has been entrusted to a persona whose imaginative outlook and social standing must be distinguished from the actual author (among other things, his voice is characterized by a false naivety and penchant for malapropisms), this persona is a crafty Leskovian construct whose relationship with the authentic *narod* is dubious, to say the least. This is not a 'told' tale in the manner of an explicitly *skaz* narrative, but rather a manipulated and 'written' narrative which makes occasional use of speech mannerism and colloquial syntax. The fact that certain characters use malapropisms first introduced by the narrator only serves to undermine the realistic status of the story and accentuate its preposterous and fantastic premise.

While Zamiatin clearly accepted the fabular texture of Leskov's narrative, he was probably unaware of the controversy surrounding its folk source. In his letter to Kliucharev, for example, he refers to the epilogue of 'Levsha' and cites the key phrases ('blasnoslovnyi sklad legendy', 'epicheskii kharakter geroia', and 'olitsetvorennyi narodnoi fantaziei mif') which indicate that the story is the product of folk fantasy. In his introduction to the published version of *Blokha*, moreover, he refers to the thematic material of the play as having derived both from a 'peripatetic folk tale' (*brodiachii narodnyi skaz*) and Leskov's story. This 'folk tale' had already been mentioned in his lecture at the State Institute of Art History: here he recalls encountering an 'oral version' of the armoury legend in the region of Tula before the Revolution. Furthermore, while wondering whether the source of this particular version might not have been Leskov himself, since the *raconteuse* in question was an old woman living in a literate family, he nevertheless referred to 'Levsha' as a 'secondary source':

Еще до революции мне довелось в г. Епифани Тульской губернии слышать устный сказ на эту тему, причем тогда, по правде говоря, особенно этот устный сказ меня не заинтересовал. Этот устный сказ представлял собою очень сокращенное и сжатое изложение лесковского рассказа, так что, помню, приходила даже в голову мысль, не был ли даже Лесков источником устного сказа — тем более, что рассказчица, старуха, жила в грамотной семье. [...] Устный сказ по словесной ткани был бледнее лесковского, а так как, повторяю, определяющую роль сыграла словесная сторона, то лесковский сказ, хотя он и был второисточником, явился определяющим фактором.[66]

It is interesting to note, nevertheless, that he ascribes the language of the narrative not to some storyteller or *skazitel´*, but to an imaginary Tula *avtor*, which means that at this time he understood the technical term *skaz* primarily in terms of a narrative mask or stylized performance, rather than simply a colloquially orientated mode of narration:

Мне хотелось и в данном случае применить на сцене полную сказовую форму — какая взята и у Лескова: весь рассказ — со всеми авторскими репликами — ведется неким воображаемым автором-туляком. И отсюда: вся пьеса должна быть разыграна некими воображаемыми туляками. Тогда естественны будут все 'мелкоскопы' в устах Царя — и тогда до конца будет использован комический эффект, заключающийся в самом словесном материале.[67]

Zamiatin devised the solution of the merrymen in order to approximate the comic, satiric, and essentially fictitious character of this author: they would assume his function as a linguistic and imaginative 'screen', commenting wittily on contemporary issues, assaulting the ear with quick-fire repartee, and showing up the stylized, and therefore fantastic and absurd nature of the spectacle. In essence, the sly and subtle wit of the original tale was replaced by an exaggerated form of pantomime comedy. Zamiatin's Tsar is much more of a buffoon than Leskov's, and bears little relationship to Nicholas I (in his letters to Dikii, Zamiatin strongly resisted all attempts to portray him realistically 'as a crass machine of discipline'). Furthermore, the carnivalized nature of the spectacle was reinforced by giving all the characters, whether 'high' or 'low' (i.e. whether monarch or peasant), the same substandard colloquial language. In addition, speech mannerisms, another device typical of folk theatre, were deployed for the purposes of characterization: Platov employs such phrases as *m-malchat´!*, *soglasno prisiage*, and *tak i tak*; the Tsar regularly intones the phrase 'nu, zdravstvui, chto li'; Levsha, who is markedly more incoherent and elliptical than the rest of the cast, peppers his speech with *tekhnicheski*; and Kisel´vrode's misquoting of Russian folk sayings results in the Tsar's one and only joke during the entire play.[68]

Keenan argues that the fantasy and the spectacle form a mask to conceal 'delicate material' just as the voice of Leskov's narrator ironically masked the meaning of the original story.[69] Topical and satirical material did, of course, creep into the play along with the merrymen. The title of the play, with its attendant associations of biting and irritation, implies a satirical bent (nothing of this kind is employed in Leskov, but there is joking along these lines in the Zamiatin–Dikii–Kustodiev correspondence).[70] Nevertheless, true to the spirit of carnival — Zamiatin refers to this himself in his lecture and 'Narodnyi teatr' — the material in question was good-natured and could hardly be constituted as seditious.[71] The first merryman, for example, jokes in his opening remarks about progress and the recent electrification campaign (Lenin's twin ingredients for the successful establishment of communism).[72] He strictly forbids 'disturbances' (*besporiadki*) on the part of the audience during the performance — such disturbances were very much part and parcel of the old *raek* performances, and thus he hints at the intolerance of authentic *balagan* on the part of the new authorities. He also makes the mistake of using the pre-revolutionary mode of address — 'Imperial Highness' — in relation to the Tsar in his prologue (343). In Act I, having donned a beard and glasses, he boasts the transformations of a magic stove which can take years off a man's life 'without damaging his brains' (345). This departs subtly from the eighteenth-century *lubok* ditty mentioned above, and is presumably a dig at the exponents of revolutionary transformation (the fact that the machine succeeds only in making its customer deaf and stupid increases the irony).[73] In his masked role as Dutch Doctor-Apothecary, he alludes to difficulties in the sphere of foreign relations (349). In his role as the *raeshnik*, moreover, he refers to an unhappy meeting between Russian and French ambassadors (355), presumably an allusion to the resumption of diplomatic relations in October 1924 which nevertheless failed to resolve the problem of debt renegotiations.[74] At this same juncture he also alludes mysteriously to the switching of sides by two Chinese generals (355), a reference, in all likelihood, to the bizarre hostilities which erupted between rival warlords Wu Pei-fu and Chang Tso-lin in September 1924, and led to a confusing change of government in Peking.[75] It is indicative of this contemporary slant that Zamiatin employs a slang term — *faraon* (373 & 387) — which could refer in general terms to the forces of law and order, but applied specifically during the February Revolution to members of the secret police (*SRIa*, IV, 553).

More significant than the number of topical allusions, none of which were going to cause censorship problems in the mid-1920s, were the changes in the plot dynamic of 'Levsha'. This resulted in an important shift in dramatic focus. Aleksandr I's visit to England after the Congress of Vienna, for example, was replaced with a new scene at the Imperial Palace featuring a fabular Tsar, a handful of incompetent generals, and Kisel'vrode, the imperial foreign minister. A further important revision, one planned as early as the first draft, involved delaying the revelation of the secret that the gunsmiths have forged tiny little shoes for the mechanical flea, and thus prevented it from executing its dance to music, until the final scene. Unlike in 'Levsha', where it precedes Levsha's departure for England in Chapter 12, this is the climactic and defining moment in *Blokha*. Furthermore, whereas this oversight causes the hero of the tale little embarrassment, in Zamiatin's adaptation, by contrast, it agitates him greatly and

contributes to the emotional turmoil which accompanies him to his
death in Act IV. The scene which takes place in London, which in
Leskov's tale conveys Levsha's fascination with the technological
superiority of the English, becomes instead an interrogation sequence,
shot with intermittent and melancholic yearning for the Motherland,
during which the hero is placed under pressure to reveal his secret
about the steel shoes. Further emotional pathos is achieved through the
introduction of a love-figure, Masha, the daughter of a wealthy Tula
merchant, whom Levsha is unable to marry because he cannot afford to
pay the huge dowry demanded by her father (in effect, the pair are the
stock *innamorati* of the commedia tradition).[76] It should be emphasized
that while the Old Believer sympathies of the gunsmiths are retained
from the original — Egupich is introduced as a 'scriptural expert'
(*nachetchik*)[77] — Levsha's depiction as a shabby, dishevelled player of
the harmonica with cockroach relics in his pockets is pure invention.
As I have remarked earlier, the denouement of the play was altered,
not only from Leskov's tale, but also from Zamiatin's own draft
proposal as outlined to Kliucharev. In Leskov, the hero returns to St
Petersburg and dies a futile death at the hands of the police before he
has the opportunity to tell the court about the English superiority in
musket-cleaning. In the early draft of *Blokha*, Levsha is handsomely
rewarded with enough money to make Masha his wife. And in the final
version he falls ill through inflammation of the liver, receives a paltry
reward of twenty kopecks for his brilliant invention, is beaten to death
by the police for disturbing the peace while playing his harmonica, and
is magically restored to life by the first merryman before disappearing
off stage arm-in-arm with his beloved Masha.

In Zamiatin's adaptation, the protagonist at the centre of the action is
more than simply a craftsman or gunsmith. In some ways, Levsha is a
comic figure akin to the fool or *durak* of the Russian folk tradition. He is
squint-eyed and poor; when we first meet him people are tripping him
up; and he is later described by his Tula compatriots as a *mukhrysh*
(358), a reference to someone who is slovenly and a slob (Dal´, II, 366).
One *topos* in the oral tradition — witnessed, for example, in the magic
tale 'Mudraia zhena' — involves a fool finding himself forced to
undertake an impossible mission by the king, his failure to do so
resulting in death.[78] In *Blokha* this receives its analogy in the
combination of cajoling bluster and threats (underpinned by the
showing of his gigantic fists) when the Cossack commander Platov
travels to Tula and enlists the support of the gunsmiths (this oppressive
atmosphere is not quite so explicit in Leskov). The fabular conceit of

the play is further underpinned by its use of the magical number three. The *durak* of folk tradition is usually the youngest of three brothers; and in the play we have three gunsmiths, each of whom may be said to represent a different quality: Siluian is associated with strength (witness his willingness to assault Masha's father in Act II); Egupich is associated with intelligence and learnedness; and Levsha, despite being a brilliant craftsman, is the simpleton (see the way in which the merrymen make fun of him for not understanding the mechanics of the peep-show in the opening sequences of Act II (356)).

As a player of the harmonica, however, one whose leitmotif throughout the play is a sad song about his beloved homeland, Levsha is also associated with music, song, and dance. By the end of the play, as Vinogradov has perceptively noted, his character has been manoeuvred out of the Leskovian sphere and into the symbolic sphere of the music-making entertainers.[79] It is significant, for example, that the very first amusement performed by the merrymen takes the form of a song to the accompaniment of the guitar (345); that the flea, when it is first glimpsed through the 'melkoscope', dances to the accompaniment of music (353); that Masha, Levsha's beloved (played, we should recall, by one of the merrymen), is the only object still 'dancing' for him after the flea has been incapacitated (387); that dancing generally is associated with the profession of the first merryman's father and the performing bear of traditional theatre (343); and that at the early stages of adaptation Zamiatin was contemplating opening the second act with the kind of round dance marriage game first used in the short story 'Kuny' ('Perepiska', 282). Unlike Leskov's tale, special weight is given to Levsha's discovery that his craftsmanship prevents the flea from dancing: his lament — 'ne tansuet' — which is repeated in the culminating scene, testifies to the pain that this discovery causes him and to the importance generally of music, song, and dance within the symbolism of the play. And it is worth remembering that his death is ultimately caused by his refusal to observe the official ban on the playing of music.

Zamiatin's decision to introduce these alterations for the stage version of the tale possesses a twofold impact. Indirectly, it might be argued, Levsha is associated with the idea of the carnival. Apart from the symbolic kinship in terms of dancing and music, it is suggested at another level by various actions and exchanges in the final scene which accentuate Levsha's anti-authoritarian defiance. The words engraved on the little shoes fashioned for the mechanical flea, for example, ostensibly involve merely a misspelling ('mater' instead of 'master'

(385)); but they can also be read as a potential pun which reflects the gunsmiths' innate sense of rebellion with regard to the task with which they have been entrusted.[80] This is accompanied by two impudent remarks addressed to the Tsar and his generals. Firstly, Levsha suggests that they must be blind if they cannot read the words, and that blindness is caused by parents hastily engaging in the act of conception: 'Скорей! А это ты слыхал: детей скоро, например, делать — слепые родятся?' (384). And secondly he accuses them of ignorance for not being able to understand the abbreviations: 'Вот ведь необразованные!'(385). The inability of the Tsar to understand the meaning of the abbreviations repeats the fruitless (cross-purpose) dialogue between himself and Malafevna in the first act (both scenes involve the misunderstanding of words). Therefore it might be argued that the play is not just about the backwardness of Russia under the Tsars and the inhuman treatment of the talented peasant artisan — as Levsha exclaims mournfully: 'Жизнь наша — копейка, судьба — индейка!' — but rather about the death and resurrection of the carnival itself. By extension, the stove which acts as the means of reification, and which is introduced by the merrymen themselves in the context of reinvigoration, comes to assume a crucial symbolic significance for the play as a whole.

The stove as an agent of resurrection, *pace* Goldt, does not derive from the tale of the miraculous, but rather from the Furnace Play (*Peshchnoe deistvo*).[81] Zamiatin refers directly to this ritual in connection with the merrymen both in 'Narodnyi teatr' (IV, 424) and in his preface to the play itself (341). In addition, along with a description of the role played by the Chaldeans, it is mentioned by Olearius in the section of his travelogue which occurs just prior to the passage quoted at length by Zamiatin in 'Narodnyi teatr' (IV, 428–29).[82]

The relevance of the Chaldeans to this ritual, and the use of the word *khaldei* to denote what is essentially a *skomorokh*-type figure (this kind of *khaldei* should not be confused with the Chaldean astronomers, popularly known as the Three Wise Men, who bring gifts of gold, frankincense and myrrh to the baby Jesus at Epiphany), is very much tied to its historical function as part of the Orthodox liturgy in the week prior to Christmas.[83] The subject or theme of this ritual is taken from Chapter 3 of the Old Testament Book of Daniel, and tells the story of three Jews — Shadrach, Meshach, and Abednego — whose refusal to swear an oath of fealty to King Nebuchadnezzar of the Chaldeans results in their being thrown into a burning furnace. Such is the force of the flames that the soldiers throwing them into the furnace themselves perish; the three boys, however, escape unharmed on account of their belief in God. The actions of the ritual are well documented from the sixteenth century onwards.[84] The 'Chaldean stove', for instance, usually took the form of a circular screen adorned by carvings and sculpted figures. Two comedians dressed as Chaldeans would bring burning coals over to the furnace. The three boys, played by novices or choirboys, and armed with lighted candles, would then be led into the stove, after which the Chaldeans would walk around it, tossing flammable herbs onto the coals so that they caught alight and burst into incandescent flames. After a brief exchange of words, the picture of the Angel of the Lord would be lowered into the furnace, the spectators would hear the sound of a thunderclap, and the boys would be led safely to freedom.[85]

This marked the end of the ceremony as far the liturgy was concerned. By the end of the seventeenth century, however, the Chaldeans had become synonymous in the public eye with the masked mummers who played games and performed tricks at Christmas. Described by Olearius as 'rascally' and 'insolent', the Chaldeans were allowed to run amok in the streets outside the church during the eight days before Christmas until the feast of Epiphany and set fire to the beards and hair of peasant onlookers: they were dressed like the masked mummers at Shrovetide, their victims were charged a copeck if they wanted to escape attack, and their own beards were smeared with honey so as not to catch fire.[86] Like much of carnival culture in Russia, these activities were officially tolerated. Furthermore, the *khaldei* were expected to rejoin the Orthodox establishment in the form of a symbolic baptism once their period of playfulness drew to a close (Olearius remarks that, unlike normal Christians, the *khaldei* could be baptized anything up to ten times during the course of a lifetime).[87] With the passage of time, as the speeches of the *khaldei* around the stove became increasingly vulgar, and their pranks became more and more offensive, the authorities became more and more alarmed until, in the middle of the eighteenth century, they resolved to ban the ritual altogether.

The idea of the stove was clearly important for Zamiatin. He could have chosen any number of comedian-style figures to 'lay bare' the devices of his play — he mentions several in his preface as 'forebears' to the Chaldeans (341) — therefore one can only conclude that their connection with the Furnace Play and antics over the Christmas period were decisive factors. It is interesting to note that the Furnace Play was associated symbolically with the idea of rebirth and revitalization. It has been argued, for example, that the ritual itself was intimately linked with the symbolism of Christmas and thus with the birth of Christ: it was performed, not on 17 December, the day in the calendar actually dedicated to the memory of the three boys, but later, during the Week of the Holy Fathers; moreover, the idea of being engulfed in flames, but not burning, is central to the symbolism of the Virgin Birth.[88] The patriarch, after inviting the Tsar to watch the ritual spectacle, would talk about the 'transformation' of the Chaldean furnace — by which he meant that a diabolical flame (because it was the work of an evil agent) was transformed into a sacred flame.[89] This idea of transformation, it has been pointed out, also informs the symbolism of fire in the folk imagination. For the peasant farmer, burning stooks symbolized the end of the old world and the beginning of the new — hence the symbolic significance of the burning of haycarts which took place outside the precincts of the church, and the smearing of honey on the beards of the *khaldei* (in Orthodox terms, honey was symbolic of heavenly sweetness).[90]

From this it would appear that Zamiatin's solution to the problem of the final scene in *Blokha* — whether it should end on an upbeat or depressing note — was more than just a piece of dramatic trickery; on the contrary, it is part of a symbolic system at the core of which lies the death of the old world and the beginning of the new. In the context of *Blokha*, this can be subjected to a variety of readings. On the one hand, it may be seen to represent the end of the old political system and the beginning of the new (an expression of solidarity with the October Revolution which is unlikely in the context). It could be approached as an expression of Zamiatin's own 'death' as a prose fiction writer and his 'rebirth' as a playwright (*Blokha* marks the beginning of a period in his career in which, for reasons as much financial as artistic, he embarks on a series of dramatic projects and film versions of his prose fiction, many of which fail to reach fruition).[91] In my view, however, the most convincing reading would be to approach the stove as a metaphor for the death and subsequent resurrection of folk-religious Rus´. This paradigm is reflected both in the imagery of the play — in the final act, Levsha talks about Tula, his *rodina*, having 'capsized' and 'sunk to the bottom [of the sea]' ('Тула-Тула первернула, ко дну козырем пошла...' (387)) — and in Zamiatin's discussion of the events of the recent past (as we have already seen, ancient Russia is described as a *pokoinitsa* in his obituary of Kustodiev (IV, 167)). Furthermore, the idea of the past resurrected in the present lies at the core of Remizov's inauguration of Obezvelvolpal and his promotion of the artist as the modern reincarnation of the *skomorokh*. His manifesto is a declaration of faith in historical continuity, in the unshakeable bonds that link the present and the past in folk-religious culture, and in the revitalizing and invigorating power of laughter throughout the ages. As he points out, even the greatest modernizer in Russian history, Peter the Great, permitted and even encouraged carnivalized modes of behaviour.[92]

Blokha signals the end of Zamiatin's interest in stylizations of Rus´ and is a fitting epitaph to the treatment of Old Russia as a literary subject in his fiction. It would be difficult to do justice to this subject, however, without examining his relationship with Boris Kustodiev at this point in his life. In his obituary, which he composed for a collection of essays in memory of the painter, Zamiatin spoke movingly of an artist whose unique and colourful vision he had been able to share only after its subject, Old Russia, lay dead and buried:

Встреча эта, когда я знал и полюбил не только Кустодиева, но и Бориса Михайловича, — случилась нескоро, лет через десять, когда пышная кустодиевская Русь лежала уже покойницей. (IV, 167)

Earlier, he had described his intense first encounter with Kustodiev the artist at a *Mir iskusstva* exhibition in 1912, where his attention had been initially grabbed by a powerfully evocative snow-scene:

На этой выставке вдруг зацепился за картину Кустодиева и никак не мог отойти от нее. Я стоял, стоял перед ней, я уже не только видел — я слышал ее, и те слова, какие мне слышались, я торопливо записывал в каталоге — скоро там были исписаны все поля. Не знаю названия этой картины, вспоминается только: зима, снег, деревья, сугробы, санки, румяное русское веселье — пестрая, кустодиевская, уездная Русь. Может быть, помимо всего прочего, эта картина так много говорила мне еще и потому, что сам я в те годы жил как раз этими же красками: тогда писалось мое 'Уездное'. Правда, Кустодиев видел Русь другими глазами, чем я — его глаза были куда ласковей и мягче моих, но Русь была одна, она соединяла нас — и встретиться раньше или позже нам было неизбежно.[93]

The inevitable meeting did take place, ten years later, when the two artists found themselves collaborating on the short story 'Rus´', which was published in an edition of one thousand copies by the Akvilon publishing house in March 1923 (*PZ*, 55). The manner in which their work came to inspire each other is revealed in Zamiatin's description of how this booklet came into being. Asked by the publishers to write a review of Kustodiev's series, which was modelled on the popular postcard designs of the pre-revolutionary era, Zamiatin spread them out on the table in front of him and became so inspired that he ended up writing a self-contained short story (see 'Vstrechi s Kustodievym'

(IV, 168)). Their artistic collaboration grew with increasing intensity after this moment. Kustodiev supplied the erotic illustrations for the émigré edition of 'Otrok Erazm' (ibid., 169). One year later he designed the cover for the reprinted book edition of *Uezdnoe*.[94] And in the winter of 1923 he painted Zamiatin's portrait (ibid., 179). Their mutual admiration may have been the reason why Kustodiev accepted the offer of work on *Blokha*, despite a crippling illness which left him paralysed from the waist down. The modest account of his contribution in 'Kak ia rabotal nad *Blokhoi*'— the title of which, curiously, echoed the title of the lecture given by Zamiatin at the State Institute of Art History — does not in any way do justice to his enormous contribution to the project. It is clear, for example, that his designs breathed life into the production and inspired the actors performing the main roles. On his own admission, moreover, Zamiatin visited Kustodiev regularly for urgent consultations on the set designs and costumes which frequently gave rise to new ideas, details, and 'stunts' (ibid., 173). The pleasure of their relationship was renewed with the comic sketch 'Zhitie Blokhi', the illustrations for which Kustodiev supplied 'in revenge' after reading Zamiatin's comical and satirical account of their earlier collaboration (ibid., 175). By this time they had become close acquaintances. Zamiatin invited the ailing painter and his family to stay in Lebedian´ in August 1926 — he rented a small room for their stay, accompanied them on short walks around the countryside, and introduced them to the provincial life which he had known ever since his childhood (Kustodiev's brother, an engineer, apparently rigged up a small motorized vehicle to improve his mobility, one jokingly dubbed 'a coffin on wheels' by the local teenagers).[95]

Zamiatin's relationship to Kustodiev and his painting is a litmus test of his changing attitudes towards the Old Russia of his youth. His obituary of the artist is essentially a lament for the passing of this world, one perfectly encapsulated in Kustodiev's painting and in the tragic circumstances of his death — as Zamiatin himself observed: 'Русь — в сущности, единственная тема его работ, он ей не изменял, и она не изменила ему — и не изменит' (IV, 177). Quoting poignantly from a fellow-artist who came to value Kustodiev's uniqueness only when he was no longer alive, and realized now that there was no one to replace him, Zamiatin gave vent to a wistfulness and nostalgia which he rarely revealed in public. The description of Lebedian´ encountered in his article — the frolicking calves, the self-satisfied geese, the carts rumbling to the local bazaars on feast days, the old women from neighbouring villages dressed in folk costume, the rosy-red apples in the gardens, the limitless fields, and the tolling of the ancient bells from the leaning tower at the bottom of the road which dated from the time of Elizabeth (ibid., 176) — paints a picture of rural idyll which could never have featured quite as simply or innocently in his early provincial fiction, even if many of the topographical elements were present. This was 'real', this was 'authentic' Rus´, now buried by Revolution and civil war, but still surviving miraculously in the heart of the Russian countryside. As Zamiatin admitted at the beginning of his obituary, Kustodiev's vision of this world had been less harsh than his own before the revolution (ibid., 167). *Blokha*, however, indicated the degree to which his attitude towards this world had softened, and the extent to which Kustodiev's 'red-faced' and 'motley' gaiety had come to infect him. It was an honest reflection of the strong roots which bound Zamiatin to the region he still described as his *rodina* one year after his mother had died. As he wrote in his 1929 autobiography: 'Думаю, что если бы в 1917 году не вернулся из Англии, если бы все эти годы не прожил вместе с Россией — больше не мог бы писать' (I, 32).

NOTES

1. *AKHRU: Povest´ Peterburgskaia*, pp. 47–48. For the publication details of 'Tulumbas' and the three other pieces which accompanied the formal inauguration of Obezvelvolpal, see note 11 of the previous chapter.
2. For discussion of the historical figure of the *skomorokh* and his official proscription by the authorities in 1678, see A. S. Famintsyn, *Skomorokhi na Rusi* (St Petersburg: Tipografiia E. Arngolda, 1889); A. A. Belkin, *Russkie skomorokhi* (Moscow: Nauka, 1975); and Russell Zguta, *Russian Minstrels: A History of the Skomorokhi* (Philadelphia: University of Pennsylvania Press, 1978).
3. *AKHRU: Povest´ Peterburgskaia*, pp. 49–50 (p. 49).
4. Ibid., p. 50.
5. There exists a screen representation of the *skomorokh* allegedly based on historical sources in Andrei Tarkovskii's *Andrei Rublev* (completed 1966, released 1971). The role of the buffoon is played by Rolan Bykov, and the episode begins with an anti-boyar song in a tavern which rapidly descends into bawdy (the *skomorokh* ends his song by dropping his trousers and baring his bottom in front of the assembled audience). For the description of this sequence in the *kinoroman*, see Andrei Konchalovskii and Andrei Tarkovskii, '*Andrei Rublev*', *Iskusstvo kino*, 1964.4, 138–200 (pp. 142–43).
6. The story does not actually use the word *chert*, but the reference to the evil assailant in the story as 'The red-haired one, you know, the very same...' ('Ryzhii, vot etot samyi...' (IV, 49)) makes this superfluous. For comparison, see 'Pribautki peterburgskikh "dedov"', in *Fol´klornyi teatr*, ed. by A. F. Nekrylova and N. I. Savushkina (Moscow: Sovremennik, 1988), pp. 395–407 (p. 401).
7. M. Chudakova, 'Eretik, ili matros na machte', in Evgenii Zamiatin, *Sochineniia*, ed. by T. V. Gromova and M. O. Chudakova, commentary by Evg. Barabanov (Moscow: Kniga, 1988), pp. 498–523 (p. 504).
8. *Blokha* (II, 341–88) was first published in 1926 by the Mysl´ publishing house in Leningrad under the title *Blokha: Igra v 4 d.*; it was reissued in a second edition shortly

afterwards (*PZ*, 55). Henceforth, unless otherwise stated, all references will be to the Neimanis version, but without the volume number. For the text of 'Skaz o tul´skom kosom Levshe i o stal´noi blokhe', see Leskov, *Sobranie sochinenii*, VII (1958), 26–59. For the sake of simplicity, this tale from now on will be referred to simply as 'Levsha'.

9.   Warner, *The Russian Folk Theatre*, pp. 72–73.
10. Kelly, pp. 18–19.
11. Annenkov, *Dnevnik moikh vstrech*, I, 266.
12. J. Douglas Clayton, *Pierrot in Petrograd* (Montreal: McGill-Queen's University Press, 1993), p. 192. For other studies or discussions of *Blokha*, see William Keenan, 'Leskov's Left-Handed Craftsman and Zamyatin's Flea: Irony into Allegory', *Forum for Modern Language Studies*, 15 (1979), 66–78; A. Matskin, 'Dikii igraet i stavit Leskova', *Teatr*, 3 (1986), 118–33 (pp. 121–27); Robert Russell, 'The Drama of Evgenii Zamiatin', *SEER*, 70 (1992), 228–48 (pp. 241–44); and Rainer Gol´dt, 'Uslovnye i tvorcheskie aspekty znaka v *Blokhe* E. I. Zamiatina', in *Poiski v inakom: Fantastika i russkaia literatura XX veka*, ed. by L. Heller (Moscow: MIK, 1994), pp. 85–100. Vinogradov's remarks on *Blokha* occur within the context of his general interest in *skaz* and Leskov's 'Levsha'. See E. I. Dushechkina's commentary to Vinogradov, 'Problema skaza v stilistike', pp. 325–34 (pp. 329–30).
13. See 'Iz knigi "Povest´ o teatral´noi iunosti"', in Dikii, *Stat´i: Perepiska: Vospominaniia*, pp. 357–64 (pp. 357–58).
14. Keenan, pp. 66 & 71.
15. Zamiatin's use of the word *skazka* is problematic here, since he does not distinguish between the folk tale (*skazka*) and the magic tale (*volshebnaia skazka*). However, judging by his remarks to Kliucharev about the 'fabular basis' (*basnoslovnyi sklad*) of Leskov's story, and the 'fabular tones' (*tona skazochnye*) which he sought for his stage adaptation, it seems reasonable to assume he is referring to the Russian magic tale in this particular context. See 'Perepiska', 281.
16. *Tsar´ Saltan* was premièred in Moscow on 21 October/3 November 1900, and *Zolotoi petushok* was staged for the first time on 24 September/7 October 1909 at Moscow's Zimin Theatre. See Gerald R. Seaman, *Nikolai Andreevich Rimsky-Korsakov: A Guide to Research* (New York: Garland Publishing, 1988), pp. 8 & 10. Diagilev's version for ballet was entitled *Le Coq d'or*, and was premièred in Paris on 24 May 1914 with designs by Natal´ia Goncharova. See Garafola, p. 405. Zamiatin was undoubtedly also acquainted with Remizov's version of the Arabian legend, 'Tsar´ Dodon', which was first published in 1920 by the Alkonost publishing house, and appeared one year later as a book edition with illustrations by Lev Bakst. See *Bibliographie des oeuvres de Alexis Remizov*, pp. 53–54.
17. Zamiatin is presumably referring here to *Russkie narodnye kartinki*, collected and described by D. Rovinskii, 5 vols (St Petersburg: Tipografiia Imperatorskoi Akademii nauk, 1881).
18. For the proper spelling, see 'Narodnyi teatr', as first published in *Blokha: Igra v 4 d. Evg. Zamiatina* (Leningrad: Academia, 1927), pp. 3–11 (p. 4).
19. 'Moia rabota nad "Blokhoi"', in Zamiatin, *Sochineniia*, pp. 570–72 (p. 572). This lecture is also held in the IMLI archives — see IMLI, opis´ 1, ed. khr. 202.
20. *Rusal´nye deistva* was the title given to three works — *Besovskoe deistvo* (1907), *Tragediia o Iude printse iskariotskom* (1908), and *Deistvo o Georgii Khrabrom* (1910) — which were stylized in the form of medieval mystery plays and published together in the eighth volume of Remizov's collected works. See *Bibliographie des oeuvres de Alexis Remizov*, p. 38. For the text of *Prints Lutonia* (1872), which was based on French author Marc Monier's *Théâtre des marionnettes*, see V. A. Kurochkin, *Sobranie stikhotvorenii*, ed. by A. V. Efremin (Moscow–Leningrad: Academia, 1934; repr. The Hague: Europe Printing, 1967), pp. 405–54.
21. Zamiatin was referring to the modern puppet-theatre of Simonovich and Efimova. In his view, they had successfully incorporated post-revolutionary material into the traditional Petrushka repertoire. He mentions Stravinskii's *Petrushka*, but argues that

he and Benois had exploited only the theme, rather than the form, of the puppet-theatre. See 'Narodnyi teatr' (IV, 426).

22. The commedia characters whom Zamiatin mentions in his first letter to Dikii — Brighella, Pantalone, and Tartaglia — are the key masked figures in *Turandot*. See Douglas Clayton, p. 119. For much of what follows, I rely on the discussion in Douglas Clayton, *Pierrot in Petrograd*, pp. 44–74, 75–102, and 103–124, respectively.

23. Ibid, p. 124.

24. Cited in ibid., p. 86.

25. The idea for the poster seems to have come from Dikii. In a letter to Zamiatin dated 23 October 1924, he writes: 'Надо составить текст афиши, которую мы хотим сделать не обычной, а от формы всего спектакля — красочной и балаганной' ('Perepiska', 297). Zamiatin's response in his letter of 30 October 1924 is interesting for the light it throws on his attitude to the production as a whole: 'Ваша затея с афишей — очень любопытна. Такая афиша равносильна выступлению раешника перед спектаклем: она сразу откроет зрителю характер спектакля. Но дело это тонкое: одно — слушать раешные слова в окружении соответствующей музыки, жестов и красок, другое — читать их напечатанными: напечатанные — они звучат гораздо грубее, и тут выбирать их надо подумавши да подумавши' (ibid., 299). Later, in his letter to Zamiatin dated 5 January 1925, Dikii recommends Leifert's book on *balagan* theatre for help with the design of the poster and programme (ibid., 333). The text of the poster is reproduced in ibid., 342; while the design of the whole poster is reprinted in colour in Lebedeva (*EV*), illustration no. 87.

26. 'Postanovochnye materialy k p´ese "Blokha"' (II, 503–06).

27. The decoration of this curtain is first mentioned in Zamiatin's letter to Dikii dated 7 December 1924: it was initially envisaged in the form of the word 'Blokha' in capital letters, accompanied by two large medallions, one with a picture of Levsha, the other with a picture of the Tsar ('Perepiska', 312). In his next letter, he writes: 'Его проект занавеса с портретами действующих лиц — очень типичен для балаганного занавеса; портреты, конечно, совершенно невероятные и непохожие (как в балагане бывает)' (ibid., 316). In a later letter to Kustodiev dated 26 December 1924, Dikii suggested the possibility of decorating the entire auditorium in the style of the *balagan* (ibid., 322), but this was rejected because of the size and sobriety of the Second Studio — see Zamiatin's letter to Dikii dated 31 December 1924 (ibid., 326). For the actual stage production, the word 'Blokha' was replaced by an image of the flea projected on to the curtain by means of a magic lantern. See Lebedeva (*RV*), p. 72. For a picture of the final version, see Lebedeva (*EV*), illustration no. 87. For a description of the stage production of Blok's *Balaganchik*, see Douglas Clayton, pp. 138–45.

28. See Lebedeva (*RV*), pp. 72–73; and Lebedeva (*EV*), illustration no. 74. For the popularity of freak shows generally at the showbooth, see A. F. Leifert, 'Balagany', in *Bloka: Igra v 4 d. Evg. Zamiatina*, pp. 23–27 (p. 24).

29. D. A. Rovinskii, 'Prikhod vozhaka s medvedem', in *Fol´klornyi teatr*, pp. 431–32 (p. 431). It is worth noting that the remarks of a modern bear-owner are recorded in Zamiatin's notebooks, presumably because the performance has clearly been adapted to new Soviet conditions. See 'Iz bloknotov 1914–1928 godov' (1989), p. 120.

30. 'Объявляю я свои науки, чтоб старики не зевали от скуки: стариков молодыми в печи переправляю и при этом мозгов совсем не повреждаю' (345). Zamiatin has modelled this sequence on a *lubok* design entitled *Galanskoi lekar´ i dobroi aptekar´*, two versions of which (one dating from the latter half of the eighteenth century, the other from the 1820s) are described by Rovinskii. See *Russkie narodnye kartinki*, I, 440–41, & 441–42. For a reproduction of the 1820s version, see Plate X. The theme of the quack physician and the miraculous reversal of the ageing process was a standard part of the pantomime repertoire in Russia. Leifert, for example, mentions a pantomime entitled 'Volshebnaia mel´nitsa; gde prevrashchaiut starukh v molodykh' as part of the programme for the Shrovetide and Easter *balagan*. See Leifert, p. 26.

31.   For cross-purpose dialogue as a device originating in the Petrushka puppet-theatre, see Kelly, p. 82.
32.   Ibid., p. 95. For the use of this device in *Balaganchik* and *Petrushka*, see Douglas Clayton, pp. 129 & 136–45. Zamiatin himself refers to this device in relation to *Tsar´ Maksimilian* in his letter to Dikii dated 22 February 1924 ('Perepiska', 291).
33.   Kustodiev produced completely independent designs for the Moscow and Leningrad productions. For the designs in question, see Lebedeva (*EV*), illustration nos. 70, 73, 74, 86–93, & 111; and Lebedeva (*RV*), pp. 70–71, 72–73 & 164–67. The audience reaction to the *lubok* stylization can be gauged by contemporaneous reports both from within the Soviet Union and abroad. Iurii Skobelev, for example, remarked that 'for over three hours while the performance ran, the laughter in the auditorium did not cease'. Cited in Russell, p. 242. In Riga, where *Blokha* was premièred on 4 January 1927, the artists reponsible for the designs and decorations had followed Kustodiev's prescriptions so successfully that the audience burst out into spontaneous applause when the first curtain was lifted, and were clearly ecstatic. See Izmagulova, 'Evgenii Zamiatin na stsene teatra russkoi emigratsii', p. 371.
34.   'Iz knigi "Povest´ o teatral´noi iunosti"', p. 358.
35.   Lebedeva (*RV*), p. 73.
36.   Ibid.; and also Lebedeva (*EV*), illustration no. 90. The Leningrad set was different: it boasted a chintz-blue sky, white polka-dot snow, pink gingerbread houses, and a bearded Tula native drinking tea from a samovar the size of a house. See ibid., illustration no. 91.
37.   The water closet was a controversial addition to the stage-design. Dikii originally gave instructions concerning the toilet scene in Act III in a letter to Kustodiev dated 5 January 1925 ('Perepiska', 331). Both Zamiatin and Kustodiev felt that this would be inappropriate. In a letter to Dikii dated 16 January 1925, Zamiatin argued that this sort of stunt had already been pulled (and with greater crudity) by Meierkhol´d in his 1923 production of *Zemlia dybom* (ibid., 341). Likewise, Kustodiev described the proposed toilet as 'unappetizing' in a letter to Dikii dated 20 January 1925 (ibid., 344). Dikii was insistent, however, and Kustodiev executed the design as requested, sending it to Moscow with the following short note of description: 'Аглицкое нужное место, белый кафель, медный кран, стеклянный градусник, зонтик, чтобы сидящий там защищен был от дождя и солнца, цветы для духа, и для приятности.' Cited in Lebedeva (*RV*), p. 73.
38.   'Iz knigi "Povest´ o teatral´noi iunosti"', p. 360.
39.   This is one of the 'fantastic items' (*butaforiia*) mentioned by Leskov in his original story. Ideas about the form of this 'barometer' are discussed in Zamiatin's letter to Dikii dated 9 January 1925 ('Perepiska', 337).
40.   Dikii, *Stat´i: Perepiska: Vospominaniia*, pp. 160 & 161.
41.   See Lebedeva (*EV*), illustration no. 73.; and Lebedeva (*RV*), p. 167. See also the stage instructions for the play itself (344).
42.   Lebedeva (*EV*), illustration no. 87.
43.   Lebedeva (*RV*), p. 74, & the colour illustrations, pp. 72–73.
44.   'Iz knigi "Povest´ o teatral´noi iunosti"', p. 359.
45.   Ibid., pp. 359–61.
46.   See the excerpts of the reviews in *Izvestiia*, *Pravda*, *Vecherniaia Moskva*, and the journal *Novyi zritel´*, as cited and discussed in 'Perepiska', 351–53 (note 1).
47.   Annenkov, I, 266.
48.   'Avtobiografiia' (written 1931), p. 13.
49.   See Dushechkina's commentary to Vinogradov, 'Problema skaza v stilistike', p. 329.
50.   See note 18 of the present chapter.
51.   'Avtobiografiia' (written 1931), p. 13. Among the Zamiatin papers in IMLI are a series of corrections made by him to Vengerova's translation (IMLI, opis´ 1, ed. khr. 128). These are interesting, not only because they provide evidence, if such evidence were needed, of the difficulty of rendering the colloquial language of *Blokha* into English,

but also because they testify to Zamiatin's somewhat less than total command of contemporary English idiom.

52. Douglas Clayton, p. 192.
53. Kelly, p. 154.
54. Cited in Annenkov, I, 269.
55. 'Zhitie Blokhi' (II, 515–16, & 518 (note 13)).
56. The favourable reaction was not restricted to the audiences. Although we have only Zamiatin's word for it, when he first read the play to the actors and actresses of MKHAT–2 while they were touring in Leningrad, they laughed so much that it was almost impossible to continue. See 'Avtobiografiia' (written 1931), p. 13.
57. See, for example, the following view expressed by an émigré critic in Riga: 'Любовь к "РАСЕЕ", любовь стихийная, любование талантами, ее гордость — ведь все это темы ЗАПРЕТНЫЕ, недопустимые в царстве интернационала. И когда Левша в городе Лондоне томится тоской по родной земле, когда он по возвращении туда жадно целует эту родную землю "Рассею", восторг советских зрителей в стране, где уничтожено самое имя России и заменено нелепыми литерами, имеет СОВЕРШЕННО ОСОБЫЙ СМЫСЛ И ЗНАЧЕНИЕ.' All emphases in the original. Cited in Izmagulova, p. 370.
58. Cited in 'Iz knigi "Povest´o teatral´noi iunosti"', p. 362.
59. Ibid.
60. Keenan, p. 72.
61. 'Afrika' (282) and Blokha (357).
62. The extent of Zamiatin's unhappiness while in England can be gauged by the letters to his wife while in Newcastle-upon-Tyne. See RN, I, 194–216.
63. Matskin, p. 122.
64. For further discussion, see Hugh McLean, Nikolai Leskov: The Man and his Art (Cambridge, MA: Harvard University Press, 1977), pp. 392–406.
65. Cited in Leskov, Sobranie sochinenii, VII, 501.
66. Zamiatin, Sochineniia, pp. 570–71.
67. Ibid., p. 571.
68. Leskov compared the witticism about the mechanical flea to a similar saying about the Germans: 'Что же касается самой подкованной туляками английской блохи, то это совсем не легенда, а коротенькая шутка или прибаутка, вроде "немецкой обезьяны", которую "немец выдумал, да она садиться не могла (все прыгала), а московский меховщик взял да ей *хвост пришил* — она и села".' Emphasis in the original. Cited in Leskov, Sobranie sochinenii, VII, 501. Kisel´vrode's comic reversal of this joke, one which rebounds because he himself is German, occurs in Act I:

КИСЕЛЬВРОДЕ Не расстраивайтесь, ваше царское величество: врет, дело ясное. Что немец! По нашей русской пословице: немцев обезьяна выдумала.
ЦАРЬ Тебя вот действительно обезьяна выдумала. (347)

69. Keenan, p. 72.
70. It is not clear who decided to call the play Blokha, or when this decision was first taken. It is significant, however, that Zamiatin puns on the title in his very first letter to Kliucharev: 'Честь имею Вас уверить, что лесковская блоха меня укусила так здорово, что на прошлой неделе я уже сделал первый эскизный набросок пьесы' ('Perepiska', 281). Later, in a letter to Dikii dated 22 Feburary 1924, he writes: 'Вот в чем горе: как она, блоха, есть существо очень прыгучее, то и вышло, что укусила она меня и Вас в очень разных местах' (ibid., 290). This idea is also the theme of the first merryman's tune: 'Дрита-дрита-дрита-дрита,/Как отцу архимандриту/Блошка спать не дает:/Уж она его кусает/Целу ночь напролет./На царя блоха насела —/Он и взад, и вперед,/Он и так, и сяк, и этак,/А блохи не найдет …' (345).
71. 'Комическое в народном театре, в Петрушке, в раешнике, непременно приправлено солью сатиры, всегда очень добродушной; такая сатира составляет основной фон всей "Блохи"' (IV, 428). Compare with the earlier 'Moia rabota nad "Blokhoi"': 'Народная комедия — не является чистой комедией... Еще: почти всегда комический элемент

смешан с сатирическим.' Cited in Zamiatin, *Sochineniia*, p. 571. On the barbed humour of the carnival *ded*, see Leifert, p. 24.

72. Keenan, p. 72. In the programme, moreover, Act II is mockingly described in terms of the 'blossoming of industrialization and living roses in the town of Tula'. See 'Postanovochnye materialy k p´ese "Blokha"'(II, 504).

73. There is further irony in the fact that in the original *lubok* engraving the quack physican hits the women three times while they are in the furnace in order to effect his cure. See the text cited in *The Lubok*, illustration no. 90.

74. The resumption of diplomatic relations took place on 28 October 1924, seven years after the October Revolution, and the first Soviet Ambassador to Paris was appointed two months later. The 'howling' refers perhaps to the public recriminations which followed owing to the two governments' inability to reach an amicable settlement over the question of debts and credits. See Edward Hallett Carr, *A History of Soviet Russia: Socialism in One Country*, 3 vols (London: Macmillan, 1964), I, 42–45.

75. A decisive part of the battle was the desertion of Wu Pei-fu's principal lieutenant in the north, Feng Yu-hsiang, on 16 September 1924. Roughly a month later, on 23 October 1924, he seized Peking on his own account and set up a provisional government with Tuan Ch'i-Jui at its head. According to Carr, this caused a considerable amount of confusion in Moscow at the time. See ibid., III, 711–12. Zamiatin has altered the names for comic effect: General 'Pei-chaiu' (Drink-Tea) and General 'Chei-syn' (Whose-Son).

76. Douglas Clayton, p. 23.

77. 'Perepiska', 321.

78. *Narodnye russkie skazki A. N. Afanas´eva*, II (1985), 130–34.

79. 'Я говорил о разрыве двух линий в "Блохе": "Левша" остается как "образ" то в "лесковской" литературной сфере, то вовлекается в круг комедийных масок совсем иного эмоционального тона.' This remark, in which Vinogradov recounts his contribution to the discussion the previous day, is contained in his letter to N. M. Malysheva dated 21 November 1926, and cited in Dushechkina's commentary to 'Problema skaza v stilistike', p. 329.

80. The words engraved on the shoes — 'Oru. Mater' — are ostensibly an abbreviation for *Oruzheinyi Master* (i.e. Gunsmith Meister), the second part of which has been misspelt. However, the first word could also be taken literally as 'I roar' (the first person singular of the verb *orat´*), especially since there is a full stop after it. Whereas 'Mater' could be taken as an abbreviation of the verb 'to swear' (*materit´sia*), the first person singular of which would be *materius´*. Read in this way, the inscription can be taken as a protest at the almost impossible position the gunsmiths have been put into by Platov, who has warned them that if they do not come up with something to trump the English, then their lives will not be worth living.

81. Gol´dt, 'Uslovnye i tvorcheskie aspekty znaka', p. 94.

82. *The Voyages and Travells of the Ambassadors Sent by Frederick Duke of Holstein to the Great Duke of Muscovy and the King of Persia, Written Originally by Adam Olearius, Secretary to the Embassy, Faithfully Rendered into English by John Davies*, 2nd edn (London: [n. pub.], 1669), p. 96.

83. It is impossible to establish with any precision the point at which the Furnace Play arrived in Russia — although believed by some to have arrived from Constantinople at some point in the fifteenth century, precise records relate only to the sixteenth and seventeenth centuries. See V. Vsevolodskii (Gerngross), *Istoriia russkogo teatra*, 2 vols (Leningrad: Teakinopechat´, 1929), I, 243; and also D. S. Likhachev, *Smekh v drevnei Rusi* (Leningrad: Nauka, 1984), p. 158. It may be worth mentioning in this context that two *lubok* versions of this ritual are described in Rovinskii's collection. See *Russkie narodnye kartinki*, IV, 770–72.

84. They are so well documented that Eisenstein included a re-enactment of the ritual in Part 2 of his film *Ivan Groznyi* — this shows the *khaldei*, the furnace, the lighting of the furnace, and the songs sung by the three boys. The sequence itself, although reduced

in length from the original screenplay, is a crucial one, since the ritual provides the background for a confrontation between the patriarch (Philip) and the Tsar, whose *oprichnina* is accused of lawlessness. See *Ivan Groznyi: Kinostsenarii S. M. Eizenshteina* (Moscow: Goskinoizdat, 1944), pp. 104–18. Coincidentally, the actress who played the third merryman so successfully in *Blokha*, Serafina Birman, here plays the role of Evfrosin´ia Staritskaia, a member of the boyar family which has come into conflict with the Tsar; indeed, the opening frames of the Chaldean sequence see her explaining to a small boy the symbolism of the ritual. See ibid., p. 105. This sequence has been described as 'the last oblique Soviet treatment of the carnival', although the scholar in question has mistaken the comedians who take part in it for ordinary *skomorokhi*. See Kelly, p. 158.

85. Likhachev, pp. 158–60.
86. *The Voyages and Travells of the Ambassadors*, p. 96
87. Ibid.
88. Likhachev, p. 160.
89. Ibid.
90. Ibid., p. 164.
91. Such an intention was conveyed privately in a letter to Iarmolinskii in March 1925, a month after the play's first performance in Moscow. See Zamiatin's letter to Iarmolinskii dated 11 March 1925, cited in Shane, p. 43. In his 1929 autobiography, moreover, he speaks about his 'betrayal' of literature for the world of film and theatre (I, 32). This is confirmed by his archives, which contain copious evidence of his various endeavours in this direction. The following are either screenplay versions of his own short stories or tales, original plays, or plays adapted from works conceived and performed abroad (the dates in parentheses relate to the time when the individual works were written): *Atilla* (1925–27), *Severnaia liubov´* (1927), *Peshchera* (1927), *Istoriia odnogo goroda* (1927), *Sensatsiia* (1929), *Afrikanskii gost´* (1929–30), *Zhizn´ Ivana* (1931), *Siurpriz* (1931), *Podzemel´e Guntona* (1931), and *Ela* (1931). See IMLI, opis´ 1, ed. khr. 130–49 & 151–64.
92. 'Великий преобразователь России был тоже скоморох, и скоморошил он дело государственное на всешутейших трапезах и на службах великого князь-папы. […] Не было дела, которое не переделывалось бы в шутку, и не было шутки, которая не претворялась бы в дело — скоморошьей дубиной дубилась Россия.' See 'Kaftan Petra Velikogo', in *AKHRU: Povest´ Peterburgskaia*, pp. 48–49.
93. 'Vstrechi s Kustodievym', ed. by A. Galushkin, *V mire knig*, 1987.6, 36–39, & 46–49 (p. 36). The reason that this source has been preferred to the version published by Neimanis is that a key half-sentence has been omitted from the latter.
94. For a reprint of the cover in question, see ibid., p. 39.
95. This information is given in a draft outline of the obituary, but not in the published version. See ibid., p. 49 (note 12).

CONCLUSION

Although the path of Zamiatin's writing career to a large extent mirrors that of Nikolai Gogol´ — by this I mean that a collection of provincial stories deeply rooted in the folk-religious imagination is succeeded by a series of more sophisticated urban tales — it is impossible to discuss his brand of literary populism without due reference to Nikolai Leskov and the Russian literary tradition to which he belongs. According to van Baak, Leskov was the 'lone wolf' of Russian literature, a writer who, through his portrayal of eccentric characters, his experiments in genre, and fascination with popular etymology openly polemicized with the fictional worlds being presented to the public in the nineteenth century by the 'aristocrats' and *raznochintsy*.[1] The challenge presented by Zamiatin, a writer whose rise to prominence coincided with the rediscovery and proper appreciation of Leskov in the second decade of the twentieth century (culminating in the publication of the previously banned *Zaiachii remiz* on the eve of the October Revolution), is of a similar order.[2] As van Baak has observed, the correspondences between these two writers went beyond formal technique to embrace the moral structure of their respective worlds and the destinies they assigned to their fictional heroes. Leskov and Zamiatin were thus 'stylizers of Rus´', writers who explored the periphery and margins of Russian provincial life, and presented their manipulated and constructed world as if through the eyes of a non-conformist experimenter.[3]

Although it is a commonplace to stress Zamiatin's debt to such writers as Leskov — Mirra Ginsburg refers to the Gogol´–Leskov– Remizov axis and the tradition of the 'told' tale in her introduction to the first collection of his short stories in English[4] — this debt has not been appreciated in all its richness and depth. One perhaps unexpected and paradoxical conclusion of this study is the degree to which Zamiatin, despite being a rational and agnostic intellectual, was fascinated and charmed by the folk-religious mind. Not only was he deeply immersed in this imaginative world — his knowledge of the rituals, customs, beliefs, oral literature, and theatre of the folk is revealed at every turn of the page — but he was able to communicate its exoticism and very Russian flavour with a sensitivity and

immediacy rare even among those of his contemporaries with a shared
artistic credo. In the introduction to this study, I invoked the character
of Senia in the short story 'Neputevyi' as a model for the revolutionary
(i.e. debauched and agnostic) activist who nevertheless embraces the
ancient churches, leather-bound ecclesiastical tomes, and old singing of
Orthodox tradition:

И голову ломают: как это Сеня, беспутник, безбожник — к игумену в милость попал?
На чем столковались они? Разве это вот, что всякую старину Сеня любил: церкви
древние, лампады под праздник, книги в старых кожаных переплетах — минеи,
триоди да цветники-изборники отеческие. Пение любил церковное, распевы всякие
знал — и знаменный, и печерский и по крюкам пел. Вот это разве? (I, 101)

It should be clear from the texts examined in this study that Zamiatin
also respected and loved the Orthodox cultural tradition, even if he
himself was not a believer. If this aspect of his writing has remained
obscured until now, it is partly because even at the time of writing, as
far as his metropolitan readers were concerned, his explorations were
perceived as exotic and appealing only to those with a certain specialist
interest and knowledge (Maksimov's description of the ignorance
surrounding the symbolism of the Feast of Prepolovenie in nineteenth-
century Russia testifies to the nature of the problem). Undoubtedly,
this kind of ignorance has been compounded by the passing of time
which, in a manner reminiscent of the Kitezh legend, has caused this
old Orthodox world largely to disappear from view. Like a deluge, the
turmoil and civil strife which engulfed the countryside after the
October Revolution, and the aggressively secular and positivist
educational policies of the Soviet state, destroyed the link between past
and present (this is illustrated forcefully by the dictionary of terms
recently drawn up as an aid for schoolchildren studying *Uezdnoe*, many
of them ecclesiastical and, from a Western point of view, basic).[5] The
aim of this study therefore has lain as much in the exhumation of the
world which Zamiatin knew as a young man growing up in Lebedian',
as in the artistic 'construct' which his provincial fiction represents.

   Another aspect of his writing which this study has tried to
communicate, and which deserves much greater emphasis as far as our
understanding of his entire *oeuvre* is concerned, is his love of language.
It is not for nothing that Voronskii drew attention to his 'worshipping'
of words; or that Shteinberg and Koni regarded his main contribution
to Russian literature in terms of his 'mining' for 'precious jewels' in the
'deep seams' of the language. The imagery of adornment and refinery
represented by the word 'jewels' is highly appropriate here, since it

conveys the great sensual pleasure to be gained from reading Zamiatin's *skaz* stylizations on a purely linguistic level; indeed, it would not be an exaggeration to say that, somewhat akin to Barthes's idea of the *plaisir du texte*, there is a vicarious and voyeuristic eroticism to be experienced in the act of reading such texts by Zamiatin. This relates not only to his use of archaisms and dialect from the folk-religious lexicon (and the associated pleasures of leafing through the dictionaries of Dal´ and Sreznevskii), but also to his appreciation of language as a visual and auditory phenomenon. Zamiatin was a sculptor who took great delight in exploiting the musical and textural value of words. The provincial fiction furnishes a myriad of cases where a word has been chosen as much for its euphonic potential as for its iconic value. Furthermore, as illustrated by his 'Skazki pro Fitu', this interest extended even to the sphere of individual letters: here we see the use of the pre-revolutionary letter *theta* (θ) both as a mode of characterization (to dub someone with the epithet 'theta', as Zamiatin satirizes Lenin, is a mode of opprobrium which refers to a superficial and second-rate mind, as well as to a person who is full of hot air) and as a visual sign (like the letter, the character in the tales is small and rotund, and his unhappy fate is to be punctured like an American dinghy).[6] The punning, allusive potential of language (witnessed in the names given to his characters) is another central preoccupation in the provincial fiction. Contrary to conventional wisdom, it can be argued that the ludic tendency in Zamiatin as far as language is concerned is far more in evidence, and intrinsically far more interesting, in the earlier than in the middle-period or later work.

Examination of these aspects of his fiction is bound to influence our overall perception of Zamiatin as a writer. The purpose of this study is not merely to relocate him within a specifically Russian and literary populist tradition, but also to demonstrate that his provincial fiction belongs to a different aesthetic altogether. It is no longer desirable, for example, to seek an understanding of his early work on the basis of principles outlined in his essays and manifestos of the 1920s. His remarks on the increasing pace of modern life, his championing of speed and efficiency of description in order to communicate our altered perceptions of reality, and his discussion of synthetic art as the means by which to convey this new reality, are only marginally relevant to a world in which technology and industrialization are totally absent. The simple people who populate these early stories owe their way of life and imaginative consciousness precisely to the fact that enlightenment and progress has yet to make a significant impact on their lives (as an example of Zamiatin's own awareness of this problem, see his ironic treatment of Marei's obsessive desire to construct a street lamp as a vehicle of enlightenment in *Sever*). As the lectures at the House of Arts demonstrate, if these stylistic devices are encountered in the early fiction, it is largely in the interests of conveying the dynamism of colloquial speech, rather than the dynamism of a particular mode of consciousness. It is part of a project of 'democratization' of the written word and the 'enrichment' of the Russian language. While this was undoubtedly a modernist project, and can best be viewed alongside the neorealist experiments of the writers initially grouped around the journal *Zavety*, it belongs to a different chapter in the history of modernism, one in which, as Eikhenbaum indicated in his essay on Leskov, the 'low' art forms of the folk are incorporated into 'high' art for the achievement of a *lubok*-style effect.

A related point concerns the aesthetic impact of this experiment on the reader. The critical responses to Zamiatin's early work, ranging from severe condemnation of the ugliness of his prose style (Derman) to an enthusiastic appreciation of its 'newly minted' quality (Voronskii) illustrate that this problem is not a straightforward one. The impact of Zamiatin's provincial fiction is certainly visceral; and if this study has attempted to emphasize the beauty, splendour, and charm of his work, it is tempered by the recognition that his prose style is informed by an aesthetic which privileges dissonance as much as harmony. The musical and textural qualities of his writing can be harsh and brutal; and this was a fact recognized by Zamiatin himself. In an unfinished article on the artist Boris Grigor´ev, for example, he referred to his writing in terms of 'beautiful ugliness' (*krasota bezobraznogo*), the famous catchphrase of the neoprimitivist exhibition held by the Knave of Diamonds painters in 1910 (for an example of Grigor'ev's work, see Plate XI). In the same article, moreover, he referred to the use of dissonance in Skriabin's piano music, and the way in which the composer had accustomed the modern ear to accept what he called 'dis-chords' (*nonakkordy*) and sevenths.[7] These comparisons testify to Zamiatin's sense of the challenge which his *skaz* stylizations presented to the modern reader. But they also provide a useful aesthetic prism through which to view and appreciate his work. Not only does his neorealism have its analogy in the neoprimitivist experiments of such painters as Mikhail Larionov and Natal´ia Goncharova, but he also incorporated motifs directly from their work as if in tribute to their common artistic endeavour — the depiction of Baryba in terms of a 'stone woman' or *kamennaia baba* in *Uezdnoe* is a particularly striking example of this.[8]

The way in which Zamiatin's aesthetic informs his attitude towards Rus´ will also now require radical reassessment. It has been customary hitherto to emphasize the cold and mercilessly detached nature of his exposé of provincial life. Undeniably, the reader of his fiction is treated to a graphic and disturbing account of vulgarity, backwardness, stupidity, bestiality, mendacity, lawlessness, injustice, corruption, inertia, and boredom; and many of his fictional protagonists are portrayed as sly, unreliable, ignorant, duplicitous, thieving, lazy, and inhumane. The pleasure to be derived from studying his fiction should not in any way detract from a sober appreciation of the overall impact of his tales, with their mordant irony and grim reflection on life's absurdities and the futile struggle against death. Yet 'detachment' is not the correct term to describe Zamiatin's paradoxical and ambiguous attitude towards the world of the provinces. He both loved and hated this world, as he himself made clear when he cited approvingly Aleksandr Blok's oxymoronic concept of 'hateful love' (*nenavidiashchaia liubov´*) to describe his feelings towards Russia ('Aleksandr Blok' (IV, 146)). Furthermore, in his article on the psychology of creativity, he confessed to 'being in love with' the negative characters in *Uezdnoe*, despite their 'ugly' and 'repulsive' personalities ('Psikhologiia tvorchestva' (IV, 368)).

Irreconcilable and conflicting elements lie at the very heart of Zamiatin's writing. He was an agnostic who encouraged his students to study the ecclesiastical literature of antiquity; a modernist who delved deep into the ancient strata of the language in order to give his prose muscularity, durability, and exoticism; and an intellectual who succeeded in evoking the life and language of the folk with tremendous resonance, and yet at the same time with an almost patrician sense of irony and humour. Unlike his Populist predecessors, Zamiatin refused to idealize the peasant; and it was precisely the mercilessness of his gaze which caused Marxist critics after the Revolution, wrongly in my view, to accuse him of reactionary sympathies. Such attacks, which were politically motivated rather than honestly felt, confused moral imperative with cynicism and a sense of superiority, and it can only be hoped that now scholars are free to engage with Zamiatin's work in an independent way this aspect of his fiction will receive due recognition.

NOTES

1. 'Leskov and Zamyatin: Stylizers of Russia', p. 313.
2. Although written from 1891 to 1895, Leskov's novel was first published in September 1917 in the journal *Niva*. Zamiatin refers to the hero — Onoprii Opanasovich Peregud — as the epitome of ignorance and philistinism in an article written by him on behalf of the editors of *Russkii sovremennik* in 1924. See 'Peregudam' (IV, 332–37).
3. van Baak, p. 313.
4. *Yevgeny Zamyatin: The Dragon and Other Stories*, ed. and trans. by Mirra Ginsburg (London: Penguin, 1975), p. 7.
5. The fact that this list contains such words as *igumen, riza, Sonnik, Katekhizis, tropar´, vsenoshchnaia, kliros, amvon, kel´ia, klobuk, kelar´, prosvira, ugodnik, vechernia,* and *krestnyi khod* gives a good indication of the degree to which Soviet society had become secularized. As far as Zamiatin's linguistic gems are concerned, however, this is only the tip of a very large and daunting iceberg. See G. V. Poliakova, 'Slovar´ k povesti E. I. Zamiatina "Uezdnoe" (iz opyta raboty uchitelia)', in *Tvorcheskoe nasledie Evgeniia Zamiatina*, II, 133–39.
6. 'Pervaia skazka pro Fitu' (III, 101–03). The joke at the heart of this tale has been lost in the editions published since its first appearance in *Delo naroda*. This is because the Greek letter *theta* (pronounced 'f' in the pre-revolutionary alphabet) became redundant as a result of the orthographic reforms of 1917–18, and its functions were assumed instead by the letter 'f' (ф). Zamiatin's prediction of an untimely end for his *theta* character may have been partly based on the redundancy of the letter itself and the likelihood that it would soon disappear — its abolition had been mooted as early as 1904, and was still very much part of the progressive agenda in 1917. See Bernard Comrie and Gerald Stone, *The Russian Language Since the Revolution* (Oxford: Oxford University Press, 1978), pp. 203–06. For earlier uses of this letter as a term of opprobrium, see Pushkin's sardonic epigram, written in 1825 and aimed at Fedor Glinka ('Nash drug *Fita*, Kuteikin v epoletakh'), in which he admonishes the poet for his long-winded psalms (Kuteikin, we recall, is the seminarian in Fonvizin's *Nedorosl´*), and expresses the hope that he will not end up by becoming a *fert* (i.e. 'dandy' or 'fop'). It is probably also worth mentioning that in Part I Chapter 4 of Gogol´'s *Mertvye dushi* the uncouth landowner Nozdrev uses the word *fertiuk*, a diminutive of *fert*, in relation to his brother-in-law. Gogol´ explains in an accompanying note (no doubt with his tongue solidly wedged against his cheek) that this word derives from *theta*, a letter considered 'by some' to be 'indecent'. See Gogol´, *Sobranie sochinenii*, V (1978), 7–236 (p. 74, note 1). It is not quite clear why this should be so, although for *fertiuk* Dal´ (IV, 583) gives 'a sullen person, a grumbler, someone who is perennially full of hot air' ('ugriumyi chelovek, briuzga, kto vechno duetsia'). Clearly there is something suggestive about the shape of the letter and the sharp exhalation of breath which is required when it is pronounced.
7. 'Boris Grigor´ev', in Zamiatin, 'O literature i iskusstve', pp. 166–67 (p. 166).
8. *Kamennaia baba* is the term given to the various stone statues of antiquity discovered by archaeologists near pagan burial mounds in Southern Russia in the nineteenth century. These statues were approximately six feet high and depicted human forms both of the male and female gender: a photograph of one such female stone statue standing outside the Hermitage in St Petersburg is reproduced in Anthony Parton, *Mikhail Larionov and the Russian Avant-Garde* (London: Thames and Hudson, 1993), p. 100 (see Plate XIIa). Natal´ia Goncharova was known to have been fascinated by these weathered figures, and transformed them into angular, quasi-cubist monsters in her paintings *The God of Fertility, Stone Woman (Still Life),* and *Pillars of Salt (Cubist Method),* all of which date from 1909 and 1910. For a reproduction of *Pillars of Salt*, see Plate XIIb; and also Mary Chamot, *Goncharova: Stage Designs and Paintings* (London: Oresto Books, 1979), p. 30. The similarity in shape and design between her stone figures and the physical description of Baryba, the main protagonist in *Uezdnoe*, is

striking. Initially, his face is described as an angular, upturned iron (I, 33); later, moreover, in the very last lines of the tale, he has been transformed into a huge, square-faced, stone woman: 'Покачиваясь, огромный, четырехугольный, давящий, он встал и, громыхая, задвигался к приказчикам. Будто и не человек шел, а старая воскресшая курганная баба, нелепая русская каменная баба' (I, 86).

BIBLIOGRAPHY

1. Zamiatin

Archive Materials

Institut mirovoi literatury imeni M. Gor´kogo Akademii nauk SSSR (IMLI), Moscow, fond 47, 625 edinits khraneniia (1903–32)

Works and Editions

O tom, kak istselen byl otrok Erazm (Berlin: Grzhebin, 1922; repr. Moscow: Izdatel´stvo 'Kniga', 1989)

Blokha: Igra v 4 d. (Leningrad: Mysl´, 1926)

Sobranie sochinenii, 4 vols (Moscow: Federatsiia, 1929)

Sochineniia: Tom pervyi, ed. by Evgenii Zhiglevich, introduction by Aleksandr Kashin (Munich: Neimanis, 1970)

Sochineniia: Tom vtoroi, ed. by Evgenii Zhiglevich and Boris Filippov, preface by Filippov (Munich: Neimanis, 1982)

Sochineniia: Tom tretii, ed. by Evgenii Zhiglevich, Boris Filippov, and Aleksandr Tiurin, preface by Filippov and Zhiglevich, and afterword on the novel *My* by Vladimir Bondarenko (Munich: Neimanis, 1986)

Sochineniia: Tom chetvertyi, ed. by Evgenii Zhiglevich, Boris Filippov, and Aleksandr Tiurin, introduction by Filippov (Munich: Neimanis, 1988)

Sochineniia, ed. by T. V. Gromova and M. O. Chudakova, with commentary by Evg. Barabanov (Moscow: Kniga, 1988)

Izbrannye proizvedeniia, ed. by A. Iu. Galushkin, preface by V. B. Shklovskii, introduction by V. A. Keldysh (Moscow: Sovetskii pisatel´, 1989)

Lectures, Essays, Journalism, and Notebooks (not published by Neimanis)

'Narodny teatr', in *Blokha: Igra v 4 d. Evg. Zamiatina* (Leningrad: Academia, 1927), pp. 3–11

'Vstrechi s Kustodievym', ed. by A. Galushkin, *V mire knig*, 1987.6, 36–39 & 46–49

'Iz bloknota 1931–1936 godov', ed. by A. Tiurin, *Novyi zhurnal*, 168–169 (1987), 141–74

'Iz literaturnogo naslediia', ed. by A. Tiurin, *Novyi zhurnal*, 170 (1988), 77–86

'Iz bloknotov 1914–1928 godov', ed. by A. Tiurin, *Novyi zhurnal*, 172–173 (1988), 89–127

'Iz bloknotov 1914–1928 godov', ed. by A. Tiurin, *Novyi zhurnal*, 175 (1989), 103–34

'Nezakonchennoe', ed. by A. Tiurin, *Novyi zhurnal*, 176 (1989), 109–33

'O literature i iskusstve', ed. by A. Tiurin, *Novyi zhurnal*, 178 (1990), 151–93

'Dvugolos´e. Iz bloknotov 1921–1928', ed. by Oleg Mikhailov, *Slovo v mire knig*, 1989.11, 76–85

'Duby (nabroski k romanu)', ed. by V. Tunimanov, *Novyi zhurnal* (St Petersburg), 2 (1993), 3–50

'Literaturnaia studiia Zamiatina', ed. by Aleksandr Strizhev, *Literaturnaia ucheba*, 1988.5, 118–43

'Tekhnika khudozhestvennoi prozy', ed. by Aleksandr Strizhev, *Literaturnaia ucheba*, 1988.6, 79–107

'Moia rabota nad "Blokhoi"' (1926), in Evgenii Zamiatin, *Sochineniia*, pp. 570–72

Ia boius´: Literaturnaia kritika: Publitsistika: Vospominaniia, ed. with commentary by A. Iu. Galushkin, introduction by V. A. Keldysh (Moscow: Nasledie, 1999)

Autobiographies (not published by Neimanis)

'"Avtobiografiia" E. I. Zamiatina' (1923), ed. by V. V. Buznik, *Russkaia literatura*, 1992.1, 174–76 (p. 175)

'Avtobiografiia' (written 1931), ed. by A. Galushkin, *Strannik*, 1 (1991), 12–14.

Correspondence

'Perepiska s E. I. Zamiatinym i B. M. Kustodievym po povodu spektaklia "Blokha"', in Aleksei Dikii, *Stat´i: Perepiska: Vospominaniia*, ed. by N. G. Litvinenko and A. G. Guliev (Moscow: Iskusstvo, 1967), pp. 279–356

'Iz perepiski s rodnymi', introduction and notes by Aleksandr Strizhev, in M. Golubkov, 'Evgenii Zamiatin: "K razrusheniiu ravnovesiia..."', *Nashe nasledie*, 1989.1, 104–09 (pp. 113–16)

'Pis´ma E. I. Zamiatina A. M. Remizovu', ed. by V. V. Buznik, *Russkaia literatura*, 1992.1, 176–80

'"Moi deti – moi knigi"*: From Evgenii Zamiatin's Letters', ed. by Julian Graffy and Andrey Ustinov, in *Themes and Variations: In Honor of Lazar Fleishman, Stanford Slavic Studies*, 8 (1994), 343–65

'Perepiska E. I. Zamiatina s V. S. Miroliubovym', ed. by N. Iu. Griakalova and E. Iu. Litvin, *Russian Studies*, 2.2 (1996), 416–37

'Pis´ma k L. N. Zamiatinoi', *Rukopisnoe nasledie Evgeniia Ivanovicha Zamiatina*, ed. by L. U. Buchina and M. Iu. Liubimova, 2 vols, Rukopisnye pamiatniki series, 3 (St Petersburg: Rossiiskaia natsional´naia biblioteka, 1997), I, 9–419

Bibliographical Materials

'Proizvedeniia E. I. Zamiatina', compiled by Aleksandr Strizhev, *Sovetskaia bibliografiia*, 1989.3., 53–57

Galushkin, A. Iu., 'Materialy k bibliografii E. I. Zamiatina', *Russian Studies*, 2.2 (1996), 368–413

Galushkin, Aleksandr, '"Vozvrashchenie" E. Zamiatina. Materialy k bibliografii' (1986–1995), in *Novoe o Zamiatine*, pp. 203–324

Translations

Yevgeny Zamyatin: The Dragon and Other Stories, ed. and trans. by Mirra Ginsburg (London: Penguin, 1975)

2. Critical Works on Zamiatin

Autour de Zamiatine: Actes du colloque: Université de Lausanne, juin 1987, ed. by Leonid Heller (Lausanne: Age d'homme, 1989)

Annenkov, Iurii, *Dnevnik moikh vstrech: Tsikl tragedii*, 2 vols (New York: Inter-Language Literary Associates, 1966)

Cavendish, Philip, 'Playing Devil's Advocate: Paradox and Parody in Zamiatin's "Ash Wednesday"', in *Russian Literature and its Demons*, ed. by Pamela Davidson (New York: Berghahn, 1999), pp. ??

Chudakova, M., 'Eretik, ili matros na machte', in Evgenii Zamiatin, *Sochineniia*, pp. 498–523

Davydova, Tat´iana, 'Antizhanry v tvorchestve E. Zamiatina', in *Novoe o Zamiatine*, pp. 20–35

de Haard, Eric, 'On Zamjatin's Narrative Art — "Lovec čelovekov"', in *Voz´mi na radost´: To Honour Jeanne Van der Eng-Liedmeier* (Amsterdam: [n. pub.], 1980), pp. 169–81

Edwards, T. R. N., *Three Russian Writers and the Irrational: Zamyatin, Pil´nyak, Bulgakov* (Cambridge: Cambridge University Press, 1982)

Eikhenbaum, B. M., 'Strashnyi lad' (1913), in *O literature: Raboty raznykh let*, ed. with commentary by M. O. Chudakova, E. A. Toddes, and A. P. Chudakov (Moscow: Sovetskii pisatel´, 1987), pp. 289–92

Faiman, Grigorii, '"Dnem i noch´iu chasovye...". Zamiatin v 1919– i 1922–gg', in *Novoe o Zamiatine*, pp. 78–88

Galushkin, A. Iu., 'Iz istorii literaturnoi "kollektivizatsii"', *Russian Studies*, 2.2 (1996), 437–78

Galushkin, Aleksandr, '"Delo Pil´niaka i Zamiatina". Predvaritel´nye itogi i rassledovaniia', in *Novoe o Zamiatine*, pp. 89–148

Geller [Heller], Leonid, 'O neudobstve byt´ russkim (emigrantom)', in ibid., pp. 176–202

Gildner, Anna, 'Stylizacje na gatunki staroruskie v twórczosci Eugeniusza Zamiatina', *Slavia Orientalis*, 37 (1988), 103–09

Gol´dt, Rainer, 'Uslovnye i tvorcheskie aspekty znaka v *Blokhe* E. I. Zamiatina', in *Poiski v inakom: Fantastika i russkaia literatura XX veka*, ed. by L. Heller (Moscow: MIK, 1994), pp. 85–100

Gol´dt, R., 'Mnimaia i istinnaia kritika zapadnoi tsivilizatsii v tvorchestve E. I. Zamiatina', *Russian Studies*, 2.2 (1996), 322–50

Gol´dt, Rainer, '"Podzemel´e Guntona": neizvestnyi stsenarii E. Zamiatina', in *Novoe o Zamiatine*, pp. 149–75

Graffy, Julian, 'Zamyatin's "Friendship" with Gogol', *Scottish Slavonic Review*, 14 (1990), 139–80

Gregg, R. A., 'Two Adams and Eve in the Crystal Palace: Dostoevsky, the Bible, and "We"', *Slavic Review*, 24 (1965), 680–87

Iangirov, R., 'Prazhskii krug Evgeniia Zamiatina', *Russian Studies*, 2.2 (1996), 478–520

Izmagulova, T. D., 'Evgenii Zamiatin na stsene teatra russkoi emigratsii', ibid., 361–75

Kaznina, O. A., *Russkie v Anglii* (Moscow: Nasledie, 1997), pp. 199–226

Keenan, William, 'Leskov's Left-Handed Craftsman 'and Zamyatin's Flea: Irony into Allegory', *Forum for Modern Language Studies*, 15 (1979), 66–78

Lampl, Horst, 'Altrussisch-kirchenslawische Stilisierung bei Remizov und Zamjatin', *Wiener slavistisches Jahrbuch*, 21 (1975), 131–45

Lazarev, Vladimir, 'Vozvrashchenie Evgeniia Zamiatina', *Sovetskaia bibliografiia*, 1989.3, 53

Lebedev, Andrei, '"Sviatoi grekh" Zenitsy Devy, ili chto mog chitat´ inok Erazm', in *Novoe o Zamiatine*, pp. 36–55

Liubimova, Marina, '"Ia byl vliublen v revoliutsii..."', ibid., pp. 56–71

Lundberg, E., 'Literaturnyi dnevnik', *Sovremennik* , 1915.1, 214

Matskin, A., 'Dikii igraet i stavit Leskova', *Teatr*, 3 (1986), 118–33

Mikhailov, Oleg, 'Zamiatinskie torosy', *Slovo v mire knig*, 1989.11, 74–75

Myers, Alan, 'Evgenii Zamiatin in Newcastle', *SEER*, 68 (1990), 91–99

Myers, Alan, 'Zamiatin in Newcastle: The Green Wall and the Pink Ticket', *SEER*, 71 (1993), 417–27

Niqueux, Michel, '*Uezdnoe* (*Choses de province*) de Zamiatin et le débat sur le peuple russe après la révolution de 1905', in *Autour de Zamiatine*, pp. 39–55

Novoe o Zamiatine, ed. by Leonid Heller (Moscow: MIK, 1997)

Poliakova, G. V., 'Slovar´ k povesti E. I. Zamiatina "Uezdnoe" (iz opyta raboty uchitelia)', in *Tvorcheskoe nasledie Evgeniia Zamiatina*, II, 133–39

Poliakova, L. V., 'Evgenii Zamiatin: tvorcheskii put´. Analiz i otsenki', ibid., I, 7–83

Postnikov, S., 'Stranitsy iz literaturnoi biografii E. I. Zamiatina', published as a supplement in R. Iangirov, 'Prazhskii krug Evgeniia Zamiatina', pp. 516–18

Primochkina, N. N., 'M. Gor´kii i E. Zamiatin (k istorii literaturnykh vzaimootnoshenii)', *Russkaia literatura*, 1987.4, 148–60

Remizov, Aleksei, 'Stoiat´ — negasimuiu svechu pamiati Evgeniia Ivanovicha Zamiatina', in M. Golubkov, 'Evgenii Zamiatin: "K razrusheniiu ravnovesiia"', *Nashe nasledie*, 1989.1, 104–19 (pp. 117–19)

Rogachevskaia, Ekaterina, 'Zamyatin's Чудеса and the Medieval Russian Tradition: Certain Aspects', *Essays in Poetics*, 21 (1996), 79–92

Russell, Robert, 'The Drama of Evgenii Zamiatin', *SEER*, 70 (1992), 228–48

Shaitanov, Igor´, 'O dvukh imenakh i ob odnom desiatiletii', *Literaturnoe obozrenie*, 1991.6, 19–25

Shane, Alex M., *The Life and Works of Evgenij Zamjatin* (Berkeley and Los Angeles: University of California Press, 1968)

Shteinberg, A., *Druz´ia moikh rannikh let (1911–1928)* (Paris: Sintaksis, 1991)

Tunimanov, V. A., 'Poslednee zagranichnoe stranstvie i pokhorony Evgeniia Ivanovicha Zamiatina', *Russian Studies*, 2.2 (1996), 387–416

Tvorcheskoe nasledie Evgeniia Zamiatina: Vzgliad iz segodnia, ed. by L. V. Poliakova, 2 vols (Tambov: Tambovskii Gosudarstvennyi Pedagogicheskii Institut, 1994)

van Baak, J., 'Visions of the North: Remarks on Russian Literary World-Pictures', in *Dutch Contributions to the Tenth International Congress of Slavists: Sofia, 14–22 September 1988: Literature*, ed. by A. van Holk, Studies in Slavic Literature and Poetics series, 12, (Amsterdam: Rodopi, 1988), pp. 19–43

van Baak, Joost, 'Leskov and Zamyatin: Stylizers of Russia', in *Literary Tradition and Practice in Russian Culture. Papers from an International Conference on the Occasion of the Seventieth Birthday of Yury Mikhailovich Lotman*, ed. by Valentina Polukhina, Joe Andrew, and Robert Reid, Studies in Slavic Literature and Poetics series, 20 (Amsterdam: Rodopi, 1993), pp. 312–24

Voronskii, A., 'Evgenii Zamiatin' (1922), in *Stat´i* (Ann Arbor: Ardis, 1980), pp. 57–91

Zolotnitskii, D. I., 'Evgenii Zamiatin i "instsenirovka istorii kul´tury"', *Russian Studies*, 2.2. (1996), 350–60

3. Reference Works

Bibleiskaia entsiklopediia, compiled by Arkhimandrite Nikifor (Moscow: Snegirova, 1891; repr. Moscow: Terra, 1990)

Bol´shoi vsemirnyi nastol´nyi atlas Marksa (St Petersburg: Marks, 1905)

Dal´, Vladimir, *Tolkovyi slovar´ zhivogo velikorusskogo iazyka*, 4 vols, 2nd edn (Moscow–Petersburg: Vol´f, 1880; repr. Moscow: Russkii iazyk, 1981)

Entsiklopedicheskii slovar´ izd. Brokgauza i Efrona, ed. by I. Andreevskii, 42 vols and 4 supp. vols (St Petersburg: Efron, 1890–1907)

Mifologicheskii slovar´, ed. by E. M. Meletinskii (Moscow: Sovetskaia entsiklopediia, 1990)

Mify narodov mira, ed. by S. A. Tokarev, 2 vols (Moscow: Sovetskaia entsiklopediia, 1980–82)

Penguin Dictionary of Saints, ed. by Donald Attwater, 2nd edn (London: Penguin, 1983)

Petrovskii, N. A., *Slovar´ russkikh lichnykh imen* (Moscow: Russkie slovari, 1996)

Polnyi pravolsavnyi bogoslavskii entsiklopedicheskii slovar´, 2 vols ([n.p.]: Soikin, [n.d.]; repr. Moscow: Vozrozhdenie, 1992)

Polnyi tserkovno-slavianskii slovar´, compiled by Father Grigorii D´iachenko ([n.p.]: [n. pub.], 1900; repr. Moscow: Moscow Patriarchate, 1993)

Slovar´ russkogo iazyka, 4 vols, 2nd edn (Moscow: Russkii iazyk, 1981–84)

Slovar´ russkogo iazyka XI–XVI vv., ed. by S. G. Barkhudarov and others (Moscow: Nauka, 1975–)

Sreznevskii, I. I., *Materialy dlia slovaria drevnerusskogo iazyka*, 3 vols (St Petersburg: Imperatorskaia Akademiia nauk, 1893–1903; repr. Moscow: Gosudarstvennoe izdatel´stvo inostrannykh i natsional´nykh slovarei, [n.d.])

4. Folk-Religious Sources

Afanas´ev, A. N., *Russian Fairy Tales*, trans. by Norbert Guterman, folkloristic commentary by Roman Jakobson (London: Routledge, [1946]), pp. 631–56

Byliny, ed. by V. I. Kalugin (Moscow: Sovremennik, 1986)

Fol´klornyi teatr, ed. by A. F. Nekrylova and N. I. Savushkina (Moscow: Sovremennik, 1988)

Golubinaia kniga, in *Russian Folk Literature*, ed. by D. P. Costello and I. P. Foote, Oxford Russian Readers series (Oxford: Clarendon Press, 1967), pp. 173–77

Izbornik: Povesti drevnei rusi, ed. by D. S. Likhachev, L. A. Dmitrieva, and N. V. Ponyrko (Moscow: 'Khudozhestvennaia literatura', 1986)

Judith, introduction and commentary by Carey A. Moore, Anchor Bible series, 40 (New York: Doubleday, 1985)

'Legenda o grade kitezhe', in *Pamiatniki literatury drevnei rusi: XIII vek*, ed. by L. A. Dmitrieva and D. S. Likhachev, Pamiatniki literatury drevnei rusi series, 3 (Moscow: Gosudarstvennoe izdatel´stvo khudozhestvennoi literatury, 1981), pp. 211–27

Molitvy i pesnopeniia Pravoslavnogo Molitvoslova, translations into Russian and commentaries by Nikolai Nakhimov (St Petersburg: Sinodal´naia tipografiia, 1912; repr. Moscow: Donskoi Monastyr´, 1994)

Narodnye liricheskie pesni, ed. with introduction by V. Ia. Propp (Leningrad: Sovetskii pisatel´, 1961)

Narodnye russkie skazki A. N. Afanas´eva (1855–64), ed. by L. G. Barag and N. V. Novikov, 3 vols (Moscow: Nauka, 1984–86)

Povest´ vremennykh let po Lavrent´evskoi letopisi: 1377g, ed. by V. P. Adrianova-Peretts, translation and commentary by D. S. Likhachev, 2nd (revised) edn, Literaturnye pamiatniki series (St Petersburg: Nauka, 1996)

Russkie narodnye kartinki, collected and described by D. Rovinskii, 5 vols (St Petersburg: Tipografiia Imperatorskoi Akademii nauk, 1881)

'Slovo o zhitii i o prestavlenii velikogo kniazia Dmitriia Ivanovicha, Tsaria russkogo', in *Pamiatnik literatury drevnei rusi: XIV–seredina XV veka* (Moscow: Gosudarstvennoe izdatel´stvo khudozhestvennoi literatury, 1981), pp. 208–29

Sobolevskii, A. I., *Velikorusskie narodnye pesni*, 7 vols (St Petersburg: Gosudarstvennaia tipografiia, 1895–1902)

The Golden Legend of Jacobus de Voragine, ed. and adapted from the Latin by Granger Ryan and Helmut Ripperger (New York: Longman, Green, 1948)

The Lubok: Russian Folk Pictures: 17th to 19th Century, introduction and selection by Alla Sytova (Leningrad: Aurora, 1984)

Vizantiiskie legendy, ed. and trans. into modern Russian by S. V. Poliakova, 2nd edn (Moscow: Ladomir, 1994)

'Zhitie Marii Egipetskoi, byvshei bludnitsy, chestno podvizavsheisia v Iordanskoi pustyni', in *Vizantiiskie legendy*, pp. 84–98

'Zhitie prepodobnogo, bogonosnogo ottsa nashego Feodosiia, igumena Pecherskogo', in *Kievo-Pecherskii paterik*, trans. by E. Poselianin (Moscow: [n. pub.], 1900; repr. Moscow: Izdatel'stvo imeni sviatitelia Ignatiia Stavropol'skogo, 1996), pp. 55–118

'Zhitie sviatykh i pravednykh bogoottsy Ioakima i Anny', in *Zhitiia Sviatykh na russkom iazyke izlozhennye po rukovodstvu Chet'ikh-minei sv. Dimitriia Rostovskogo s dopolneniiami iz Prologa*, 12 vols (Moscow: Sinodal'naia tipografiia, 1903–11), I (1903), 185–92

'Zhizn' i deianiia avvy Simeona, Iurodivogo Khrista radi, zapisannye Leontiem, episkopom Neapolia kritskogo', in *Vizantiiskie legendy*, pp. 53–83

'Zhizn' i deianiia blazhennogo Simeona Stolpnika', ibid, pp. 25–36

5. Critical Sources on Folk-Religious Culture

Afanas'ev, A., *Poeticheskie vozzreniia slavian na prirodu*, 3 vols (Moscow: Soldatenkov, 1865–69; repr. Moscow: Indrik, 1994)

Alissandratos, Julia, *Medieval Slavic and Patristic Eulogies* (Florence: Sansoni, 1982)

Belkin, A. A., *Russkie skomorokhi.* (Moscow: Nauka, 1975)

Bernshtam, T. A., *Russkaia narodnaia kul'tura pomor'ia v XIX – nachale XX v.* (Leningrad: Nauka, 1983)

Chicherov, V. I., *Zimnii period russkogo narodnogo zemledel'cheskogo kalendaria: XVI – XIX vekov*, Trudy instituta etnografii im. N. N. Miklukho-Maklaia (new) series, 40 (Moscow: Akademiia nauk SSSR, 1957)

Clarke, K. W. and M. W., *Introducing Folklore* (New York: Holt, Rinehard & Winston, 1963)

Douglas Clayton, J., *Pierrot in Petrograd* (Montreal: McGill-Queen's University Press, 1993)

Dushechkina, Elena, 'Russian Calendar Prose: the Yuletide Story', *Elementa*, 1993.1, 59–74

Ermolov, A., *Narodnaia sel'skokhoziaistvennaia mudrost' v poslovitsakh, pogovorkakh i primetakh: I: Vsenarodnyi mesiatseslov* (St Petersburg: Suvorin, 1901)

Famintsyn, A. S., *Skomorokhi na Rusi* (St Petersburg: Tipografiia E. Arngolda, 1889)

Florovsky, Georges., *Puti russkogo bogosloviia*, 2nd edn (Paris: YMCA, 1981)

Frierson, Cathy A., *Peasant Icons: Representations of Rural People in Late Nineteenth-Century Russia* (New York: Oxford University Press, 1993)

Goddard Elliott, Alison, *Roads to Paradise: The Lives of the Early Saints* (Hanover, NH: University Press of New England, 1987)

Gromyko, M. M., *Traditsionnye normy povedeniia i formy obshcheniia russkikh krest'ian XIX v.* (Moscow: Nauka, 1986)

Hennessey Olsen, Alexandra, '"De Historiis Sanctorum": A Generic Study of Hagiography', *Genre*, 13 (1980), 407–29

Heffernan, Thomas J., *Sacred Biography: Saints and their Biographers in the Middle Ages* (New York: Oxford University Press, 1988)

Ingham, Norman W., 'The Limits of Secular Biography in Medieval Slavic Literature, Particularly Old Russian', in *American Contributions to the Sixth International Congress of Slavists: Prague, 1968, August 7–13: Vol. II: Literary Contributions*, ed. by William E.

Harkins, Slavistic Printings and Reprintings series, 81 (The Hague: Mouton, 1968), pp. 181–99

Ingham, Norman W., 'Genre Characteristics of the Kievan Lives of Princes in Slavic and European Perspective', in *American Contributions to the Ninth Congress of Slavists, Kiev, September 1983: Vol. II: Literature, Poetics, History*, ed. by Paul Debreczeny (Columbus, OH: Slavica, 1983), pp. 223–37

Ivanits, Linda, J., *Russian Folk Belief* (Armonk: Sharpe, 1992)

Kallash, V. V., and N. E. Efros, *Istoriia russkogo teatra* (Moscow: Ob˝edinenie, 1914)

Kelly, Catriona, 'Life at the Margins: Woman, Culture and Narodnost'', in *Gender Restructuring in Russian Studies: Conference Papers – Helsinki, August 1992*, ed. by Marianne Liljestrom, Eila Mantysaari, and Arja Rosenholm, *Slavica Tamperensia* series, 2 (Tampere: [University of Tampere], 1993), pp. 139–59

Kelly, Catriona, *Petrushka: The Russian Carnival Puppet Theatre* (Cambridge: Cambridge University Press, 1990)

Kliuchevskii, V. O., *Drevnerusskie Zhitiia Sviatykh kak istoricheskii istochnik* (Moscow: Tipografiia Gracheva, 1871; repr. Farnborough, England: Greg International, 1969)

Komarovich, V. L., *Kitezhskaia legenda: Opyt izucheniia mestnykh legend*, Monuments of Early Russian Literature series, 5 (Moscow: Akademiia nauk SSSR, 1936; repr. Berkeley: Berkeley Slavic Specialties, 1982)

Kondakov, N. P., *Ikonografiia Bogomateri*, 2 vols (St Petersburg: Tipografiia Imperatorskoi Akademii nauk, 1914–15)

Likhachev, D. S., *Smekh v drevnei Rusi* (Leningrad: Nauka, 1984)

Matossian, Mary, 'The Peasant Way of Life', in *Russian Peasant Women*, ed. by Beatrice Farnsworth and Lynne Viola (New York: Oxford University Press, 1992), pp. 11–40

Pomerantseva, E., *Mifologicheskie personazhi v russkom fol´klore* (Moscow: Nauka, 1975)

Ramers, Samuel C., 'Traditional Healers and Peasant Culture in Russia: 1861–1917', in *Peasant Economy, Culture, and Politics of European Russia: 1880–1921*, ed. by Esther Kingston-Mann and Timothy Mixter (Princeton: Princeton University Press, 1991), pp. 207–32

Rovinskii, D. A., 'Prikhod vozhaka s medvedem', in *Fol´klornyi teatr*, pp. 431–32

Smirnov, Vas., 'Chort rodilsia', in *Tretii etnograficheskii sbornik*, Trudy Kostromskogo nauchnogo obshchestva po izucheniiu mestnogo kraia series, 29 (Kostroma: [n. pub.], 1923), pp. 17–20

Smirnov, Vas., 'Potonuvshie kolokola', ibid., pp. 1–4

Trofimov, A., *Sviatye zheny Rusi* (Moscow: Entsiklopediia russkikh dereven´, 1993)

Tserkovno-narodnyi mesiatseslov na Rusi I. P. Kalinskogo, ed. by E. Malinina and N. Artemova, afterword by V. Anikin, Zabytaia kniga series (Moscow: Gosudarstvennoe izdatel´stvo khudozhestvennoi literatury, 1990)

Vsevolodskii (Gerngross), V., *Istoriia russkogo teatra*, 2 vols (Leningrad: Teakinopechat´, 1929)

Warner, Elizabeth A., and Evgenii S. Kustovskii, *Russian Traditional Folk Song* (Hull: Hull University Press, 1990)

Warner, Elizabeth A., *The Russian Folk Theatre* (The Hague: Mouton, 1977)

Worobec, Christine D., *Peasant Russia: Family and Community in the Post-Emancipation Period* (Princeton: Princeton University Press, 1991)

Zabylin, M., *Russkii narod, ego obychai, obriady, predaniia, sueveriia i poeziia* (Moscow: Berezin, 1880; repr. Moscow: Kniga 'Printshop', 1989)

Zelenin, D. K., *Ocherki russkoi mifologii: Tom 1: Umershie neestestvennoiu smert´iu* (Petrograd: Tipografiia A. V. Orlova, 1916)

Zguta, Russell, *Russian Minstrels: A History of the Skomorokhi* (Philadelphia: University of Pennsylvania Press, 1978)

Ziolkowski, Margaret, *Hagiography and Modern Russian Literature* (Princeton: Princeton University Press, 1988)

6. Texts and Critical Works (General)

Alekseev, M., 'Zametki o Gavriiliade', in *Pushkin* (Leningrad: Nauka, 1972), pp. 281–325
Anderson, George K., *The Legend of the Wandering Jew* (Providence: Brown University Press), 1965
Andreev, Leonid, 'Iuda', in *Sobranie sochinenii*, ed. by I. G. Andreeva, Iu. N. Verchenko, and V. N. Chuvakov, 6 vols (Moscow: Gosudarstvennoe izdatel′stvo khudozhestvennoi literatury, 1990–96), II (1990), 210–64
Bakhtin, Mikhail, *Rabelais and His World*, trans. by Hélène Iswolsky (Bloomington: Indiana University Press, 1984)
Barthes, Roland, *The Pleasure of the Text*, trans. by Richard Miller (Oxford: Oxford University Press, 1990)
Bibliographie des oeuvres de Alexis Remizov, ed. by Hélène Sinany (Paris: Institut d'Études Slaves, 1978)
Blok, A. A., 'Stikhi o prekrasnoi dame' (1901–02), in *Sobranie sochinenii*, ed. by V. N. Orlov, A. A. Surkov, and K. I. Chukovskii, 8 vols (Moscow–Leningrad: Gosudarstvennoe izdatel′stvo khudozhestvennoi literatury, 1960–63), I (1960), 74–238
Blok, A. A., *Balaganchik* (1906), ibid., IV (1961), 7–21
Blok, A. A., *Roza i krest* (1913), ibid., pp. 168–246
Bruce Lincoln, W., *Passage Through Armageddon: The Russians in War and Revolution* (New York: Simon & Schuster, 1986)
Carr, Edward Hallett, *A History of Soviet Russia: Socialism in One Country*, 3 vols (London: Macmillan, 1964)
Chamot, Mary, *Goncharova: Stage Designs and Paintings* (London: Oresto Books, 1979)
Clay, Catherine B., 'Russian Ethnographers in the Service of the Empire (1856–62)', *Slavic Review*, 54 (1995), 45–61
Danilevich, L., *Poslednie opery N. A. Rimskogo-Korsakova* (Moscow: Gosudarstvennoe muzykal′noe izdatel′stvo, 1961)
Davidson, Apollon, *Muza stranstvii Nikolaia Gumileva* (Moscow: Nauka, 1992)
Dikii, Aleksei, 'Iz knigi "Povest′ o teatral′noi iunosti"', in *Stat′i: Perepiska: Vospominaniia*, ed. by N. G. Litvinenko and A. G. Guliev (Moscow: Iskusstvo, 1967), pp. 357–64
Bresky, Dushan, *The Art of Anatole France* (The Hague: Mouton, 1969)
Eikhenbaum, B., 'Leskov i literaturnoe narodnichestvo', in *Blokha: Igra v 4 d. Evg. Zamiatina* (Leningrad: Academia, 1927), pp. 12–15
Eikhenbaum, Boris, 'Leskov i sovremennaia proza', in *Literatura: Teoriia: Kritika: Polemika* (Leningrad: Priboi, 1927; repr. Chicago: Russian Language Specialties, 1969), pp. 210–25
Eikhenbaum, B. M., 'Illiuziia skaza' (1918), in *Skvoz′ literaturu* (Leningrad: [n. pub.], 1924; repr. 'S-Gravenhage: Mouton, 1962)
Forsh, Ol′ga, 'Za zhar-ptitsei' (1910), in *Sobranie sochinenii*, ed. by M. Belousova, commentary by A. V. Tamarchenko, 8 vols (Moscow–Leningrad: Gosudarstvennoe izdatel′stvo khudozhestvennoi literatury, 1962–64), VI (1964), 48–63
Forsh, Ol′ga, 'Afrikanskii brat' (1922), ibid., pp. 243–57
Freud, Sigmund, 'The Taboo of Virginity' (1918), in *Standard Edition*, trans. and under the general editorship of James Strachey, 24 vols (London: The Hogarth Press, 1953–74), XI (1957), 191–208
Fuhrmann, Joseph T., *Rasputin: A Life* (New York: Praeger, 1990)

Garafola, Lynn, *Diagilev's Ballets Russes* (New York: Oxford University Press, 1989)

Gogol´, N. V., 'Maiskaia noch´, ili utoplennitsa' (1831), in *Sobranie sochinenii*, ed. by S. I. Mashinskii and M. B. Khrapchenko, 7 vols (Moscow: Gosudarstvennoe izdatel´stvo khudozhestvennoi literatury, 1976–79), I (1976), 54–80

Gogol´, N. V., *Mertvye dushi* (1842), ibid., V (1978), 7–236.

Gor´kii i sovetskie pisateli: Neizdannaia perepiska, Literaturnoe nasledstvo series (Moscow: Izdatel´stvo Akademii nauk SSSR, 1963)

Gorodetskii, Sergei, 'Mucheniia sv. Iustiny' (1912), in *Stikhi* (Moscow: Gosudarstvennoe izdatel´stvo khudozhestvennoi literatury, 1964), pp. 124–25

Grechishkin, S. S., 'Arkhiv Remizova', in *Ezhegodnik rukopisnogo otdela Pushkinskogo Doma na 1975 god*, ed. by M. P. Alekseev and others (Leningrad: Nauka, 1977), pp. 20–44

Gumilev, Nikolai, 'Iudif´', in *Sobranie sochinenii*, ed. by G. P. Struve and B. A. Filippov (Washington: Kamkin, 1962–), I (1962), 227–28

Heard Hamilton, George, *The Art and Architecture of Russia* (New Haven: Yale University Press, 1954)

Hellman, Ben, *The Poets of Hope and Despair: The Russian Symbolists in War and Revolution (1914–1918)* (Helsinki: Institute for Russian and East European Studies, 1995)

Hoffmann, E. T. A., 'The Story of Serapion', in *Great Short Stories of the World*, ed. by B. H. Clarke and M. Lieber (London: Heinemann, 1926), pp. 256–65

Ivan Groznyi: Kinostsenarii S. M. Eizenshteina (Moscow: Goskinoizdat, 1944)

Ivan Iakovlevich Bilibin: Stat´i: Pis´ma: Vospominaniia o khudozhnike, ed. by S. V. Golynets (Leningrad: Khudozhnik RSFSR, 1970)

Jensen, Peter Alberg, *Nature as Code: The Achievement of Boris Pilnjak: 1915–1924*, Institute of Slavonic Studies series (Copenhagen: Rosenkilde and Bagger, 1979)

Khodasevich, Vladislav, '"Prokliatyi prints" A. Remizova', in *Sobranie sochinenii*, ed. by John Malmstad and Robert Hughes (Ann Arbor: Ardis, 1983–), II (1990), 509

Kiukhel´beker, V. K., *Agasfer* (1832–46), in *Izbrannye proizvedeniia v dvukh tomakh*, ed. by N. V. Korolevaia (Moscow–Leningrad: Sovetskii pisatel´, 1967), I, 76–138

Koz´menko, M. V., '"Limonar´" kak opyt rekonstruktsii russkoi narodnoi very', in *Aleksei Remizov: Issledovaniia i materialy*, ed. by A. M. Gracheva (St Petersburg: Izdatel´stvo 'Dmitrii Bulanin', 1994), pp. 26–32

Konchalovskii, Andrei, and Andrei Tarkovskii, '*Andrei Rublev*', *Iskusstvo kino*, 1964.4, 138–200

Korolenko, V. G., *V pustynnykh mestakh* (1890), in *Sobranie sochinenii*, ed. by S. V. Korolenko and N. V. Korolenko-Liakhovich, 10 vols (Moscow: Gosudarstvennoe izdatel´stvo khudozhestvennoi literatury, 1953–56), III (1954), 110–228

Kristeva, Julia, *Visions capitales* (Paris: Réunion des Musées nationaux, 1998)

Kruchenykh, A., 'Deklaratsiia zaumnogo iazyka', in *Manifesty i programmy russkikh futuristov*, ed. by Vladimir Markov, Slavische Propyläen series (Munich: Fink, 1967), pp. 179–81

Kunina, Irina, 'Vstrecha s Blokom', *Literaturnoe obozreñie*, 1991.9, 92–97

Kurochkin, V. A., *Prints Lutonia* (1872), in *Sobranie sochinenii*, ed. by A. V. Efremin (Moscow–Leningrad: Academia, 1934; repr. The Hague: Europe Printing, 1967), pp. 405–54

Lebedeva, V., *Boris Mikhailovich Kustodiev* (Moscow: Nauka, 1966)

Lebedeva, V., *Boris Kustodiev: The Artist and the Work* (Moscow: Progress, 1981)

Le Fanu, Mark, *The Cinema of Andrei Tarkovsky* (London: BFI, 1987)

Leifert, A., 'Balagany', in *Blokha. Igra v 4 d. E. Zamiatina*, pp. 23–27

Leskov, N. S., 'Zapechatlennyi angel' (1873), in *Sobranie sochinenii*, ed. by V. G. Bazanov and others (Moscow: Gosudarstvennoe izdatel´stvo khudozhestvennoi literatury, 1956–58), IV (1957), 320–84

Leskov, N. S., 'Skaz o tul'skom kosom Levshe i o stal'noi blokhe' (1881), ibid., VII (1958), 26–59
Leskov, N. S., 'Prekrasnaia Aza' (1888), ibid., VIII (1958), 291–302
Leskov, N. S., 'Gora. Egipetskaia povest'' (1890), ibid., pp. 303–89
Letopis' zhizni i tvorchestva F. I. Shaliapina, ed. by Iu. Kotliarov and V. Garmash, 2 vols, 2nd edn (Leningrad: Muzyka, 1989)
Levin, Eve, Sex and Society in the World of the Orthodox Slavs (Ithaca, NY: Cornell University Press, 1989)
Manouelian, E. R., 'Judas: apocryphal legend into symbolist drama', Slavic and East European Journal, 37 (1993), 44–66
McLean, Hugh, Nikolai Leskov: The Man and his Art (Cambridge, MA: Harvard University Press, 1977)
Mel'gunov, S. P., Legenda o separatnom mire (Paris: [n. pub.], 1957)
Mel'nikov-Pecherskii, P. I., V lesakh (1875), 2 vols (Moscow: Gosudarstvennoe izdatel'stvo khudozhestvennoi literatury, 1958)
Merezhkovskii, D. S., 'Griadushchii Kham', in Polnoe sobranie sochinenii, 17 vols (Moscow: Vol'f, 1911–13), XI (1911), 1–36
Murav-Lavigne, Harriet, Scandalous Folly: The Discourse of 'Iurodstvo' in the Works of Dostoevsky (Ann Arbor: Ardis, 1985)
Mushchenko, E. G., V. P. Skobelev, and L. E. Kroichik, eds., Poetika skaza (Voronezh: Izdatel'stvo Voronezhskogo Universiteta, 1978)
Nichols, Robert L., 'The Friends of God: Nicholas II and Alexandra at the Canonization of Serafim of Sarov, July 1903', in Religious and Secular Forces in Late Tsarist Russia, ed. by Charles E. Timberlake (Seattle: University of Washington Press, 1992), pp. 206–29
Parton, Anthony, Mikhail Larionov and the Russian Avant-Garde (London: Thames and Hudson, 1993)
Prishvin, M. M., V kraiu nepuganykh ptits (1907), in Sobranie sochinenii, ed. by N. P. Smirnov, 6 vols (Moscow: Gosudarstvennoe izdatel'stvo khudozhestvennoi literatury, 1956–57), II (1956), 1–163
Prishvin, M. M., Za volshebnym kolobkom (1908), ibid., pp. 163–93
Prishvin, M. M., 'Svetloe ozero' (1909), ibid., pp. 395–475
Remizov, Aleksei, 'Mariia Egipetskaia' (1907), in Sochineniia (St Petersburg: Shipovnik [I–VII] and Sirin [VIII], 1910–12; repr. Munich: Fink, 1971), VII (1912), 45–46
Remizov, Aleksei, Chto est' tabak (St Petersburg: Troinitskii, 1908)
Remizov, Aleksei, Posolon' (1908), in Sochineniia, VI (1911), 13–135
Remizov, Aleksei 'Tragediia o Iude printse iskariotskom' (1908), ibid., VIII (1912), 91–184
Remizov, Aleksei, 'Russkie zhenshchiny', in Dokuka i balagur'e (St Petersburg: Sirin, 1914), pp. 13–91
Remizov, Aleksei, Za sviatuiu Rus' (St Petersburg: Otechestvo, 1915)
Remizov, Aleksei, Ukrepa: Slovo k russkoi zemle o zemle rodnoi, tainostiakh zemnykh i sud'be (Petrograd: Tipografiia Sirius, 1916)
Remizov, Aleksei, 'Slovo o pogibeli Russkoi Zemli', in Ognennaia Rossiia (Revel: Bibliofil, 1921), pp. 10–24 (first publ. in Skify, II (1918))
Remizov, Aleksei, 'Tulumbas', 'Kaftan Petra Velikogo', 'Obezvelvolpal', and 'Manifest', in AKHRU: Povest' Peterburgskaia (Berlin: Grzhebin, 1922), pp. 47–48, 48–49, 49–50, & 50–51, respectively
Remizov, Aleksei, 'Mariia Egipetskaia' (written 1915), in Trava–Murava (Berlin: Efron, 1922), pp. 39–45
Remizov, Aleksei, Vzvikhrennaia Rus' (Paris: Tair, 1927; repr. Moscow: Sovetskii pisatel', 1991)

Rosenthal, Charlotte., 'Remizov's *Sunwise* and *Leimonarium*: Folklore in Modernist Prose', *Russian Literature Triquarterly*, 19 (1986), 95–112

Rothman, William, *The "I" of the Camera* (Cambridge: Cambridge University Press, 1988)

Rouart, Marie-France, *Le Mythe du Juif errant* ([Paris]: [José Corti], 1988)

Rybakov, B., *Iazychestvo drevnei Rusi* (Moscow: Nauka, 1987)

Seaman, Gerald R., *Nikolai Andreevich Rimsky-Korsakov: A Guide to Research* (New York: Garland Publishing, 1988)

Sergei Konenkov (Leningrad: Avrora, 1977)

Shklovskii, Viktor, 'Iskusstvo kak priem' (1917), in *Gamburgskii schet: Stat´i – Vospominaniia – Esse* (Moscow: Sovetskii pisatel´, 1990), pp. 58–72

Slobin, Greta N., *Remizov's Fictions: 1900–1921* (Dekalb: Northern Illinois University Press, 1991)

Sobranie sochinenii S. V. Maksimova, introduction by P. V. Bykov, 20 vols, 3rd edn (St Petersburg: Prosveshchenie, [1908–13])

Sologub, Fedor, 'Alchushchii i zhazhdushchii', in *Rasskazy* (Berkeley: Berkeley Slavic Specialties, 1979), pp. 305–14

Solov´ev, V., 'Smysl´ liubvi', in *Sobranie sochinenii V. S. Solov´eva*, ed. by S. M. Solov´ev and E. L. Radlov, 2nd edn, 9 vols (St Petersburg: Prosveshchenie, [n.d.]), VI, 356–418

The Fall of the Romanoffs, introduction by Alan Wood (London: Herbert Jenkins, 1918; repr. Cambridge: Ian Faulkner, 1992)

The Serapion Brothers, ed. with introduction by Gary Kern and Christopher Collins (Ann Arbor: Ardis, 1975)

The Voyages and Travells of the Ambassadors Sent by Frederick Duke of Holstein to the Great Duke of Muscovy and the King of Persia, Written Originally by Adam Olearius, Secretary to the Embassy, Faithfully Rendered into English by John Davies, 2nd edn (London: [n. pub.], 1669)

Tolstoi, A. N., 'Ivan da Mar´ia', in *Polnoe sobranie sochinenii*, ed. by A. S. Miasnikov, A. N. Tikhonov, and L. I. Tolstoi, 15 vols (Moscow: Gosudarstvennoe izdatel´stvo khudozhestvennoi literatury, 1951–53), I (1951), 153–56

Turbin, V., 'Kitezhane. Iz zapisok russkogo intelligenta', in *Pogruzhenie v triasinu: Anatomiia zastoia*, ed. by T. A. Notkina (Moscow: Progress, 1991), pp. 346–70

Uspenskii, B., '"Zavetnye skazki" A. N. Afanas´eva', in *Anti-mir russkoi kul´tury*, ed. by N. Bogomolov (Moscow: Ladomir, 1996), pp. 143–64

Uspenskii, G. I., *Vlast´ zemli* (1882), in *Polnoe sobranie sochinenii*, ed. by N. F. Bel´chikov, B. I. Bursov, and B. P. Koz´min, 14 vols ([Leningrad]: Akademiia nauk SSSR, 1949–54), VIII (1949), 7–121

Vernadsky, George, and Michael Karpovich, *A History of Russia: Volume 1: Ancient Russia* (New Haven: Yale University Press, 1943)

Vinogradov, V. V., 'Problema skaza v stilistike' (1925), in *Izbrannye trudy: O iazyke khudozhestvennoi prozy*, afterword by A. P. Chudakov, commentary by E. V. Dushechkina (Moscow: Nauka, 1980), pp. 42–54

Voloshin, Maksimilian, 'Kitezh' (1919), in *Stikhotvoreniia v dvukh tomakh*, ed. by B. A. Flippov, G. P. Struve, and N. A. Struve (Paris: YMCA, 1982), I, 233–35

Walter White, E., *Stravinsky: The Composer and his Works*, 2nd edn (London: Faber and Faber, 1966)

Wells, Herbert George, *The Sea Lady* (London: Methuen, 1902)

Zhukovskii, V. A., *Stranstvuiushchii zhid* (1851–52), in *Polnoe sobranie sochinenii*, 3 vols (Moscow: Marks, 1906), II, 474–93

INDEX

PLATE I.   Evgenii Zamiatin. Reproduced from Evgenii Zamiatin, *Sochineniia* (Moscow: Kniga, 1988), p. 2

КАКЪ НАХИМЪ ШУМЯТ, | Кому клинъ дать кому станъ | Какъ вечоръ меня милой | Какъ тебя мне нелюбить.
САРАФАНЪ БАБЫ ДѢЛЯТЪ, | Кому весь бы Сарафанъ. | Цѣловалъ да миловалъ | Немогу тебя забыть
Ой вы дѣвки : | Вышла дѣвка молода | Крѣпко къ сердцу прижималъ | Ой вы дѣвки ;
Ой вы бабы молодыя : | Порасхвасталась она : | Онъ сударушкою называлъ | Ой вы бабы молодыя !
| Ой вы Дѣвки ; | Ты сударушка моя |
| Ой вы бабы молодыя ; | Вѣрно любишь ли меня ;

PLATE II.   Peasant lithograph *c.* 1871 entitled *Russkaia pesnia*. Reproduced from *The Lubok: Russian Folk Pictures: 17th to 19th Century* (Leningrad: Aurora Art Publishers, 1984), illustration no. 166. Original held in the Russian Museum, St Petersburg

PLATE III. *Egorych-the-Beekeeper*.
Sculpture in wood by Sergei
Konenkov *c*. 1907. Reproduced
from *Sergei Konenkov* (Leningrad:
Avrora, 1977), illustration no. 44.
Original held in the Karelian
Museum of Fine Arts,
Petrozavodsk

казанный инокъ
Еразмъ еще во чревѣ
матери посвященъ былъ
Богу. Родители его дол-
гіе годы ревностно, но
тщетно любили другъ
друга и, наконецъ, исто-
щивъ всѣ суетныя сред-
ства, пришли въ оби-
тель къ блаженному
Памвѣ. Вступивъ въ
келью старца, жена
преклонила предъ нимъ
колѣни, но стыдъ жен-
скій запечаталъ ей уста,
и такъ молча предстояла
старцу. Блаженному же
Памвѣ и не надо было

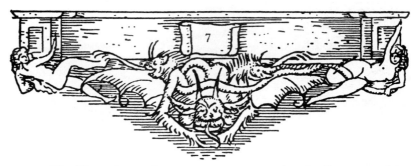

PLATE IV.   Kustodiev's illustrations accompanying the first page of the
1922 Berlin edition of 'O tom, kak istselen byl otrok Erazm'.
Reproduced from Evg. Zamiatin, *O tom, kak istselen byl otrok Erazm*
(Berlin: Grzhebin, 1922; repr. Moscow: Kniga, 1988), p. 7

образъ голубиный, сѣвъ на крестѣ могильномъ и уронивъ на землю вѣнокъ, предались плотскому неистовству. — Онъ ее заклюетъ! Освободи ее, добрый старецъ! — вскричалъ отрокъ Еразмъ къ блаженному Памвѣ. Старецъ Памва поднялъ глаза на бѣсовъ — тѣ истаяли дымомъ на виду у всѣхъ, не окончивъ своей непристойной игры. Старецъ же возложилъ на Еразма руки, сказавъ: — Счастливъ удѣлъ твой, братъ

Еразмъ, и тяжелъ онъ, ибо уже раскидываютъ надъ тобой бѣсы свою сѣть, но они ищутъ лишь цѣнной добычи. И, чтобы блюсти Еразма отъ козней бѣсовскихъ, блаженный Памва поселилъ его въ своей кельѣ. Юный инокъ Еразмъ служилъ старцу, подавая ему воду

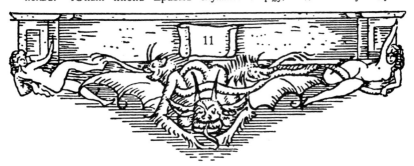

PLATE V. 'Henceforth thy husband shall no longer be like unto the ploughman who tills the sand, but his labours shall bear fruit'. Kustodiev illustration from the 1922 edition of 'O tom, kak istselen byl otrok Erazm'. Reproduced from Evg. Zamiatin, *O tom, kak istselen byl otrok Erazm* (Berlin: Grzhebin, 1922; repr. Moscow: Kniga, 1988), p. 11

Адамова. Такъ сказавъ, вышелъ старецъ: уже проступала вечерняя кровь на непорочно-бѣлой одеждѣ стѣны, и чугунное било зва-ло братію въ храмъ. Еразмъ же разрѣшенъ былъ старцемъ отъ церковной молитвы и остался въ келіи одинъ. Опечаленный палъ Еразмъ передъ обра-зомъ и жарко молился, вопія: Умилосердись, преподобная, научи меня познать честное тѣло твое, дабы могъ я достойно прославить тебя. Но здѣсь услышалъ онъ сзади тихій, едва слышимый смѣхъ. Обратившись изумленно, искалъ онъ, кто могъ взойти въ келію — и увидѣлъ лишь на рѣшеткѣ окна двухъ играющихъ голубей. Въ тотъ же часъ вспомнилъ Еразмъ голубей на могильномъ крестѣ

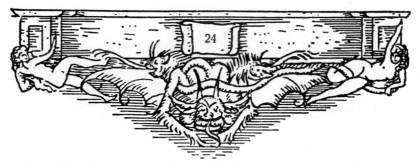

PLATE VI.   Erasmus unveils the 'fourth secret' of St Mary of Egypt. Kustodiev illustration from the 1922 edition of 'O tom, kak istselen byl otrok Erazm'. Reproduced from Evg. Zamiatin, *O tom, kak istselen byl otrok Erazm* (Berlin: Grzhebin, 1922; repr. Moscow: Kniga, 1988), p. 24

КАКЪ ПРАВЕДНЫЙ ЗАМУТІЙ
ЖЕНЪ ОТЪ БЕЗПЛОТІЯ
ИСЦѢЛЯЛЪ

PLATE VII.   'How the virtuous Zamutius cured women of
infertility.' Kustodiev illustration from reprinted facsimile
edition of Zamiatin's 'Zhitie Blokhi' (1929). Reproduced
from Evgenii Zamiatin, *Sochineniia* (Moscow: Kniga, 1988),
p. 171

PLATE VIII.   Kustodiev's poster design for the Moscow production of *Blokha*. Reproduced from Victoria Lebedeva, *Boris Kustodiev: The Artist and His Work* (Moscow: Progress, 1981), illustration no. 87

РУССКІЙ РАЁКЪ

Хозяинъ райка... Вотъ смотри гляди, большои городъ Парижъ, побываешъ уго
ришъ гдѣ все помодѣ, былибы денежки только въ камодѣ, все лишь и гуляи,
только денги давай; вонъ какъ смотри барышни порькѣ сель катаются на шлю
бахъ въ широкихъ юбкахъ, въ шляпкахъ модныхъ никуда на годныхъ; а вонъ
немного по ближе большой мостъ въ Парижъ, вонъ какъ по немъ франтики
съ бородкими гуляютъ, барышнямъ улыбкою головкой кивяютъ, а упрахож-
ихъ зѣвакъ изъ кармановъ платочки летаютъ, бррр... хорошо штучка
 да послѣдняя! Зрители: ХА ХА ХА ХА!

PLATE IX.   *Lubok* engraving in copper *c.* 1858 entitled *Russkii raek*. Reproduced from *The Lubok: Russian Folk Pictures: 17th to 19th Century* (Leningrad: Aurora Art Publishers, 1984), illustration no. 138. Original held in the Historical Museum, Moscow

PLATE X.   *Lubok* engraving in copper c. 1820s or 1830s entitled *Galanskoi lekar' i dobroi aptekar'*.
Reproduced from *The Lubok: Russian Folk Pictures: 17th to 19th Century* (Leningrad: Aurora Art
Publishers, 1984), illustration no. 90. Original held in the Russian Museum, St Petersburg

PLATE XI.   Portrait of Nikolai Rerikh *c.* 1917 by Boris Grigor'ev. Reproduced
from Tamara Galeeva, *Boris Grigor'ev* (Moscow: Galart, 1995), illustration no. 17.
Original held in the Tret'iakov Gallery, Moscow

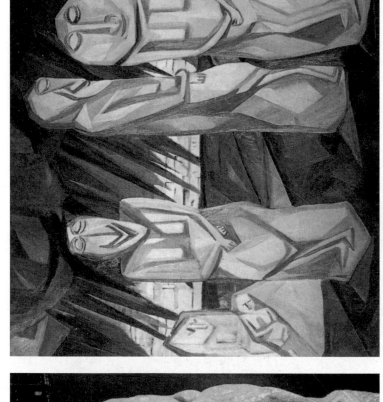

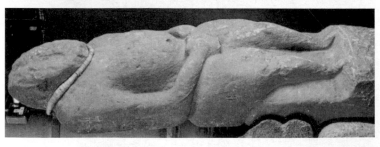

PLATE XIIa.   Russian Stone Baba dating from the eleventh century. Reproduced from Anthony Parton, *Mikhail Larionov and the Russian Avant-Garde* (London: Thames and Hudson, 1993), p. 100. Original held in the Pitt Rivers Museum, University of Oxford. Reproduction by the kind courtesy of Princeton University Press

Plate XIIb.   Natal'ia Goncharova's *Pillars of Salt c.* 1911. Reproduced from Anthony Parton, *Mikhail Larionov and the Russian Avant-Garde* (London: Thames and Hudson, 1993), *p.* 100. Reproduction by the kind courtesy of Princeton University Press. Original held in the Tret'iakov Gallery